Sounds English

Sounds English

Transnational Popular Music

Nabeel Zuberi

University of Illinois Press

Urbana and Chicago

Library of Congress Cataloging-in-Publication Data
Zuberi, Nabeel, 1962–
Sounds English : transnational popular music / Nabeel Zuberi.
p.   cm. — (Transnational cultural studies)
Includes bibliographical references, discography, and index.
ISBN 0-252-02620-9 (cloth : alk. paper)
1. Popular music—Great Britain—1981–1990—History and criticism.
2. Popular music—Great Britain—1991–2000—History and criticism.
3. Music—Social aspects—Great Britain. 4. Popular culture—Great Britain—
History—20th century. I. Title. II. Series.
ML3492.Z83   2001
781.64'0941—dc21   00-009647

C 5 4 3 2 1

Contents

Acknowledgments

Without my planning it, this book became a transnational production, a version of England and Englishness written in the United States, India, and Aotearoa/ New Zealand.

I want to thank my colleagues in the Centre for Film, Television, and Media Studies at the University of Auckland for their friendship and support: Gregory Bennett, Annie Goldson, Roger Horrocks, Margaret Henley, Shuchi Kothari, and Laurence Simmons. Many thanks to the Department of English for its financial support for travel to conferences, and for the opportunity to present material from the dance music chapter in its staff seminar. Salaams to the Centre for the Study of Social Sciences in Calcutta, which invited me to present some of the work on Britpop at its conference entitled "Globalisation: The Case of Music," in February 1998. Many thanks to the University of Auckland Research Committee for providing funds for a research trip to London. The students in my Popular Music graduate seminar from 1998–2000 will recognize many of the issues taken up in these pages. Their lively engagement and critical nous inform many of the book's arguments.

I thank Ien Ang and Jon Stratton, editors of the Transnational Cultural Studies series, for their advice and comments on the manuscript. Thank you to Tony Mitchell and the anonymous readers for the University of Illinois Press for their very useful suggestions. Loads of gratitude to Richard Martin, Carol Betts, and Veronica Scrol of the press for their editorial guidance and patience during the production of this book.

Some material in chapter 1 appears in "The Last Truly British People You Will Ever Know?: Skinheads, Pakis, and Morrissey," in *Hop on Pop: The Politics and Pleasures of Popular Culture,* edited by Henry Jenkins, Tara McPherson, and Jane Shattuc (Duke University Press, forthcoming).

I am deeply grateful to my family in the U.K. Love to my parents, Muhammad Mustafa Zuberi and Parveen Zuberi, my sister, Samia, and my brothers, Sameer and Fawzi, who gave me emotional and financial support throughout my graduate education and also sent me countless tapes, CDs, videos, and press clippings. I have been blessed with a family in Ahmedabad that also kindly provided me with a room of my own for writing. Much love to Pushpa Kothari, Tarun Kothari, Geeta Kothari, Abhijit Kothari, Rita Kothari, Shamini Kothari, Bina Handa, Sushil Handa, Arjun Handa, Aditya Handa, Pradip Vakil, and Gita Vakil, all of whom have made a Pakistani-Brit feel that India is also home.

This book began life as a Ph.D. research project in the Department of Radio-Television-Film at the University of Texas at Austin. I extend my respect and thanks to the members of my dissertation committee: my supervisor, Mary Desjardins, for her kind support and careful intellectual guidance; Mia Carter, for her inspiration, friendship, and encouragement; John Downing, for his shining example as a teacher, intellectual, and dear friend; and Doug Kellner and Janet Staiger, for their critical lessons in the classroom. Work with Mia Carter, Barbara Harlow, and Neil Nehring in the English Department at UT helped me to see the 1980s and 90s in terms of the nation's longer histories.

Much of this book carries traces of conversations and musical exchanges with friends and colleagues. Big shout-out to Jonathan Ayres, Patrick Burkart, Sean Campbell, Sandra Carter, Gareth Davies, Ken Feil, Nick FitzHerbert, David Gerstner, Forrest Green III, Misha Kavka, Eriko Kobayashi, Caspar Melville, Anne Morey, Sarina Pearson, Dushun Phillips, David Riddle, and Stephen Turner. Special thanks to Rónán Lynch and Tom McCourt for the many animated sessions on music. Big up to Saghir Shaikh for his care, insights into nationalism, and technical know-how at the most crucial moments. Major gratitude to Ash Corea and John Downing for their love and support through both hard and good times in Austin, and for making their house both a home and a model for the public sphere.

Most of all, I want to thank my partner and best friend, Shuchi Kothari, for her love, counsel, and editorial advice. She lived with me through this book and everything else in all these places. This book is for you, Shuchi, with my love.

Sounds English

Introduction
English Semidetached

I read somewhere that no musical vibrations are ever lost: that even
though they are dispersed they will go on vibrating through the cosmos
for eternity.
— Gordon Burn, *Alma*

Sound
falls round me like rain on other folks.
— Ntozake Shange, *I Live in Music*

A criminal may improve and become a decent member of society. A
foreigner cannot improve. Once a foreigner, always a foreigner. There is
no way out for him. He may become British; he can never become
English.
— George Mikes, *How to Be an Alien* (1946)

Sounds English examines popular music culture in the 1980s and 1990s as an arena for debates on English and British national identity. I focus quite narrowly
on English sounds since the idea of England and its Englishness has for so long
dominated economic, political, and cultural life in the United Kingdom of Great
Britain and Northern Ireland; the latter is the long-winded term with which the
state imprints itself on my passport. When the English have confidently defined
what it means to be British, they have really meant a national identity with Englishness at its core. By taking apart the idea of England we might be able to imagine significantly different British futures. Jacqueline Rose suggests that

> the term "national identity," as scrutinized by recent literary theory, has undergone
> a strange and uneven division of roles. Identity—as a psychic phenomenon in its

coercive, self-contradictory, internally ambivalent contours, or more simply identity gone mad—has taken off to the post-colonial; while "national"—as in the cultivation of virtue and character—has tended to remain at home. So Englishness, while
subject to historical and political critique, has escaped psychic exposure. Or to put
it another way, in discussions of Englishness, relatively little has been said about the
potential insanity of the moral life.[1]

An examination of popular music culture sheds light on these often obscured
aspects of English life.

The hegemony of Englishness seems to be in crisis. The last twenty years of
national navel-gazing should be seen in terms of the longer durée of at least the
postwar period. Most of Britain's dominions have been liberated from colonial
rule since 1945. The end of empire and the need for cheap labor brought many
migrants from the former colonies to the "mother country." This settlement
unsettled older conceptions of the white body politic. A generation of nonwhite
citizens has been born and raised on the national soil and tarmac. To many Britishers, this intrusion is even worse than the cultural imperialism of the United
States. Anglo angst about the changing contours of the national also accompanies the U.K.'s protracted and stuttering incorporation into a new Europe. The
European Union may soon displace the British union, which also faces the challenge of devolution from Irish, Scottish, and Welsh nationalisms. The nation-
state undergoes the many pressures of globalization. While New Right and New
Labour governments have supported the integration of the U.K. into a transnational finance economy, they still invoke sentimental and often quite narrow
notions of national community, from the heritage land of warm beer and village-
green cricket to Cool Britannia.

Popular music has registered and responded to these political, economic, and
cultural changes. The music discussed in *Sounds English* gives some insight into
the 1980s and 1990s, using pop recordings as the material culture for history-work.
For some readers, this book may resemble *The Rock 'n' Roll Years,* a British television documentary series in which each episode included the major newsreel foot-
age of a particular year spliced together with a soundtrack of its pop hits. The
music often provided a surprising and extremely prescient commentary on the
images and news stories. But this book should not be mistaken for a comprehensive history of popular music and national identity in the 80s and 90s. Some readers might be disappointed that I've neglected a number of obvious musical med-
itations on the national condition. The folkie left-populism of Billy Bragg is
absent, as is the London-Irish mapping of the Pogues, the ornery northwestern
angles of The Fall, and the post-Thatcher postfeminism of the Spice Girls. There

are fewer female than male musicians in this book, though I've examined the construction of both femininity and masculinity in the work of various artists.

Sounds English does include musicians such as the Smiths, Morrissey, Oasis, Blur, Pet Shop Boys, Tricky, Massive Attack, Goldie, A Guy Called Gerald, Roni Size, Bally Sagoo, Fun^da^mental, Echobelly, Cornershop, Talvin Singh, and others in order to highlight debates about gender, sexuality, race, ethnicity, and class in relation to the construction of the local, national, and transnational in popular music and cultural studies discourse. I have chosen these artists because they have generated a critical mass of both journalistic and academic writing around issues of Englishness. Rather than focus exclusively on production or consumption of popular music, I examine popular music culture as a collection of discourses that make sense of *and* help define musical activities.

I'm concerned less with music as a reflection of national history and geography than how the practices of popular music culture themselves construct the spaces of the local, national, and transnational. How does the music imagine the past and place? How does it function as a memory-machine, a technology for the production of subjective and collective versions of location and identity? How do the techniques of sounds, images, and activities centered on popular music create landscapes with figures? The book attempts a kind of sonic topography.

Recorded History and Memory

A central assumption behind this book is that recorded music culture has a significant role in private and public memory. According to Michel Foucault, popular memory "exists in the world rather than in people's heads, finding its basis in conversations, cultural forms, personal relations, the structure and appearance of places and, most fundamentally . . . in relation to ideologies which work to establish a consensus view of both the past and the forms of personal experience which are significant and memorable."[2] Foucault is concerned with the reproduction of "official" governmental notions of the past. It has to be acknowledged that England does often resemble an old curiosity shop holding one of those going-out-of-business sales that never ends; customers gaze at the antiquities in the shop window, chatter about the good old days, and mourn their passing. One is inclined to believe Tom Nairn's diagnosis that Ukania is a small, insular monarchy in Europe enthralled by the "glamour of backwardness."[3]

However, *Sounds English* takes issue with the view that the economic, political, or cultural elite simply hands down a carefully packaged version of the national to the transfixed populace. Popular culture is a site of struggle, albeit on an uneven playing field. Despite Thatcherite and Blair-y nationalism's many spectacular and banal victories, Britishness and Englishness remain strongly contested. The field of popular music culture reveals a much wider, more variegated terrain of popular memory, national belonging, and identification than the apparently singular theme-park nation of a place for everyone and everyone in his place. Even the heritage critic Patrick Wright admits that the notion of heritage is not singular and straightforward. The past is "the area not just of publicly installed illusion and ideology but also of everyday historical consciousness—of stories, memories, and vernacular interpretations which differ (sometimes in fully conscious opposition) from that superior 'History' which, while it has always spoken with easily assumed authority, is distinguished not just by its laurels but also by the difficulty it experiences in achieving its gloriously neutral 'truth.'"[4]

Popular music is part of vernacular history and itself a set of cultural technologies that produces politically *correct* and *incorrect* forms of "history." *Sounds English* takes up Raphael Samuel's call for "alternative histories which take as their starting point the bric-à-brac of material culture, the flotsam and jetsam of everyday life."[5] This book positions itself against the postmodern jeremiads that claim we live in a period of waning historicity in which commodity culture has simply reduced history to the apolitical play of images, surfaces, sound bites, and bytes. My five essays argue that words, music, audio samples, and video and photographic images in popular music culture contribute to the production of historical knowledge, activating memory and bringing the past into dialogue with the present. As George Lipsitz suggests: "For some populations at some times, commercialized leisure is history—a repository of collective memory that places immediate experience in the context of change over time. The very same media that trivialize and distort culture, that turn art into commodities, and that obscure the origins and intentions of artists also provide meaningful connection to our own pasts and to the pasts of others."[6]

Morrissey's invocation of images from 1960s "kitchen sink" films or 1970s skinhead culture is not only an homage to the catalog of trendy pop-culture iconography but a historical gesture grounded in the present realities of northern working-class life. When the Pet Shop Boys parody Oscar Wilde's trial in their *DJ Culture* video, the citation forces late Victorian fin-de-siècle sexual anxieties forward to a Britain policing homosexual desire and representation. When Massive Attack mixes its mumbling raps with roots reggae bass lines and almost subliminal Jamaican samples from the seventies, this tells us something about the history of cultural exchange and digitally enabled diasporic consciousness in Bristol. And when Fun^da^mental fixes the speech fragments of Malcolm X and Louis

Farrakhan to its Bollywood samples and hip-hop rhythms, Nation of Islam militancy rubs up against post-Rushdie British Islam in Bradford and London.

Quotations, covers, versions, samples, and remixes have cultural currency, not just as examples of a hip bricolage or detournément—a formalist jiggery-pokery for art's sake—but as popular cultural forms that have resonance with the politics of everyday life. This mediated activity is not merely a world of simulation, simulacra, and blank parody, but involves an aesthetics of engagement, self-definition, collective practice, and desire. While the logic of music industry capital determines that recycling, repackaging, remixing, and revivalism allow corporations to sell the same product again and again, such commodified repetition can also be productive in new contexts. The retro mode of pop music does not connect just to the seemingly hyperreal world of an institutionalized pop history and discourse, but to aspects of the specific *and situated* pasts and presents of people. As Jon Savage argues, "the media definition of post-modernism presupposes a lack of political, social or even narrative content. The fragment is all, and cannot refer to anything outside its closed loop. But a younger generation, many of whom aren't yet represented in the mainstream media, takes this loop-de-loop for granted to the extent that they quite naturally assemble new narratives out of the ruins of pop's past narratives which resonate as powerfully to their audience as any record has done over the last forty years."[7]

Changes in music culture have encouraged its role as a memory-engine. Technological developments such as digitization have increased the storage capacity of musical machinery—the instruments of production and the equipment of consumption. Twentieth-century music is an almost infinitely expanding archive or museum of sounds. Record companies mine rock's past in their back catalogs. Well-known and neglected recordings are recontextualized in new genealogies. Obscure musics from the past form new genres and market categories like "lounge music" and "world music." Boxed sets of multiple compact discs reprocess and compile the famous act's every recorded breath and cough. New technologies of dissemination and the globalizing strategies of media corporations facilitate the commodification of sounds from all over the world, available now in the West on an unprecedented scale.

The post-Presley rock music formation in the English-speaking world is almost fifty years old and institutionalized. This has made it more self-conscious about its own history, now organized into encyclopedias, canons of recorded classics, coffee-table books, Halls of Fame, Hard Rock cafés, and television series. The music press, particularly in the U.K., has been a crucial mediating institution, a font for many of popular music's ideologies and ways of thinking about music history. Popular music studies is also a growing academic field, gaining some institutional ground over the last fifteen years or so, and now a part of the tertiary education curriculum in many countries. A number of journals and professional bodies such as the International Association for the Study of Popular Music are devoted to serious scholarship on popular music's production, consumption, aesthetics, and social meaning.

Placing Cultural Studies and Popular Music

Sounds English charts popular music discourse as produced by musicians, journalists, listeners, fans, and academics. Many of the field's theoretical impulses have come from broader debates within cultural studies. This book uses music to work through some of the overlapping questions in popular music studies and cultural studies. Chapter 1, on the Smiths, Morrissey, and Britpop, incorporates a discussion of subcultural theory's politics of gender, race, and class as it traverses the de-industrialized landscape of Manchester and the north of England. This chapter also looks at the notion of *authenticity* in rock music and criticism. Chapter 2, on the Pet Shop Boys' queer memory-work, continues a discussion of authenticity in relation to stardom as it looks at the new vistas of consumerism in the (post-)Thatcherite metropolis. Chapter 3 examines the discourse on popular music's politics in the era of an ostensibly hedonistic rave/DJ/dance-floor culture that appears to have to some extent displaced guitar rock music and its ideologies. Chapter 4 investigates the debate on new technologies in the production and consumption of music—in particular, arguments about the effects of digitization and visualization on black British diaspora aesthetics in music. The concept of diaspora and its sibling term "hybridity" are further explored in chapter 5's discussion of the themes of travel and home in British Asian music.

In all five chapters, the music itself offers theories and ways of conceptualizing the local, national, and transnational that overlap with and sometimes contradict the claims of academic writing and journalism. I consider the music itself as *theoretical,* not merely an object used to test the applicability of various theories and analytical methodologies. Recorded music comments on arguments in other cultural spaces. I've tried to use commodified music and performance to open up from a different angle some well-known issues in the postdisciplinary fields of popular music studies and cultural studies.

Sounds English offers a critique of common-sense notions of Englishness and Britishness at the heart of cultural studies. This book is an attempt at what Jon Stratton and Ien Ang propose as "a British cultural studies which does not ex-nominate Britishness but exposes it."[8] Little Englandism tends to think of the island nation's culture as developing in isolation, according to its own pristine logic, its fundamental features as essentially separate and distinct from the stuff outside. This remains a strong current in English thinking even though the nation's past and present are inextricably linked to people and places beyond its borders. This book forces the somewhat cozy national(ist) model for cultural studies to come to terms with its colonial legacy, postcolonial others, and its imbrication in transnational economies.

Music from other places has been integral to the history of British music culture. Diana Jeater recounts how in the 1970s she "revised for her school exams playing Bob Marley's 'Exodus' over and over again, so that I can't hear it now without associating it with the English country garden where I grew up. I'm not sure what Marley would have felt about this. I was white and English, but much of the way that I thought about the world was structured by my contact with black music and my sense of connection with my black contemporaries."[9] Jeremy Gilbert describes how, as a white teenager in the northwest of England in the late 80s, listening to records by the New York–based 1960s group the Velvet Underground offered him *jouissance* and androgyny beyond the phallocentric sex and gender regime of most rock music, and constituted him as a part of a disseminated community of fans.[10] While *Sounds English* concentrates on music produced by British/English recording artists, a wide range of music from other places and other eras informs these English sounds, including New York disco, Chicago house, Detroit techno, Kingston reggae, Los Angeles rap, Dusseldorf electronica, and Bombay film music. English pop music and its others have interconnected geographies and shared myths of place and identity—of clubs, venues, concerts, and the histories of performers and listeners.

This book is aligned with various approaches we might place under the rubric of transnational cultural studies.[11] This broad field has questioned the national as the fundamental unit of economic, political, and cultural life. At the same time, *Sounds English* doesn't claim that the era of the nation-state is over in the globalized cultural economy. Though it has been weakened by transnational forces, the state has contributed to its own reconstitution. The hyphen in the term "nation-state" might be more elastic as the nation-state continues to withdraw from its role in social welfare and public service, but the state has been instrumental in facilitating the increasingly rapid and deregulated movement of transnational finance capital. The nation is by no means on the verge of disappearance. This book examines theories that complicate the national, but it also maintains that the national, local, and regional, as well as the transnational, are important sites of power as well as focus for subjective and collective identification.

Paul Willemen argues that "a kind of promiscuous or random form of alleged internationalism . . . an evasive cosmopolitanism masking imperial aspirations" is rife in discussions about global culture. This "discourse of universalist humanism is in fact an imperial and colonising strategy."[12] Willemen warns of conflating nationalism with national specificity; for example, black British cinema is distinctly British, but not nationalistic.[13] Nationalism and national specificity are two discourses that may overlap in different conjunctures, but "the concern with socio-cultural specificity is different from identity searches and debates. The specificity of a cultural formation may be marked by the presence but also by the absence of preoccupations with national identity." According to Willemen, "the construction of national specificity in fact encompasses and governs the articulation of both national identity and nationalist discourses."[14]

Thatcherism is a powerful state formation in the landscape described by this book. Its mobilization of narratives of national belonging and exclusion permeates all the chapters. But articulations of the national are not bound by Thatcherism or the New Right. Thatcherism is by no means a coherent ideological phenomenon in its definition of the nation. In fact, no single tradition of the imagined community can account for the different histories within any nation. As Anne McClintock points out, "there is no single narrative of the nation. Different genders, classes, ethnicities and generations do not identify with, or experience the myriad national formations in the same way; nationalisms are invented, performed and consumed in ways that do not follow a universal blueprint."[15] The musical performers, recordings, and activities described in this book attest, not so much to a happy cultural pluralism, but to the multiple, contesting, and sometimes overlapping spatialities within the nation's borders.

Any study of how the national is represented should also be attuned to the ways in which different axes of power operate *together*. Catherine Hall suggests that terms like "race," "class," "gender," and "sexuality" "are often produced as a litany, to prove political correctness, but that does not necessarily mean that the forms of analysis which follow are really shaped by a grasp of the workings of each axis of power in relation to the others."[16] McClintock reiterates this point: "race, gender and class are not distinct realms of experience existing in splendid isolation from each other; nor can they be simply yoked together retrospectively like armatures of Lego. Rather they come into existence *in and through* relation to each other—if in contradictory and conflictual ways."[17] Many variables are at play at any one time, so that case studies should carefully trace out the contradictory ways in which these relationships function in historically specific moments and over time. Though it often seems that the neo-Nazi skinhead, the Conservative Party, and the World War II veteran are united in their hate and fear of particular "others," it is impossible to ignore the sometimes affiliatory, sometimes contradictory impulses and narrations of national identity along and across axes of gender, generation, sexuality, ethnicity, and so on.

As Salman Rushdie suggests in a typically pithy example, cultural theory and criticism must be able to acknowledge and account for people like the "Asian businessman in Handsworth who made his pile by employing his fellow Asians in sweatshops to make, of all things, the Harrington jackets beloved by the skinheads who were also, as it happened, fond of bashing the odd Paki."[18] Such a businessman would probably have been an ethnic poster-boy for Thatcherism, applauded by the leader for his private enterprise and held up as a model of British-Asian citizenship. To take another example of strange bedfellows: some radical Islamist groups in the U.K. have had meetings with the British National Party with a view to potential alliances on some issues.

The national can be a slippery concept. Eve Sedgwick suggests that there is "simply no normal way to partake of the national, no single kind of 'other' of what a nation is to which all can by the same structuration be definitionally opposed": "The 'other' of the nation in a given political or historical setting may be the pre-national monarchy, the local ethnicity, the diaspora, the trans-national corporate, ideological, religious, or ethnic unit, the sub-national locale or the ex-colonial, often contiguous unit; the colony may become national vis à vis the homeland, or the homeland become national vis à vis the nationalism of its colonies; the nationalism of the homeland may be coextensive with or oppositional to its imperialism; and so forth."[19]

For example, the Falkland Islands became British along certain lines when Margaret Thatcher wanted the nation to go to war; miners became the "enemy within" when they protested pit closures and went on strike; the regionally specific mythical working-class soap-opera neighborhoods of *Coronation Street* and *East Enders* are coded as recognizably English, not merely by the simple fact that their locations are inside the nation's boundaries but because their specific local landscapes have come to represent some broader, populist notion of "our place"; black British soccer players may be booed and showered with monkey noises from their own club's racist fans, but celebrated for their contributions to the national team's efforts; the children of Irish Catholic migrants may become the exemplars of quintessentially English pop music; the vindaloo might be the British national dish.

The contours of the national overlap and blur with the local, regional, and transnational. Culture cannot be contained by the boundaries of the state or smaller community units within it. Local identities within the nation-state are reshaped and reconstituted as part of global processes. At the same time, the national is not simply bypassed by transnational and local economies; neither the local or national can be assumed as stable ground against which cultural change is measured.

In relation to music production and consumption, Simon Frith argues that the "cultural imperialist model—nation versus nation—must be replaced by a postimperial model of an infinite number of local experiences of (and responses to) something globally shared." He writes: "In this context the 'local' is defined by reference not to a specific geography or community but, rather, to a shared sense of place that is, itself, part of the global picture. In such a mapping process, one's sense of musical locality depends both on the immediate material circumstances (venues, audiences etc.) and also on 'reference' groups, on identities and fantasies that are themselves mediated globally. 'Locality' is produced as our sense of difference from the global—it is not a spontaneous expression of given, hard-held local traditions."[20]

Arjun Appadurai notes that many ethnographic descriptions have "taken locality as ground not figure, recognizing neither its fragility nor its ethos as a property of social life. This produces an unproblematized collaboration with the sense of inertia on which locality, as a structure of feeling, centrally relies." He argues that cultural analysis needs to move away from this mode of ethnography, "from a history of neighborhoods to a history of the techniques of the production of locality."[21] This book examines how musical techniques articulate local, national, and transnational "imaginaries." Appadurai points out that "the world we live in today is characterized by a new role for the imagination in social life. To grasp this new role, we need to bring together the old idea of images especially mechanically produced images (in the Frankfurt School sense); the idea of the imagined community (in [Benedict] Anderson's sense); and the French idea of the imaginary (imaginaire) as a constructed landscape of collective aspirations."[22]

Benedict Anderson describes the nation as *imagined* because "the members of even the smallest nation will never know most of their fellow-members, meet them, or even hear of them, yet in the minds of each lives the image of their communion." It is a *community* because, "regardless of the actual inequality and exploitation that may prevail in each, the nation is always conceived as a deep, horizontal comradeship."[23] He attributes the development of a national consciousness to the technology of printing, which made possible a vernacular language that bound together different constituencies into a community. Mass reproducibility allowed for the dissemination of this new, standardized language. Novels and newspapers defined national space and national time for a limited community of readers, and so created the consciousness of a distinct national culture.[24]

Anderson's work has prompted many productive analyses of the national as *textual practice*. His thesis underlies much of this book's analysis of how audiovisual technologies—music recordings on vinyl and compact disc, digital machines, music video, and film—as well as print, imagine subjects and collectives.

However, Slavoj Zizek cautions that "a nation *exists* only as long as its specific *enjoyment* continues to be materialized in a set of social practices and transmitted through national myths that structure these practices. To emphasize in a 'deconstructionist' mode that the Nation is not a biological or transhistorical fact but a contingent discursive construction, an overdetermined result of textual practices, is thus misleading: such an emphasis overlooks the remainder of some *real*, nondiscursive kernel of enjoyment which must be present for the Nation qua discursive entity-effect to achieve its ontological consistency." Zizek stresses the psychological attraction and function of the "Nation-Thing," not just its textuality.[25] Appadurai has also suggested that Anderson's thesis doesn't adequately account for the affective side of nationalism, the libidinal rather than rational impulses that result in "full attachment" to the national.[26] *Sounds English* considers the elements of fantasy, yearning, and desire in the construction of local, national, and transnational imaginaries. Zizek argues, using an appropriate example for this study:

> The element which holds together a given community cannot be reduced to the point of symbolic identification: the bond linking together its members always implies a shared relationship toward the Thing, toward enjoyment incarnated. This relationship toward the Thing, structured by means of fantasies, is what is at stake when we speak of the menace to our "way of life" presented by the Other: it is what is threatened when, for example, a white Englishman is panicked because of the growing presence of "aliens." What he wants to defend at any price is *not* reducible to the so-called set of values that offer support to national identity. National identification is by definition sustained by a relationship toward the Nation qua Thing. This Nation-Thing is determined by a series of contradictory properties. It appears to us as "our Thing" (perhaps we could say *cosa nostra*), as something accessible only to us, as something "they," the others, cannot grasp; nonetheless it is something constantly menaced by "them." It appears as what gives plenitude and vivacity to our life, and yet the only way we can determine it is by resorting to different versions of the same empty tautology. All we can ultimately say about it is the Thing is "itself," "the real Thing," "what it really is about," etc. If we are asked how we can recognize the presence of this Thing, the only consistent answer is that the Thing is present in that elusive entity called "our way of life." All we can do is enumerate disconnected fragments of the way our community organizes its feasts, its rituals of mating, its initiation ceremonies, in short, all the details by which is made visible the unique way a community *organizes its enjoyment*.[27]

Enjoyment can be commodified in sounds, images, writing, and rituals. This book acknowledges that media organizations and industries shape the value and affect of popular music and its practices. However, my primary focus is the mediation and reception of musical commodities during their social life. Some economic approaches to media culture pay scant attention to the changes in use value of musical commodities as they are disseminated and circulate from musicians and music companies through networks of consumer-listeners. Critical political economists are sometimes reluctant to grant the symbolic power of cultural forms at the micro-political level. They suggest that cultural studies' recent emphasis on consumption is complicit with the values of the New Right and neo-liberalism, which have tried to construct citizens as consumers. Admittedly, some studies of consumption and active audiences do seem celebratory, uncritical of social and economic power relations in consumer capitalism.[28]

Sounds English, however, is not concerned to show popular music culture simply as a site for resistance and anti-hegemonic practice. Music is a contradictory space, but it does offer modes of address for listening subjects to make sense of location, history, and identity. As subjects in late capitalist society we have been overdetermined and interpellated within capitalism. Our subjectivities have been shaped by commodified culture, so we make sense of the world through it. As Jeremy Gilbert says, "commodification and dissemination are not things that simply *happen* to our cultures, they are the very medium in which those cultures exist and function."[29]

The critique of cultural populism in cultural studies comes not just from political economists. Simon Frith and Jon Savage argue that the media and academia increasingly perpetuate notions of musical taste and value defined largely by the market.[30] In his recent *Performing Rites,* Frith articulates a typical critique of academic populism:

> The populist cultural studies line that popular consumer culture serves people's needs, and that by denigrating it we therefore denigrate those needs and thus the people themselves, misses the point. The issue is whether people's lives are adequate for human needs, for human potential. The political argument, in other words, concerns culture as reconciliation versus culture as transformation. . . . Culture as transformation, in other words, must challenge experience, must be difficult, must be unpopular. There are[,] in short, political as well as sociological and aesthetic reasons for challenging populism. The problem is how to do this while appreciating the popular, taking it seriously on its own terms. And I know this is where my own tastes will inform everything that follows, my own tastes, that is, for the unpopular popular, my own belief that the "difficult" appeals through the traces it carries of another world in which it would be "easy." The utopian impulse, the negation of

everyday life, the aesthetic impulse that Adorno recognized in high art, must be part of lower art too.[31]

Here Frith advocates a familiar modernist position, that of the critical avant-garde and the vanguard left. While I'm sympathetic to many of his criticisms of cultural populism's market values, I do think much of the hostility to the notion of active audiences and consumers, as well as the desire to return to an apparent origin of meaning at the level of production, is a symptom of the waning power of academic intellectuals to define political and aesthetic value and taste for the public.

Why is it so hard for some academics to acknowledge that *the masses* can think through their consumer desires and activities? Here, for example, is Frith's disparaging description of fans: "people who are certainly well enough organized to express their views—and indeed, organize fan clubs in order to do so—but whose terms of judgement are, for just that reason, likely to be a bit peculiar."[32] For Frith, fandom is a troubling presence for the sociological enterprise. In *Performing Rites,* a book with the construction of musical value as its central question, he admits that he likes the Pet Shop Boys, disco, and other pop music, but he also consistently distinguishes an academic posture from more *emotional* investments, demarcating his roles as rock critic, sociologist, and fan. The fan must be disavowed, though the repressed returns repeatedly throughout his book. *Sounds English* admittedly shares some of the tropes of (male) fan literature.[33] I have not separated my own (apparently "subjective") investment with this music from an (apparently "objective") academic analysis.

In a critique of Frith's antipopulism, Jim Collins warns that critical theory and cultural studies can become a form of left professionalism: "The academic's own self-location depends all too often on a foundational narrative, featuring the ever popular critical distance equation, in which Intellectuals resist the Marketplace, fighting a desperate battle against Mass Culture as the last defenders of critical discrimination."[34]

In an essay titled "The Cultural Study of Popular Music," Frith argues that a social anthropology or sociological approach to music production is "a more accurate, empirical account of popular music as a cultural process" than one based in the analysis of consumption. These two approaches construct popular music as a different kind of object. He believes that pop music ultimately provides a home for rootless, white middle-class intellectuals, where they can locate their fantasies of active and political consumption. Pop culture becomes a site for this intellectual to figure out his or her identity in a world that doesn't provide stable communities for identification.[35] Frith cites Dick Hebdige's *Hiding in the Light,* to illustrate this tendency. In his introduction to that collection of essays, Hebdige argues that one of his concerns is "the relations we are all forced to contract . . . with the quintessential *modern* category—the nation state." He admits that he has "tried to escape the English tradition, to find my own 'elsewhere,' to stage manage my own symbolic defection."[36]

Sounds English also maps a defection from the nation, though it realizes that a cleancut departure is not entirely possible. As Jacqueline Rose astutely and eloquently observes,

> talk of the postmodern predicament—belonging everywhere and nowhere at the same time—has never felt quite right. There is something about this vision of freewheeling identity which seems bereft of history and of passion. As if the anxiety of belonging, itself the product of stories which stretch back in time, could be redeemed in the present by dispersal, the heart miming, shadowing, beating to the tune of a world whose contours can no longer confidently be drawn. Loss of confidence may be welcome, especially where it was misplaced, coercive, or oppressive (you might want to argue that confidence is always one of these three). But it is far from clear that the mind leaps from here into freedom. Hearts can retrench; the body which feels weak reaffirms itself. The carapace of selfhood and nations cannot be willed—does not fall so easily—away.[37]

The following five chapters form a personal narrative of voluntary and involuntary exile that places race and ethnicity at the heart of the national question. As a middle-class Pakistani-Brit, I find that popular music culture has provided a home through which I can negotiate the very idea of "home." However, this hasn't been the comfortable place of resistant, subversive, politically correct consumption, as Frith suggests. I've loved *and* argued with this music.

Sociological approaches tend to posit a pre-formed identity that then engages with music that fits with that identity's experience. But our responses to music are much more complicated. They don't fall into taste formations according to this simple fit. In terms of my cultural and more specifically musical identifications, I'm as white, queer, English, and black as I am a Pakistani. My identification with the music described here shaped my formation as an English subject, though ironically, I had to leave England and write a book in order to really become English. Inevitably, *Sounds English* also carries some of the nostalgia of the English diaspora. The autobiographical surfaces at various points in this book, but I've tried to tone down the self-indulgence, to think of the written self as a critical construct, a staging of experience, and to always contextualize the production of the personal, thinking through the complex relations of class, gender, sexuality, race/ethnicity, and geography.

Pop music may not change the world in the avant-garde aesthetic revolutionary praxis that Frith and elements of the vanguard Left advocate; but it can en-
gender a series of mechanisms, feelings, and affect that contribute to a sense of
place and politics, as well as a way to begin thinking of personal and collective
change. Identifications with musical performers, genres, and individual texts, and
participation in various music activities, have helped me come to terms with my
own troubled Englishness and Britishness, my belonging and unbelonging, affection for, anger with, and alienation from national culture. This process is shot
through with ambivalences. As Jon Stratton and Ien Ang state, the "imbrication
of the colonizer and the colonized is deep and complex."[38] Listening and dancing, thinking and writing about music with a measure of self-consciousness about
the limits of identity politics have provided methods for the decolonization of
my mind and body. Pleasurable forms of consumption and production such as
music journalism, academic work, and stints as a radio DJ all have contributed
to the mixed-up (trans)national narrative of this book.

1

The Last Truly British People You Will Ever Know

The Smiths, Morrissey, and Britpop

Worked upon and reinterpreted, the landscape becomes a historical
landscape; but only through continual and active reworking.
—Carolyn Steedman, *Landscape for a Good Woman*

I didn't murder any moors, did you?
—"Moors Murderer" Myra Hindley in a letter to fellow killer Ian Brady

Union Jacking

Saturday, 8 August 1992, Los Angeles, California. Tickets for Morrissey's show
at the Hollywood Bowl sell out in twenty-three minutes, breaking a longstanding record held by the Beatles.[1] At the very same time in north London, Morrissey plays support slot to the English pop group Madness at its "Madstock" re-
union concert. Dressed in blue jeans and an open-necked gold lamé shirt, he
cavorts across the stage against a huge photographic backdrop of two 1970s skinhead girls. During the song "Glamorous Glue," from his latest album, *Your Arsenal,* he swirls a Union Jack flag around himself and lyrically laments that London is dead because it looks to Los Angeles for its everyday language.

This performance of Britishness is interrupted by a volley of homophobic in-
sults, sieg-heils, and small projectiles hurled by skinhead fans of Madness. Morrissey's use of the loaded national signifiers of the Union Jack and skinhead also
sparks various forms of abuse from antiracist sections of the audience, many of
whom have been concerned with the renewed and vigorous recruitment of skinheads by extreme right-wing organizations and the rising number of racist attacks
against Britons of African, Caribbean, and Asian descent. Outside the concert
venue in Finsbury Park, National Front and British Movement supporters hold

aloft British flags in opposition to a Troops Out (of Northern Ireland) march. Rattled by the Madstock crowd's response to his show, Morrissey leaves the stage, never to return that night. A press statement issued on his behalf the next day claims that he was forced to abandon his performance after being hit in the face by an orange-juice carton and a fifty-pence coin thrown by National Front skinheads.

This musical moment spills over with national/transnational ironies: a pop star in London tells his audience that local language and culture are dead at the hands of American cultural imperialism while he spectacularly sells out a concert in Los Angeles; a performer known for his androgyny and Oscar Wilde obsession is abused by the macho, determinedly hetero English skins he seems to celebrate; and the war in Northern Ireland looms large (if offstage) as an English singer of Irish-Catholic descent wraps himself in the Union Jack.

In the weeks following the Madstock debacle, sections of the nominally left-liberal British music press criticized Morrissey's flirtation with nationalist imagery. When he refused to respond to charges of racism or account for his actions, journalists exhumed any questionable references he had made in songs about Asian immigrants, black music, Americanization, National Front youth, and football (soccer) hooligans. Contentious interview statements about reggae's being vile, the negative effects of the Channel/Euro Tunnel, and the decline of Englishness uttered during Morrissey's solo career and as lead vocalist for the successful Manchester group the Smiths were cited as evidence for the prosecution.

Former fans of Morrissey, the Anglo-Asian indie rock group Cornershop, burned a poster of him outside the offices of his label, EMI, in London, a gesture that earned the band some press coverage as pop situationists. But this action was also motivated by a genuine concern with the singer's brush with fascinatin' fascism at a time of increased racist violence.

Photographs in the music press soon after the Madstock incident showed Morrissey smirking at the camera in a t-shirt that bears a 1980 Nick Knight photograph of an angry skinhead with "Made in London" tattooed on his forehead. The skinhead defiantly sticks two fingers up at the camera as he is led away handcuffed by a policeman. In other press and promotional photographs Morrissey wears a t-shirt emblazoned with the St. George's cross of the English flag. In one picture he proudly displays a Britain-shaped badge on his denim jacket. Morrissey's new album *Your Arsenal* featured two provocative *nationalist* tracks: "We'll Let You Know" lends a sympathetic ear to the point of view of English soccer hooligans; "The National Front Disco" voices a boy's desire to join the fascist party. The song's title may be inspired by Bill Buford's literary-journalistic account of attending such a disco in the "highly ordered, middle-class town" of Bury St. Edmunds in East Anglia.[2]

Morrissey's scrawled name was photographed alongside British National Party graffiti on a wall in London's East End, where British fascists have had some popular success since the 1930s days of Oswald Mosley and his blackshirts. In September 1993, Derek Beackon, a candidate from the British National Party, was elected as a municipal councillor in the Millwall ward of the London borough of Tower Hamlets (he later lost his seat, though the BNP retains about 25 percent of the vote). This was the hard Right's first seat on a local council since the National Front won two seats in Blackburn, Lancashire, in May 1976. The BNP also had considerable voter support in neighboring east London boroughs in the May 1994 local elections.

The electoral strength of the BNP is less an issue than the fact that its presence validates the racial harassment and violence carried out by some white men who themselves may not be members of far-right organizations. Bangladeshi-British residents face regular assaults to their bodies, homes, and businesses in east London neighborhoods. In 1992–93, there were eight thousand officially recorded incidents of racial violence in the U.K. Between 1992 and 1994, fifteen people died in Britain as a result of racially motivated attacks. This national experience of racism has been compounded by post-1989 political developments in Europe that have seen the rise of the far right as an electoral force in France, Germany, Russia, Belgium, Austria, and Italy, and an increase in the official number of racist attacks in these nation-states.[3]

In this racially charged atmosphere, the British music press's response to Morrissey's theatrical evocation of the "national" was polarized. He was either vilified as a racist Little Englander or defended as an artist whose music seriously investigates what it means to be British and English. In *Vox* magazine, his defender Tony Parsons claims that Morrissey has been unfairly pilloried as the "Pik Botha of pop" and makes an "unlikely Heinrich Himmler."[4] Parsons inadvertently highlights the problematic explored in this chapter. The Right and the Left both disavow racist nationalism in English and British culture by equating fascism with foreign elements. They resist the possibility that the very banality of English racism is what sustains it. Englishness rests on common-sense, commonplace notions of "the people," who is *really* English, and who doesn't belong to the national community. This Little Englandism relies on turning inward to an island nation of sedimented values, untouched by any trace of its colonial history.

However, Morrissey's brand of Little Englandism is not simply conservative, but both regressive *and* progressive in its conflicted representations of femininity, masculinity, class, race, ethnicity, and region in relation to what becomes identifiably "national" geography and history. I'm not interested in putting Morrissey in the academic dock to denounce him as a "racist" in a name-calling gesture that doesn't get us very far. Rather, Morrissey provokes an examination into the continuing power and resonance of certain notions of "Englishness" at a broader and deeper level in the landscape and its figures.

This chapter focuses on how Englishness is readily and regularly invoked in popular culture through representations of the nation's working class. In popular *music* culture, the Smiths and Morrissey activate collective memory about this proletarian, plebeian past in contradictory ways, reworking it in song lyrics, music, record-sleeve design, performance, and statements to the press. In particular, I examine how Morrissey uses the imagery of working-class women from the late 1950s and early 1960s and the skinhead from the late 1960s onward in his work as a member of the Smiths (1983–87) and as a solo recording artist (since 1987).

I compare the imagery of working-class women from the 1950s and early 60s with other recent cultural memory-work about this period and its landscape. Morrissey's recalling of this past (located in the particularities of northern England) shares similarities with other cultural productions that question the dominant patriarchal image of the English working-class past. Gordon Burn's novel *Alma* (1991) and a number of films, including Terence Davies's *The Long Day Closes* (1992) and Mike Newell's *Dance with a Stranger* (1984), also return to this period (often termed the "age of affluence") of profound economic and social change for the working class. Morrissey grew up in the northwestern English city of Manchester and has been fascinated with an image of the declining industrial north inherited from the British new wave or "kitchen sink" realist films of the late 50s and early 60s. I'm concerned with Morrissey's "feminizing" of the landscape and its relationship to the violence of Thatcherism. How is the "age of affluence" made to resonate with New Right Britain in the 1980s and 1990s?

The 1950s-1960s past to which Morrissey is drawn also saw the emergence of British cultural studies as an intellectual formation, with the working class a central concern in the writing of Raymond Williams and Richard Hoggart. As Geoff Eley notes: "This was of course a working class defined as a 'whole way of life' by popular culture, not the working class of production and exploitation defined by Marx. As commentators sought to make sense of the postwar changes, they were drawn increasingly toward this ground of culture. Indeed, through a discourse of nostalgia in the making, the idea of the working class has been continually repositioned somewhere beyond political economy, where culture seems or aspires to be a 'safe' place, whether for left or for right."[5]

This working class has been defined in *cultural* rather than explicitly political terms. This may have been politically disabling but nonetheless has shaped the development of working-class subjects. Valerie Walkerdine argues that the work-

ing class has been constructed as a fantasy or fiction in the (left and right) bourgeois imagination, as a problematic group that needs to be transformed. These
fictions have had a truth value that is part and parcel of the regulation and classification of the working class. According to Walkerdine, such fantasies, rather like
the Western fictions of the East that Edward Said discusses in *Orientalism,* tell
us more about their creators than they do about the working class; but, she adds,
"if fictions can function in truth then fictions themselves can have real effects.
Subjects are created in multiple positionings in material and discursive practices,
in specific historical conditions in which certain apparatuses of social regulation
become techniques of self-production. These are imbued with fantasy. We cannot separate something called 'working-class experiences' from the fictions and
fantasies in which . . . that life is produced and read."6

Walkerdine argues that the Left positioned the *white* working class as a problem during the 1970s and 1980s because it was perceived as hindering antiracism
and antisexism. Meanwhile, the Right, throughout the extended tenure of Margaret Thatcher's and John Major's Conservative governments, attacked organized
Labour, emphasized individualism over mass-movement politics, and sentimentalized and depoliticized working-class history. As Eley suggests, this "reconfirmed
the working class as a phenomenon of culture as opposed to politics."7

In the 1980s and 90s, English working-classness becomes increasingly signified
through commodity culture. We see the emergence of a working-class *heritage* in
various products. For example, films, television shows, advertisements, postcards,
posters, product packaging, and popular music perpetuate and refigure notions
of working-class history and geography through what the historian Raphael Samuel calls "retrochic." Through such commodity forms, cultural producers and
consumers create and perpetuate forms of historical knowledge, and sometimes
generate unofficial forms of history that draw on popular memory. In this context, commercial popular-cultural memory is one important battleground on
which working-class identity and its relationship to national identity are contested and negotiated.

The Left's culturalism has tended to perpetuate particular versions of working-
class identity, some of which conflate the national working-class with the *white*
working-class. Such specific evocations of whiteness continue to be used to immediately signify a broader Englishness and Britishness. It therefore becomes necessary to take apart this taken-for-granted whiteness of the national working class.
Following a discussion of Morrissey's reframing of working-class women, I will
turn my attention more explicitly to this goal in a discussion of the skinhead and
soccer hooligan in the singer's iconography. Walkerdine's point that the bourgeois
construction of the working class is similar to orientalism's construction of the

racial, ethnic other offers a way of thinking about the representation of the skinhead in relation to the discursive regime that creates the ethnic other in Britain.

As a longtime fan of the Smiths and Morrissey, I use my discomfort with the
star's apparent fascination with English nationalism to examine the skinhead's
place as a working-class subject in British cultural studies, and the gendered,
racialized, and ethnic assumptions behind some of this writing. But rather than
just lay out yet another history of discourse about the subcultural skinhead, I trace
out his representation in relation to his antithesis, the *Paki*—the South Asian in
Britain—the object of the right-wing skinhead's wrath, the body at the receiving end of the Doc Marten boot. The stereotypical contours of the Paki emerge
at the same time the skinhead is created as a folk devil in the late 1960s. Both are
products of the English environment, and both are framed by academic, political, and journalistic discourse. As a creation (or fiction, in Walkerdine's terms),
the Paki is dependent on the skinhead's presence, a figure in the white youth's
shadow. Where is this British Asian, the designated Paki, to be situated in the
national landscape? My analysis is prompted by Homi Bhabha's call for critical
intervention to "shift from the *identification* of images as positive or negative, to
an understanding of the *processes of subjectification* made possible (and plausible)
through stereotypical discourse. To judge the stereotyped image on the basis of a
prior political normativity is to dismiss it, not to displace it, which is only possible by engaging with its *effectivity;* with the repertoire of positions of power and
resistance, domination and dependence that constructs the colonial subject (both
coloniser and colonised)."[8]

As well as imaging skinheads, Morrissey has also recorded two songs directly
about Britain's South Asians: "Bengali in Platforms" deals with an immigrant's
attempt to assimilate into English culture through wearing Western fashion; and
"Asian Rut" describes a violent clash between an Asian and some white youths.

The following questions of the pop star Morrissey underlie my analysis: Are you
really racist or have you just been brave enough to confront certain realities that
the English on the right and left want to dismiss as "politically incorrect"? Are you
a trickster figure forcing Britishers to confront painful fractures in the national
body? Or are you just another miserable Little Englander who wishes Britain was
still white? And are the answers to these questions mutually exclusive?

A fan's relationship with an English pop star can be opened up to ask broader
questions about the national-cultural condition and reveal something of the ways
in which Pakistani-British subjects, often derided as Pakis, are positioned in British
culture and its "cultural studies."

Morrissey's looking backward shares some similarities with other strains of

British rock music. The chapter concludes with some observations on the nostalgic mode in "Britpop," a media term used to describe a varied collection of guitar groups in the 90s, most prominently Oasis and Blur. Like Morrissey, the memory-work of Britpop seems to be a patriotic/xenophobic reaction to both U.S. cultural hegemony and multicultural Britain, a celebration of hackneyed narratives, images, musical tropes, and ways of representing England. During the mid-90s tabloid-fueled rivalry between the rock groups Oasis and Blur, familiar scenes of white working-class life and lower-middle-class suburbia saturated their songs and product packaging. These musicians captured the sounds and shapes of a "timeless" national popular culture. The landscapes on their CD covers have been reproduced countless times before as immediate signifiers of Englishness: the greyhound races, the canal lock, the semi-detached suburban house. These images allow young Britons to revel in the familiar continuities of "our way of life" while claiming some critical distance from clichéd versions of the past and the English landscape. In an ambiguous fluctuation between intimacy and disavowal, Britpop's camp gestures seem part of an ironic attitude to national history.

Musically, most Britpop groups revive the tried-and-trusted riffs and motifs of English pop and its high points, from the Beatles and Kinks to glam rockers Bowie and Cockney Rebel and punk acts like Wire and the Buzzcocks in the late 1970s. In the concluding part of this chapter, I argue that Britpop is part of the (re)invention of a specifically British rock/guitar pop tradition, an assertion of an indigenous national and distinct version of U.S. rock, at the moment that rock and "what it stands for" seem to be in crisis.

Like Morrissey's performances, the retro mode in these strands of British rock music also reveals a white English masculine identity to be in a state of flux, if not crisis. This may not signal the "passing of hegemonic whiteness," but a shift in consciousness about white ethnicity when faced with feminism and the globalizing popular cultural influences of North America and Europe, as well as the African-Caribbean and Asian diasporas at home.

In the marketplace for popular music, in high-street megastore displays in the U.K. and elsewhere, Morrissey and Britpop acts have vied for attention alongside a number of rapidly multiplying and hybridizing dance-floor genres and subgenres such as techno, jungle/drum'n'bass, bhangra, and trip hop. Representing a modern, indeed futurist, multiracial, multicultural Britain that includes Caribbean and Asian elements, musicians like Goldie, Massive Attack, Bally Sagoo, Tricky, and even Britpop-sounding groups like Echobelly challenge pervasive, banal nationalisms and redefine the "British" in British music (if not its Englishness).[9]

Stardom and Fandom

As a star, Morrissey has a measure of cultural power to circulate commodified representations of the national through audiovisual media. While recognizing institutional and economic determinations in the production of media meaning, we should also, as Georgina Born suggests, pay attention to cultural production in its "imaginary social and aesthetic dimensions." "Only in this way," she states, "is it possible to grasp for any specific cultural production how these different moments and forms may come, in various ways to be politicized." Born argues that we should "think about 'imagined communities' in relation to the politics of cultural production . . . What kind of 'community' do aesthetic strategies articulate/imagine?"[10] In this case, we might ask what kind of England is imagined through Morrissey's pop strategies.

The social meaning of music arises through the complex intersection of not just production, but distribution and consumption. Marcia Landy argues that the

> interfaces between stardom and value production are located in the heterogeneous, seemingly dissimilar ways in which images as products circulate throughout the culture at many levels and at great speed, revealing the protean, mobile, affective, and effective nature of capital through the forms of its cultural commodities. . . . In tracing this complicity between economic and cultural phenomena, questions of subjectivity and affect shed light on the creation, perpetuation, and transformation of affective value that cannot be measured solely in terms of a cash nexus. Cultural discourses are saturated with affect, circulating seemingly independent of the marketplace. Affective representation is closely tied to social representations that circulate knowledge involving sexuality, gender and national identity. . . . Stardom is a complex mode of production and reception. Like production generally, the creation of this commodity entails manufacture, distribution, consumption, reproduction, and recycling, all of which are dependent on a close affiliation with prevailing hegemonic discourses, especially in relation to affective value's role in the process not as excrescence or superstructure but as the heart of cultural creations. The importance of affect in the determination of value construction lies in its revealing the interested and constitutive, rather than innocent and essential, character of subjectivity.[11]

"Affect" has been one of those slippery concepts used by theorists to explain the way people experience the media. In an essay on the "affective sensibility of fandom," Lawrence Grossberg defines "affect" as "closely tied to what we often describe as the feeling of life. . . . But feeling, as it functions here, is not a subjective experience. It is a socially constructed domain of cultural effects. . . . Affect is what gives 'color,' 'tone' or 'texture' to our experiences." For Grossberg, affect is organized and thus produces "mattering maps," which are like "investment portfolios" that attempt to "organize moments of stable identity, sites at which we can, at least temporarily, find ourselves 'at home' with what we care about."[12]

However, Grossberg believes that the place of music in people's lived realities should be understood socially rather than psychologically; the psychological is the realm of "experience" whereas the social is where "determination and power" are situated. As Dave Laing argues, this is too simplistic a division between the psychological and social, and "denies the importance of the subject and the subjective, and of the psychoanalytical, in the processes of power as well as those of responding to music."[13] Neil Nehring also questions Grossberg's splitting of emotion from affect, in which emotion is seen to be an "internal or personal matter" whereas affect depends on broader determining social structures. Grossberg's dismissal of emotion seems to reproduce the critical division between the personal and the political, private and public, feeling and thought, body and mind.[14]

These criticisms back up my own suspicions that sometimes in film, television, and media studies, "affect" is a term favored by academics to dress up their own "guilty" pleasures, investments, and feelings about popular culture; the notion of "affect" can be a rhetorical device that distances an academic understanding of popular culture from the emotionally charged engagement of bodies outside the university. (Feelings, nothing more than feelings . . .) But, of course, fans are scholarly and academics do get "worked up" about popular cultural forms. I've used the Smiths and Morrissey to (dis)orient myself in a number of ways.

As a Pakistani who grew up in Britain during the 1970s and 1980s, I've been produced as a British citizen ("naturalized" in 1973) through English institutions and shaped by U.K. racism. My subjectivity has also been formed in some significant measure by the presence of the skinhead.[15] My mother, brother, sister, and I joined my father in Britain in July 1968, when I was five years old. This was just a few months after Enoch Powell, the godfather of New Right cultural racism and a Member of Parliament from the Midlands region where we first lived, made his infamous speech predicting civil war and "rivers of blood" if immigration from the former colonies in the Caribbean and the Indian subcontinent were to continue. According to Powell, who had a taste for the exotic metaphor, allowing more black people into the country was like piling bodies on a funeral pyre.

By 1968, with the postwar economic boom and swinging London receding from view, the skinhead was emerging from its subcultural precursor, the "hard mod." Powell's public pronouncements gave skins (and others so inclined) the license to indulge in "Paki-bashing." I was hit for being a Paki only a handful of times.

Otherwise, there was constant harassment throughout my childhood in the 70s and the reminder that I was a "Paki cunt nignog wog sambo black bastard" from children, teenagers, and adults at bus stops, in the playground, outside the school gates, at the soccer match, in pubs and streets. "Enocky nocky nocky nock" was a gleeful taunt from some kids, the words often accompanied by saliva showered in my general direction. During soccer matches for the primary school team or in kickabouts in the park, other players would curse racist abuse as they lunged into the tackle. These were the rules of the game. Even after I left school, the racist verbals came from people of all ages, and the threat of violence always seemed near the surface of life.

"Where is the place that you move into the landscape and can see yourself?" poses Carolyn Steedman in her analysis of the failures of Marxism and psycho-analysis to account for the experiences of working-class women and girls.[16] "What binds together images and sounds in personal memory with images and sounds in collective memory?" asks Annette Kuhn in another critical autobiography.[17] My "experience" isn't emblematic of British Asian life; has anyone encountered the "typical British Asian"? My analysis of white British rock seeks neither to reproduce the false cultural binary of Pakistani diasporic identity against white Englishness nor to proclaim right-on militant Asianness against racist whiteness. On the other hand, I have no desire to act as a cheerleader for British metropol-itan multikulti hybridity either. Though many of us are hodge-podge black white brown, the often tortuous complexities of growing up brown in a deeply racist society are frequently obscured in the rush to validate and celebrate the hybrid and hyphenated self or to claim a normative politically correct identity "sorted" for the race/class wars. British/English racism has done some long-term psychic damage. I needed to leave England for repair work.

The embodied, ontological reality of racism made me a Paki. I've occupied a place outside Englishness, despite at the same time being interpolated by many well-worn marks of so-called quintessentially English culture. Inside and outside Englishness, belonging and unbelonging, by taking apart white Englishness in this chapter I also acknowledge that aspects of both its whiteness as signified by Morrissey, and forms of power and knowledge that produced "the Paki," have together shaped my identity as a British subject and pop music fan. Therefore, in this meditation on Mozzer, I use and abuse him as a kind of enabling device to explore the question of my own national identity or lack of it, my affection for England, and my anger with it.

If one had to choose a pop star, Morrissey seems singularly appropriate for this purpose, given the powerful discourse of "the self" and "the fan" in his body of work. He has self-consciously developed a pop persona through song lyrics, record-sleeve design, and interview pronouncements. Steve Redhead notes that Morrissey's cultivation of his own image of ambiguous sexuality and celibacy, however mannered, is a working on "techniques of the self" as outlined by Foucault.[18] Foucault stresses not only "the technology of domination and power" but also "the history of how an individual acts upon himself, in the technology of the self." These are "techniques which permit individuals to affect, by their own means, a certain number of operations on their own bodies, their own souls, their own thought, their own conduct, and this in a manner so as to transform themselves, modify themselves."[19] Morrissey's own fandom is essential to his work. His citation of films, literary figures, pop stars, and the "cover stars" on his record sleeves and in the songs themselves point to his own imaginative engagement as a fan. His video collections *Hulmerist* and *Introducing Morrissey* present live performances during which streams of devoted fans leap up on to the stage and kiss or hug Morrissey in slow motion before being led off by a roadie. While I've loved the Smiths and Morrissey, just like the skinheads and others at Madstock, I'm ready to throw a few awkward verbal projectiles in his direction.

The Smiths, the Music Press, and Rock Authenticity

A brief outline of Morrissey's career with the Smiths will help to contextualize the representation of the English working class in the group's sounds and images. The Smiths were (Steven) Patrick Morrissey: voice; Johnny Marr: guitar; Andy Rourke: bass; and Mike Joyce: drums. This traditional four-piece rock group was formed in Manchester. Its first single, "Hand in Glove," was released in May 1983 on the independent Rough Trade label. Exposure on John Peel's influential late-night radio show on BBC Radio One and music press coverage put the group on the national musical map. The Smiths became the front page darlings of the weekly *New Musical Express (NME)*, which featured regular interviews with Morrissey. Though Morrissey (words) and Marr (music) co-wrote the group's material, the press focused on the singer, who became spokesperson for the group, providing witty, literate, and provocative pull-quotes for the features pages of the major weeklies *NME, Sounds,* and *Melody Maker.*

The role of the national music press in the ascent of the Smiths, particularly the weekly large newspaper format "inkies," cannot be overstated. The British music press is a powerful force in the production of popular music discourse and a vital institution in the mediation of stardom. The Smiths arrived on the national popular music scene when sales of the weeklies were falling as monthly glossy four-color (life)style magazines like *The Face, I-D, Blitz,* and the teen-oriented bi-weekly *Smash Hits* dominated the pop publishing market. If the *NME,*

Sounds, and *Melody Maker* represented broad rock constituencies of musicians and listener-consumers, the new lifestyles magazines signaled the transformation of publishing to niche-market oriented magazines in a more "user-friendly" format: less ink on your fingers, smaller-sized pages, less text, more photographs, fewer features, more short interviews. As John Williams later put it in *I-D* magazine, this was "the moment when *The Face* takes over from the *NME* as an arbiter of style, when cocktail bars replace dingy pubs, when second-hand Flip finery replaces mock-prole utility clothing, when Roland Barthes replaces Leon Trotsky as a name to drop, when irony replaces authenticity and postmodernism comes too soon."[20]

Some music journalists promoted the so-called new pop (a term coined by *NME* writer Paul Morley) as a way out of punk's and rock's musical and ideological ossification, as a line of escape from the grayness and dourness of early 1980s Britain under Thatcher. Artists such as Sheffield's ABC and the Human League, the tweedy cleancut Haircut One Hundred, and Scottish groups like the Fire Engines and Altered Images were perceived to write classic pop songs; they presented themselves as bright and "shiny" audiovisual packages, but with a sharp understanding of the pop industry's machinery and an ironic attitude to its fabrications.

The transition from post-punk to new pop was exemplified in the work of West London–based Scritti Politti, who in the late 1970s had recorded EPs with song titles like "Hegemony," designed record sleeves with extracts of Gramsci's writings, and even made a BBC2 television documentary showing how anyone could go about recording and releasing music on one's own record label for a relatively small amount of money. By the early 1980s, Scritti Politti was releasing a series of singles with sleeves that pastiched the chic packaging of pricey consumer products like Dunhill cigarettes and Napoleon Brandy. From scratchy rock guitar and reggae bass lines the group's sound was transformed into synthesized dance music with expensive New York production and references to Aretha Franklin. Along the way the Scrits, as some affectionately dubbed them, even recorded a double A-side single entitled "Asylums in Jerusalem"/"Jacques Derrida," which convinced some academic critics and serious journalists that pop culture's politics had shifted from (at least a trace of) quasi-Marxist commitment and praxis to postmodern play, political ambiguity, and the hedonism of the dance floor. Pop writers like Morley and Ian Penman at the *NME* brought high theory to high-street pop culture, with Nietzsche, Derrida, and Barthes turning up in the review and features pages to enliven discussions of pleasure, textual ambiguity, and the body.

New pop seemed a slightly askew, cracked-mirror image of Thatcher's consumerist dream. Its emergence overlapped with the influence of the style magazines dedicated to shopping for trendy products. But new pop also coincided with the increasing interest in African-American dance music culture such as hip-hop/rap. *The Face* and *I-D* tended to focus on the fashions and music of London's cliquey club culture and publicized new imported American records that were, in turn, embraced by a burgeoning domestic dance-floor market.

Whether new pop's imitation of Thatcherite values was a sly mimicry is arguable. Wham!, formed by George Michael and Andrew Ridgely in Watford, on the outskirts of northwest London, began their recording career with the independently released twelve-inch dance single "Wham Rap," in which they defiantly celebrated the joys of weekend nightclubbing with their unemployment benefit money. You could still have "soul on the dole." By the time the Watford boys were *Smash Hits* cover idols, they had released "Club Tropicana," a song about a nightclubbing paradise where there was "fun and joy for everyone." Thus, Wham! predicted the flight to Ibiza and the rave scene.

In contrast, the Smiths just said No. Simon Reynolds suggests that "New Pop, far from being a bright new beginning, turned out to be merely the inauguration of global designer-soul, the soundtrack to the new yuppie culture of health and efficiency. In the face of the benign totalitarianism of leisure capitalism and its off-the-peg self-improvement, the Smiths glamorized debility and illness, advocated absenteeism, withdrawal, the failure to meet quotas of enjoyment."[21] Reynolds loved the Smiths because of their negation, their celebration of illness and the abject. As a rock critic he has tended to attack music that smacks of good health, well-being, and "social adjustment." The Smiths appeared to represent everything antithetical to London-based consumerism and the government lie that the nation was fit and working again after the "permissive society," Labour welfarism, and national self-doubt.

For the weekly rock press the Smiths were a new old-fashioned pop group in the authentic rock tradition. They played guitars, not electronic instruments. They wrote three-minute songs that were released primarily as seven-inch vinyl singles—the vintage pop form—rather than the longer twelve-inch single format of dance music that stressed the rhythmic groove as much as the singer's voice. The Smiths remained on the independent label Rough Trade rather than sign with a major company. This position on the margins of the corporate capitalist recording industry gave them greater rock credibility. Despite the group's "indie" status, the Smiths still managed chart success with fifteen Top-30 hits and seven Top-10 albums in Britain between late 1983 and mid-1987, when they split up. They became popular with American college students. Rock authenticity was further secured by Morrissey and Marr's decision to resist using the promotional music video for much of the group's career, unlike nakedly commercially mind-

ed new-pop artists like Duran Duran and Culture Club who embraced the visual format. The Smiths were also considered more authentic because they could
"cut it live," touring extensively and using "real" instruments, rather than the
synths of the dressed-up groups.

From a well-documented Manchester music scene, the group was seen to
emerge from a real community that was embedded in their songs, images, and
press pronouncements; in short, in almost every aspect of their performance.
The Smiths were proudly local, indigenous and thoroughly English in their
accent. Morrissey sang in a Manchester accent about everyday life in a recognizable north. The group's very name encapsulated ordinary Englishness. They
dressed down, were stylish but not flashy. At a time when, according to Will
Straw, there was "an intensification of the discourses of celebrity" and the renewed involvement of young adolescents in popular music consumption through
music video and magazines, the Smiths seemed to stand apart from these developments while backhandedly exploiting these very conditions.[22]

Notions of "authenticity" grounded in rock ideology still remain powerful in
the music press and fan discourse, even though some journalists and academic
critics have sought to question these assumptions. Simon Frith, for example, critiques the suggestion that "pop music becomes more valuable the more independent it is of the social forces that organize the pop process in the first place; pop
value is dependent on something outside pop, is rooted in the person, the *auteur,*
the community, or the subculture that lies behind it." Frith proposes instead that
"the question we should be asking is not what does popular music reveal about
the people but how does it *construct* them."[23] Steve Redhead also argues that "the
view that musical forms can express community of any kind is indeed fraught with
difficulty. There is, initially, the objection that the community is itself constructed, to some extent, through the medium of the musical form. . . . But even more
testing is the question of the pre-existence of 'given' communities at all. There is
the argument [made by Colin McCabe] that we 'are all members of numerous
communities, which hold often contradictory beliefs and attitudes.' Pop and rock
music's association with nationalism and regionalism becomes ever more crucial
for the question of how pop can be politicised, as the internationalisation—even
globalisation—of pop music culture continues apace."[24] The weekly rock press,
for example, continues to advocate a kind of pop nationalism and assumes a community, constituency, and demographic of readers and fans that are predominantly
white and male.

In a polemic against rock values, Jeremy Gilbert argues that in rock press discourse, "authenticity is guaranteed by the presence of a specific type of instrumentation (rhythm guitar, bass, drums, voice). The singer is all-important, and

it is crucial that he (it was always he) be authentic and sincere, because his fundamental role is to represent the culture from which he comes."[25] According to Gilbert, this is part of a conservative reaction against new constituencies or communities of music listeners in Britain: "As young people started to dance to music without words—made originally for black queens—the boys in the indie press began their desperate rearguard action, and it isn't yet over. We've seen it every time a pallid vocalist backed by a conventional four-piece has been heralded as the second-coming of those great saviours, The Smiths (who appeared at just the moment when faced with post-punk experimentation, New Pop and the first stirrings of electronic dance, British Rock last looked in danger of collapsing), and we'll see it again."[26]

Notions of rock authenticity are rooted in a 1960s rock ideology that sees music as reflecting the genuine and potentially radical voice of the people/folk. There are, in fact, many authenticities, some of which correspond to different segments of the pop market defined by musical genre and different fan constituencies.

Grossberg takes the view that any notion of authenticity is a lie. The way pop stars function in these economic conditions negates any sincere intentionality on the part of the musician or authentic reception on the part of the listener-consumer: "the star is a mobile sign which can be linked to any practice, product or knowledge, freed from any message or set of values. The star is no longer an individual measured by their creativity, their authentic relation to their performance, or even the possibilities of an audience projecting its fantasies on to them. The star is a commodified and mobile sign, moving across the broad terrain of cultural tastes and entertainment."[27]

Keith Negus points out that Grossberg displaces the meaning of popular music purely to the play of signs rather than arising out of concrete origins and relations with audiences. Though there has undoubtedly been a proliferation in pop discourse, in the repertoire of signs available within pop music culture, Negus contends that "these signs are not simply connected to other signs but to very specific social conditions and life experiences." He uses the "star texts" of Bruce Springsteen and Bob Marley to point out that "the issue of authenticity is not so much about the way in which an act truthfully represents its 'real' origins, but about the way in which the affective relationship between artist and audience is mediated and articulated. Notions of authenticity cannot be explained as myths which conceal more real conditions, nor as mobile meanings continually emerging out of a sea of endlessly circulating signs. At some point these meanings connect human beings."[28]

I would agree that while authenticities are fabricated, they have power and currency because they are stitched into the fabric of the everyday lives of music listeners. The way listeners feel and think that music is authentic does not always correspond to particular community values, for we can be members of many contradictory and overlapping communities. In a study of country music's development, Richard Peterson also suggests that authenticity isn't static, but "continuously negotiated in an ongoing interplay between performers, diverse commercial interests, fans, and the evolving image." The continuing authenticity of country music for its producers and fans is due to the fact that authenticity is a "renewable resource," drawn upon in different shapes again and again.[29] In his discussion of a different musical field—world music and its fans—Timothy Taylor argues that authenticity is, as Martin Stokes describes, "a discursive trope of great persuasive power,"[30] sometimes a marketing tool, but also a real thing in which musicians and listeners believe.

The concept of "authenticity" continues to preoccupy scholars in the still loosely defined domain of popular music studies. The authentic is invoked or implicit in academic debates about the commodification of music and its mediation by technology, in questions of music's representation of specific communities, and in arguments about musical value and taste. Meanwhile, music listeners mobilize the concept in debating whether "selling out" to MTV and corporate record companies is a betrayal of authenticity; dance music fans celebrate an authentic "underground" against the mainstream; and members of the hip-hop nation pronounce the importance of "keeping it real."

Flip unmaskings of the manufactured "lies" behind authenticities fail to understand the power of discourses of authenticity in the institutionalization and currency of commercial music. While claims to authenticity require the work of fabrication, we should be aware of the multiple and shifting political positions and rationales different social agents occupy when they lay claim to the authentic.[31]

A cursory glance through *The Smiths: All Men Have Secrets,* a collection of fan letters about the role of Smiths songs in their lives, reveals that the songs function in myriad ways across a hugely varied body of listeners. For example, the songs inhabit and invoke memories of joblessness, love affairs with Belgians, and the death of a grandmother.[32] The many Smiths/Morrissey fanzines (e.g., *Miserable Lies, Wilde about Morrissey, Jammy Stressford, Sing Your Life*) and World Wide Web sites and newsgroups spend much of their time in the exchange of consumer collectibles associated with the star, but they also confirm the broad array of identifications, pleasures, and irritations with the star's cultural production, as well as initiate fan activities that only marginally depend on the star.

As for my own fandom, in the 1980s the Smiths were part of a north of England battered by Thatcherite policies. Chronic unemployment was a result of the decline in manufacturing industries. Even middle-class university students and graduates like myself seemed downwardly mobile, spending intermittent and sometimes long periods on the dole in an economic climate where academic qualifications didn't translate into full-time jobs, never mind careers. Higher education kept at bay the dole's subsistence lifestyle and the terrifying alternative offered by the privatized hell of the growing service and financial sectors. Tertiary education at least provided some kind of narrative of a future. Hugo Young notes in his biography of Margaret Thatcher that in 1981 a "Tory backbencher returned from a visit to Hartlepool, in North-east England, with the intelligence that according to the town's director of education it was now statistically more probable that a young person would get to university than get a job."[33] However, with cuts in government spending on education throughout the 1980s, some of us chose and were able to escape to foreign parts.

In 1984, Morrissey caught the narrowing possibilities with close-to-the-bone humor when the Smiths presented their "Heaven Knows I'm Miserable Now" hit on BBC1's primetime *Top of the Pops* amidst a studio audience whipped up by relentlessly perky disc jockeys. A swiveling Morrissey in nerdy national health spectacles lipsynched his words of woe with a hearing aid in one ear (an homage to 1950s American heartthrob Johnnie Ray) and a bunch of gladioli protruding from the back pocket of his blue jeans. Johnny Marr's light and lustrous guitar lines counterpointed the combination of drolery and melancholy in Morrissey's words, which claimed that even managing the near impossible—finding a job—was no guarantee of happiness.

At the height of their national success in 1986, the Smiths played the London Palladium, an old-world theatrical venue famous for its regular royal command performances. The concert was the culmination of a tour promoting their fourth album release and number-one hit *The Queen Is Dead*. On stage, Morrissey aggressively wielded a placard bearing the record's title, like a totem designed to exorcise any spiritual trace of the monarchy from the concert hall. Teenage Morrissey clones who had followed the group around on their national tour stood in the balcony seats beside me, mouthing every word of every song.

The album's title track, which opened the group's live set, assaults the official version of England and English history hyped by Margaret Thatcher and the ideologues of the New Right. As a stubborn indictment of one kind of born-again cultural nationalism, it jabs at the symbol of the "national family"—the royals. Accompanied by the slashing and thrashing, abrasive guitar of Johnny Marr, and thundering bass and drums of Andy Rourke and Mike Joyce, Morrissey's lyrics sound out England's ugliness and lack of possibility. This might be William Blake's dream of England as Jerusalem, but it's turned into a nightmare in which its subjects are like captured animals. The singer goes on to ridicule the monarchy with swipes at a disabled queen and a Prince Charles who likes to dress in his mother's clothes. "The Queen Is Dead" also alludes to Michael Fagin, who in the early 1980s broke into the queen's bedroom to have a heart-to-heart chat with Her Majesty. In the song, such an entry into the royal chambers with a sponge and a spanner suggests that the hermetically sealed space of the palace can be disrupted with the ordinary, grubby items of everyday English life.

Jon Savage argues that the recording "fused existential desolation and the hardest, most spacious rock possible into what remains the most accurate emotional map of nonmetropolitan English life in the '80s."[34] In its description of a grim, urban landscape that offers no hope of finding a home, of a place to belong, there's little hope for community. Neither the pub nor the church can save you from alienation. In such writing, Morrissey dissolves the distance between public and private matters. The Smiths' lyrics repeatedly obsess over everyday humiliations and the misery of not belonging, but such personal traumas are placed in the concrete public context of the urban landscape.

In rock mythology, the *street* is where the boys are, where the (political and sexual) action is, the road to empowerment, or at least the place where the lads hang out and try to look cool. But many Smiths songs with Marr's melancholic guitar lines articulate the loneliness, danger, and violence of city streets. On "Never Had No One Ever," from *The Queen Is Dead,* Morrissey sings about the unease of walking on streets you have known all your life. "The Death of a Disco Dancer," a song from the Smiths' last studio album, *Strangeways, Here We Come* (1987), suggests that any hope for a common culture of nonviolence is evidence of ignorance about these urban realities.

The sense of not completely belonging to a landscape and the vulnerability and fear on the streets had a resonance for me as a fan in the 1980s. I saw the Smiths in concert for the first time at Leeds University on a biting cold February night in 1984. After the show, my younger sister and I waited alone for the last bus home to Ilkley, at a bus stop in front of the university's Georgian facade. Our ears still hummed from the loudness of the PA system. Across the street, the neon sign for the Islamabad Restaurant was glowing red. Suddenly four white skinheads burst through the restaurant's doors into the street and hurtled toward us like skittles about to topple over. Two Pakistani waiters in white jackets stormed out of the doors a moment later. They tripped one skin and kicked him repeatedly as he lay jerking around on the pavement. His mates gawped at the scene from our side of the street, only a few feet away from us, unsure whether to enter the fray or give their comrade up to the Pakistani kicks.

A number of thoughts raced through my head: the three skins might kick the shit out of us in revenge and frustration. Worse still, they might hover interminably, spit expletives, or just mutter "Paki" at us like a thousand and one times before. I hoped that silence and quiet deference would assuage the fist and boot. Sometimes it seems eminently reasonable to comply to the passive, emasculated middle-class Asian stereotype when you're middle-class, Asian, outnumbered, and scared.

Fortunately the skins retreated, mumbling and grumbling their way up the street. Safely on the 783 bus, I was warmed by the thought that our fellow Pakistanis had wrought justice on some of the fascist bastard sons of Enoch, who doubtless had tried to disturb the peaceful consumption of curries after a few pints down at the local. The deserved kicking was like payback for all the years of schoolyard abuse. Though I had been a mute witness to the violence, the incident proved that we Asians were not the passive race the whites made us out to be. The Smiths' "Barbarism Begins at Home," which Morrissey had sung only minutes earlier, seemed shockingly appropriate. The Smiths uncovered the violence that was "normal" in northern homes, schools, and streets. My near run-in with the skinheads in Leeds also presaged the solo Morrissey song "Asian Rut," in which the narrator passively watches an Asian boy getting his head kicked in by white youths. Though I, of course, had watched a white skin being assaulted.

It's Grim Up North: The Landscape, Women, and Violence

In Morrissey's oeuvre, the local flavor and minutiae of Englishness/Britishness are registers of an obsession as deep and murky as the waters of the Manchester-Liverpool canal. Morrissey's particular fascination with the white English working class can be charted through record sleeves, songs, videos, and the visuals of his gigantic concert stage backdrops. The northern English landscapes of Smiths songs present the proletarian proto-city of back-to-back houses and grimy, rain-sodden streets. Many of the group's plaintive guitar motifs and geographical references in lyrics conjure up a Manchester beautifully sorry for itself and its postindustrial urban wasteland. This is still a powerful image of Manchester and the urban north, even though European money, the shift to service industries, and redevelopment have transformed the inner city in the 1990s.

The Smiths' psychogeography maps a bleak cityscape based on black-and-white images of seedy Manchester, Leeds, and Bradford in the kitchen-sink movies of the late 1950s and early 60s. The music seems to photograph the industrial north in economic decline. Morrissey's lyrics, his wistful vocalese, and Johnny Marr's plangent guitar arrangements lovingly draw a wasteland of bus stops, bedsit flats, dilapidated railway lines, canals, and iron bridges.

On the inner sleeve of their album *The Queen Is Dead*, in an iconic image, the Smiths stand in front of Salford Lads Club on the corner of Coronation Street, the original location for Granada Television's long-running soap opera. *Coronation Street* has come to represent the quintessential northern working-class street and neighborhood lodged in popular memory.[35] In the 1930s, the photographs and ethnographic descriptions of Mass Observation and George Orwell's *The Road to Wigan Pier* revealed the poverty, color, and stoicism of this kind of mythical working-class street. For Richard Hoggart in *The Uses of Literacy*, this "landscape with figures" and its neighborly working-class culture were threatened by American-style mass consumerism.[36] In the early 1960s, the kitchen-sink films (most of which were directed by middle-class men) turned this urban landscape into a poetic mirror for the existential desolation and class resentments of angry young working-class men (but very few angry young women). By the 1980s, this vision of the north had been pastiched and parodied endlessly to the point of cliché: aye, we all knew about "dark satanic mills" and how it was "grim up north"; but this mythology of "northernness" still had political and cultural resonance twenty years later in a period when the north was suffering from Thatcherite policies and those mills were being replaced by malls and McDonald's.

The sense of the north as still alien to the relatively affluent south was captured by the conceptual pranksters the Justified Ancients of Mu Mu in their 1992 hit single "It's Grim Up North." The track essentially consists of a list of northern British towns read portentously, like an obscure religious litany (in a Scottish accent), over a propulsive electronic beat. Sound effects of hooting factory horns (and dark satanic mills?) intersperse the track with the beat, finally segueing into a disco-meets-Wagner electronic mock orchestral version of "Jerusalem." On BBC1's *Top of the Pops* the group appeared in costumes suggesting they were druids invoking some pagan spirit of the land. The sleeve notes for the single dwell on this strange wasteland (for many southerners) just up the motorway from London and Birmingham:

> Having stepped from the wreckage of their 1968 Ford Galaxy American police car Rockman Rock and Kingboy D (the Justified Ancients of Mu Mu) found their ice-cream van. Heading East up over the Pennine-straddling M62, they pull their ice-cream van onto the hard shoulder. Behind them to the west, they can still make out the sprawling conurbation of Greater Manchester and those surrounding Lancashire towns, proud in their decline. Further west, somewhere beyond where Liverpool used to be, a dirty sunset sinks into the Irish sea. To the east the sky is already dark, the Yorkshire towns seeking solace in their Pennine valleys, but up here on this unhealing gash across the backbone of England the immediate landscape is a desolate moorland, with none of the grandeur of the highlands or the classic English beauty

of the Lakes. Three bedraggled sheep huddle for shelter in a ditch, the drizzle toughens, then climbs to a solid rain. Heavy goods vehicles plough by, tacographs on overload. A leaded grime smears the verges, sodden silk cut packets wonder whether they are biodegrading. A crow flies north. Through the downpour and diesel roar, Rockman Rock and Kingboy D can feel a regular dull thud. Whether this is the eternal echo of a Victorian steam-driven revolution or the turbo-driven kick of a distant northern rave is irrelevant. Thus inspired, the Justified Ancients of Mu Mu climb into the back of their ice-cream van and work.[37]

The Smiths' recovery of an endlessly commodified image of the north and its representational tropes is also a marker of regional and economic difference. Like the late 80s t-shirts that read "Manchester—Born in the North, Return to the North, Exist in the North, Die in the North," the Smiths directed dissident gestures to the more affluent south. Morrissey cites snatches of kitchen-sink film dialogue in songs, and the group's recordings even directly sample from these films. Record sleeves reproduced stills from some of the kitchen-sink films and used photographs of northern celebrities of this era as "cover stars." A young Pat Phoenix, who played the feisty Elsie Tanner in *Coronation Street,* appears on the cover of the single with the Virginia Woolfian title "Shakespeare's Sister." Shelagh Delaney, author of *A Taste of Honey* (and later the screenplay for the film *Dance with a Stranger*), graces the sleeves of the single "Girlfriend in a Coma" and the American compilation release *Louder Than Bombs.* Rita Tushingham, star of *A Taste of Honey,* is the face on a version of "Hand in Glove," on which the Smiths collaborated with the 1960s pop singer Sandie Shaw. Tushingham's lack of Hollywood glamour expresses Morrissey's rejection of the Hollywoodization of British culture. She also appears in the video for "Girlfriend in a Coma," in a sampled clip of *The Leather Boys,* one of the few kitchen-sink/British new wave/social realist movies to deal directly with homosexuality. The actor Colin Campbell, from the same film, is on the cover of the Dutch release of the single "Ask." Liverpool's early rock 'n' roller Billy Fury is the sartorially elegant cover star of the single "Last Night I Dreamt Somebody Loved Me." On the "What Difference Does It Make" single, a young Terence Stamp holds a glass of milk in a still from *The Collector.*

When these records were released in the mid-1980s it was unusual to see such faces on record sleeves. Most pop musicians tended to present themselves as part of their packaging or, like acts on the independent Factory and 4AD labels, have an "arty" abstract design that created an enigmatic identity around the group through stylistic association. The Smiths rarely appeared on their record jackets. The "cover stars" on their releases undoubtedly reflected Morrissey's own emotional biography and affective investments. But these images, with lyrics and music, also reverberated as part of collective memory in a movement between the past and the present, circulating alongside a host of other popular representations of the working-class past: retro postcards in gift shops depicting children in long shorts and the cloth-capped masses at 1930s soccer matches, photographs of cobbled streets in theme pubs, the films of Terence Davies, and television ads exploiting the image of a cozy, communal-heritage north to sell bread (e.g., Hovis) and cakes. Morrissey uses the technologies and commodified spaces of pop music culture to rework popular memory with his personal fan's gallery. For example, the audio sample of the song "Take Me Back to Dear Old Blighty" from the 1962 film *The L-Shaped Room,* which opens "The Queen Is Dead," is a nostalgic invocation to think of Britain past in relation to its perilous present.[38]

In her discussion of kitsch and camp objects, Susan Stewart suggests the personal and collective function of Morrissey's images and samples from the past:

> Such objects serve to subjectify all of consumer culture, to institute a nostalgia of the populace which in fact makes the populace itself a kind of subject. Kitsch objects are not apprehended as the souvenir proper is apprehended, that is, on the level of the individual autobiography; rather, they are apprehended on the level of collective identity. They are souvenirs of an era and not of a self. Hence they tend to accumulate around that period of intense socialization, adolescence, just as the souvenir proper accumulates around that period of intense subjectivity, childhood.[39]

The resurrection of old celebrities in a new context, filtered through the domain of Smithsdom—in songs, record sleeves, interviews, advertising—forms a strategy of remembrance that dwells on the power of the photograph. This is a probing of the past that works through defamiliarizing the familiar. The past as image is filtered through a fetishism for rock 'n' roll style. In the world of pop music, the look has always been as important as the noise. When the fan dwells on the Smiths record sleeves he or she attends to the bouffant hairstyle and knitted mini-dress of Vivienne Nicholson, the leather jackets of 1950s rockers, Pat Phoenix's kiss curl, the way Shelagh Delaney holds her cigarette. History is informed by rock 'n' roll spectacle and vice versa.

The tinted pictures of these women celebrities imbue them with a glamour of the English everyday, something rare in the dominant imagery of working-class women in the 1950s and 1960s. Nearly all visions of femininity from this period yield hardworking, self-sacrificing mothers, often passively tied to their televisions and radios, sometimes consumption-mad girls bent on upward mobility by any means necessary, sexually promiscuous "sluts and slags," and women set on trapping young men into marriage and parenthood. Women in this received image of the north, present in films like *A Kind of Loving, Saturday Night and*

Sunday Morning, and *Billy Liar,* take second place to the troubled subjectivities
and escape narratives of angry young men.

Because this patriarchal social realism in British new wave films, the Griersonian
documentary tradition, novels, and nonfiction (including British cultural studies) has almost come to stand in for a timeless Britishness or Englishness, feminist historians and cultural critics in the 1980s and 90s have been engaged in a
thorough re-examination of this version of the past. Carolyn Steedman, for example, outlines the project of a feminist rewriting of working-class history at the
beginning of *Landscape for a Good Woman:*

> The fixed townscapes of Northampton and Leeds that Hoggart and Seabrook have
> described show endless streets of houses, where mothers who don't go out to work
> order the domestic day, where men are masters, and children, when they grow older,
> express gratitude for the harsh discipline meted out to them. The first task is to par-
> ticularize this profoundly a-historical landscape (and so this book details a mother
> who was a working woman and a single parent, and a father who wasn't a patriarch).
> And once the landscape is detailed and historicized in this way, the urgent need be-
> comes to find a way of theorizing the result of such difference and particularity, not
> in order to find a description that can be universally applied (the point is not to say
> that all working-class childhoods are the same, nor that experience of them produces
> unique psychic structures) but so that people in exile, the inhabitants of the long
> streets, may start to use the autobiographical "I," and tell the stories of their life.[40]

Echoing Steedman's points, Annette Kuhn tells her own story as a "scholarship girl" because someone like her is not to be found in the standard accounts
of the working-class past: "The only young women in Hoggart's account are the
undifferentiated, briefly flowering girls in flimsy frocks and bright lipstick, the
scholarship boy's flighty, factory-working sisters, giggling together on their way
to the cinema or the dance hall. The scholarship girl does not belong with them,
either. If she wants a role in this story, the scholarship girl must, it seems, create
it for herself."[41]

In a related vein, Beatrix Campbell returns to Wigan Pier in the mid-1980s to
revisit the elisions in Orwell's famous text, and to examine changes in the constitution and representation of the English working class under Thatcherism.[42]
Such feminist memory-work in recent years produces revisions and remakes that
subvert dominant ideas about gender and sexuality in the working-class landscape.

While Morrissey's retro work is nowhere as radical a reassessment of the past,
it does open up a supplementary space for discussion of representations of English working-class femininity. Vivienne Nicholson and Myra Hindley, two
women from the 1960s that appear in the Smiths pantheon, illustrate how popular memory becomes activated in the present through commodity culture.

These vintage images tell us something about the consumerism and *violence* of Thatcherism. But why should images of working-class life in the 1950s and early 1960s have had currency in the 1980s?

During the Thatcher years working-class life was profoundly restructured. The turn to the "age of affluence" makes sense because the urban landscape was also transformed in that period, throwing working-class identity into flux. This was the point when the real landscape of Coronation Street—the long terrace—was being demolished to be replaced by huge council blocks of flats. The old cityscape's power to evoke a mythical working-class community was most forceful at the point of its near disappearance.

According to Labour and Conservative governments of this period, consumerism and new technology were supposed to save British capitalism. In the Thatcher era, there was an ideological drive toward a consumer society and service economy. Thatcher promised economic mobility for the working-class in the new Britain. She stressed individualism, working-class enterprise in the form of small businesses, the private ownership of property, and shares in former nationalized industries. She sought a radical change in the class formation of the nation.

In 1957, the Conservative prime minister Harold Macmillan told the nation that "most of our people have never had it so good. Go round the country, go to the industrial towns, and you will see a state of prosperity such as we have never had in my lifetime—nor indeed ever in the history of this country." From 1951 to 1964, John Hill points out, "Total production (measured at constant prices) increased by 40 per cent, average earnings (allowing for inflation) by 30 per cent, while personal consumption, measured in terms of ownership of cars and televisions, rose from two-and-a-quarter million to 8 million and 1 million to 13 million respectively."[43] Macmillan would say that "the class war is over," assuming a new social and political consensus in Britain, and claiming that postwar prosperity was eroding fundamental class divisions. According to many commentators on both left and right, the working class was apparently disappearing through a process of "embourgeoisment"—the adoption of middle-class values.

Hill says that "it was the ideological achievement of the period to focus on the local shifts and transformations while concealing the essential continuity of the 'outer boundaries.'"[44] The working class's relative economic relation to the middle class remained essentially intact throughout the late 50s and early 60s even though higher disposable income, for young workers in particular, marked the emergence of new patterns of consumption. But just as Margaret Thatcher's ideology of a classless consumer capitalist society resulted in chronic high unemployment and the emergence of an underclass, so the promise of prosperity in the 1960s evaporated as Britain's manufacturing industry was mismanaged and run down by successive Conservative and Labour governments. While 1950s and 1960s Conservative and Labour ideologies were based on consensus, and Thatcher's New Right policies broke with consensus to create a new hegemonic structure in Britain, both in their respective historical periods promised working-class voters upward mobility if they dissociated themselves from their traditional institutions (the trade unions and the Labour Party) and their "out-of-date" ideologies.

The paradox of Thatcherism was that it promoted "Victorian values" of moral restraint as it fostered consumer desire. As Matthew Collin suggests,

> The Thatcher dream was about breaking free from the past, casting off restraints, entering a paradise of untrammeled entrepreneurial and consumer opportunity; the idea that anything was possible if you had the will to conquer and a good credit card. Yet while libertarian capitalist doctrine elevated consumer materialism to a creed, Thatcherite assaults on collectivism, pursued through a range of policies, intentionally created a society that was fragmented and individualised. Its economic libertarianism was tempered with a grim authoritarian edge, its contradictions and harsh side-effects mercilessly policed. It simultaneously advocated and curtailed freedom. . . . Thatcherite Conservatism offered a blueprint for achievement with a Victorian morality built in.[45]

With these contradictions in mind, the figure of Vivienne Nicholson on two of the Smiths record sleeves can open up a discussion of the related discourses of femininity and consumerism, and their relationship to Englishness. A national social(ist) realist tradition has tended to castigate women as the passive consuming subjects of mass culture. The Smiths' use of Viv Nicholson's image draws attention to this discourse, considers the problem of consumerism, but is not judgmental against women.

Morrissey has said that he was drawn to Nicholson because she is a "survivor." The cover star of "Barbarism Begins at Home" and "Heaven Knows I'm Miserable Now" was a working-class woman and wife of a trainee Yorkshire miner. She won £75,000 on the soccer pools in 1961, when her family was living in poverty. Her autobiography, *Spend, Spend, Spend* (turned into a successful 1970s TV drama by Jack Rosenthal), describes how she spent her winnings on Jaguars, race horses, trips abroad, and five husbands. According to Catherine McDermott, Nicholson's autobiography "suggests allegiance to a totally different set of cultural values than those promoted by the establishment. Given relatively unlimited funds, her spending spree included hair dyed champagne blonde to match a new Chevrolet Impala, a holiday in Las Vegas, and a Spanish style bungalow in Yorkshire called the Ponderosa."[46]

The cover of "Barbarism Begins at Home" presents Nicholson, hands on hips, in a riding cap, a mini-dress, and knee-length boots incongruously standing in front of a coalmine with a suitcase beside her. She is about to embark on a trip to Malta. The picture offers a defiant escape, Nicholson's "hip" fashion in the foreground starkly at odds with the dark, drab colliery rigging in the background. The image subverts the mythical iconography of the industrial north in, for example, the British documentary movement, where the coalmine is the site of the heroic male worker. In the context of the mid-1980s, the photograph also suggests the loss of working mines as the government forced pit closures in the north of England and took on the National Union of Miners in one of the most violent and protracted industrial disputes since the 1926 General Strike.

Nicholson's defiant pose reasserts the transgressive power of working-class women chided for their close relationship to fashion, pop music, the transistor radio, television, and dancing. To some extent, female consumerism questions the masculine order in the 50s and 60s. It provides women in the home with a measure of control over domestic space and time. In the case of women working outside the home, consumerism in the form of makeup, stylish clothes, and perfume was a declaration of independence in a spectacular manner, publicly demonstrating that one had economic power that wasn't simply tied to the income of a father, boyfriend, or husband.

On the cover of "Heaven Knows I'm Miserable Now," a bouffant-headed Nicholson stares glumly at the camera, one hand in the pocket of a smart winter coat as she stands in a typical dingy street of terraced houses. The plush coat contrasts with the gray surroundings. Like the other photograph of her, this image draws attention to the aspirations of working-class women, just as Carolyn Steedman does in the account of her mother's desire for Christian Dior's New Look coat in the 1950s. Lest you think that the cry against female consumerism had disappeared by the 1980s, Beatrix Campbell reminds us of a strain of leftist writing that bemoans the loss of a particular kind of working-class identity. This lineage stretches from Orwell and Hoggart in the 1940s and 50s to Jeremy Seabrook in the early 1980s: "The complaint from the moral school of socialism against material goods is always about the working class having them. . . . All this anti-consumerist talk is so anti-mass pleasure; it makes my spine shiver with fear that Big Brother Orwell is going to take away my fridge and hi-fi, that he'll melt down the Beach Boys and the Supremes, Blondie and Bob Marley, and there will be no more discos, no more late-night movies on TV, no more Fred Astaire and Ginger Rogers, no more 'Soap'; he won't allow us our pleasures."[47]

If we turn to the infinitely more controversial figure of England's most famous female murderer, Myra Hindley, Morrissey again exhumes the nation's collective memory of a "problematic" woman. Part of the reaction to Hindley is rooted in a discourse of consumerism. The B-side of "Heaven Knows I'm Miserable Now" (with its Viv Nicholson sleeve) is a song called "Suffer Little Children," also the final track on the Smiths' eponymous debut album.

The title is taken from a chapter in *Beyond Belief,* Emlyn Williams's account of the so-called Moors Murders.[48] Between November 1963 and October 1965, Myra Hindley and Ian Brady killed several children and buried them on Saddleworth Moor, just north of Manchester. They also recorded the torture of these children. The audio tape of Lesley-Anne Downey's last minutes was played at their trial. Brady and Hindley were sentenced to life imprisonment in 1966.

In "Suffer Little Children," Morrissey, only a few years younger than these children at the time of the murders, invites us to follow him over the moor to this northern landscape of death. He imagines himself lying down beside the dead bodies. The ghosts of the children—John Kilbride, Lesley-Anne Downey, and Edward Evans—still promise to haunt the city in the song. The people of Manchester share some collective culpability for their deaths—"Manchester has so much to answer for." Over Marr's low-key, slow guitar chords, reminiscent of the Byrds' Rickenbacker guitar sound, Morrissey's voice is mournful. But there is also a bitter sarcasm in his suggestion that Manchester finds it easier to deal with the collective memory of the Manchester United team that died in the 1959 Munich air crash than to cope with the troubling memory of this "team" of children buried on the moors. The maudlin atmosphere of the track thickens as a child weeps in the recording.

The controversy around this song reveals the stakes of this kind of cultural necrophilia. Some relatives of the children thought the song in bad taste. The tabloid press attacked the Smiths, and following suit, a few retail outlets briefly refused to stock any Smiths records. Some consumers even mistook the picture of Viv Nicholson on the "Heaven Knows I'm Miserable Now" single for a photograph of Myra Hindley. Morrissey personally telephoned the victims' parents and Rough Trade issued a public relations release, which eventually diffused yet another short-lived pop scandal.

However, the reaction to this musical memorial for the murdered children (in the commodity form of seven- and twelve-inch vinyl singles) highlights the link between popular memory and mass-reproduced images. Morrissey uses celebrity photographs from a period in which the mass-reproduced photograph in popular magazines like *Picture Post,* newspapers, television, and consumer culture had an accelerated social power. *Pop Art in Britain* commented on the power of these images in their potentially infinite repetition.

In the 1980s, the public confusion over the photograph of Nicholson on the Smiths record sleeve resulted from the continuing impact of one photograph of

Myra Hindley. As Joan Smith points out, the famous police mug shot of Hindley, "hard as nails and icily sexy . . . played a key role in forming her public image." According to the London tabloid the *Evening Standard,* "the murderer with the Coronation Street name and the signature bleached hair" has become a symbol of evil.[49] In the novel *Alma,* a "fictional autobiography" of the 1950s British singer Alma Cogan, Gordon Burn meditates on this notorious black-and-white photograph of Hindley: "That she has an existence independent of the image that has represented her for twenty-one years—the trowel nose, the defiant eyes, the peroxide hair—is a mystery that seems hard to get to grips with. Hindley was twenty-three when she was arrested. Now she's forty-four. It is as if by changing her appearance, and keeping her current identity secret, she has effected some kind of escape."[50]

Burn's novel deals with the changes in the landscape of postwar British popular culture, a woman's memory, and indeed, collective memory. The fictional middle-aged alcoholic Cogan (the real singer died in 1966, the year Hindley and Brady were jailed) narrates her life story in 1987 as real historical events unfold on the Manchester moors. At this time the imprisoned Hindley and Brady confessed to more killings and helped the Greater Manchester police search for the bodies of other children. Burn remarks that Hindley easily found her old haunts on Saddleworth Moor, even after twenty years in prison.

In the novel's concluding pages, Cogan anonymously meets up with an obsessive fan who shows her his exhaustive collection of Alma memorabilia, the most rare and precious being a tape recording of Downey's torture. Cogan listens on headphones to the horrific drama of Hindley and Brady's conversation and Downey's agonies. The murderous couple have tuned their radio to Radio Luxembourg, which happens to be playing Cogan's hit version of "The Little Drummer Boy." Burn also informs us of the chilling fact that Brady bought a pop record for Hindley after each murder.[51]

The force of songs and images to initiate personal and collective memory-work has only intensified since Hindley was caught by police cameras in the mid-sixties. The issue of her parole and Lord Longford's campaign in her support occupied the media fairly regularly throughout the 1980s and 1990s. In 1994, Home Secretary Michael Howard decreed that she should never be freed. In September 1997, a portrait of Hindley in the Royal Academy's *Sensation* exhibition "sparked an explosion of national outrage." *Myra,* painted by part-time artist and care worker Marcus Harvey, is a black-and-white literally *digital* facsimile of "the police mugshot of the staring peroxide blonde murderess" made up entirely of children's handprints.[52] In 1998, Hindley's appeal against Michael Howard's decision was rejected. She will never be released, despite Lord Longford's and her own claims that she has reformed.

In a 1988 essay on Margaret Thatcher and another murderess, Ruth Ellis (who in 1955 was the last woman to be executed in Britain), Jacqueline Rose argues that "the symbolic order is gendered" and femininity is often "used to draw a line around the limits of what a society will recognize of itself."[53] Rose looks at Thatcher and Ellis together as examples of female violence, the former as one who legitimized state violence in its many forms (in particular, the Falklands War, and her calls for the return of the death penalty) and the latter as one involved in individual illegitimate "out-of-control" female violence.

There are clear parallels between Ellis and Hindley. Much of the attitude to Ruth Ellis's "sanity" and "femininity" at her murder trial was shaped by the conflation of her working-class consumption and style—blonde hairdo, lipstick, perfume—and an "aggressive" sexuality. Hindley too had freshly dyed hair and in smart clothes sat impassively in the dock during her trial. This femininity in the eyes of both juries made these women personifications of calculating murderous evil. They became British embodiments of the femme fatale.[54]

I want to make some speculative points about the violence of English life and about collective (national) fantasy and its relationship to the feminine, using Rose's arguments, but also inspired by the way Morrissey and others exhume Myra Hindley in the 80s and 90s. Rose argues that right-wing ideologies like Thatcherism "harness fantasy to reason" and "thrive on and strain against the furthest limits of psychic fantasy."[55] She suggests that considerations of the place of fantasy in public life should avoid the rigid dichotomy that either (1) fantasy is a rational projection of individual self-interest or (2) that fantasy is an illogical irrationalism, "a simple counter-image of the law":[56]

> It seems to me that it must be limiting to talk of images and identifications in relation to politics as if what we are dealing with belonged to a straightforward economy of desire. Desire may well be the necessary term, but only if we define it as something which includes not irrationality—what is at stake here is not some rational/irrational dualism—but a logic of fantasy in which violence can operate as a pole of attraction at the same time as (to the extent that) it is being denied. If this logic is "deadly and irreducible," it is so only in so far as it repeats a paradox inherent to the organization of the social itself. One of the things that Margaret Thatcher is doing, or that is being done through her, is to make this paradox the basis of a political identity so that subjects can take pleasure in violence as force and legitimacy while always locating "real" violence somewhere else—illegitimate violence and illicitness increasingly made subject to the law.[57]

Following Margaret Thatcher's third consecutive election victory, in 1987, Rose posed the question: "What if Thatcher was re-elected not despite the repugnance that many feel for her image, but also in some sense because of it? What if that force of identity for which she is so severely castigated somewhere also operates as a type of pull?"[58]

Rose's thesis overlaps with the anarchist punk group Crass's feminist classic "Mother Earth," from its 1980 album *Stations of the Crass.* The song voices a psychic mechanism of simultaneous attraction to and disavowal of violence in the British public's reactions to the murderer. Hindley is perceived as the anti-mother whom the public wants to see rot in jail. Crass rants that the populace wants to tear her apart, urinate on her grave, yet also aggressively yearns to have sex with her; the public is horrified by her crimes but would also love to have seen Hindley and Brady committing them. By convincing themselves that Hindley is "beyond the pale," people are assured that they are civilized, normal, and virtuous. Crass argues that this obsession with Hindley is not to be distinguished from the violence of the social. In its punkish rage, "Mother Earth" also screams that the public's fantasy and voyeurism are sustained by the famous mug shot of Hindley.

Morrissey's invocation of Hindley is not as direct as Crass's brilliant exposure but emerges on the same cultural terrain as a number of other representations of Hindley (the Sex Pistols had used her mug shot for shock effect in the late 70s). What such examples as "Suffer Little Children," "Mother Earth," and *Alma* illustrate is that violence is gendered and embedded in the landscape and national fantasies.

Aspects of Thatcher's own star image in the 1980s bear a resemblance to Hindley's "look" as well as the way violence and social landscape are configured through a female icon. While the prime minister played up the role of Mrs. T., the petit-bourgeois family woman keeping the nation's housekeeping in order with sensible budgeting, she was also the Iron Lady, Boadicea, a warrior-queen for new Britain. A critique of Margaret Thatcher risks being misogynistic. In the form of a puppet caricature in television's satirical *Spitting Image,* Thatcher was a double-breasted-suited-booted boss who scolded her wimpy "wet" ministers as she stood at the urinal in the men's toilets. This image captured English desires for the Victorian discipline of Mother England. The dominatrix persona may have contributed to the success of the 1987 film *Personal Services,* which features Julie Walters as a brothel owner/madam who realizes with Thatcherite foresight that this form of private enterprise can be very profitable. Even government ministers and city stockbrokers pay for their "slap and tickle," and some favor the receiving end of the S/M whip. Iain Sinclair's mapping of the capital city points to the compelling violence in Thatcher's image: "The City is termite territory: thousands of heads-down workers serving an unacknowledged queen, a fear motor buried deep in the heart of the place. A dominatrix with carmine lips. Which is why all those drones, wideboys, and compulsive hustlers responded so feverishly to the imago of Margaret Thatcher. She made it all right: greed was good, work was holy, the clouds were frivolous nonsense. There was no such thing as society, no time beyond or behind the present—no cosmology, but the great darkness, the worship of her achievements."[59] Thatcher was "dead hard." This formed part of her attraction. Maggie's military might torpedoed the *Belgrano* ("Gotcha!" said the *Sun*'s headline), sending Argentinian sailors to their deaths in the South Atlantic. In *The Krays* (1990), Billie Whitelaw plays Violet Kray as a Thatcher type (with Saatchi and Saatchi hairstyle to match) devoted to the ambition of her gangster sons in the 1960s. After all, they were East Enders who aspired in enterprise-culture fashion to be wealthy London gents.[60]

Morrissey, who provocatively brings the violent core of the national to the surface in much of his work, responds to the image of Thatcher as executioner by flipping it over. "Margaret on the Guillotine," the closing track from the aptly titled 1988 album *Viva Hate,* is a fantasy of the prime minister's own execution. To a lilting lullaby melody, Morrissey plaintively suggests that the people's dream to have Margaret on the guillotine be realized. Singing the dream can make it real. Ironically, in a telling indictment of state violence, the recording resulted in the police's searching the singer's home for any further seditious material. Morrissey's violent fantasy is curiously echoed in Elvis Costello's song "Tramp the Dirt Down" from the 1989 album *Spike.* Disgusted with the disregard for life shown by Thatcher and her policies, the singer yearns to stomp on her grave if she should die. The violence of the lyrics contrasts shockingly with the song's bittersweet Irish folk-ballad arrangement and Costello's lilting vocal delivery.

I believe such songs respond to the violence of Thatcherism but also to something deeper in the English landscape and its figures. In an August 1992 postscript to her article on Ruth Ellis and Margaret Thatcher, written after Thatcher was no longer the Conservative Party leader, Jacqueline Rose warns that it's "too easy . . . to say that what Thatcher carried psychically has now gone away; too easy to load on to her something which, in the course of her administrations, seemed at moments out of control if not mad. If Thatcher thrived on the ideology and mechanism of the scapegoat (the victim to be expelled), it would be a strange irony now to see ourselves as innocent of that process because we have so entirely lodged it in her."[61] The responsibility for the violence of Thatcherism should not be so easily shaken off by the public. Rose concludes that this is not the time "when dismissal of Thatcher and her psychic agendas is appropriate. The risk is that, like any good—or rather bad—act of repression, the extent to which we require her to bear the burden will be in exact proportion to the grotesque-ness with which those agendas return."[62]

▄ ▄ ▄

Morrissey's imaging of working-class women is a reaction to a dominant mascu-line version of the north. It reworks that landscape in Steedman's terms but also has its limitations. While it may feminize and queer-y representations of place, it remains resolutely white. In Tim Broad's video for one of the Smiths' final songs, "Stop Me If You Think You've Heard This One Before," Morrissey and a pack of androgynous male and female teenage Morrissey clones weave through the Manchester streets on bicycles. They make their way to Salford, the site of the original Coronation Street, then pose outside the Salford Lads Club, reproduc-ing the photograph of the Smiths on the album *The Queen Is Dead.* In the neigh-borhood, the streets of Victorian back-to-back houses are empty except for a lit-tle girl with a doll. The cyclists plaster posters of Oscar Wilde and Shelagh Delaney against a wire fence and red brick wall. Morrissey wanders around, staring up at the old buildings, symbolically taking back this mythic macho landscape for himself and his fans.

But Salford and other inner-city areas like it across the north have been peo-pled by others, who are just *not there* in popular representations of the working-class landscape. Where are the Asians and African-Caribbeans who are British? The Coronation Street ethos with its grime, dim light, damp, and romantic seed-iness—a "structure of feeling" about a decaying industrial England—is part of my mind's landscape. I recognize the salty humor and northern vernacular po-etics in Morrissey's work. But he seems to deny that we nonwhite Brits belong in this mythical black-and-white documentary landscape past or present, even though we have walked and continue to walk those same streets in Salford, Brad-ford, Leeds, Liverpool, and Manchester. This Coronation Street picture is not the only working-class past and landscape worked upon in popular memory, but it remains one of the strong currents of a *timeless* Englishness circulated in com-modity form.

There are two images of this mythic landscape and past that powerfully crys-tallize its hostility to nonwhites. The first is from Terence Davies's autobiograph-ical film *The Long Day Closes* (1992), set in working-class Liverpool during 1955–56. In a fleeting but crucial scene, young women chat happily as they prepare for a weekend night out. They send eleven-year-old Bud to buy some Chanel No. 5 perfume (Richard Hoggart would have been pissed off). The scene of family reverie is interrupted as Bud rushes out into the hallway. He stops in his tracks. A black man stands at the open front door. Hearing Bud's shocked yelp, the rest of the family bursts out into the hall. The camera takes the stranger's point of view as the family huddles together at a safe distance. The man smiles and politely asks in a Caribbean accent if Mona lives there. Bud's sister tells him curtly that there's no Mona at that address. One of Bud's brothers angrily tells the black man to "frig off." The West Indian backs out of the front door, almost in a glide. There is then an ellipsis. The film cuts to the men and women cheerfully leaving for their night out some time later. Nothing of the encounter is mentioned. The ellipsis suggests the problem of explaining the presence of the nonwhite migrant in an English landscape reconstructed whole in memory. Whether this was deliberate or not on the part of the filmmaker, it points out the representational gap between blackness and this working-class landscape of the imagination.

The other image of the working-class neighborhood that haunts me is a 1950 *Picture Post* photograph by Bert Hardy taken in Tiger Bay and reproduced on a retro postcard I bought in a London shop in the late 80s. The photograph captures a Welsh landscape but looks like the typical Coronation Street setting, exactly the kind of black-and-white image one might expect to see on a vintage Smiths record sleeve. A young black boy stands in the shadow of a wall of a row house on a working-class street corner. He has his right arm in front of his face in what looks to be a vulnerable gesture of shyness. The dark and mottled wall towers over him. A street sign on the wall, well above his head, reads Gladstone Street, a trace of the British Empire hanging over this new postcolonial British subject. The picture is split into two by the edge of the wall. Beyond the corner is a range of row houses that resembles the mythic thoroughfare of a Coronation Street. The light reflects brightly off the rain shining on the road and pavement. Its whiteness starkly contrasts with the darkness of the boy and the imposing wall. The landscape is bleak and the buildings dwarf the little body. He doesn't seem to belong in this place, just as I didn't really belong.

Many African-Caribbeans and Asians could never fully claim this place as our own, despite the fact that throughout the postwar period black people have had ordinary and extraordinary lives in such streets. Will there ever be a time when images of Asians in these British streets will seem banal and "natural," when the representations of national-popular culture acknowledge that we belong in this landscape just like any another Brit? And not just as exotic coloring for an essentially white nation.

Despite its problematic assimilationism, and a traditional and violent Pakistani father set against an idealized English mother, the 1999 film *East Is East* begins to tell the stories of the brown people in Salford. The film's box-office success depends in part on its drawing on the tradition of *Coronation Street* humor. The world of its family is not too unfamiliar to white English audiences. Yet the film's writer, Ayub Khan Din, has pointed out that the marketing department at the BBC, which originally developed the script, believed that a film with "a bunch of Pakistanis wasn't going to make its budget back." Even when FilmFour took on the project, there were no brown faces in the promotional posters.[63]

Unlike Morrissey's ambivalent yearning for Coronation Street, Tony Wilson, head of one of Manchester's most famous record labels, Factory Records, foregrounds the city's multicultural heritage in his description of his grandfather's sense of belonging: "And his blood and all the other blood in Little Germany— which is what they called Whalley Range in the 1890s—became part of the general blood of this village—just as the Jewish blood of the thirties, the West Indian of the fifties, the Asian of the sixties, and the Chinese of the moment became the blood of the village. So in my village the blood ran easily from black gay clubs in mid-West America through techno arenas in the Mediterranean to the heart of rock."[64] The village is, of course, another powerful myth with which to make a narrative of the city's past but Morrissey doesn't want to acknowledge Manchester as a community made up of a succession of migrant groups and settlers. He yearns instead for the organic working-class community of white people.

National Fronting: Hooligans, Skinheads, and Pakis

The photograph of the Smiths on the corner of Coronation Street is a pastiche of documentary photography of working-class youths that dates back to the late Victorian period. Photography was used by reform movements and police in the regulation and surveillance of the working class. Many Victorian photographs present working-class boys standing in front of the institution responsible for their "correction." Lord Baden-Powell, founder of the Boy Scout movement, argued that the late Victorian hooligan had the kind of energy and resourcefulness that could be harnessed in the service of nation and empire. The "young offender" who needs to be "sorted out" has been a common folk devil in British media since reformers surveyed and surveilled the slums and urban jungles in the nineteenth century. As Seth Koven points out, the rough lad of the slums was also the focus of sexual attraction for many late Victorian and Edwardian upper-class social reformers.[65]

British pop music has played with this discourse of youth deviance for some time, most spectacularly during the punk moment in the late 1970s. Punk photography in fanzines, the music press, and record sleeves shows scruffy young men and women with deliberately vacant looks, leaning against blank walls. The Sex Pistols assumed a Dickensian street-urchin look in some of their promotional photographs. The relatively sedate picture of the Smiths in front of an old Victorian boys' club designed to keep rough lads off the streets and occupied in athletic pursuit comments on the revival of "Victorian values" in Thatcherite Britain. With its emphasis on law and order, the Conservative government repeatedly called for "short, sharp, shock" treatment for juvenile offenders. The title of the Smiths' final studio album, *Strangeways, Here We Come,* refers to a Victorian Manchester prison and, even more directly, comments on an ideology that marries youth and deviance.

Morrissey's attraction to working-class young men is an act of identification with the marginalized "deviant" outsider, and partly a homoerotic attraction. Apart from the cover stars from northern working-class culture, Smiths sleeves have presented many images from gay culture: Jean Marais from Jean Cocteau's *Orphée* ("This Charming Man" single); Warhol superstar Candy Darling ("Sheila Take a Bow"); from Warhol's *Flesh,* the rippled torso of Joe Dallesandro (*The Smiths*); Richard Davalos, from the movie *East of Eden* (*Strangeways, Here We Come*); a nerdy, bespectacled James Dean ("Bigmouth Strikes Again"); a Cocteau model (*Hatful of Hollow*); a young and ebullient leaping Truman Capote ("The Boy with the Thorn in His Side"); and Elvis Presley as a pimply, androgynous high-school kid with sideburns ("Shoplifters of the World Unite").

The address of many of Morrissey's songs is gender-unspecific, unlike the conventional boy-sings-to-girl/girl-sings-to-boy approach of most pop tunes. More obviously gay songs like "Hand in Glove" and "Reel around the Fountain" waver between the epiphanic moment of human connection and inevitable loss. The former song captures the pleasure and risk of being public about one's desire, but also the sense that it can never be this good again. In the latter, Morrissey suggests the sexual coming-of-age of a child with an older man in the pedestrian surroundings of a garden patio. "This Charming Man" is the story of a brief encounter between the song's narrator, who has a punctured bicycle tire, and a man who offers a lift in his car.

The gay sensibility in many Smiths songs holds together what Richard Dyer suggests is "a fierce assertion of extreme feeling with a deprecating sense of its absurdity."[66] In one of the Smiths' most beautiful songs, "There Is a Light That Never Goes Out," the love is so great that the singing voice doesn't mind if he and his lover get killed in a road accident with a truck or a bus. That would be a beautiful death. Such songs often explore what Andy Medhurst calls "the double-edged nature of romantic love—simultaneously wanting it desperately to happen but convinced of the impossible ridiculousness of any such desire."[67] Medhurst argues that this tone or attitude is a "structure of feeling" common to contemporary gay culture and is related to the bittersweet tone of nostalgia found in gay camp.

Though Morrissey has played with homoerotic images and lyrics, Al Wiesel in *QW* magazine indicts the star for never making any direct statements about his sexuality, other than his celebrated celibacy during much of the Smiths' early career. Of Morrissey's Oscar Wilde obsession, Wiesel argues that the singer "adopts Oscar Wilde's mantle—complete with reactionary Victorian baggage, Morrissey's love dares not speak its name; like his politics, the singer has deliberately kept his sexuality ambiguous."[68] Wiesel suggests Morrissey's attraction to skinheads is primarily a sexual one.

Working-class youths turn up in many of Morrissey's lyrics, often in their relationship to violence. Rusholme ruffians, sweet and tender hooligans, suedeheads, and skinheads constitute some of the roughnecks in his pop vocabulary of "aggro." They inhabit street corners and alleys waiting to stick the boot in as Morrissey's subject walks through the city. In one interview, the star recalls the threat of violence from Perry Boys (a working-class subculture of the 70s) in Manchester: "The memories I have of being trapped in Piccadilly bus station while waiting for the all-night bus, or being chased across Piccadilly Gardens by some 13 year-old Perry from Collyhurst wielding a Stanley knife!"[69]

A critique of male violence in Morrissey's work exists alongside a fascination with machismo, "hardness," and the homosocial dynamics of working-class subcultures. This is played through quite archly in the camp scenario of the Smiths' rockier fast track "Sweet and Tender Hooligan," in which a young thug stands trial for attacking an old man and strangling an old woman in bed. They are victims of domestic accidents. Morrissey sings that the hooligan should be shown lenience because he is unlikely to commit the crime again. However, he adds ironically, this may only be the case until the next crime.

By the time Morrissey gets around to the skinhead and the soccer hooligan, a homoerotic attraction works through a discourse that created these working-class representatives of Englishness, one preoccupied with what Phil Cohen describes as a "male physicality at once envied, feared and despised, especially by those who secretly or openly wished to participate in a bit of male bonding with the rough trade as part of their reclamation of the working class."[70] British cultural studies has nurtured this fascination with the angry white working-class male, often at the expense of British Asians. As Leon Hunt notes, youth cult fiction or "Youthsploitation" such as Richard Allen's novels *Skinhead* and *Suedehead* emerges as the "low counterpart of the blossoming British subcultural theory" in the early 1970s: "Subcultural theory coincided with a specific subculture, one which was also to sell a lot of paperbacks—the skinheads. Skins and pre-Hebdige subculturalists were seemingly made for each other. It was all here—a strong sense of class identity (although the suedehead incarnation complicates this with the appropriation of 'city gent' trappings), a spectacular dead-end of resistance, a sense of 'authenticity.'"[71]

In *Subculture: The Meaning of Style,* Dick Hebdige suggests that we can observe "played out on the loaded surfaces of British working-class youth cultures, a phantom history of race relations since the War." Where to locate the British Asian in this dynamic? In a troubling passage, Hebdige describes the interaction between Pakistanis and reggae-loving skinheads in the late 1960s and early 1970s. There have been black as well as white skinheads. The activity of "Paki-bashing" is an outcome of the awkward alliance between African-Caribbean and white youth: "'paki-bashing' can be read as a displacement manoeuvre whereby the fear and anxiety produced by limited identification with one black group was transformed into aggression and directed against another black community. Less easily assimilated than the West Indians into the host community . . . sharply differentiated not only by racial characteristics but by religious rituals, food taboos and a value system which encouraged deference, frugality and the profit motive, the Pakistanis were singled out for the brutal attentions of skinheads, black and white alike. Every time the boot went in, a contradiction was concealed, glossed over, made to 'disappear.'"[72]

In other words: "We don't have to kick each other's heads in, if we can beat someone else up." The objects of this violence are represented as a catalog of anthropological details that fix their difference from the host nation. And while black and white unite, even if temporarily and only as an act of imagination, the Pakistanis "disappear" like the "contradiction" itself. The tentative love affair between black and white youth cultures effaces the agency of the Pakistani, and race relations continue at the expense of the alien unassimilable Asian. A playground racist joke I remember stretches this vanishing to its limit: "What's transparent and lies in the gutter? A Paki with the shit kicked out of him."

Pete Fowler's 1972 article on the emergence of the skinhead explains that Asians basically stick to themselves and have middle-class values. He is hopeful that the skinhead love of reggae and appropriation of working-class macho Jamaican rude-boy style signals a coming together of the races through shared class experiences. Asians with their middle-class aspirations are excluded from this racial and class-based compact. Des, a "garage worker and a Skin of three years standing," explains his antipathy to Asian settlers: "I'll tell you why I hate the bloody Paks. I'll tell you a story. A week or so ago I was walking down the street with a couple of mates. I wanted a light for my fag, so I walk up to this Pakki git and ask him, 'You got a light, mate?' And what do you think the fucker did? I'll tell you. He walks—no, runs—into this shop and buys me a box of matches! Now I ask you! What the fuck could I do with a bleeder like that but hit him? And another thing.

Have you ever been in their restaurants? Have you seen the way they *grovel* round you, the way they're always trying to please you? I hate them, that's all."[73]

The Paki here is an obsequious, sniveling creature. His reluctance to resort to violence is seen as a weakness. His emasculation is doubly assured when one compares him to Afro-Caribbean youth. White male identification with (and desire for) blackness, from Mailer to Marky Mark, Jagger to Vanilla Ice, involves a worship of certain tropes and images: black cool, machismo, the Stagger Lee/ gangsta/outlaw figure, the natural, strong, physical, sensual self that has rhythm but can also fight to protect his rights. Blacks are militant, whereas Asians are passive in such white supremacist ideology. And Asians are middle class, which for white middle-class writers is strictly uncool.

In another example of mid-1970s cultural studies writing on the skinhead, John Clarke explains: "Paki-bashing involved the ritual and aggressive defence of the social and cultural homogeneity of the community against its most obviously scapegoated outsiders—partly because of their particular visibility within the neighbourhood (in terms of shop ownership patterns, etc.) by comparison with West Indians, and also because of their different cultural patterns (especially in terms of their unwillingness to defend themselves and so on)—again by comparison with West Indian youth."[74]

The fragmented left-wing culture of academics and the socialist press in the 1970s often measured "political resistance" by the individual and collective aptitude and readiness for violence if necessary. Spectacular forms of protest are part of a romantic mythology of praxis that permeates popular cultural forms. The Clash captures this urge for glamorous action, taking to the streets and "manning" the barricades in the "White Riot" punk single of 1977. Singer Joe Strummer wishes that he could riot just like the black people did during the previous year's Notting Hill carnival. The "hardness" or toughness of the working-class male (black or white) is lumpen-potential for class action. In popular music culture, particularly the influential British music press circa 1977–78, "street credibility" and working-class credentials were a boon. In "multi-racist Britain," Philip Cohen points out that "many White working-class boys discriminate positively in favour of Afro-Caribbean subcultures as exhibiting a macho proletarian style, and against Asian cultures as being 'effeminate' and 'middle-class.' Such boys experience no sense of contradiction in wearing dreadlocks, smoking ganja and going to reggae concerts whilst continuing to assert that 'Pakis stink.'"[75] The skinhead's seduction by the far Right proved an unfortunate embarrassment for the Left. In skinhead music and culture such as Oi! (a kind of skinhead punk), the rhetoric of class becomes increasingly articulated through the ideas of race and nation.[76]

Notions of white masculinity are essential to these rightist and leftist national fantasies. Since Asians are not hard, have been emasculated, and are "stuck in their own ways," they are even less fit for identification as integrated members of the nation. The skin, however misguided he may be, is the genuine article, as British as fish and chips and a pint of bitter, whereas Asians are an alien enclave threatening English working-class communities. Nick Knight exemplifies this position in *Skinhead,* a book of photographs appropriated by Morrissey: "Asian immigrants had a different, closed way of life and did not blend with traditional working class or East End ways of living. Inner city areas faced the threat of the settlement by immigrants or demolition and removal to overspill areas."[77]

John Clarke argues that skinhead style "represents an attempt to re-create through the 'mob' the traditional working class community as a substitution for the *real* decline of the latter."[78] On a similar, though less explicitly Althusserian, note in a book on rock style, Paul Du Noyer explains that the skins "were aggressively working class, taking traditional styles (big boots, braces, short hair) up to the point of parody. In fact it was the exaggerated uniform of an old proletariat that had vanished along with the blitz."[79] Subcultural analysis in the 1970s took skinheads as texts to decipher, compiling their fashion fetishes and expanding on their other activities. This research was concerned with how the skinhead represented himself (rarely *her*self). The skinhead's style was a mark of his agency, an act of partial, if misplaced, resistance. He was a semiotically charged naif who signified the breakdown of postwar social consensus.

The 1970s saw the rise of the National Front and British Movement, far-right political parties actively recruiting skinheads. The NF's youth paper, *Bulldog,* was sold outside the Leeds United soccer ground when I was a student. It could also be found at gigs by Oi! bands and at certain local pubs. At antiracist events and marches in support of the IRA hunger strikers, and, in fact, just walking in Leeds streets, the possibility of confrontation with fascist skins was always present. Before we knew who Dick Hebdige was, we learned to identify the socialist skin from the fascist skin by the color of the laces on his Doc Marten bovver boots.

By the mid-1980s, there had been a subtle shift in the cultural studies approach to the skin. The style in which the skinhead is represented, rather than represents, becomes the primary concern. Under the influence of Foucault's work, regimes of representation and discursive power become more important than the skinhead's sartorial agency. In his essay "Hiding in the Light," Hebdige uses Nick Knight's photos of skinheads (and some other pictures of punks) to illustrate his argument that the sociological imagination represents "youth" as janus-headed: youth-as-fun/youth-as-trouble. The skinhead is either a criminal threat or a victim in the concrete jungles of the inner city, the "object of Our fear" or "object of Our compassion."[80] These are the two skinheads we encounter most often.

From the vantage point of the mid-90s, David Muggleton criticizes subcultural analysis for the relegation of the subcultural members' own voices. He argues that the Marxist paradigm obscures "the level of biography, of phenomenology, of how the subculture is lived out, experienced and interpreted by its members," an analytical problem "symptomatic of a realist epistemology and totalizing theory which results in the imposition of an a priori framework upon the phenomenon in question."[81] This is what happens when mostly middle-class academic men create their own fantasy image of the working class.

Before turning to Morrissey's own riff on cultural studies discourse of the skinhead, it's worth laying out the way the skinhead's "brother in arms," the soccer hooligan, has been defined. I'm not conflating the skinhead and the soccer hooligan, but popular discourse often places the two closely alongside each other. Notions of the "British hooligan" have cemented themselves in the public consciousness for several reasons. The tabloid press held soccer supporters responsible for the 1980s disasters at Heysel and Hillsborough, even though unsafe facilities and bad policing were partially responsible for the deaths at these stadiums in Brussels and Sheffield, respectively. British soccer fans have developed a reputation for going abroad, getting drunk, and pissing in the fountains of the continent's city squares before fighting pitched battles with opposing fans and/or local police. The soccer hooligan has become something of a national institution and embarrassment. When England plays another national soccer team, home or abroad, sociologists, police experts, and various pundits appear in the media to explain this "English disease."

With the transnational corporatization of the game in the 90s, grounds are now better equipped, tickets more expensive, and soccer is fashionable once again with the middle classes. Fans are also better organized, and alternative soccer fanzines and a growing body of soccer literature and literary journalism have flourished in recent years. Bookstores are full of autobiographical accounts of "my years as a hooligan" and the like, which almost amount to a literary genre. One of the finer soccer novels, *The Football Factory*, by John King, has a smart-arse tabloid journalist-wanker mouth a common perception about the apparent waning of soccer fan violence:

> The hooligans faded away after Heysel, Dobson confided, lowering his voice because the subject was a taboo which turned off the sponsors. Before that they were a bloody nuisance, but they shifted papers and journalism's all about circulation figures. My theory is they either got into drugs like ecstasy which destroyed their violent tendencies and/or organised crime, or got married and settled down, and the kids today can't afford to go very often which means there's no new blood coming through to fill their shoes, Dr Martens if you like, so the hooligan drifted towards extinc-

tion, just like the dinosaur. The police became experts in the field of crowd control and introduced video cameras and the yobs decided enough was enough. A few tough sentences and they handed in their Stanley knives and started new lives. There's a pitch invasion now and then, but it's just a handful of idiots pissing in the wind, if you'll excuse my French. Football violence is dead and buried. Society is much more better balanced these days. The Tories have eradicated the class system. The angry young men of yesteryear are either sitting in bed smoking cannabis or wandering around their local homestore trying to decide what shade of paint to buy for the baby's room.[82]

But against this populist interpretation of soccer violence, King's novel and its sequels, *Headhunters* and *England Away,* elaborate the continuing desire for and organization of soccer aggro by some supporters.

Morrissey's "We'll Let You Know" examines this idea that soccer hooligans are a declining English species. The words and music accentuate the pathos of their plight. Over a plaintive acoustic guitar the voice of the singer here is the collective voice of the soccer hooligans. They are mournful and will explain to the listener how they feel. The defense for bad behavior is (like the Smiths' "Sweet and Tender Hooligan") couched in ironic terms: being herded through the turnstiles into the soccer ground like animals makes them violent; the songs they sing in the stands do not mean anything. A long instrumental break follows these words as an electric guitar wails tremulously. The previously subdued music builds up to a crescendo as a sample of chanting soccer fans provides a kind of melancholic Greek chorus. The fans may appear morbid and unfriendly, but speaking for them, Morrissey says they are the "last truly British people you will ever know." The music comes to a shuddering halt as he repeats, "The last truly British people you will ever, never, want to know." The music shifts momentarily to the kind of fife-and-drum military band march heard at Protestant, Orange Day parades in Northern Ireland, and evokes a hard-line, right-wing British nationalism. The music fades away into silence almost as soon as it begins, a decaying echo of the past to match the doomed end of these British subjects. Repeated listening to the song convinces me that Morrissey does not so much celebrate acts of soccer violence as he romanticizes soccer hooligans as tragic figures.

"The National Front Disco," which immediately follows "We'll Let You Know" on *Your Arsenal,* is as aggressive in its rock guitar sound and forward-looking in lyrics as "We'll Let You Know" is musically restrained and elegiac in tone. The song describes the enthusiasm of a boy who wants to join the NF despite the protestations of his parents. Morrissey voices the boy's racist slogans like "England for the English" and adopts an empathic perspective with his desire for revenge. But he also takes the position of the boy's parents, who are so exasperated with their son's right-wing ambitions they cannot come to utter the horrible full name of the organization. They trail off after the phrase, "the national." We also hear a voice skeptical about the arrival of a white nation expunged of its alien elements. The power of the song lies in its articulation of desire. The boy longs for independence from his parents and yearns for a utopian elsewhere, back to the future of the white English nation. As Armond White puts it, Morrissey "risks the anger of people who want to pretend that the kids are always all right or that fascism has no attraction."[83]

Morrissey taps into a structure of feeling among some young white working-class males that is present in a number of other texts. In *The Football Factory*, a soccer hooligan discusses the attractions of fascism in a volatile economic and political climate:

> The cunts in charge of his firm had shifted their resources around to save a few bob and thirty people had ended up on the dole. Top management within the firm had awarded themselves big increases on the savings made. Fascism was an attractive proposition. Listening to speakers at local, clandestine meetings and their calls for the hanging of child molesters, rapists and the scum in the Tory party made a lot of sense. Blokes with the same attitude went along and the social workers and students with placards shouting Nazi at them from behind police lines just made him more determined. He wasn't into the Combat 18 bit but was gearing up for the big push. He was white, Anglo-Saxon, heterosexual and fed up of being told he was shit.[84]

Cracker, Granada Television's detective show starring Robbie Coltrane as a hard-drinking, gambling but brilliant police psychologist, also theatricalizes this white working-class angst in a 1994 storyline that brings together skinheads, soccer, and Pakistanis in an ideologically ambiguous and charged space.

The episode entitled "To Be a Somebody" centers on Alby, a white working-class Liverpool fan and factory worker (played by Robert Carlyle). Alby is miserable after the death of his father from cancer and the breakup of his marriage. He cannot get on with his fellow shop-floor workers. On his way home from the nightshift one morning, he stops by a cornershop to pick up a newspaper and a bottle of milk. These cost him one pound and four pence. He has only a pound, and the fastidious Pakistani shop owner will not let him take the goods until he has produced the extra four pennies. They argue and Alby storms out of the shop empty handed. At home he shaves his head, returns to the shop with his late father's British army bayonet, throws four pence at the Pakistani, calls him a "thieving Paki" repeatedly, then stabs him to death.

After the murder, Alby scrawls the number 9615489 in blood on the shop wall.

We learn later that this refers to the 96 Liverpool fans killed in the Hillsborough disaster on 15 April 1989. Alby intends to kill exactly 96 people. He targets a female tabloid journalist who has written a story blaming Liverpool supporters for the Hillsborough disaster. A university criminologist who comes up with a psychological profile of the Pakistani's murderer is also confronted by Alby. The academic's profile describes the killer as a typical white racist skinhead. Alby tells him that he listens to Mozart and is nothing like this working-class stereotype. Then he stabs the criminologist to death, and photocopies his head. He also kills a police detective and turns up at a Manchester United v. Liverpool match in the Manchester end with plans to explode a bomb, before finally being apprehended.

We learn that Alby and his father witnessed the terrible events at Hillsborough and Alby's father couldn't bear to go to another soccer match after this disaster. During interrogation, Alby tells the police psychologist that he became a skinhead because that's what everyone—the police, the politicians, and the media—expects of white working-class soccer fans. He has transformed himself into this folk devil as a protest against a discourse that marginalizes the white working class. At one point, Alby says that the politicians and the bourgeois lefties listen to the blacks, Pakis, and queers but have no time for the white working class.[85]

Though he somewhat strangely ignores the racialization of soccer aggro, Paul Smith does make the useful point that "hooliganism cannot responsibly be regarded as simply an irrational, inexplicable violence" but as "a practice rooted in a particular segment of class struggle."[86] Against the criminologists, sociologists, and authors of government reports, Smith reminds us that soccer violence is working-class *ressentiment* even though the state wishes to deny continuing class divisions in Britain. While Smith convincingly argues that accounts of soccer violence like Bill Buford's *Among the Thugs* tend toward a "modernist masculinism" in their flirtation with collective violence, he ignores the homosocial attractions and fantasies of warrior-masculinity in hooliganism, which have been theorized in relation to fascism by Klaus Theweleit.[87]

In his discussion of the Nation-Thing, Slavoj Zizek argues that "what truly disturbs liberals is . . . enjoyment organized in the form of self-sufficient ethnic communities." The disenfranchised white working class's belief in a white English ethnicity is something Morrissey is prepared to grapple with. His "dodgy" politics have provided the opportunity for me to attempt to examine the national fantasy he seems to perpetuate. Zizek claims that the "truly radical critique of ideology should therefore go beyond the self-congratulatory 'social analyses' which continue to participate in the fantasy that sustains the object of their critique and to search for ways to sap the force of this underlying fantasy-frame itself."[88]

On Morrissey's 1995 album *Southpaw Grammar,* the track "Reader Meets Author" interrogates the desire to know the working class. Possibly with a hint of self-deprecation, Morrissey castigates middle-class types for their fascination with the working class. The latter are happier with knives than books. The tourist to the working-class neighborhood hears the sad voices of the proles and starts to imagine things.

What kind of imagination is at work in the representation of these national icons? Morrissey feels compassion for these defiantly British subjects. Skinheads are beautiful losers. Morrissey is drawn to them because they signify a dying national. But the skinhead is also attractive because he is "unsullied by matters of the mind," a common fantasy about the proletariat. The skin is not intellectual but physical, even though this physicality sometimes manifests itself in violence. In a 1993 *Vox* interview, Morrissey says: "They don't need to use their imaginations all that much—they act upon impulse—and that's very enviable. Theirs is a naturalness which I think is a great art form, which I can't even aspire to."[89] Parsons believes that Morrissey's attraction to "shaven-headed machismo has nothing to do with right-wing tendencies and everything to do with the grudging admiration he feels for lives that can be lived without angst. The attraction is not political but psychological."[90]

The assessment by Parsons too neatly separates the political from the psychological. Morrissey's approach is aesthetic and erotic but also has political implications. Despite the representation of the fascist skinhead's homosocial world its homosexual implications are rarely acknowledged. Morrissey opens up this possibility, and this is why he met with skinhead homophobia at the Madstock concert. By using the image of skinhead girls, he also draws out their androgyny. But Morrissey's skinheads are also noble savages. His love affair with "hardness," a tough working-class masculinity, is politically questionable. Eroticizing and aestheticizing the skin's hypermasculinity may question that masculinity's construction (as in the Canadian filmmaker Bruce La Bruce's *No Skin Off My Ass*) but such a gesture of serious camp does not necessarily undermine masculine power. A preoccupation with macho working-class lads, historically one aspect of gay culture, transgresses class and sexual boundaries. But sometimes this masculinity's attractions and its romantic power are not easily separated from its nationalist racial politics.

Pat Kane describes the tortuous politics of this romance in his review of a Morrissey concert at Glasgow Barrowlands in February 1995. After a lackluster start, the band and Morrissey warm up only when they begin the song "The National Front Disco." Kane notices that some people in the audience sing along weakly with the chorus line of "National Front . . . National Front":

At that moment, something smelled extremely rotten in the state of adult rock. But as the song appropriately dissolved into white noise frenzy, Morrissey adjusted his jacket, stepped forward and began to croon, rather beautifully, Moon River, the old tear-jerker covered on the current CD.

I'm gagging at his audacity. Is Morrissey taking this anthem of the white trash, Enoch Powellite, sixties-seventies generation and forcing us to confront how the most virulent hatreds can seethe alongside the most gauzy and romantic fantasies? Are we being presented with both the banality of England's evil, and the evil of England's banality? One dearly hopes so: for what also gives these seven minutes their queasy power is the faint possibility that Morrissey perhaps understands this tumerous England, and its skin-headed carcinogens, far too well. "We're after the same rainbow's end," runs Moon River's key line.[91]

In the live video *Introducing Morrissey,* before the band breaks into "The National Front Disco," the singer utters the enigmatic phrase "Because we must" to the audience. The song is the centerpiece of the live set, the high point of a generally flat stage presentation. As the live rendition of the song reaches its final guitar white noise crescendo, the arena is filled momentarily with a blinding white light.

The beginning of *Introducing Morrissey* features stagey shots of a skinhead in various locations in some of London's oldest working-class neighborhoods. Street and railway signs of Lambeth and Arsenal are shot in close-up. This is vintage London with its idealized white inhabitant claiming his territory. Barnor Hesse argues that British nationalism relies on "the infinite enumeration of its own particularisms" that define the authentically national. Increasingly the national is defined through the local: "national identity begins to refer less to the nation than to the region or the neighborhood. The historical formation of the nation is perhaps relegated to a symbolic abstraction while the generational formation of locality is elevated to the concrete heritage of indigenous "whiteness."[92]

Julian Evans suggests that other songs on *Your Arsenal* that appear to be about love—"It's Gonna Happen Someday" and "Tomorrow"—could just as well articulate a "totalitarian longing" for a white England. Evans defends Morrissey's opening up of this can of worms: "To have any kind of discussion about Englishness, as he has discovered, is practically impossible now—though it may be worth remembering in the future Claude Lévi-Strauss's warning in his autobiography: we should question carefully, even sadly if we wish, 'the future of a world whose cultures, all passionately fond of one another, would aspire only to celebrate one another in such confusion that each would lose any attraction it could have for the others and its own reasons for existing.'"[93]

It's doubtful that we have approached quite this state of affairs, or that globalization has dissolved national cultural distinctions despite Lévi-Strauss's lament for "those old particularisms, which had the honor of creating the aesthetic and spiritual values that make life worthwhile and that we carefully safeguard in libraries and museums because we feel ever less capable of producing them ourselves."[94]

The ambiguities in Morrissey's "nationalist" position become less ambiguous and more troubling when he makes statements that wouldn't sound amiss on the lips of Enoch Powell or Margaret Thatcher. On the Bengali inhabitants of London's East End, Morrissey remarks: "I suppose there has been a complete invasion." When the interviewer Tony Parsons suggests that this has enriched the national culture, he replies: "No, not at all." Then Morrissey suggests, like Evans, that "it's a subject that can't really be discussed. Because if you try to open it out and have the broad discussion it's almost like admitting that there is a case for racism."[95] Like Lévi-Strauss, Morrissey wants to make the distinction between the maintenance of cultural distinctions and racism. There's a reluctance on Morrissey's part to admit that cultural nationalism may take the form of racism.

He does, however, admit the limits of his own Little Englandism: "I think it's the village atmosphere, the small-mindedness, which is still very much a part of me. I can't shake it off. I can't become internationalised and I don't think of the world as a place that is mine. I don't feel that I can go anywhere I choose to go. But I think I've pounded my Englishness into the ground. It's just me. I don't claim to have a copyright on the English stamp."[96]

But what claim does the British Asian have on the English stamp? In "Bengali in Platforms," from *Viva Hate* (1988), the Bengali who wears unfashionable platform shoes is trying to make the English love him through a (failed) impersonation of Westernness. He's a pathetic creature, hoping to gain friends by dressing like a Britisher. I have to admit that Morrissey's description of the sartorial inadequacies of the Bengali reminds me of the recent Asian migrants we saw in post-punk Birmingham and Bradford, who always seemed to dress in unfashionable seventies gear (dodgy color-coordination, bell-bottoms, and platforms) and about whom my brothers, my sister, and I had a supercilious middle-class assimilated laugh. But, according to Morrissey, the integration of such a sorry sight into the national way of life is impossible. The Bengali should give up any desire to become Western. The alien must be told this because a sense of belonging is hard enough to achieve for the alienated local, so the outsider has little chance of ever feeling at home in England.

"Asian Rut," from *Kill Uncle* (1991), about an Asian boy fighting with white thugs to avenge the killing of his friend, further suggests Morrissey's attitude to Britain as a multiracial nation. The narrative is presented as a warning. The Asian is likely to be beaten and pushed against sharp fence railings if he seeks revenge.

The melodrama of the scene is amplified with mawkish music that recalls the northern brass band soundtrack from old Hovis Bread television commercials set in a vintage heritage north. "Asian Rut" ends with Morrissey telling the listener that he comes upon this scene by accident on his way to a more civilized place, though he doubts he'll arrive at such a location. The tone is one of defeat and inevitability, feelings encouraged by some dirge-like cello playing. The Asian will get beaten up because he doesn't belong. That's the way it is. Violence isn't celebrated in the song, simply deemed the only possible consequence of the presence of nonwhites in the nation.

Morrissey's staging of the white working class in Little England shares some of the features of George Orwell's representation of the "proles" in *1984*. Patrick Wright suggests that in Orwell's dystopian novel "the past is imagined as the hopelessly redemptive trace of values which are all but totally buried by a destructive and inferior present. Thus human value comes to be associated with an everyday life which has been shredded and is no longer capable of supporting anything except particularistic argument and quarrel."[97]

In a 1990 interview Morrissey opines: "Even people who are quite level-headed and quite capable of happiness feel that this country is absolutely shambolically doomed."[98] His work suggests, not so much how wonderful the past was (though it was *our* white English past), but how awful the present is, and how dreadful the future is certain to be.

This millennial angst is captured in the Smiths' song "Panic," from the mid-80s. At the time, I thought the hit tune was about the urban rioting in 1985 and/or the rockist fear of dance music, with its chorus of "Hang the DJ." To a Marr rhythm-and-guitar sound reminiscent of glam rockers T. Rex, Morrissey maps out various British towns and localities where there is unexplained "panic." The promo video by Derek Jarman, another anti-Thatcherite nostalgist, features a photogenic lad with close-cropped hair and a classically proletarian donkey jacket who wanders pixilated through the rubble and graffiti of London's East End. The graffiti attacks the London Docklands Development Council, which reshaped the East End landscape in the Thatcher era. In the lyric, Morrissey wonders if English life will ever be like it used to be. With the rest of the Morrissey back catalog in mind, the song now feels like a yearning to arrest change, a desire to return to an England before Thatcher (but also to an England before the immigrants arrived).

On the left and right, the myth of a Little England and its white ethnicity betrays a reluctance to imagine a different future for Britain that isn't defined by a normative whiteness and cultural insularity. As Jesus-Martin Barbero points out, in the search for the quintessentially national—in this case, "the last truly British people you will ever know"—that which is native is defined within stricter limits: "transformed into the touchstone of identity, the indigenous would seem to be the only thing which remains for us of the 'authentic,' that secret place in which the purity of our cultural roots remains and is preserved. All the rest is contamination and loss of identity."[99]

As a studious fan I want to concede to Morrissey the escape clause of irony— that he doesn't really mean it, and he's just provoking Brits to think about the past, juggling the images, sounds, notions and potions of our collective memory. This is the attraction of tricksters. Listening to the songs repeatedly suggests to me that Morrissey is a ventriloquist, posing different voices against each other. You're never very sure which voice belongs to him. On the other hand, the ambiguities of this kind of queer English tricksterism also leave me frustrated. I sometimes feel that it's about bloody time the English got beyond irony as a device to deal with their limited repertoire of the national. As much as an ironic mode has the potential to critique certain versions of history, irony can serve to evade realities and new possibilities as it takes apart the same decaying body of national cultural concerns again and again with its blunt scalpel.

I remain caught in a bind: irony can be exasperating, but then again, who wants politically correct music? The ironies of being English or British are hard to escape whether one is Morrissey, a skinhead, or a Paki. And maybe irony is a necessary mechanism through which certain versions of the national must be invoked and thus disempowered, before being eventually disavowed. One hopes that camping this national robs it of its power. But irony and camp can also keep the crushing ordinariness of English racism at bay without destroying it. As Hanif Kureishi has remarked to an American journalist: "Very few people in England would want to be considered not to have a sense of humor, and the English are very self-conscious about not being considered to be stony-faced about things. So if someone says, 'You fuck off home, you Paki,' you have to laugh about it, and that works all the way through. The levels of irony—you would get lost in them over here."[100]

Bittersweet Symphony: Britpop and the "Death" of Rock

Since the Madstock event in 1992, when Morrissey claimed that London was dead and that we look to Los Angeles for the language we use, Britain has witnessed a revival of pop nationalism. "Britpop" has done the balance of trade no harm and (re)invented a national tradition of guitar rock and pop, partly in reaction to the emergence of American grunge groups like Nirvana and Pearl Jam, but also as opposition to the hegemony of dance music in Britain.

In its April 1993 issue, *Select* magazine offered a populist and nativist response to invasion with the words "Yanks Go Home" boldly on its cover. On a two-page spread inside, the monthly indulges in English camp juvenilia with a photomontage that imitates the credit sequence of *Dad's Army,* a 1970s sitcom about a group of inept part-time male members of the Home Guard meant to protect Britain should Hitler's troops step foot on national soil. "We are the boys who will stop your little gang," went the theme tune to the show, sung by the vintage musical hall duo Flanagan and Allen. Instead of swastikas moving toward the map of Britain to be repulsed by Union Jacks, *Select* features Union Jacks and British pop faces staving off the American threat of Kurt Cobain and his Stars and Stripes cohorts. In the accompanying article Andrew Harrison argues that it's time to reclaim the Union Jack:

> No other nation in the world is as neurotic about its national emblem as the British. . . . Yet Morrissey waves the Union Jack in a hamfisted way, and suddenly he's a Nazi. . . . Morrissey's summer offensive was hysterically tactless, but he knew there was a void at the centre of pop in 1992. It no longer talked about life in Britain, like the Smiths once did. . . . The British are tired of being ashamed of themselves and of any feeling for their country. They want the best notions of Britishness rescuing from the idiot stormtroopers, and in their own tiny way, the bands in this issue do some of that . . . Because if good people won't try to give Britain its culture back, there are plenty of evil people who will.[101]

The Union Jack has returned as a popular icon of born-again British optimism and neo-swinging London, particularly with the national success of 60s nostalgists Oasis and the global export phenomenon of the Spice Girls.

In the same issue of *Select,* Jarvis Cocker of the group Pulp also enumerates "Englishness" in pop as the "sense of the romantic in the everyday"; he cites the Kinks as an example of a quintessentially British group that wrote and recorded songs about recognizably native subjects with an authentically national accent and tone. "Ordinariness" is often conflated with Englishness. The accretion of local detail and attention to the particular is crucial.

Pulp's 1995 album *Different Class* features the hit "Common People," which, echoing Morrissey, is about a young wealthy woman who wants to slum it because she thinks "poor is cool." The CD sleeve notes present various cutouts of the group's members superimposed on photographs of instantly recognizable British locations: a cobbled city square with a coach/bus in Devon; with donkeys at the seaside; watching a couple snogging on the grass in a heath; posing in front of a red double-decker bus; seated in a minimally decorated café (or should I say "caff"); in a supermarket car park; and in the background of an awkward teen scene in which an Asian schoolboy smokes and chats up a white schoolgirl as they lean against some park railings.

The gushing sleeve notes for the Oasis hit album *(What's the Story) Morning Glory?* also allude to this English everyday: "As you are dragged on this trip abandon, you hear a council estate singing its heart out, you hear the clink of loose change that is never enough to buy what you need, boredom and poverty, hours spent with a burnt out guitar, dirty pubs and cracked pavements, violence and love, all rolled into one, and now all of this."

Britpop incorporates such a sentimentalized notion of Englishness, which emerges from the need to state and preserve England's difference from other places and peoples. This difference of the national is, as Martin Cloonan suggests, mediated through an attention to the specificities of the local. Just as Morrissey invokes East End and Manchester landscapes to signify aspects of Englishness, so these other groups dwell on the particular "unique" details that mark local/ national difference.[102]

Sonically, Britpop groups generally reproduce British guitar rock/pop styles from the mid-1960s Beatles and other British Invasion groups through glam rock (Cockney Rebel, David Bowie, T. Rex) in the early 1970s to late 1970s punk-era groups like the Buzzcocks and the Jam. The music is white guitar music robbed of any black influences. Simon Reynolds believes it enacts the "symbolic erasure of Black Britain" in its nostalgia for a traditional British musical look and sound.[103]

The "Britpop" tag was promoted by the weekly inky rock press, which has suffered declining sales over the last two decades. The mainstream tabloid press, which has had regular pop columns since the early 1980s, has used the music's success in its national boosterism. According to Jeremy Gilbert, just "the name 'Britpop' makes clear what it is that this reaction offers as an alternative. It offers a coherent, inclusive yet restricted sense of community. This is specifically British music; not American, not European (and therefore not black, not queer, experimental, not dangerous), not even aware that anywhere else exists."[104] Britpop celebrates a form of rock/pop classicism, an invention of a quintessentially national guitar group tradition.[105]

In its sleeve packaging and subject matter, Britpop often seems to fetishize an old English working-class culture. Many of these musicians are supposedly middle-class young males enjoying a homosocial flirtation with the rougher elements. The group Blur has been accused of this tendency by some critics, especially on its hit album *Parklife,* a romp through the clichés of lower-class work and leisure.[106] Blur and Oasis are the most commercially successful and clearly retro of

Britpop groups, wearing their influences quite openly and often referring to their historic pop sources explicitly in songs.

Like Morrissey and the Smiths, Oasis comes from Manchester. Guitarist/song-writer Noel Gallagher and his lead-singing younger brother, Liam, behave like classic traditional rock 'n' roll stars, much to the delight of a salivating press. The Gallaghers have developed a reputation as bad boys prone to the odd punch-up, trashing of hotel room, or unruly drunkenness and foul language on airplanes. The photogenic Liam seems to have modeled his aggressive pop persona on Robert De Niro's Johnny Boy character in Martin Scorsese's film *Mean Streets.* Like Blur, Oasis has promoted the so-called new laddishness, a backlash against feminism and political correctness fueled by popular magazines like *Loaded,* which feature soccer, pop music, hedonistic lifestyles, and photo spreads of scantily clad young women.

While Jon Savage has been broadly critical of the musical conservatism and masculinist tendencies of many Britpop acts, he argues that Oasis articulates the anger of a marginalized working-class Anglo-Irish. In the early 1950s many Irish migrants settled in Britain's cities, including Liverpool and Manchester. The children of these migrants have been an energizing force in British popular music, for example, Johnny Rotten/John Lydon in the Sex Pistols and Public Image Limited, Kevin Rowland in Dexys Midnight Runners, and Morrissey and Marr in the Smiths. As Sean Campbell argues, the Irishness of these "quintessentially English" performers has been repressed in the history of British popular music. It is something to be noted but then obscured in a narrative of British national identity that for obvious reasons finds the question of Ireland's relationship to Britishness too troubling.[107]

According to Savage, Oasis represents an authentic community and a place.[108] In contrast, the members of middle-class Blur pose as prole lads nostalgic for ye olde England with its lovable cockneys, old beer ads, and nights down the grey-hound races. Steve Sweeney-Turner, however, believes that Savage takes a "modernist" position on musical authenticity. According to Sweeney-Turner, critics like Savage

> read into Blur a variety of conservatisms with regard to both gender and ethnicity [which] is due to their own critical desire for the very authenticities which Blur actively problematise in their work. However, once one renounces such modern concepts of authenticity, a quite different reading of Blur emerges—one which, while not necessarily characterizing them as revolutionaries in either gender or ethnicity, certainly manages to trace the subtle shakings of received categories which they actually do effect in their work. In this—their irony, their kitschness, their campness,

and their intertextuality—Blur may be seen as assembling a form of postmodern "Englishness" which operates without recourse to any essentialist or reductive notions of culture, race, class, or gender.[109]

Sweeney-Turner believes that Britpop has criticized New Right notions of Englishness, though he does acknowledge that "the problematic residue of a certain nationalism remains within its structure." Britpop may be a sign of the general ethnicization of British society within which many white people also want to have an "identity" based on ethnicity to which they can lay claim.

I would caution against too swift a dismissal of the nostalgia and "regressiveness" of Britpop. The anti-Britpop polemics tend to gloss over the differences in the way aspects of the national are represented in the work of a broad range of musicians. Arguments about Britpop are often too neatly racialized. To understand sound as cleanly divided between white and black can verge on the essentialist. There is no *necessary* correspondence between the guitar rock/pop group format, musical genre, and whiteness. Guitar groups like Echobelly and the Voodoo Queens have proved that more than a backward-looking Englishness can be fashioned from a familiar set of vintage "English guitar pop" sonic signifiers. The political value of a musical form vis-à-vis gender, race, the national, and so on cannot simply be read off the formal aesthetic elements of a piece of music. At least a "postmodern" argument such as Sweeney-Turner's is open to the changing meaning of musical sounds and images and the different ways musicians revive, reinvent, and rekindle old images and sounds.

Diatribes against Britpop also often partake of a modernist condition common to the music press in Britain, for whom the imperative to peddle the novel musical artist, genres, and styles creates and maintains the demand for the hot new music product. Since dance music is the area where completely new technological-sonic sounds are being created, these emergent experimental genres and subgenres tend to be celebrated as the frontier of musical exploration. For some the aesthetic and institutional traditionalism of rock is plain old-fashioned. Even successful musicians like Radiohead and the Verve who have worked in the rock idiom are now commonly referred to in music press and record company promotional discourse as "post-rock," thus disavowing associations with an apparently has-been musical field. The currency of post-rock suggests that rock as a generic form survives after its ideological foundations have been discarded. Rock's demise has meant that guitar musicality can be conceived according to discourses not based on particular notions of authenticity, virtuosity, and masculine performance. The end of the rock era has also meant that types of music marginalized by the rock canon can now be reconsidered.

In the 1990s there was a growing perception that Anglo-American rock's hegemony in the popular music field was over at the same time that rock discourse lay firmly embedded in postwar social life in Europe, North America, and Australasia. To draw the history of this discourse in broad strokes: rock was born in the relative economic affluence of the 1950s and centered on the idea of "youth." The teenage, generational rebellion of rock 'n' roll in the 1950s became in the 1960s a constellation of sociopolitical values in opposition to a perceived mainstream or dominant society. Rock 'n' roll was assigned the status of art and given a political meaning as Rock. The decline of affluence in the late 1960s and global recession brought on by the OPEC oil crisis in the 1970s put liberal welfare capitalism's consensus values in jeopardy. Musically, punk in Britain signals this breakup of the postwar consensus. According to Grossberg, in the 1980s rock loses its political power in the context of New Right politics and an emergent postmodern structure of feeling. Grossberg is careful to describe rock not as a musical style per se but a set of conditions and practices, and a kind of political affect (a negation of rationalized everyday life in a capitalist society) that is depleted of its oppositional value in the 80s and 90s. Grossberg's view seems overly pessimistic since many rock genres, like punk and "heavy rock" in the form of grunge and Riot Grrrl music for example, have been revived and retuned to convey political criticism and "the negation of everyday life" he posits as the central purpose of rock music.[110]

These more recent trends occur against the back beat of rock's institutionalization. Post–Elvis Presley rock in the United States and Britain is now middle aged. Its canon has been produced by baby-boomers in umpteen *Rolling Stone* encyclopedias of rock and in television documentary series like the BBC/PBS collaboration *Dancing in the Street.* Rock is institutionalized in record labels, boxed-set releases, countless media outlets, Halls of Fame, and now even has its own university courses. If one were cynical: a largely white male pantheon of Great Performers is taken for granted with some belated acknowledgment of African-American musicians and styles and a few sidebars devoted to the contribution of women to the tradition and heritage of "rock's rich tapestry."

Grossberg suggests that rock music is no longer at the center of the media economy for youth. It may have been replaced by video game culture. The notion of youth has itself fragmented, partly from the baby-boomers' troubled investment in their own youth, but also as a result of new social movements and identity politics. Gays, lesbians, women, blacks, and other ethnic groups have fragmented the rock constituency. Grossberg believes that "there is almost a complete absence of any compelling, viable images of rebellion. All that is left is the fact of marginality and the struggle for identity."[111] Admittedly, cultural difference and identity have been commodified in the fragmentation of the popular music market, but does this mean that all "political" value has been shredded?

What seems more telling about these "rock anxieties," as Dave Laing terms them, is the fact that rock's ability to speak for any one community has become highly questionable. The white boys simply cannot define the counterculture any more. Susan McClary questions rock's limited conception of "politics" and its own social significance (as touted by musicians and critics): "For theorists of popular music, the sixties may have been the worst thing ever to have happened: because some small percentage of the music produced during those few years articulated protests against the Vietnam War or class oppression, our attention has been distracted from the issue more consistently fought over in popular music—even during that paradigmatic decade. More than that, in positioning the physicality of music in opposition to whatever the political substance of the 'real stuff' was supposed to be, such theories reinscribe the polemics against the body that have characterized attempts at policing music throughout western history."[112]

The challenges of feminism, lesbians and gays, and social movements around racial/ethnic identity have contributed to the decentering of rock and its apparent "death." This applies to British guitar rock as much as its American counterpart. Britpop seems like a yearning for an indigenous rock tradition faced with the domination of a more nebulous transnational dance-floor culture. Feminism's challenge to rock masculinism changed guitar group music during the 1980s. Some groups returned to regressive laddishness and macho antics as a response to feminism—the Happy Mondays and Oasis being the most notable examples. This backlash is markedly different from the "sensitive," more androgynous masculinity of groups like the Wedding Present, Felt, the Pastels, and Belle and Sebastian, with their vulnerable male voices and softer Velvet Underground chords.

This less macho attitude hasn't necessarily meant that male musicians, journalists, and fans have been more open to girls and women participating in the indie rock scene. As Laura Lee Davies notes, the attraction of groups like the Smiths was that they justified an indulgence in "little-boy-lost tendencies" and offered a place to sublimate a fear of sex and relationships with women.[113] This urge can be dressed up as intellectual androgyny and/or sensitive "New Man masculinity." On a similar note, Jon Savage reckons that the nostalgic fan mode of Nick Hornby and other male journalists writing about music, soccer, and 1970s pop culture has legitimized a middle-class populism, another disappointing response to the gains and possibilities brought about by feminism.[114] Despite male anxieties and backlash, women have become increasingly audible and visible in white guitar pop-rock.

These developments do not suggest that "rock is dead" but rather that rock has reformulated itself. Obviously, many male and female musicians still play and listeners continue to enjoy established and developing musical genres such as indie rock, heavy metal, and its many subgenres. Robert Miklitsch thinks the "mantra about the death of rock" might be "a projection of the white male baby-boomer's rapidly aging body." This notion of rock as a decaying and dying body is disabling for popular music studies. Miklitsch is right to insist that we would do better to think of musical forms or genres themselves. Such a turn will lead theorists to the historicity of the music and the diverse ways in which people live with it.[115]

In popular music studies, feminism and queer cultural politics have focused on what many simplistically see as guitar rock-pop's nemesis—dance music culture—to place issues of the body, gender, sexuality, race, and ethnicity more firmly on the agenda for theorists and critics. The hard-held ideologies of rock have come under strain. The culture of the word and song, which provided a politics of representation, has been threatened by a musical culture that seems more concerned with the beat than the voice, with bodies moving rather than speaking. Instead of taking up the guitar, bass, and drums, many would-be musicians in Britain have chosen turntables and computer technology to make music. This isn't to suggest, like a Decca executive who refused to sign the Beatles, that "guitar music is on the way out," but to register an important shift in the very notion of musicianship. Driven by the digital revolution, dance music production and consumption have also reconstructed music-based leisure in Britain through complex networks of music scenes and practices that cross national borders; and, unlike rock music, dance music has not been defined primarily by the British-U.S. axis of musical power.

In a 1991 article on music communities and scenes, Will Straw contrasts alternative rock (within which we can place the Smiths, Morrissey, and a phenomenon like Britpop) with dance music genres. He argues that musicians and listening constituencies for alternative rock tend to privilege the canonical, traditional, and local, whereas dance music scenes privilege the novel, the redirective, and "international circuits of influence over the mining of a locally stable heritage." A now dominant dance music mainstream and its margins seem to have "heightened the insularity of white, bohemian musical culture."[116]

Through clubs, DJs, specialist music shops, and a dance music press, British cities like London and Manchester are closely connected to protean music scenes in, for example, Chicago, Detroit, Berlin, Amsterdam, Paris, and New York. Straw argues that popular music theorists critical of the development of an increasingly transnational media economy run the risk of celebrating musical practices which seem to be rooted in "geographical, historical and cultural unities."[117] Therefore, whenever we encounter what seems like a unified, coherent, and locally constructed sense of Englishness, we must be aware of its uneven imbrication with forces outside as well as inside the nation's borders. Englishness is always shaped in transnational conditions.

2

U.K. Public Limited Company
England's Consuming with the Pet Shop Boys

The Britishness is that we live in Britain and our experience of life is of Britain and that's what we're about. . . . It's kind of a "gimmick" for the Pet Shop Boys.
—Neil Tennant

In his 1992 essay "Anglo-America and Its Discontents," Simon Frith suggests that the period of British-American global pop domination, which began around 1964 with the Beatles and the British Invasion of the U.S., may well be coming to a close. The U.K. may remain a fermenting talent pool with a tightly integrated national media infrastructure, but as a market it's simply not as important as it used to be. Dave Laing argues that the "platinum triangle" formed by North America, Britain, and Australasia is being superseded by other regions such as Asia and Latin America. The regional and geo-linguistic perspective is now central to the globalizing strategies of media and communications industries.[1]

How does this affect England? Both Frith and Laing believe that economic and political integration of the European Community with deregulation of national media industries has made continental Europe a more important network for popular music production and consumption. A unified European market potentially provides a greater profit return on the same product, and these nations share a similar mix of public and private media institutions.

With the decline in Europe's state broadcasting systems, a channel like MTV Europe figures more prominently in the dissemination and marketing of popular music. Corrina Sturmer speculates on whether such a "European" institution will lead to transnational identifications that contest national imaginaries and affiliations: "Is the imaginary Europe of MTV a product of the irresistible attraction of popular 'low' consumer culture, a consequence of American cultural imperialism? Are we being spoon-fed 'Euro-pudding'? Is MTV the new lingua franca of European popular culture, diluting local styles and sounds in its flow, or does it open avenues of opposition for Europe's youth resisting either oppressive national identities or the values and life-styles of an older generation? Does it open spaces for new and different identities to emerge across Europe?"[2]

These new European tendencies may challenge "Englishness," though this may not necessarily be cause for much celebration. Insular nationalisms might not be replaced by a benign, more open "internationalism" but by the siege mentality of Fortress Europe. The hard-won political rights of various movements and organizations at the national level could be compromised in a new federated Europe. As this economic and political bloc emerges, the contours of a European identity are still quite ill-defined. Europe continues to be in flux, between East and West, North and South, the Christian-secular and Islam, torn by military conflicts and ethnic nationalisms, and unsure how it marks itself apart from the United States. Europe's political and cultural imaginary still appears shadowy compared with the more defined lines of its economic vision.

Even though the business-class traveler from "U.K. p.l.c." in the Pet Shop Boys' track "Single" (from the 1996 *Bilingual* album) wants to think of the continent as "home," Europeanness is far from seriously undermining identifications with "Englishness." In 1993 the electronic pop duo took part in MTV Europe's official launch in the former Soviet Union. The station was to be shown for two hours a week on state TV across the CIS, and for an additional 41 hours on various terrestrial stations in Moscow, reaching a potential audience of 88 million homes, 210 million people.[3] From a British perspective, Frith sees the Pet Shop Boys as exemplars of the changing global configuration of pop music and the end of Anglo-American hegemony. The group sells more units in Europe than America; their videos have more exposure on European television channels than on U.S. MTV.

The Pet Shop Boys seem to be a transitional act, "old-fashioned" in certain respects; they have a clearly defined pop-group star identity, and they write and record traditional song structures; on the other hand, they have played a role in the transformations in music production and consumption associated with dance-floor culture. Neil Tennant and Chris Lowe use electronic instruments and work within and across dance-floor genres such as house, Hi-NRG, techno, and many other subgenres. Their tracks are radically remixed by DJ producers for twelve-inch singles designed for dance-floor utility. For a number of pop critics, their computer music and stardom have brought up issues of authenticity, authorship, technology, and postmodernism. While negotiating the changing pop music landscape themselves, their work has commented on popular music discourse and the transformations of the Thatcher period, particularly the debate around consumerism. The Pet Shop Boys are also well known for their "Englishness." As the carriers of a residue of middle-class nationalism, the group has mapped a history and geography of London during the AIDS crisis.

When Tennant and Lowe appeared in Moscow for MTV-Europe, they also shot some of the video for the single "Go West" in Red Square. This track was a massive hit across Europe in 1993. Originally recorded by the disco outfit Village People in the 1970s, "Go West" is a utopian tune that appropriates Horace Greeley's famous slogan to suggest San Francisco as a gay promised land. In a further semiotic slippage, "Go West" becomes an anthem for post-communism in the early 90s. A gay American song is reborn as a song for a new Europe.

In the video the Statue of Liberty is a black disco diva whose torch sends out radio waves to the east, broadcasting American messages to the world. This image of cultural imperialism is juxtaposed with shots of Soviet imagery framed like constructivist photographs and films. A phalanx of Soviet sailors who might have manned the Potemkin becomes a male voice choir singing the chorus "Go West" as it stomps its way up a staircase that ascends to heaven and away from the Soviet Union. The hammers and sickles and statue of Lenin, shot in documentary style, are crumbling and fading monuments compared with the video's computer-enhanced images of the present. The Pet Shop Boys wander around Red Square in brightly colored rubber suits, like sheathed aliens, as Muscovite passersby look askance at them.

Another PSB song also taps into the decline of Soviet communism, but its treatment of national myth might be equally applicable to England. "My October Symphony" from *Behavior* (1990) poses precisely the historiographical questions addressed in the group's career-long meditation on Englishness. Tennant (himself a history graduate) voices the dilemma of a Soviet composer during *Glasnost*. He wonders what he should do, now that the national myth of the October Revolution has been debunked. Should he rewrite or revise his symphony now that revelation appears to have replaced revolution? Are socialist realism and historical materialism to be nudged aside by such enlightenment? The fall of the revolution becomes the autumnal crisis of the nation. All these years, the people have faithfully marched to celebrate the Soviet revolution; now what do they do? If Soviet history-making is bunk, do we replace the collective remembering of the Bolshevik revolution with the Menshevik revolution or honor those who have fallen in war, but without invoking our communist legacy? The stakes of popular memory are dreadfully clear, but the composer's dilemma isn't resolved.

The song's story is inspired in part by Shostakovich's career and his composi-tions for Eisenstein's monumental film *October* (AKA *Ten Days That Shook the World*), which fixed the national myth of the Bolshevik Revolution. The Pet Shop Boys' track sounds like proto-disco, a light 1970s Barry White shuffle beat with wah-wah guitar. The disco sound has now itself become vintage. The elegiac string motifs of the Balanescu Quartet bring a simulation of Soviet classical sound up against disco rhythm, in homage also to the Salsoul Orchestra, which brought strings together with Afro-Latino disco rhythms in the 1970s. Jay Henry's mourn-ful gospel backing vocals reiterate Tennant's questions.

A similar historiographical quandary is examined by the Pet Shop Boys' col-laborator Derek Jarman in his super-8 film *Imagining October.* In Eisenstein's house, he shoots the film theorist Peter Wollen turning the pages of the filmmak-er's 1920 copy of John Reed's *Ten Days That Shook the World.* Trotsky's name has been blocked out with black ink. History and popular memory have been erased from the book by state power, which has attempted to enforce a collective for-getting. Jarman's film moves between the Soviet Union and Britain. "Step for-ward into the past that is not / Into the merrie old land of was," proclaims an intertitle. *Imagining October,* like the PSB's "My October Symphony" is "politi-cal," but as Jarman writes, the film "doesn't take a direct line; it's simpler than that, its didacticism is ironic, the problem is no longer one of opposition, but the fiendishly complicated dynamic of the post-industrial state. Both systems are coping with the problems, problems of inheritance."[4] Like Jarman, the Pet Shop Boys' music is critical of the monumental histories written and imaged by the British state as responses to "problems of inheritance" during the 80s and 90s.

A Brand of Englishness

When an interviewer asked Neil Tennant and Chris Lowe if there was "anything peculiarly British about the whole Pet Shop Boys way of doing things," Tennant replied that "there is a kind of caricature of Britishness that goes on . . . of Brit-ish reserve. We kind of play up to it."[5] The group's stylized restraint emerges from a characteristically middle-class, English approach to aesthetic (under)statement. In 1991, Tennant positioned the group in the following terms:

> I see us in the tradition of Joe Orton and Noël Coward in that we are serious, com-ic, light-hearted, sentimental and brittle, all at the same time. Orton and Coward belonged to a bourgeois theatre tradition. The thing that always fascinated me about that is that it bites the hand that feeds it. That's what it's there to do. It's a constant critique of middle-class life and values. The point being that they're all utter hypo-

crites. It seems to me that Pet Shop Boys belong to a kind of middle-class tradition similar to those playwrights. We are of the middle class and, at the same time, we attack that kind of life. Just as we are of pop music and attack it at the same time.[6]

Michael Bracewell argues that the Pet Shop Boys share a conservative and "sentimental nationalism" that transcends left and right political boundaries, and is evident in the work of John Betjeman, Philip Larkin, W. H. Auden, and Jarman. According to Bracewell, these artists are inspired by a myth of England as pre-industrial arcady.[7] In a similar vein, Lawrence Driscoll outlines "a British tradition of middle-class dissent, a tradition which flickers consistently throughout British history."[8] This body of work is rooted in English romanticism's response to industrialization. In Victorian England, such middle-class dissidence was associated with effeminacy, homosexuality, the aesthetics of high culture, and the belief that the national landscape and quality of life were being ruined by the cities and their factories.

Though Neil Tennant does not share this dissident tradition's anti-urbanism, his lyric writing and singing technique owe a great deal to its middle-class structure of feeling. In the BBC Radio Four program *With Great Pleasure,* in which celebrities select their favorite extracts of literature to be read over the air, Tennant picked the likes of Betjeman, Larkin, and Noel Coward for inclusion. The Englishness performed inheres in the tone as much as the content of the work. The restraint of articulation is a peculiarly English form of communication.

The Pet Shop Boys provide a kind of immanent critique of middle-class Englishness. As Bracewell notes, "the Englishness of the Pet Shop Boys manipulates mannered language (the undefended argot of the urban bourgeoisie) and forces it to comment on itself."[9] Critique and homage to a certain old England of the imagination coexist. Nostalgia is built into this discourse. I think Alison Light pinpoints this feeling of bittersweet melancholy about national identity in the prologue to her study of middle-class literary conservatism between the two World Wars:

> Certainly as the writing began to take shape, I noticed how prevalent was a farewell tone, and I must wonder why. Is it because we are really at the end of that Englishness, that voice and grammar which drew so much on histories of imperialism and whose modern transformations, which carried such authority between the wars, are now finally exhausted? Is indeed the very idea of an English nationality—of something which, in Rupert Brooke's words, could be forever England—inevitably tinged with the elegiac? Is it because we are watching the collapse of so many of the sodalities which this century has created, and of the epistemological frameworks which gave us collective forms of belonging and belief, that even a history of conservatism

must become an epitaph? No doubt, like all historical feelings, it is also personal. I grew up in a city fortified against foreigners; as a child I learnt the names of battles from the war memorials which overshadowed all our sea-front strolls. As someone who once played on bombsites and listened avidly to stories of the Blitz and of "our finest hour," maybe my own sadness has seeped into this writing: a sort of melancholy recognition that those ways of being English, foolish and even vicious as they often were, were a form of identity and community in which I too was brought up, and whose disappearance, however, is also bound to hurt. . . . But these thoughts are perhaps more fitting to a peroration than a prologue.[10]

Though the Pet Shop Boys are younger than Light, they work within and through this ambivalence about a disappearing Englishness.

When I saw the group in Detroit during its 1991 *Performance* tour, I was struck by the incredible familiarity of the English scenes enacted on stage. The group had stationed its musical technology behind the curtain while the proscenium became a set for elaborately choreographed song-and-dance sequences featuring Tennant, Lowe, and a host of male and female dancers. The prohibitions and discipline of a middle-class English upbringing and socialization were theatricalized in scenarios almost exaggeratedly Foucauldian, but also influenced by the camp of *Carry On* films and musical theater. *Performance* takes us through the boys boarding-school's discipline and punishment, its sexual repressions, fantasies, and illicit behavior. A schoolmarm chides and then canes boys caught masturbating in the dormitory. The beds become those of a hospital ward in which Chris Lowe is put in a cage and given electric shock treatment. During the song "Suburbia," several women vacuum in unison. During "Opportunities (Let's Make Some Money)" and "Shopping," dancers in pig heads sit at computers monitoring the rise and fall of share prices.

The show opens up with "This Must Be the Place I Waited Years to Leave" a song about the misery of school life. Like the Smiths' song "The Headmaster Ritual," it remembers the English school discipline of body and mind, the regimentation of teachers and preparation for exams. This colonial form of education had a long tenure in Britain. The discipline meted out to Tennant is not unlike the petty cruelties inflicted on Morrissey on the soccer field in his Manchester school in the early 70s.

When I was at school in the 1970s, humanism stood beside patriotism in both the curriculum and our orderly lines in the corridors. At school assembly, we sang military anthems like "Onward Christian Soldiers" and the headmaster told us stories of self-sacrifice in expeditions to the South Pole. The regime taught us to keep our ties straight, our mouths shut, speak only when spoken to, know our place, and "knuckle under." The order of things was drilled into us. Many of us resented it and resisted in small ways, wearing punk badges on our lapels and drawing fanzine cartoons of burning Union Jacks.

In May 1979, the month Margaret Thatcher became prime minister for the first time, I took my "O" Level exam in English at Ilkley Grammar School, a West Yorkshire comprehensive that still liked to think it was a grammar school. The Ordinary Level, or General Certificate of Education, required the class to familiarize itself with texts representative of English society, culture, and national values. There was no American literature on the syllabus, nor translated European writers like Kafka and Camus. We never read anything by a woman, not even an English woman. Instead we studied, revised, and wrote about a couple of Shakespeares, some Canterbury Tales, and the William Golding novel about English schoolboys who get stuck on an island and revert to savagery. We were required to master the meters of John Betjeman and Philip Larkin, both poets who presented a picture of middle-class England with detail, a touch of critical humor, and a heavy dose of melancholy.[11]

While colonial values were intact in its national affect, this education told us next-to-nothing of what had been done to other peoples and places in the name of England, Britain, and Empire. As far as the syllabus was concerned no one had ever written a novel or a poem of any consequence in Africa, India, or the Caribbean. The literature curriculum fixed on the details and idiosyncrasies of the English, the national identity of an island untouched even by the European continent. Asian and black British migrants were simply invisible. This was not an England of imperial expansion, but one gazing at the little picture—the miniature, not the grand canvas. And unlike Morrissey's working-class landscape, this Little England of the imagination was devoted to the middle class.

Raymond Williams's description of coming to England from Wales, in his autobiographical novel *Border Country* (1960), seems quite familiar to me as a middle-class Pakistani-Brit looking back at the 1970s: "England seemed a great house with every room partitioned by lath and plaster. Behind every screen in every cupboard, sat all the great men, everybody. If you wanted to see them, you could see them; that was what they were there for. But you must cool your own heels first; a necessary part of decorum. If you went out of your own cupboard, to see a man in another cupboard, still you must wait for the cupboard door to be opened, with proper ceremony, and by a proper attendant."[12]

Stay in your cupboard, the place to which you have been assigned. A place for everyone, everyone in his place. Middle-class Anglo-Britishness was founded on this kind of identity-thinking. It is not too much to suggest that the operations of the cupboard are not hugely different from the operations of what Eve Kosofsky Sedgwick describes as "the epistemology of the closet," a closet in which the Pet Shop Boys have been for much of their career in public.[13]

Postmodern Media and (Gay) Authenticity

In any discussion of the Englishness of the Pet Shop Boys, one cannot ignore the changing configurations of pop stardom, mediation, and notions of authenticity in popular music during the last two decades. As I discussed in chapter 1, authenticity is a crucial component of discourse on popular music by fans, journalists, and academics. Part of the Pet Shop Boys' authenticity, or lack of it (depending on the critical point of view), has focused on the issue of the group's sexual identity.

At the genesis of their music career in the mid-80s, Tennant and Lowe formed the Pet Shop Boys Partnership and have been with the EMI label ever since (on its Parlophone imprint). They have studiously managed their development as recording artists and pop commodities with precision and care. Repeatedly described as postmodern ironists by the music press, they are often praised/chided for their understanding of/collusion with the giant transnational machine of the music industry. They have styled, marketed, and disseminated their image and product through the vast and differentiated pop music media. Tennant and Lowe appear to know exactly how the record business works and have provided a critique of contemporary pop processes from inside the music industry machine. This is not to claim that they are radical or to let them off the hook entirely, but to suggest that pop discourse involves complicated and multiple notions of authenticity and politics. Many recording artists endeavor to repress the contradictions of working in transnational capitalist media industries while they boast a political significance to their recorded output. The Pet Shop Boys have continually criticized such hypocrisy and grandstanding, which they associate with the ideology of rock.

The group's life over the last decade and a half has coincided with a fundamental shift toward a new consciousness about "image" construction. Pop has always been visual, "the look" absolutely crucial in the selling of the star-commodity. Style and fashion, record sleeves, dance and movement in performance have always been integral to the identities of performers, fans, and subcultures. But this period has witnessed the widespread expansion of music video and the greater symbiosis of popular music and feature films.

In the 1980s, English pop music offered attractively packaged product in the new palaces of urban consumption. Record stores became more like department stores. The new superstores like the HMV Shop near Oxford Circus, Tower Records in Picadilly Circus, and the Virgin Megastore at the corner of Oxford Street and Tottenham Court Road, all in London's West End, occupied several floors across acres of prime urban real estate. They displayed a wide range of commodities, from computer games, magazines, books, t-shirts, and music videos to a huge selection of carefully genre-delineated compact discs, records, and cassettes. One could wander around for hours, almost getting lost in the megastore's many sections, dizzy at the range of products. If such a landscape offered the music-junkie flaneur, that wandering observer, possible bliss in record collecting and the discovery of the unexpected, obscure gem, it also reflected broader developments in consuming lifestyles.[14]

Stan Hawkins argues that the Pet Shop Boys signal changes in the relationship between consumerism and masculinity in this period. In advertising, the display of male bodies becomes common (in, for example, the commercials for Calvin Klein products and Levi Strauss 501 jeans). Shopping is now taken for granted as a part of the urban male's domain. This, according to Hawkins, is a modification to feminism, rather than a questioning of patriarchy. New masculinities, including gay/queer identities, are linked, he claims, to a new economy of consumer desirables.[15]

The Pet Shop Boys have often been associated with the white middle-class urban gay economy of the "pink pound." Chris Heath's two travelogues about the group in Asia and North America revive the classic trope of the rock-band-on-tour account, but instead of telling us the story of trashed hotel rooms and sexual exploits with groupies they spend many pages following Tennant and Lowe on their shopping excursions in foreign parts.[16]

The group itself offers a vast array of products, including multiple mixes of each single, their *Disco* and *Disco 2* mix albums, recordings featuring other singers such as Dusty Springfield and Liza Minnelli, and soundtrack productions for *Scandal* (1989) and *The Crying Game* (1992). In this way their star image is dispersed across a range of text-commodities and their authorship seems fragmented. The recognizable, blank faces of Tennant and Lowe appear in flat Mapplethorpe-style portraits in advertising flyers, magazine articles, record covers, and videos. On the surface, the Pet Shop Boys seem to provide evidence for Grossberg's assertion that stars have become simply mobile signs to shift an array of different products.

The group appeared in magazines like *Smash Hits* (for whom Tennant was once an editor) and *The Face* in which photography was as at least as important as written text. The graphic design of *The Face,* in particular the work of Neville Brody and Malcolm Garrett, was enormously influential in the 1980s, transform-

ing the look of the new "lifestyle" magazines and other publications as well as
the advertising for banks and other businesses seeking new youth consumers. Dick
Hebdige contrasts *The Face*'s style of social commentary to the documentary
photojournalism of *Picture Post,* which had provided the kind of mythical images of community and the national-popular that Morrissey brought into a new
context with the Smiths record sleeves. In "Squaring Up to *The Face,*" Hebdige
writes about the new style publication with a mixture of admiration and anxiety. The magazine is all sensuous surface, quintessentially postmodern in its taste
for quotation. History disappears in its play of signs, as politics are erased from
its textures. At best, *The Face*'s politics are about style. He concludes that the
magazine "reflects, defines and focuses the concerns of a significant minority of
style and image conscious people who are not, on the whole, much interested in
party politics, authorized versions of the past and outmoded notions of community. The popular and the job of picturing the popular has changed irrevocably
even since the 1950s."[17]

Like much left-liberal music criticism of the period, Hebdige's commentary
laments the shift from the politics of punk to postmodernism. "Youth" now functions as a discourse centered on consumption. In fact, in a discussion of the July
1981 uprisings/riots in various English inner-city neighborhoods, Hebdige remarks
that even youthful rebellion centers on consumption, even if it is in the "illegitimate" act of looting—"the right to work subsumed in the right to consume."[18]

The conventional wisdom in both academic writing and journalism in the 1980s
was that punk's musical and political authenticity had been replaced by postmodern cynicism, a sign of the (Reagan/Thatcher) times. But the ideology of popular authenticity had not disappeared, only changed uniforms, from an ethic demanding control of the means of production into control of one's image in a
corporate record industry. One of the powerful impetuses of the punk ethic in
1976–77 aimed for independence, a measure of self-sufficiency, a small-time cottage cooperative industrialism that could bypass the large music corporations.
Indie labels like Rough Trade and Factory formed The Cartel to distribute their
releases. "Complete Control," as the Clash had sung in frustration with its label
CBS in 1977, was now wishful thinking. The belief that one could make music
that escaped the "system" was replaced by more pragmatic concerns such as the
negotiation of publishing rights, single releases, in short, the circulation of the
musician and his or her music as a commodity-image within the dominant transnational music industry.

David Hesmondhalgh usefully adapts the political economist Graham Mur-
dock's distinction between allocative and operational control to describe the
developing relation between small and large record companies in the 1980s and

1990s. Allocative control consists of the overall economic policy of a company; operational control involves the day-to-day running at a lower level, decisions concerning the use of resources already allocated, processes that have a degree of autonomy but are still delimited by the goal of the larger organization.[19] While Hesmondhalgh applies this distinction to major and indie labels, it could define the parameters within which many recording artists signed to major labels conceive of "creative control" over their careers and the product they release. The authenticity of musicians is now often measured by the extent to which they can negotiate and regulate their profits, just as media corporations facilitate the manufacture and circulation of musicians as multiple commodities.

I argued in chapter 1 that ideas of authenticity ground popular music consumption with affect. As David Buxton points out, "Rock stars, as agents of consumer discipline, help to define the norms and limits of the existing sociohistorical consumer, and thus individual possibilities. They anchor a chaotic aesthetico-ideological discourse and represent it in a 'humanized' form by investing the human body itself. Thus the record managed to achieve an enhanced social usefulness far exceeding the mere 'need' for recorded music."[20] As listeners and consumers, we need to *believe* in some aspects of star images and personae—that, for example, the Pet Shop Boys are who we think they are. Magazines like *Smash Hits* regularly feature pop stars (including the Pet Shop Boys) who tell us about their ordinary daily habits and lifestyles—what they eat for breakfast, the books they read, the films they like—in short, the pop star's range of consumer choices. The star's consumer sovereignty can by extension be the fan's consumer freedom but this needs to be anchored to the fan's belief that the star is a unique subject.

Andrew Goodwin reiterates the importance of the continuing belief in a real flesh-and-blood person behind the popular music star: "the aesthetics of rock and pop . . . remain thus locked into an essentially Romantic discourse of self-expression, even where mimesis, truth, and faithfulness to 'reality' are stressed (in rock's classical/realist appeal) or where manipulation, self-consciousness, and artifice are trumpeted (the modernist, or postmodernist address). . . . what is really at stake for pop fans and critics is related to a romantic aesthetic concerning suppositions about intentions, feelings, and sincerity."[21]

Goodwin cites the Pet Shop Boys live in *Performance* to illustrate his argument because many critics consider them as emblematic of the postmodern star-as-sign. While Tennant and Lowe barely addressed the audience during the concert, choosing instead to play parts in a dramatic diegesis on stage, audience members still responded to the first-person address of the songs as if the Pet Shop Boys had stepped out of the theatrical fiction on stage to address the audience directly. Tennant then reacted directly to fans like a pop star at a conventional concert, even though he was playing a role on stage. The boundaries of the traditional rock concert and stage persona were breached to some extent, but not entirely broken down.

The desire for an authentic identity underlying the artist is also striking in the debates around the Pet Shop Boys' homosexuality. The "gayness" of their musical content has never been in much doubt but calls for them to be open about their sexual identity have been contested. Whether this is the result of the epistemology of the English closet or not, the relative merits of the Pet Shop Boys' pop strategy have been scrutinized by a number of writers as part of a discourse on sexual identity and queer politics in the 1980s and 90s.

Tennant publicly came out only in 1994, in an interview with *Attitude* magazine. Prior to the "post-Out" 1996 album *Bilingual,* a sympathetic critic might argue that the group's well-documented (to the point of cliché) irony and camp are akin to what Jonathan Dollimore terms *transgressive reinscription,* "a turning back upon something and a perverting of it typically if not exclusively through inversion and displacement." Dollimore argues that "reinscription is an oppositional practice which is also a perspective and language (sensibility?) constantly interpreting and re-presenting all sections of a culture including its dominant and subordinate fractions, its conventional (e.g., heterosexual) as well as deviant (e.g., homosexual) identities." Repetition is intrinsic to the process of resistance and transformation: "the task is to repeat and, through the repetition to displace."[22]

One might argue that the Pet Shop Boys' "irony" is about repeating the tropes of middle-class Englishness, though it's arguable if these tropes have been completely displaced. There does seem to be a residue of both this nationalism and the closet. Dollimore adds that an important aspect of transgressive reinscription is a kind of representational ambivalence, in which "identification with, and desire *for,* may coexist with parodic subversion *of* the norm." This sounds like gay camp's simultaneous proximity and distance to its object of affection/disavowal. Ann Powers also notes that the Pet Shop Boys "use camp, but also step outside to critique it, showing the artifice of the artifice. And they're as likely to camp entrenched gay customs as to stick a pin in the straight status quo."[23]

On the other hand, Joseph Bristow suggests that very little about this sort of reinscription is transgressive. Tennant and Lowe may dress up as leather men on the cover of *Smash Hits* (12–25 August 1987), and their use of gay imagery cannot be dissociated from their commercial success, but Bristow adds, "there is nothing militant in the Pet Shop Boys' songs, although a gay audience will detect allusions and subtexts in the lyrics. . . . As long as the music is in demand and the money keeps rolling in, then gayness of a semi-invisible kind is allowed for."[24]

The American magazine *Outweek* in May 1991 was even more critical: "Let's get it out in the open: The Pet Shop Boys, Neil Tennant and Chris Lowe, are gay. They won't say so, but a lot of other people have, and every nuance of their music, lyrics, personal style and sensibility *screams* it. . . . The Pet Shop Boys owe a lot to gay men. We gave them their material. We are their audience and their brothers. We made them stars, yet they stay in the closet. It's time they paid that bill."[25] John Gill also criticizes the group for its failure to declare its sexual identity sooner. He argues that the "open secret" of the Pet Shop Boys' gayness has ultimately functioned to repress discussion of sexuality as represented in the group's music. In this way, the Pet Shop Boys "fit the bourgeois English tradition of discreet perversion and collusion with the establishment."[26]

In the Pet Shop Boys' defense, Simon Watney claims a central place for the group in gay culture's response to the AIDS epidemic: "Disco music has been at the heart of gay youth culture for two decades, so it is hardly surprising that pop music has responded to the epidemic far more pragmatically and directly than any other culture medium. Indeed nothing is more indicative of our determination to live through this appalling tragedy than the intensity of contemporary gay dance and 'rave' culture, which articulates the complexity of our lives and feelings with passionate precision. No band has responded to this challenge with more integrity and musical imagination than the Pet Shop Boys, who more than anybody else have helped 'get us through' these bad times."[27] In November 1995, *The Independent* claimed that the Pet Shop Boys "still get most of the Western World to dance to the queerest things. Album units shifted globally are about 25 million."[28]

These different critical positions reveal the hotly contested terrain of the group's public gay identity. Is the decision to not state their gay identity a desire on the part of the Pet Shop Boys to be queer rather than gay, a resistance to the categorizations and reifications of identity politics, or a cop-out to heterosexual hegemony and a profit-driven strategy?

If we use the term "queer" in the way defined by Alexander Doty, as a variety of discourses that question, criticize, and attack the dominant heterosexual symbolic order, then pre-1996 Pet Shop Boys music seems to fit this description.[29] Pamela Robertson suggests that queerness "includes gay- and lesbian-specific positions as well as non-gay and non-lesbian ones."[30] But then again, the PSB never called themselves "queer" either.

In his "coming out" interview, Tennant suggests that identity politics is constraining, but he uneasily defends himself: "I've never wanted to be a part of this separate gay world. I know a lot of people will not appreciate hearing me say that. But when people talk about the gay community in London, for instance, what do they really mean by that? There is a community of interests, particularly around the health issue, but beyond that what is there, really? There's nightclubs, music, drugs, shopping, PAs by Bad Boys Inc. Well I'm sorry, but that really isn't how I define myself. I don't want to belong to some narrow group or ghetto. And I think, if they're really honest, a lot of gay people would say they felt like that as well."[31]

Tennant is equivocal about his long silence on his sexual identity, as he further elaborates in an interview with *Bay Windows* in 1996: "The gay label doesn't really bother me, as long as it's not something that is restrictive. I just don't think one should live one's life as a gay man. I don't think that sexuality necessarily implies a lifestyle package that comes with it. . . . As I write the words in the Pet Shop Boys' songs, I deal with [being gay] in them. I always have done that. I probably deal with them slightly more openly now, which I quite enjoy doing. Although 'Metamorphosis' [is] a rap [on *Bilingual*] about growing up gay and realizing what you are and how you are going to deal with it and all that stuff, I suppose I wouldn't have done that a few years ago." In 1997, Tennant told the *Gay Times:* "Our songs speak to gay people because the lyrics are written by me, and I'm a gay man. But I would hate for us to be categorized, to be disloyal in some way, as a gay group. We make singles for whoever wants to like it. We make pop singles that we hope would attract a wide audience as well. To be honest, I'm kind of against the categorization of splitting up our society into communities of race or sexuality or any other classification. I would like society to be one community. I know that isn't possible, but I think it's something we should all aim for."[32]

One thing is clear beyond this utopian call for "one community" against identity politics: the Pet Shop Boys are unlikely to have made the kind of music they did if they hadn't been closeted. Their particular evocations of England in the 1980s and 90s depend on a repression that is part of that residue of English nationalism's effect on the body. Nevertheless their body of work has created a selective aural map of queer urban Britain. Their hit music has commented on the New Right celebration of consumerism. Their songs have mourned during the AIDS crisis when government legislated the suppression of homosexual representation using the rhetoric of the "national family."

Capital Ventures

In the mid-1980s, the Pet Shop Boys released a cluster of hit singles, sonic snapshots of Thatcherite London in the yuppie boom period before the Black Monday stock market crash in October 1987.

Opening with the kind of rhyme about guns and suicide usually heard on gangsta rap tracks, "West End Girls" (1985) exploded internationally as their first chartbuster. The promotional video undoubtedly fostered record sales outside Britain. Music video was crucial in the British Invasion of the U.S. in the mid-80s, soon after MTV began broadcasting on cable.

At a moment when images of England, its heritage, and tourist sites were being sold on the international market through Merchant-Ivory films and television dramas, the Pet Shop Boys semi-vérité video of London's busy West End was a smart device for promoting a new pop group. Tennant and Lowe are pictured among the familiar sights of London, such as the Houses of Parliament, Tower Bridge, Leicester Square, and double-decker buses, iconic images of the nation captured for the "tourist gaze" and mass-reproduced in postcards, books, films, and television.

John Urry claims that in today's media-saturated world, "people are tourists most of the time whether they are literally mobile or only experience simulated mobility through the incredible fluidity of multiple signs and electronic images."[33] Jonathan Culler argues that "the tourist is interested in everything as a sign of itself. . . . all over the world the unsung armies of semioticians, the tourists, are fanning out in search of the signs of Frenchness, typical Italian behaviour, exemplary Oriental scenes, typical American thruways, traditional English pubs."[34] Tourism has been one of Britain's few growth industries in the last two decades.

The video for "West End Girls," directed by longtime collaborator Eric Watson, operates within the visual regime of tourism. But stock images of London are repeated with a slight difference, displacing the practice to some extent. The video shares the stylistic strategies of what John Taylor terms "oppositional photography," which critiques English Heritage and the conventions of British tourism:

> Though oppositional photographers separate themselves from standard tourist fare, they do not segregate themselves from the reassuring imagery of "normal" tourism. Opposition depends on harnessing the dominant modality of tourism, especially the identification of core English values which are constantly repeated. Oppositional photographers rework the language of tourism, and play with its appearance and concerns. They take part in a constant dialogue with the everyday practices of tourism and with its standard imagery. Their success depends upon their ability to embrace the cliché and alter it, making it appear new in ways which are surprising and not necessarily subtle.[35]

This photographic practice seems akin to Dollimore's notion of "transgressive reinscription."

The "West End Girls" video tourism shows Tennant and Lowe as they move through central London. At the beginning of the video we hear the noises of the hustling-bustling city that are part of the sound recording of "West End Girls." The camera cruises past Chris Lowe on the street and rests on two vintage child dolls in a shop window. A sequence of quick cuts follows with shots of skinheads, young black men, and a member of the working-class "casual" subculture who all return the mobile gaze of the camera. The video runs through the same sequence of images, but much faster, then freezes on the casual staring back at the camera. Cut to Tennant and Lowe who walk purposefully along an almost empty Berwick Street in Soho during the foggy early morning. A shabbily dressed man (who may be a homeless person) accompanies them.

Both Pet Shop Boys stand in front of a red garage door. Tennant is dressed affluently, Lowe the silent, rough lad. In its videos and record sleeves, the group repeatedly plays on the suggestion that Tennant and Lowe come from different social classes. The song's chorus is "East End Boys and West End Girls," possibly an allusion to working-class young men who have sexual encounters with women and/or men of the higher orders in the consumer hub of the city. The image is as flat as one of Mapplethorpe's portraits. Tennant directly addresses the camera. Lowe with a characteristically blank expression seems to melt into the landscape, the red ridges of the garage door running across his torso.

A number of other images of the Pet Shop Boys place them in the London landscape, suggesting a gay couple or a gay encounter waiting to happen. The sleeve for the "Heart" single presents Tennant in a suit and bowler hat as a city gent on a bench (possibly on a tube train) while Lowe stands behind him. Tennant has his hands clasped as he looks down humbly, a Magritte-like figure, the embodiment of the uptight middle-class commuter-drone. Lowe is a futurist blur, but still recognizable as a youth in trendy sport-designer wear. On the sleeve for the single "Rent," Tennant and Lowe stand together at the far end of a railway platform staring directly at the camera. Again the perspective is flat, with the direct address to the camera of Mapplethorpe figures or models in a catalog for designer clothes.

Echoing Walter Benjamin's seduction by the shop windows in the Paris arcades, Tennant raps in a pinched English accent about the West End's commercial landscape of posters, moving bodies, voices, and exchanges of all types. London is a galaxy of signifiers and glimmering surfaces offering infinite choice, promising a supply to meet any acquisitive demand. The financial speculation of "a hard or soft option" has the whiff of sexual connotation. Urban desire is both sexual and economic.

In slow motion the steadicam passes through one of the new shopping malls in central London, probably the Trocadero at Piccadilly Circus. Young women return the camera's gaze on the words "West End girls" in the chorus. The camera-eye cruises through Leicester Square, past the amusement arcades and highest density of movie theaters in central London. The theater marquees reveal traces of Britain's "glorious" past—Rank and the Empire Ballroom. The chorus sounds the city in more depressing terms. This is where East End boys and West End girls meet, but it's also a dead-end world. The city's possibilities are not all they are cracked up to be.

On the South Bank of the Thames, the Pet Shop Boys pose in a pastiche of a postcard image. Tennant addresses the camera while Lowe looks off screen as the "classic" skyline of the Houses of Parliament lurks darkly in the background. We cut to an iconic red double-decker bus headed for Aldgate, near the City, the capital's financial district. Tennant and Lowe stand against the metallic frame of the NatWest tower, a major banking center. Through these still shots the video reproduces the tourist postcard's representational tropes.

As the instrumental break in the middle of the song swells and a trumpet solo works its way into the electronic pulse, we are swept up in an ascension-to-heaven shot over Tower Bridge and Westminster. The image is now black and white rather than color. This is the epiphanic moment of the song and video. As we look down upon London with a bird's-eye view of Westminster, the shot becomes a negative, an inverted representation of the city. The image is a palimpsest. It turns the view of London into an abstraction as beautiful and strange as the famous map of the London Underground.

As Michel de Certeau notes of the view of New York from the World Trade Center, the viewer takes voluptuous pleasure in seeing the whole city with a totalizing eye. Such elevation "transforms the bewitching world by which one was 'possessed' into a text that lies before one's eyes. It allows one to read it, to be a solar Eye, looking down like a god": "Is the immense texturology spread out before one's eyes anything more than a representation, an optical artefact? It is the analogue of the facsimile produced, through a projection that is a way of keeping aloof, by the space planner urbanist, city planner or cartographer. The panorama-city is a 'theoretical' (that is, visual) simulacrum, in short a picture, whose condition of possibility is an oblivion and a misunderstanding of practices."[36] This "concept-city" of the planners, politicians, and panopticon is juxtaposed against the practices of everyday urban life at ground level—activities that have insinuated themselves against official surveillance and the regulations of urban life.

Back to earth in color, the camera now drives around Trafalgar Square, taking in the vista of the National Gallery famous from Humphrey Jennings and Stewart McAllister's film *Listen to Britain*. But rather than dwell on this museum of national art treasures, we pass South Africa House, where demonstrators are assembled in a continuous anti-apartheid vigil. Again, the imperial and colonial legacy of the city is a suggestive trace. We also become very conscious of the camera's role as driver, rather than walker, as the image lurches for a moment when the car slows down at a traffic light, changes gear, and speeds up again. The apparatus of both travel and visualization heighten the sensation of movement through the heart of the city.

On foot again, the camera focuses on Leicester Square, where people queue for movies like *Fletch* and *Desperately Seeking Susan,* American products that dominate the mediascape. Then we are a few yards away in Piccadilly Circus, with the statue of Eros at its center, a sexually charged rendezvous point. Neil Tennant in closeup addresses the camera with the song's chorus. Through a video special effect, purple neon behind him, with its bright exclamation-mark sign, bleeds across his face a little. This flaneur does not have visual mastery over this landscape; he melts into the buildings.

This is a cityscape of commerce but also one of other stories and images. In contrast to the "concept city," this city, as de Certeau poetically describes it, is one of people moving in myriad directions:

> The ordinary practitioners of the city live "down below," below the thresholds at which visibility begins. They walk—an elementary form of this experience of the city; they are walkers, Wandersmänner, through whose bodies flow the thicks and thins of an urban "text" they write without being able to read it. These practitioners make use of spaces that cannot be seen; their knowledge of them is as blind as that of lovers in each other's arms. The paths that correspond in this intertwining are unrecognized poems in which each body is an element signed by many others to elude legibility. It is as though the practices organizing a bustling city were characterized by blindness. The networks of these moving, intersecting writings compose a manifold story that has neither author nor spectator, shaped out of fragments of trajectories and alterations of spaces: in relation to representations, it remains daily and infinitely other.[37]

The video for "West End Girls" presents different Londons, hinting at the mobile erotics of the city as well as the monumental architecture of its past and present. For the city planners and business interests, the West End is the landscape of idealized consumer desire and tourist pleasure. The Pet Shop Boys show us that it is also a place for encounters between East End "boys" and West End "girls." Consumer desire is linked to sexual desire, something embodied in the figure of the flaneur.

The flaneur has been a controversial figure, a problematic metaphor for the modern and postmodern experience, an exemplar of the mobility of people, media, and mass reproduction. In the writings of Baudelaire and Benjamin, the flaneur wanders aimlessly through the city as part of the mass but is also not completely of it, eyeing the sights and sites with a distracted gaze. Critics have argued that this modern figure is the omnipotent bourgeois male subject, getting "a bit of the other" as he cruises the streets taking in the prostitute and the rent boy, the objects of his gaze as well as figures in an economic exchange. The visual regime of the city is organized by this mobile spectator who is separated from the objects of his gaze by his social and economic privilege and power.

However, flânerie need not be defined by this male bourgeois subject and these particular regimes of looking. The act of walking through the city is different for subjects and groups determined and inflected by sexual orientation, gender, race and ethnicity. The urban nomadism of the flaneur is also related to the notion of (gay) camp, which, according to John Durham Peters, "glides across the surface and never hammers the stakes too deep into the ground."[38] While de Certeau's description of walking in the streets is rather abstract and misty-eyed in its poetry, it does suggest, as Steve Pile points out, "the innumerable ways in which walking in the streets mobilizes other subtle, stubborn, embodied, resistant meanings. The streets become haunted by the ghosts of other stories. The city becomes a ghost town of memories without a language to articulate them because walking is a transient and evanescent practice. The proper spaces created for the city by the view from above—whether embodied in the visual regimes of the panoptic gaze or cartography—are interrupted, resignified and torn by the everyday practices of moving by foot."[39] The "West End Girls" video juxtaposes these different ways of constructing the city landscape.

London's mobilization of consumer longing and sexual desire is worked through in a number of other early PSB songs. In the single "Opportunities (Let's Make Lots of Money)" (1986), Tennant plays the yuppie bent on a get-rich-quick scheme. He will be the brains while his partner can provide the brawn for their enterprise. The video features Tennant in a suit with a dollar-sign pin, standing in front of a giant American car in a parking garage. He sings to the camera from a manhole, as leather-jacketed working-class lad Lowe wanders silently and enigmatically around the garage in the studied, sullen manner of his early pop persona. The song's narrator has the cultural capital of an elite university education and could have had an academic career, but is now determined to make some serious money.

Sex and loadsamoney also share the lyric turf of "Rent" (1987). The title suggests rent boys and male prostitution. But "Rent" is also a song about the way that romantic and sexual relationships have an economic dimension. The singer loves the sung-to because he pays the rent. The "heterosexual" video narrative, directed by Derek Jarman, features a "kept woman" (played by Margi Clarke) who looks exceedingly unhappy as she watches her fat capitalist sugar-daddy gorge himself at a banquet. She manages to get away from this Groszian caricature in a limousine driven by chauffeur Tennant. At King's Cross Station, she warmly receives Chris Lowe, who with a duffel bag over his shoulder is a migrant from the north hoping to find a job and a new life in the capital.

Thatcherism's economic-political ideology is most directly dissected in "Shopping," the anthemic chorus of which sounds like a celebration of unbridled consumerism. But with the tone of a sharp Brecht/Weill diatribe, the song attacks the Conservative government's sale of national assets and its heritage pimping. The lyrics refer to the "Big Bang" in the City of London, the electronic revolution that linked London more efficiently to the globe's other money markets. During its first tour, the group and accompanying dancers donned the quintessentially yuppie uniform—suit, tie, suspenders, and striped shirt—as they hopped and pranced on stage with cellular phones during "Shopping."

The songs I've discussed could be described as "city symphonies" of the 80s, when Thatcherite policies promoted a brief financial boom in the south. If "West End Girls" (1985) was the first of the group's songs (and videos) to map the changing landscape of London, then "The Theatre," from the *Very* album (1993), is almost like the B-side to the A-side of affluence that is "West End Girls." After the stock market crash in October 1987, it was clear that Thatcherite consumerism and rampant greed had not come up with the goods.

"The Theatre" is inspired by a statement from a Conservative Member of Parliament who callously and carelessly remarked that the homeless were the people you stepped over when you left the theater. The song's chorus repeats this from the perspective of the bums. Again, the Pet Shop Boys use an aspect of gay middle-class urban life—the West End theater—to comment on the politics of urban space. The songscape presents the glitter and possibility of the city but undercuts it. Tennant's multitracked voice takes the point of view of a homeless person who observes the busy activity of the street, its bright lights and wealth. Young people come to London from Scotland and the north of England. The song's vision of the city as the dead-end of migration is familiar from Mike Leigh's film *Naked* (1993). The tube stations, thoroughfares, alleyways, and nooks and crannies of the West End have become resting places for the homeless poor. If the shop windows and malls are the focus of "West End Girls," here it is the world underneath the bright facades. The encounter between rich and poor takes place when the crowds leave West End theaters after a night's entertainment to stroll up The Strand, where they are reminded of these other bodies on the streets. The sound recording apes the big production numbers of West End musicals with its full orchestra, thunderclap sounds, pantomime laugh samples, and the diva backing vocals of Sylvia Mason-James. The accusing voice of the homeless person singles out the theater-goer and wonders if he or she will catch the flaneur's eye. The song brings the invisible homeless into the spotlight, *les miserables* of the London streets, while the musical of the same name plays on and on (and on) in the West End.

In these songs about the landscape of consumer culture, the Pet Shop Boys provoke many of the same questions debated at the end of the first Thatcher decade by the left intelligentsia, in particular the New Times project associated with the journal *Marxism Today*. New Times argued that the period brought to a head certain tendencies within capitalism. Consumerism was now more important to the shape of the economy than ever before. Citizenship and consumer identity were more intimately linked. Thatcherism had been successful in developing a discourse of individualism and freedom using the rhetoric of consumer democracy. According to Frank Mort, the Left had to respond to these changes: "For more and more people it is outside work, outside the formal political structures, in the world of holidays, home interiors and superstores, that they have a sense of power and freedom to express themselves, to define their sense of self, to mould the good life."[40] Mort acknowledges that critically thinking through consumerism is a difficult task. The Left must question its own "Calvinist tendencies" and the productivism of Marxist theory; it must respond to how the cultures of politics and economics have been transformed by the language and images of consumption.

Mort articulates a position that encapsulates an influential strand of cultural studies: "Commodities and their images are multi-accented, they can be pushed and pulled into the service of resistant demands and dreams. High tech in the hands of young blacks or girls making-up are not simply forms of buying into the system. They can be very effectively hijacked for cultures of resistance, reappearing as street-style cred or assertive femininity."[41] Many researchers have turned to the study of active audiences, of the creative consumer, no longer perceived as the dupe of the culture industries. This tendency has been criticized for its "cultural populism," its romanticization of consumer sovereignty and its misunderstanding of power relations.[42] There is a huge body of literature around this debate, too enormous to discuss here at length, but a number of criticisms made by Christopher Norris crystallize a negative view of New Times developments.

Norris argues that New Times is indicative of the Left's capitulation to consensus politics; the Labour Party has dumped its old alliances with the unions and the working class in favor of the New Right myth of the classless society and upward mobility. Labour merely promises market values with a smiley face, a kinder, gentler, caring version of Thatcher's and Major's policies. According to Norris, the notion of false consciousness is now unfashionable and seen as outdated in left circles, so scholars celebrate "semiotic democracy" as they ditch ideological analysis and sideline the study of the economic base.[43]

A number of political economists hold Foucault's influence accountable for the attention to micro-power relations rather than the macroeconomics and politics of corporations and government. And critical theorists in the lineage of the Frankfurt School argue that radical cultural studies has been co-opted, its cultural relativism mirroring the market value of pluralism, as differences of many kinds are commodified. This range of (post)disciplinary arguments fills the latest cultural studies anthologies, as the paradigm pendulum swings from production to consumption and back again.

Much cultural studies work does celebrate the apparent resistances of the subjective and subcultural consumer without due consideration of institutional and economic forces. On the other hand, the tradition of negation in Marxist approaches often fixates on the radical ideal of a European modernist avant-garde as it fails to consider the myriad modes of contemporary consumption or the possible political valences of practices of representation within commodity culture. Aspects of queer discourse have attempted to interrogate and move beyond this dichotomy of celebration versus pessimism, to aim for what Robert Miklitsch calls a "critical-affirmative" approach to commodity fetishism in post-Fordist capitalism.[44]

The Pet Shop Boys explore the link between sex and capitalism in their songs, using the tropes of the pink cultural economy. This work presses against what Michael Warner calls a

> blockage against sexual politics in the Marxist tradition . . . and the close connection between consumer culture and the most visible spaces of gay culture: bars, discos, advertising, fashion, brand-name identification, mass-cultural camp, "promiscuity." Gay culture in this most visible mode is anything but external to advanced capitalism and to precisely those features of advanced capitalism that many on the left are most eager to disavow. Post-Stonewall urban gay men reek of the commodity. We give off the smell of capitalism in rut, and therefore demand of theory a more dialectical view of capitalism than many people have imagination for.[45]

In a 1988 piece in the *Village Voice,* Frith writes that the Pet Shop Boys "start with a delight in shopping but never without an undertow of regret." While Morrissey and the Smiths symbolically withdraw from the world of enterprise culture, the Pet Shop Boys engage with the promise of consumption, even if it evaporates. But Frith also links their music to the release of consumer desire espoused by Thatcherism, a desire set against gay desire, which must be policed by the state because gay culture "makes explicit what is implicit in 'enterprise culture,' that if all needs can be met in the marketplace, then *any* act of exchange is legitimate."[46] Of course, the Pet Shop Boys' teasing out of this "irony" also happens during the AIDS epidemic, so that sexual as well as economic desire may not pay dividends. The stock market may crash, but sex can be even more dangerous. In this context, the Pet Shop Boys do not share the abandon of 1970s gay disco but, as Walter Hughes notes, "the familiar bass line is sheathed and numbed by a prophylactic irony."[47]

Mourning Becomes Electronic

PSB music has used the landscape of London and the peculiarities of Englishness as elements in the work of remembrance during the AIDS crisis. King's Cross Station is one location in the group's musical version of the London A-to-Z map book. An important point of entry into the capital from many points in the north, King's Cross is also a red-light district, and an area with several gay pubs and clubs. In the 80s and 90s much of it had been gentrified.

"King's Cross," the final track on the album *Actually* (1987), seems to refer to cruising around the area. The lyrics suggest legal and police punishment if gay men are discovered in this public space. With its doomy keyboard setting and echoing horn interruptions, the song presents an apocalyptic vision of the city that places AIDS dramatically at this London hub. Tennant's flaneur-narrator finds himself lost by the station one night. There he is confronted by dead and wounded. The place is like a battlefield, the song a lament for the dead. The vision echoes the use of the First World War in Jarman's *War Requiem* (1989), a historical displacement that resonates with the deaths of young men with AIDS today: "So many friends dead or dying—since autumn: Terry, Robert, David, Ken, Paul, Howard. All the brightest and the best trampled to death—surely even the Great War brought no more loss into one life in just twelve months, and all this as we made love not war."[48]

When the Pet Shop Boys toured for the first time, in 1989, they performed "King's Cross" with a back projection of a specially made Jarman film. In grainy black and white, a hand-held super-8 camera wanders along the area's streets and meanders through the station. Jarman ekes out a gloomy beauty from the place as the camera tracks past the gasworks, rubbish-strewn streets, and glimpses liaisons in the labyrinthine station. The film incorporates some of the video for

"Rent," which shows a nervous Chris Lowe arriving at King's Cross, repeating the experience of thousands of young migrants from the depressed north, many of whom would end up homeless on the streets. The Pet Shop Boys remind us of the area's partially hidden history and geography, when gentrification and urban development threaten working-class communities and gay social life.

This remapping of London along with a number of other texts about London in this period seems to be an example of what Frederic Jameson describes as "a new kind of spatial imagination capable of confronting the past in a new way and reading its less tangible secrets off the template of its spatial structures—body, cosmos, city, as all those marked the more intangible organization of cultural and libidinal economies and linguistic forms."[49]

Mike Leigh's film *High Hopes* (1988) places its plucky socialist couple in the beleaguered council flats of King's Cross. At the end of the film, Shirley, Cyril, and Cyril's mother gaze down at the station and neighboring St. Pancras. Cyril's mother, Mrs. Bender, recalls the days her husband worked on the railway tracks. The family looks across the roofs to the huge drumlike structures of the gasworks, which represent an older London before gentrification. Mrs. Bender is one of the last original residents on a street of council houses that have been sold off to yuppies. Patrick Wright's book *A Journey through Ruins* is a kind of flanerie that describes the end of such neighborhoods as the Conservatives whittled down the state housing sector, discredited the intervention of government in architecture, and encouraged private developers to take over once civic spaces.[50]

Isaac Julien also made the contested meanings of King's Cross, its history, and the relationship between territory, identity, and the "spatial politics of surveillance" explicit when he staged a performance version of his film *Looking for Langston* on the streets: "The *Langston* performance was first staged in the King's Cross area of London which has a reputation for sex and sleaze. Listen to the Pet Shop Boys singing. Because of the railway station, King's Cross is also a gateway into England, a doorway between north and south. The performance used Camley Street in particular, a street that is notorious as a cruising ground for straights— it has a special geography. The proposed redevelopment of the area also means that there are certain political ramifications to the location. The whole space is going to be knocked down and renovated into a kind of Covent Garden yuppie village."[51]

Another countergeography to Thatcherite topography is presented in Patrick Keiller's film *London* (1993), a journey through the capital and its suburbs. A collection of mock postcard images of the capital, the film represents another history through location. Old buildings reveal the hopes and utopian dreams of previous times. Listening to the gateposts at the entrance to a park in Vauxhall reveals the (sound) quality of contemporary urban social life. Keiller's voice-over narration, performed by the actor Paul Scofield, is a hybrid of BBC documentary diction, classic marine/island travelogue à la Conrad and Defoe, a lecture on the city's architecture, and a revival of the Romantic view of the city and its crowds, which is opposed to the puritanism of the state in the past and present. The writings of eighteenth- and nineteenth-century European exiles stranded in London punctuate the piece.

A history of queer London is uncovered in Alan Hollinghurst's *The Swimming-Pool Library* (1989). The novel's erudite upper-class narrator/antihero works on the Cubitt *Dictionary of Architecture.* He cruises the London streets and underground stations, enjoying sex with black and white working-class young men. The swimming-pool library of the book's title is the locker room in a Victorian social and athletic club in the West End where upper-class men meet working-class boys and men. Like the Salford Lads Club in the Smiths' iconography, this was built by wealthy philanthropists as an institution for working-class boys, designed for the inculcation of the appropriate athletic, military, and homosocial values required for citizenship and the imperial project. But such clubs were also places where men of different social classes could meet each other and have sex.

The action of *The Swimming-Pool Library* is set in the immediate pre-AIDS moment of the early 1980s, of which the narrator comments elegiacally, but with some portent: "My life was in a strange way that summer, the last summer of its kind there was ever to be. I was riding high on sex and self-esteem—it was my time, my belle époque—but all the while with a faint flicker of calamity, like flames around a photograph, something seen out of the corner of the eye."[52]

Hollinghurst superimposes the erotic landscape of 1980s London on a geography and history of the Edwardian "Brideshead" moment of empire and aestheticism. A colonial officer's desire for the black male "other" in the Sudan rubs up against black and white British queer sexuality in the 1980s, when the narrator is asked to read an aging gay aristocrat's diaries and ghostwrite his memoirs.

This kind of imaginative historiography shares affinities with the library "detective work" of Neil Bartlett's *Who Was That Man? A Present for Oscar Wilde,* which uncovers fragments of gay London before that famous moment of homosexual definition in 1895. This Benjaminian history is a document of British Museum library research into "perverted" or "pornographic" texts, and a constellation of autobiographical fragments about wandering in the city. Bartlett's love-hate fan obsession with the gay martyr hero Wilde exposes the national and class contradictions in the icon's life and work. It sketches the lives of many other working-class drag queens and rent boys who came up from the East End to have relationships with the rich and famous in the West End. These boys and men have been forgotten while Oscar is remembered. For Bartlett, the city's structures can provide a cartography of desire: "1981 was the first year that I actually lived here, and that was when I discovered that a city has nights as well as days. That summer the city was full of men, hidden, just waiting for me. I'd be walking up the Strand, dressed to kill, and then I'd find myself looking up from the street to all the nineteenth-century facades above me, and fantasize that all the buildings of the West End had seen other men before me living a life after dark, that somehow the streets had a memory."[53] The urban landscape holds memories of the past in its bricks and mortar. Buildings and monuments signify collective myths.

The Pet Shop Boys' pop songs, and these films and writings, incorporate a spatial imagination that unlocks these meanings and gives us other obscured histories of these famous and not-so-famous city locations. Faced with homophobia during the epidemic, and with the government's abnegation of national health, Bartlett points out that such "a rewriting of history becomes a truly dangerous activity": "In any formation of my desires, my sense of history has a very particular role to play. We are, in many obvious ways, written out of history. At the same time, we are acutely conscious of the shifting history of our traditions, our heritage."[54] In the case of the Pet Shop Boys, this heritage meets and interrogates the official heritage of Tory nation-building.

Because a middle-class English conservatism is present in PSB music, Tennant knows many of the tropes and images of a Conservative Little Englandism inside out. He cannot completely refute the English conservatism that is one element in party-political Conservatism. This limitation is also the strength of Pet Shop Boys music, as essential a structure of its English *irony* as the repression of homosexuality. The song "Your Funny Uncle" (a B-side ballad), about the awkwardness between gay men and the parents of a dead young man at his funeral, suggest that irony in the Pet Shop Boys work has less to do with a knowing, tooclever-by-half pose, than with the painful gap between knowledge and the inability to utter the truth.

In *Policing Desire,* Simon Watney describes how he was impelled into AIDS activism when he attended a similar suburban funeral for "Bruno," a gay man with AIDS. Bruno's parents were unable to deal with the fact that their son had the virus. They couldn't grieve openly with friends and relatives, and neither could the two gay men at the funeral who had been Bruno's lovers: "Their grief had to be contained within the confines of manly acceptability. The irony of the difference between the suffocating life of the suburbs where we found ourselves, and our knowledge of the world in which Bruno had actually lived, as a magnificently affirmative and life-enhancing gay man, was all but unbearable."[55] The Pet Shop Boys do not escape the repression exemplified by the suburban funeral in Watney's account, but they do open up these English repressions for investigation through small gestures.

The title of a song on *Actually,* "It Couldn't Happen Here," for example, is the kind of phrase that usually springs from Little Englanders who believe that this nation is separate, different, discrete, an island unto itself: nothing can touch us, because we're English; that sort of thing only happens in foreign parts; it couldn't happen here. The Pet Shop Boys deform the phrase into a meditation on the effects of AIDS. This is not a critique of gay denial of the epidemic's reality, but a cliché of nationalist sentiment turned into an elegy for lost times. You cannot "go all the way" any more. With the real and synthesized dirgelike strings on the track and "classical" allusions, the chorus is full of doubt; the gains of 1970s sexual liberation have been threatened, even turned back; it couldn't happen here, but it has. What do we do next?

"Being Boring," from the album *Behavior,* is another example of a deliberately banal statement used to suggest *and* contain the pre-AIDS range of sexual freedoms, pleasures, and practices. This coming-of-age and coming-out narrative reflects on pleasurable times as the singer refers to his and his friends' "never boring" lives in the 1970s. Now in the 90s, many of these friends and the lovers he has kissed over the years are gone. Bruce Weber's promotional video combines the style of his Calvin Klein advertising spreads with the flickering nostalgia of an old black-and-white home movie. Beautiful young female and male models bathe, swim, dance, kiss, and embrace in a huge Gatsby-style mansion. A tuxedo-wearing black boy dances on stairs, and a ballerina on a bicycle adds a Felliniesque flavor to the pleasure circus.

"In all home movies is a longing for paradise," writes Derek Jarman.[56] Jarman's own film for "Being Boring," projected during the Pet Shop Boys' first live tour in 1989, was in fact his first film, *Studio Bankside,* a black-and-white collection of architectural still-lifes and portraits of places and friends shot in the London neighborhood at the beginning of the 1970s. Such records are vital links to past lives and times destroyed or transformed by the epidemic. As Simon Watney points out: "For those of us who came out before the early 1980s, the past often seems like a prelapsarian dream, impossibly distant. This in turn makes many of us feel older than our natural years. Old photographs take on a new poignancy, not simply of nostalgia, but in relation to our awareness of what our lives might have been like if this catastrophe had not happened, and if it had not been tacitly aided and abetted by governments, newspapers, religions and political parties all around the world."[57]

Mourning and melancholia pervade the wistful images and sounds of *Behavior*. A photograph on the album cover shows Lowe seated while Tennant stands. Both look directly at the camera and hold huge bouquets of red roses, the flowers for graves. And *Behavior* is elegiac in its sounds. "Being Boring," like "My October Symphony," is a somber electronic shuffle with clearly recognizable elements of 1970s disco music, which now often signifies the moment of gay liberation before AIDS. The album was produced in Munich by Harold Faltermeyer, who engineered Donna Summer's electronic disco records during the 1970s. In its longer twelve-inch mix, "Being Boring" recalls the hyper-erotic languid string orchestrations and bubbling rhythms of Summer's "Love to Love You Baby" or "I Feel Love," both part of a gay disco canon. In the cautious AIDS era the hyper-eroticism and ecstasy of disco music becomes almost a substitute for real sex, or at least a sonic condom. Walter Hughes, for example, suggests that the "bland insouciance" of the Pet Shop Boys "seduces us with the promise of low-risk disco," but the group still confronts us with "a return of our repressed anxieties." Hughes likens the nursery-rhyme chorus "watch them all fall down," from "Domino Dancing," to "the computing of sexual contacts, the counting of T-cells, the calculation of casualties."[58]

The funereal soundtrack of "Dreaming of the Queen" tells us that "there are no more lovers left alive." The centerpiece of 1993's *Very* album, like the Smiths' "The Queen Is Dead," the track revisits the national family as it taps into the nation's collective unconscious and fantasy life. Tennant wrote the words for the song after reading that the most common dream in England was to have the Queen visit for tea. In the song, Lady Di comes along too.

According to Brian Masters, author of *Dreams about H.M. The Queen and Other Members of the Royal Family*, "up to one third of the country has dreamt about the Royal Family."[59] In the royal dream's most popular incarnations, the queen or other royal invites the dreamer round to Buckingham Palace for a cuppa tea or during a public walkabout the royal agrees to accompany the dreamer to his or her modest home. Invariably, the royal member is surprisingly *ordinary*, and often hard up, in need of some extra cash, which the commoner kindly provides. As Tom Nairn writes of the public's imagined royals, "what the dream seizes is a dialectic of the transcendent and everyday."[60] It is this dialectic that accounts for the monarchy-obsession, despite the divorces, Diana's death, and tabloid torments of the last few years. Sue Townsend's satirical novel *The Queen and I* plays on this dream as the royal family is abolished by a left-wing Labour government and the queen et al. are forced to become just like the rest of the citizenry; the royals are moved to a modest council house, have to do their own shopping at the local supermarket, and queue up at bus stops just like everyone else. The royals are made ordinary.

In the Pet Shop Boys' fantasy narrative, the queen, sitting down for some tea, is appalled at the breakup of yet another royal marriage. The family's continuity is threatened because love has died. But Di sees it from another perspective, responding with an apocalyptic vision in which all the lovers have died. The dream ends with Tennant waking up in a sweat. On the somber tone of the recording, one can hear electronically reproduced royal trumpets, a string orchestra, and church bells for a funeral or a wedding. The song takes the decline of a marriage and the ill fortunes of the national family and uses them to register gay loss and mourning. The Pet Shop Boys draw on the kind of personal and collective affect engendered by the image of Diana in her life and, in fact, anticipate the debate about national affect engendered by her death.[61] Diana's failed marriage to Charles becomes a way to talk about the death of lovers in the epidemic. The song also crystallizes Annette Kuhn's point that the "nation as family is founded on repressions." "Dreaming of the Queen" both brings to the surface some of these repressions and highlights the "difficulty of an imagined community of nationhood that takes the family as an ideal."[62]

The national homophobic ideology of the heterosexual nuclear family is interrogated with a swipe at wartime jingoism in the single "DJ Culture," particularly its promotional video directed by Eric Watson. In the sleeve notes for their singles compilation *Discography,* the group states: "1991 was the year of the conflict in the Gulf. This song was written as a response to both the conflict and public reactions to it." "DJ Culture" refers to the life of the discotheque and its escapist techno-utopian attitudes, but it also suggests analogies between the spectacle of the dance floor in the rave era and the television spectacle of war. The Gulf War was managed through television, a military exercise turned into leisure pursuit, the Nintendo war in which the extermination of thousands of Iraqi citizens and destruction of their cities became a video simulation. Dead and wounded bodies disappeared through the machinery of military and media technologies.

"DJ Culture" presents various simulations and popular representations of war in its words and images. The hip-hop beat of the recording is supported by a computer-generated video game target with the camera moving through this virtual world. This cuts to an overhead shot of soldiers in a desert landscape choreographed in a dance that mimics them sliding along the sand in battle, dragging their wounded legs behind them. At intermittent points in the video, Tennant and Lowe appear in the khaki uniform of British officers, seated in front of a back projection of sand and incongruous beach umbrellas. They look like char-

acters in one of countless British army farces or like dead souls stranded in the
surreal stage set of a Samuel Beckett play. At the end of the video, Lowe, stiff
upper lip not quite intact, disgustedly wipes some bird shit from the top of his
military cap.

Tennant compares the war to a soccer match, as he stands dressed as a soccer
referee while male and female dancers leap about mimicking the warmup exer-
cises of first-division players of a bygone era. For many Englishmen in the 1980s
and 90s, the national game has been a common metaphor for war. Right-wing
English soccer supporters have thought of themselves as an English army invad-
ing foreign territories to battle with police and opposition fans. As I suggested
in chapter 1, the soccer field and its environs have been places to exhibit a sense
of national pride. In the video, Lowe is dressed up like a "vintage" soccer supporter, wearing a scarf and hat of the team colors. This sentimental image of the
soccer supporter has disappeared, but sport and militarism, bound together in
British imperialism, continue their perverse coupling.

"DJ Culture" joins its satirical critique of national militarism to the government's regulation and policing of gay identity by using the image of Oscar Wilde.
Tennant appears as Wilde in a courtroom presided over by Lowe, who is robed
as judge Mr. Justice Wills. "And I, my Lord, may I say nothing," words Tennant
repeats a number of times in the song, are almost identical to Wilde's words after being found guilty in Richard Ellmann's account of the trial: "And I? May I
say nothing, my Lord?" Wilde's near-fainting in Ellmann's version of the trial is
transformed into Tennant's defiant gesture in the dock. The political stakes are
gay representation. In the video, Victorian matrons, some in drag, some black,
wag their fingers in moral disapprobation.

In 1895, the *London Evening News* accused Wilde of trying to subvert the
"wholesome, manly, simple ideals of English life." In 1988, section 28 of the Local Government Act stipulated: "A local authority shall not (a) intentionally promote homosexuality or publish material with the intention of promoting homosexuality; (b) promote the teaching in any maintained school of the acceptability
of homosexuality as a pretended family relationship." This legislation further
centralized power in the Westminster state and policed gay representation. New
Right rhetoric enforced sexuality within a family structure as crucial to national
well-being.

In November 1987, the most famous proponent of "Victorian values," Margaret Thatcher, stated that "a nation of free people will only continue to be great
if family life continues and the structure of that nation is a family one." In their
muted English way, the Pet Shop Boys do with the royal family what thousands
of gay disco dancers have done with Sister Sledge's disco track "We Are Family,"

adopting a celebration of family as an anthem for gay community. The Pet Shop Boys' queer nationality is not as militant and in-your-face as that of their contemporaries in ACT UP or Queer Nation in the United States, though it is as ambiguously and multiply positioned in relation to discourses of nationhood.[63]

On the album *Bilingual,* the group frames Englishness within the European community. The songs describe Tennant's "coming out" as well as England's coming to the end of the Tory torment. The national now circulates in relation to Brussels, Bonn, and Barcelona. The sound of the album owes more to uptempo Latin rhythms. "The Survivors" finds Tennant's narrator crossing a London bridge and walking past Embankment Gardens. He ponders the memorials of those who have died and is grateful for the fact that he is alive. In "To Step Aside" Tennant wonders whether market forces will ever provide what history has denied the workers he sees from his window.

While mourning those lost to AIDS and "showing us the money," the Pet Shop Boys remain ambivalent about the pleasures of DJ culture; they are anxious about its yearning for escape and its disavowal of reality; but they also celebrate and bring together the ecstatically dancing collective with their proto-disco tracks. *Bilingual*'s final track is "Saturday Night Forever," a title that recalls *Saturday Night Fever.* The singer doesn't care what the serious commentators think; he's off for a drink, a chance to meet "someone gorgeous" and dance his head off at the local club in the British weekend ritual. And he'll keep doing this even though he knows it's not going to last.[64]

3

E Is for England
Civilization and Its Discotheques

He felt that you had to party, you had to party harder than ever. It was
the only way. It was your duty to show that you were still alive. Political
sloganeering and posturing meant nothing; you had to celebrate the joy
of life in the face of all those grey forces and dead spirits who controlled
everything, who fucked with your head and livelihood anyway, if you
weren't one of them. You had to let them know that in spite of their best
efforts to make you like them, to make you dead, you were still alive.
Glen knew this wasn't the complete answer, because it would all still be
there when you stopped.
—Irvine Welsh, *Ecstasy*

"Britain, for fuck's sake, chill out!"
—a character in the film *Human Traffic* (1999)

The combination of recreational drugs, rhythmic electronic music, and dancing bodies transformed the economy of leisure in Britain during the 1980s and
90s. Clubbing was expected to be worth about four billion pounds a year by
2000. Club culture has revitalized the night-time economy of many cities, some
of which now advertise the attractions of their famous dance clubs in official
tourist literature. The prominence of nightclubs reflects the reordering of city
centers, and civic spaces in general, from places of production to primarily those
of consumption. The arts and "culture" have become increasingly important
in reconstituting the image of cities like Manchester, Bristol, and Birmingham
as they have developed more intimate "globalized" connections with other places. Dance scenes in various U.K. locales maintain transnational links with club
culture in, for example, New York, Chicago, Detroit, Miami, Amsterdam,
Berlin, and Paris through networks of specialist record shops, music companies, the dance press, as well as the movement of musicians between these places. The promise of foreign dance floors is now a feature of tourism to the is-

land of Ibiza, to Goa and Kerala in India, and parts of Australia, Thailand, and Japan.

The sounds of a rapidly multiplying number of dance music genres and subgenres hold together this dispersed imagined community of the dance floor. Electronic music, rave, or DJ culture can now claim a centrality in popular music culture once occupied by guitar rock. I use the three terms above interchangeably to designate music produced in recorded form (vinyl and compact disc) primarily for listening and dancing at discotheques rather than performed "live" on stage by musicians.

A clutch of recent histories by pop journalists and some work by academics signal the institutionalization of dance music and its associated activities. I'm interested in how the cultural politics of DJ culture have been theorized in the context of the New Right and New Labour, a widespread disillusionment with representative politics, and in particular, young people's disaffection with traditional forms of left-wing organization. If the mythologies of community, rebellion, opposition, and authenticity in the "rock formation" have been found lacking in certain respects, what can we say of the praxis of an emergent "dance formation"? What are the continuities and discontinuities in writing about popular music culture given these recent developments? In this chapter, I focus on popular music's relationship to the body, the technologization of everyday life, and the politics of public space. In this survey of writing, my approach is critical yet affirmative, and it attempts to be dialogical in the manner of a DJ mix with its grooves, sampled riffs, and, of course, those vital moments of dissonance in the (hip-hop) mix—the scratches. At stake is how we might define the "political" in our analysis of popular music culture.

We Are E

The grand narratives of DJ culture in the U.K. usually share a genealogy of influences dating back to musique concrète and the European avant-garde, down to 1970s disco, dub reggae, the German group Kraftwerk, and, in the 1980s, New York hip-hop, Chicago house music, and Detroit techno. Rave historians and the dance press love lists. Delirium, Shoom, Trip, Future, Spectrum, and Land of Oz—the names of U.K. rave events and clubs in the late 1980s and early 90s—constitute a psychedelic chronology. Typical DJ culture historiography is supported by the compilation of a canon of great works, influential records released in the culture's most prized format, the twelve-inch vinyl single, and now collected on compilations with titles like *Mastercuts* and *Classic Rave*. Despite the anonymity of many performers behind the soundtracks to dancing in the last decade or so, DJ culture now has its pantheon of auteurs who tour the globe just like any self-respecting rock band. Even the technology has its galaxy of black-and-silver stars—the Technics SL1200 Mk2 turntable, the Roland TB-303 bass line and TR-808 drum machine, the AKAI S-900 sampler.[1]

At the core of the U.K. dance formation's own histories is 3-4 methylene-dioxymethamphetamine (MDMA), better known as Ecstasy, or just plain E. The designer drug follows a long line of illegal recreational drugs such as marijuana, LSD, amphetamines, and amyl nitrate, which over the years have been ritually consumed in the British will to weekend oblivion after the drudgery of the working week. Here is a fanzine trying to describe the thrill of the drug–dance-floor experience in April 1988, soon after Ecstasy was widely available in the country: "Technological psychedelia; heavy funk at 1000 mph; waves of light and sound and colour; persistent movement; deep space; travelling at the speed of light along a kaleidoscopic black hole; Heaven: a synthesised orgasm; synchronised noise; Shoom! the sound of blood rushing to your brain; the inner space of a crystal ball; shock; luminous experience; a million thoughts and fantasies; a glorious nightmare; a frightening dream."[2]

More than a decade later, many of the dance histories make quite serious claims for Ecstasy. This technological insertion into the populace seems to have produced a shift in national consciousness, a physiological and psychological adjustment in the body politic.

The oral history *High Society* — subtitled *The Real Voices of Club Culture* to assure the reader of its definitive, authentic rendition of history — collects the reminiscences of clubbers and ravers during the late 80s and 90s, documenting their first time, the "off your face" antics, myriad hallucinations, loved-up smiles and hugs on the dance floor, the friendships struck and cemented on E and drug cocktails, and the adventures in foreign parts.[3] The dropping of an E at a dance event is now almost a rite of passage for the British teenager. In 1994 a Home Office survey estimated that up to a million Britons had tried Ecstasy. Approximately a million tablets of E were dropped every weekend, which at ten quid (sixteen U.S. dollars at that time) a dose represents an industry turning over half a billion pounds annually, supported by 2 percent of the population.[4]

The novelist Irvine Welsh has termed those who have grown up with Ecstasy the "Chemical Generation." The rave scene has even produced a genre of literature by this youth constituency, though much of it seems to verge on what the critic Hari Kunzru describes as "chemical pornography, texts which exist only to record heroic acts of consumption." A collection of dance fiction, *Disco Biscuits,* takes its title from the slang for Ecstasy pills.[5]

One of the recent chunky histories of the movement, *Energy Flash: A Journey through Rave Music and Dance Culture,* by Simon Reynolds, has the alternative title *Generation Ecstasy* for the U.S. market.[6] *Energy Flash*'s cover features a bright-orange sparkling star in an ocean of computer-generated bubbles, presumably a simulation of the whoosh or surge up the spine when the drug hits the user; in fact, the graphics seem to more closely resemble soap bubbles in a 1970s TV commercial for laundry detergent. The book's title comes from a classic record of the scene, a 1990 track by a New York producer, Joey Beltram. Reynolds exhaustively covers the period, focusing on the Ecstasy-mediated experience of listening on the dance floor to the ripples, rhythmic bursts, and bass lines of the scene's crucial records. The influential tracks of the period are the focus of his more "trainspotter-ish" account, a correlative to the Ultimate Record Collection that forms one of the templates of a predominantly masculine rock historiography.

In contrast, covering much of the same ground in regard to musical influences and periodization, Sheryl Garratt's *Adventures in Wonderland: A Decade of Club Culture* features the author as Alice tripping through a psychedelic geography of clubland. The book's cover features a rainbow spectrum and the smiley face, the once ubiquitous symbol of E-d up bliss. As a former editor of the lifestyle magazine *The Face,* Garratt is more concerned with the activities on the nation's dance floors than with the sonic qualities and merits of particular dance tracks.[7] Also in the vein of social and cultural history, Matthew Collin and John Godfrey's account of the rave scene, *Altered State: The Story of Ecstasy Culture and Acid House,* in its title argues that the nation-state has undergone a chemical reaction, its collective affect irrevocably transformed.

In his somewhat contradictory style, the DJ Trevor Fung suggests E's role in a psychic as well as geographical departure from uptight Britishness in his description of clubbing in Ibiza: "We'd definitely all changed. . . . We'd taken our British reserve, that guard down. Wearing black, sitting at the bar, too cool to talk to anyone—all that had gone. Over there everyone was talking to each other, you were a different person. Happier, because of the sun as well as the Es. It wasn't *just* the drugs. We didn't have drugs all the time. Es were just an excuse. We probably needed it to express ourselves then, but it was all in us all the time. It was fun. We'd all just come out of ourselves."[8]

Here the drug is a catalyst for a change in English psychology that will go on to influence dance-floor culture back home in the British Isles. The good-time holiday dance music or so-called Balearic beats of Ibiza nightlife were taken back to England together with Ecstasy in an attempt to extend that summer feeling or Ibiza vibe in clubs during the drizzly, chilly days of the British autumn. In the music press, Ecstasy is now routinely invoked as one of the main factors in the apparent end of English reserve. The mood of the nation has changed. We can now express ourselves. The collective public grieving for Diana with tears on the tarmac may have been an indication of this sea-change.

However, according to most accounts, in the early 90s the drug and its empathetic effects were dulled by burn-out, abuse, and the adulteration of Ecstasy pills with other substances. In a 1993 article written when the utopian dream of rave community had soured, Reynolds asked if rave culture was "living dream or living death." With hindsight, the drug was held accountable: "the intransitive, go-nowhere aspects of rave culture are almost chemically programmed into MDMA itself. Among all its other effects, E incites a sort of free-floating fervour, a will-to-belief—which is why the most inane oscillator synth-riff can seem so numinously radiant with MEANING. But at the end of even the most tearing night out, there can be a disenchanting sense of futility; all that energy and idealism mobilized to no end (except to line the pockets of the promoter, and Mr Evian)."[9] Here the drug *defines* the range of possibilities for Reynolds.

More broadly, Matthew Collin charts the wider historical trajectory of British urban dance-floor culture *through* the isolated drug experience and its long-term use:

> The first rush begins with the honeymoon period—the beatific, loved-up, evangelical phase. Within a year or so, that early excitement begins to fade and many experience diminishing returns. A few accelerate into excess, abuse sometimes leading to the emergence of physical or psychological problems. The third stage is the come-down: disillusionment, reduced use, and attempts to readjust to the fact that the initial high is gone for ever. Finally comes the re-entry to the post-Ecstasy world, a time of reassessment and regaining of equilibrium. The myriad manifestations of the culture often reflect this pharmacological narrative, each scene experiencing its own individual honeymoon, comedown and re-entry phases.[10]

Most of the dance-floor histories represent Ecstasy as the star of DJ culture, the motor of dance-floor development. This version of events is even applied to the music: house music is the sonic embodiment of early E bliss, the more frenetic and paranoid sound of Jungle emerges from the "dark side" when Ecstasy pills become impure and crack cocaine enters the club economy. Admittedly, musical forms have a history with drugs, and Ecstasy's role in dance-floor culture is crucial, but I'm wary of a kind of technological determinism or rather pharmacological determinism as an explanatory framework for the social meaning of DJ culture. Ecstasy and other drugs flow through DJ culture's veins, but the chemical repertoire needs to be considered alongside a number of other economic, political, and cultural factors.

DJ culture can be analyzed in the context of the changing economies of urban consumption, the politics of lifestyle, and the state's regulation of public space and prevention of sociability. For many scholars, the electronic sounds of DJ culture, produced by sequencers, drum machines, and digital samplers, have revived the question of technology in popular music studies. I deal with this area of concern in more detail in chapter 4.

Since this is a culture of dancing, many critics have turned to the body, the subject on the dance floor, and how history, place, and identity are written on the body or embodied in dancing. Other critics have turned to the dancing collective. Dance-floor discourse continues along avenues of analysis already established in academic and journalistic writing about popular music, but it has also developed new lines that depart from the conceptual schemas used in studying what Lawrence Grossberg terms the "rock formation."

Body Politics

Underlying the varied study of DJ culture is the question of its value, its politics or lack of politics. Many critics seem to pursue the same basic question: How can a series of cultural practices devoted to abandon, to "getting out of it" on drugs, and to dancing for hours be considered "political" in any sense? The music itself says little in terms of language. Much dance music, including some of the canonized classics, have few lyrics, opting instead for exhortations to get up on the dance floor disco-style, or the heavy breathing oohs and aahs of the sexual encounter, emotive ejaculations like "Can you feel it," "Pump up the volume," and short samples of mass-media sound bites. Such an aesthetic undermines the ideology of folk and rock music as defined by rock critics and popular music scholars. Lyrics speak a position, reflect a place, locality, and situation from where the singer speaks, sings, and so vocalizes community. For left-liberal critics, folk and even commercialized rock music's politics of opposition are grounded in the notion of a counterculture. But dance music is not centered on representation. It doesn't necessarily say anything at all. According to its "rockist" critics, it is music you dance to, not music for listening, music for the body, not the mind, for pleasure, not political commitment. This view persists despite Germaine Greer's assertion that "the most significant part of the rock revolution, because it did happen, was that kids got into their bodies."[11]

In response to the rockist point of view, much of the recent writing about dancing bodies comes from the fields of feminist theory and queer discourse. The musicologist Susan McClary believes that the limited sociological imagination of a great deal of popular music scholarship has marginalized the music itself and its effects on the body. She points out that the music itself—especially as it intersects with the body and destabilizes accepted norms of subjectivity, gender and sexuality—is precisely where the politics of music often reside. . . . music is foremost among cultural "technologies of the body," that is, a site where we learn how to experience socially mediated patterns of kinetic energy, being in time, emotions, desire, pleasure, and much more. . . . These patterns inevitably arrive already marked with histories—histories involving class, gender, ethnicity; music thus provides a terrain where competing notions of the body (and also the self, ideals of social interaction, feelings and so on) vie for attention and influence.[12]

McClary argues for the importance of theories and cultural studies of music that do not "reinscribe the polemics against the body that have characterized attempts at policing music throughout western history."[13]

Having been subjected to this polemic in its "Eastern" version and raised in a Pakistani household in the West Midlands and West Yorkshire, I can testify to the transformative aspects of dance music on my own sense of embodied self in early 1980s pre-rave England. Islamic doctrine regulated the legitimacy of bodily pleasures for my brothers, my sister, and me. Dancing was discouraged, particularly for girls. "Disco" was a dirty word reeking of sexually suggestive movements and public displays of affection; slow dancing in embraces; snogging in the shadows. When we wanted to go to a school disco my parents usually acquiesced, but only after protracted negotiations, heated argument, tears, and the imposition of strict curfew limits. The parental policing was more rigorous if my sister wanted to attend. We were trained to not discuss sexuality, which was tied to marriage. Even an "innocent" romantic relationship with a boyfriend or girlfriend was out of the question. When we drove through, say, Birmingham, Bradford, and Leeds, my parents would frown at the "shameless" romantic couples entwined on the streets. We were often reminded that white people and West Indians tended to be lax about sexual morality.

These limits from my Pakistani Muslim upbringing were supported by the disciplines engendered by English racism. Like many middle-class migrants, my parents wanted the best education for their children, so we grew up in "good areas," in predominantly white schools and neighborhoods. I learned to not stick out, to hide my cultural difference, so I wouldn't suffer abuse and racial humiliation. The goal was to make my body as unobtrusive as possible. One of the few places I felt embodied in a pleasurable way and intermittently suspended the feeling of racial otherness was the soccer field, playing for the school team and local clubs.

At the age of eleven, I was determined that the white English girls I had begun to desire would never be attracted to me because I was a Paki. One of my friends told me, "Nabeel, girls would really fancy you if you were white. You're good looking enough." This was meant as a compliment. I now realize that if he'd said, "Nabeel, girls really fancy you because you're brown," I'd have probably been just as messed up. But anyway, I convinced myself that since I was brown, not white, English girls were inaccessible. I cut my losses, postponed desire. I didn't belong with the English anyway. Study hard at school, make it to university, get a job, and then my parents would find a Muslim girl and sort out an arranged marriage. Choosing this route meant less hassle with the folks. I did my homework and passed exams. My *passion* and anger went into punk music and its associated politics.

Punk was a noisy vehicle for my rage at both English and Pakistani regimes. Punk ideology also proved appropriate for the sublimation of sex since its style was predominantly asexual or antisexual. In a host of songs and press interviews with punk rockers of the late 70s, sexual intercourse is represented as messy, masochistic, and sadistic, but almost always as short lived as the duration of the average two-and-a-half minute punk single. Punk's musical jerkiness and the pogo dance seemed to simulate frenzied masturbation. The packed, moving crowd at the chaotic punk gig provided the sensory compensations of having your face mashed into leather jackets smelling of patchouli and glue. And one could indulge in the commodity fetishism of buying a record, admiring the cover and label on the bus home, and the anticipation as one placed the needle in the groove on the bedroom record player. Record collecting is a well-documented and stereotypical form of arrested sexual development for boys.[14] My sexual identity succumbed to something then deemed "more important" than cheap pleasures— namely, politics; Rock against Racism, the Anti-Nazi League, CND, flirtations with anarchism and even the Socialist Workers Party. Through these involvements, the erasure of my body could continue without too much embarrassment.

Though 1970s punk and disco shared some history, for example, their art school and bohemian club origins in America and the U.K., most punks officially hated disco music, which was considered mechanical, mindless, and escapist. "Death Disco," by Public Image Limited, confirmed the punk attitude. Disco was about love and dancing, nothing serious like rioting or supporting the Sandinistas. The commercial hegemony of *Saturday Night Fever* exemplified the decline of Western civilization. Dance music was only righteous if it was black American soul music, the voice of an oppressed people from the ghetto demanding R-E-S-P-E-C-T. The *New Musical Express* informed us weekly as to what was politically correct music.

Many of us who came of age in the punk and postpunk era eventually found its literal politics and poetics rather limited. Its sounds and poses became as rigid as the bombastic rock tradition it derided. By the early 1980s, the postpunk intelligentsia was leaving behind the battlements of punk for the new sensual frontiers of funky rhythms and deep bass frequencies. We began to study low-end theory. Hip-hop electro, Washington go-go, New York garage, rare groove (recycled 1970s funk), and then house music provided the rhythmic soundtrack.

When I went clubbing with friends to the Warehouse in Leeds or the Garage in Nottingham almost every weekend during the early 1980s, I began to know and feel my body differently. By putting myself out there on the dance floor on my own, haltingly at first, I felt my way into the music's ebbs, flows, and spaces, moving arms, feet, knees, hip, and head, watching other dancers, until I perceived a shape to my own movements within the music. Eventually, I convinced myself that I could dance, though each visit to the club began awkwardly, standing around trying to act nonchalant with a sophisticated long brown cigarette and a drink, before venturing onto the dance floor and into the groove.

I had made myself invisible for so long. Now I felt embodied in public. This new body consciousness and confidence was also marked by a shift from the dressing-down of the postpunk look of gray or black shirts and trousers and long overcoat (beloved of Joy Division, Cabaret Voltaire, and Echo and the Bunnymen fans) to the dressing-up of baggy trousers and smart jackets in a "New Romantic meets Leeds Goth" style. If we had pessimism of the intellect, we should now at least demonstrate optimism of the will. "Fuck Art, Let's Dance" was a popular t-shirt slogan at the time.

I was still nervous about talking or dancing with women at clubs. My dance-floor pleasures, in some ways, were like the desexualized dancing of boys and girls, men and women on E in the AIDS era, except I wasn't compelled to hug anyone with a big grin on my face. Sometimes on the dance floor, all consciousness of my mind and body felt in flux in moments of oblivion, bliss, yes, even *jouissance*. And the feeling was facilitated on many occasions by recreational substances. This was a performance-enhanced privatized experience but also communal; I felt my individuality as a dancing member of the crowd.[15] Then my friends took off and I went home alone, rather like a cliché from the Smiths' great disco song "How Soon Is Now?"

Dancing has been important in the construction of social identities, though marginalized by left-liberal masculinist rock ideology. In the last two decades, feminism and queer politics are largely responsible for taking popular dance culture seriously. Back in 1979, the film critic Richard Dyer wrote an essay called "In Defense of Disco" that gave serious consideration to the main features of disco music—romanticism, eroticism, and materialism—despite its reputation as "po-litically beyond the pale" for leftists.[16] The late 80s and early 90s witnessed a proliferation in disco discourse.

For example, Walter Hughes argues that disco music has played a crucial role in the formation of post-Stonewall gay male identity in the West. He uses the term "disco" in an overarching sense to describe not just a specific 1970s genre, but music designed for dancing. Hughes believes that "disco is less a decadent indulgence than a disciplinary, regulatory discourse that paradoxically permits, even creates a form of freedom." Disco creates a discipline of the body and self through its invocation to the dance floor: "By submitting to its insistent, disci-plinary beat, one learns from disco how to be one kind of gay man; one accepts with pleasure rather than suffering, the imposition of a version of gay identity."[17]

In the surrender to disco's relentless rhythm, one's social identity as a man "becomes recategorized alongside the black woman and the machine that together relentlessly draw him into the empire of the beat."[18] Here Hughes refers to the prevalence of African-American divas such as Donna Summer, Diana Ross, Gloria Gaynor, and Loleatta Holloway on many disco records. In disco and soul, the gospel-style vocals of the black woman are secularized as the voice of abject suf-fering, a subject position with which gay men can identify. Hughes adds that the text(ure)s and audience of disco music put into doubt fixed identity categories as the music offers subject positions that fluctuate between black and white, male and female, gay and straight. At the same time, a humanist conception of the self and identity is denied through the body's merging with the music's machine-like repetition, increasingly marked in the electronic disco music of house, tech-no, and related genres in the 1980s and 90s.

Angela McRobbie was one of the first scholars in the field of British cultural studies to consider the role of dance in the lives of girls and women. Since the mid-1980s, she has analyzed dancing and the fantasy work of dance narratives like *Flashdance* and *Footloose* in relation to female subjectivities. She also turned her attention to the rave scene in the early 90s, partly because her teenage daughter was involved in these events.

McRobbie believes that Ecstasy and a fear of AIDS make the rave a relatively asexual place so that women are less likely to be seen as sexual objects. Howev-er, the desexualizing of the dance floor can also lead to the maintenance of the male homosocial behavior of traditional subcultures, where females are margin-alized as the lads hang out and dance together. She also notes that female be-havior in the early rave scene stages a spectacular return to childhood in its re-treat from sexuality and the responsibilities of adulthood. Rave girls dance in shorts and halter tops with pacifiers in their mouths and whistles around their necks. This style was a common feature in the early rave scene, with boys as well as girls displaying small robots and dolls on their bodies, particularly during a period of so-called Toytown rave, which featured many tracks that sampled children's television shows. Performers and dancers in the rave scene sometimes supplemented such fashion accessories with rubber suits and surgical masks as a sartorial comment on the health fears of the time. They often used products such as Vicks VapoRub with these masks to intensify the effects of Ecstasy. McRobbie wonders what kind of politics such a willfully regressive subculture can produce:

> There is nothing like the aggressive political culture found in punk music. It is as though young ravers simply cannot bear the burden of the responsibility they are being expected to carry. There are so many dangers (drugs, cigarettes, alcohol, unprotected sex, sexual violence and rape, ecological disaster), so many social and political issues which have a direct bearing on their lives and so many demands being made of them, to be fully responsible in their sexual activity, to become good citizens, to find a job and earn a living, and find a partner and have a family in a world where marriage has become a "temporary contract," that rave turns away from this heavy load and dips headlong into a culture of avoidance and almost pure abandonment. It does this in as visible and as spectacular a way as many of its subcultural predecessors and thereby provokes a stern social reaction. As a result, a dialogue is established, one which, as in the past, includes the intensification of policing and social control. The question then is . . . can it provide a cultural politics?[19]

McRobbie salvages rave subculture by focusing on how the traditionally "feminized" space of the dance floor, a space of consumption, can ultimately facilitate cultural production. The scene produces forms of subcultural capital for young women that transform consumption into production. Participation as listeners and dancers often leads to the acquisition of job skills; though women are still marginalized in music production, they have become involved as DJs, designers, and taken part in the management and organization of dance-related events. This valuable experience may lead to careers and economic independence.

Maria Pini's ethnographic research on women in the same period confirms McRobbie's point that the desexualizing qualities of Ecstasy create an environment where girls and young women feel relatively safe from the culture of the sexual pickup. Patriarchal notions of sexuality and the male gaze are put on hold in the rave experience. Dancers melt into a communal, blissed-out non-phallic *jouissance*. Pini suggests that this might be indicative of a general feminization of youth. But how is this dance-floor practice political? For Pini, "this politics is not one concerned with 'changing the world' but rather with the constitution of a particular mind/body/spirit/technology assemblage which makes for alternative experiences of the self."[20]

In *Writing on Drugs,* Sadie Plant states that "MDMA was the interior technology for the digital age, the wetware for the software revolution, the molecular adjustment that allowed a generation to explore the new machine interface."[21] Like a number of dance-floor theories, including those of Walter Hughes, these arguments draw on strands of post-human discourse, in particular Foucault's ideas of "technologies of the self" and Teresa de Lauretis's more specific focus on gender as technology. This technologization of the body in theory has been developed by Donna Haraway in her notion of the cyborg as an empowering model for an anti-essentialist politics of identity. Pini herself invokes Rosi Braidotti's related idea of the nomadic subject, as someone living in transition, believing in strategic essentialism but never taking any kind of gendered, sexual, ethnic, or national identity as permanent.

For Pini the combination of drugs, music, and the body undoes a sense of the socialized female self. However, the rave participants she interviews talk of the rave's "positive vibe" and often draw on new-age discourse about the mind and spirit, which seems to refute the argument that a humanist conception of self has completely disappeared. If the self in the rave is not the clear "bounded" individual of traditional Cartesian identity discourse, Pini makes the crucial point that social definitions of gender and sexuality do not completely disappear on the dance floor: "The experience of rave cannot be detached from the sexually specific body. . . . Even Utopian claims about rave's apparent ability to erode sexual differences (as well as other social differences) has to be grounded within the sexually-specific, because this perceived erosion obviously has particular implications for femininity. For example, a woman's perception that rave affords her an 'ungendered' sense of self clearly implies an escape from a body which is always already specifically coded, and such a claim would carry different implications and speak of different issues were it uttered by a man."[22]

Pini's cautionary remarks are valuable because some of the writing on the rave phenomenon tends to overstate the experience's dissolution of cultural differences. Either ravers dissolve into some kind of one-world unity vibe or, as Antonio Melechi argues, they become part of an "aesthetics of disappearance" in which the body is lost.[23] Pini's work historicizes the rave experience and is significant in its ethnographic consideration of how rave participants actually make sense of their own experience. While Ecstasy and dancing increases empathy with one's fellow beings, the women interviewed remind us that the rave scene fosters a sense of collectivity off the dance floor too. Women travel to raves together, forge friend-

ships, and develop a collective identity.[24] Drug use on the dance floor must also
be historicized. As a number of commentators have pointed out, the impurity
of Ecstasy pills and the emergence of cocaine and marijuana on the scene brought
the return of the male gaze. Ecstasy is often described as engendering more poly-
morphous desire. And for the past few years, most of the glossy dance publications prominently feature photographs of young women at clubs in their Won-
derbras, hot pants, and high heels.[25]

The technologization of self need not result in progressive gender relations. For
example, the members of one well-known sound system or DJ collective known
as Desert Storm wear military combat gear and celebrate their hardcore techno
sessions for their stamina and toughness. The pummeling beat forms part of the
homosocial ethos of their raves. The harder the beats, the better. Hillegonda
Rietveld argues that this makes the dance floor as phallocentric as the heavy-metal
stadium concert.[26] The punching beats and subcultures of industrial beat, hardcore techno, and the extremely fast gabber (180 bpm), popular in Scotland,
Holland, and Germany, are popular mainly among the lads. However, it is
difficult to generalize about gender relations across the varied terrain and multiple genres and scenes that constitute DJ culture.

Better Living through Chemistry

The much invoked drugs/technology/music interface and various forms of post-
human theory applied to dance music are symptoms of the increasing technologization of everyday life. Lawrence Grossberg laments that rather than dance to
music we like, we like the music we can dance to. Simon Reynolds goes one step
further, arguing that we now like the music we can drug to.[27] Drugs have become
essential components in the synergy of consumer pleasures and leisure practices.

The time-honored anxieties and moral panic about recreational drugs have also
been part of the discourse on Ecstasy. Even for sympathetic cultural commentators, the feelings of euphoria and communal bliss associated with the rave scene
at the end of the 1980s were short-lived. In the early 90s the purity of Ecstasy
pills declined as MDMA came mixed with amphetamines and LSD. Histories,
memoirs, and fictions document the increasing use of E with a cocktail of drugs.
Cheaper narcotics like temazepam are now a part of the roster of prescription
drugs that have fueled the good times but also resulted in cases of intermittent
psychosis and some fatalities.[28]

In late 1995, a middle-class teenager, Leah Betts, collapsed and went into a coma
as a result of dropping E. She became the first celebrity victim of the chemical

generation as her decline and death were sensationally monitored over several weeks by the tabloid press. Her parents launched a campaign against Ecstasy use, mounting massive billboards that featured a photograph of her with the drug slang word "Sorted" set beside her face in giant letters for black irony. Betts's death did little to prevent more young people from taking the drug.

Despite the painfully predictable outrage of the tabloids and television, Ecstasy use has become increasingly regulated through various institutions. Clubs and some local councils generate pamphlets and flyers on the safe use of the drug. Promoters are encouraged to provide a cheap or free water supply to prevent dehydration at dance venues. The music and youth press now commonly report new research on Ecstasy and other drugs, outlining the effects and potential dangers of drug use and abuse. Research on MDMA has developed alongside its use in dance-floor culture. On his website and in books, Nicholas Saunders has collected a vast body of information on the drug, including scientific research, the spiritual and creative activity it has unleashed, and its effects on the individual and society.[29]

Ecstasy has to some extent become a domesticated consumer product, part of the weekly leisure routine, a middle-class drug. Dance magazines will often carry pictures of the pills with cute vernacular names such as "fluffies" and "snow whites" and present charts of the top ten drugs on the scene at any given moment. Ecstasy's widespread use and regulation suggests a shift to a less moralistic attitude toward recreational drugs in general. As a designer drug, Ecstasy's manufacture and consumption may reflect the respectability of various "performance-enhancing" chemicals in contemporary life and a less outraged approach to drug use. Though still illegal, Ecstasy can sit comfortably alongside Prozac, Viagra, steroids, and various weight-loss drugs in the medicine cabinet. Drugs are increasingly conceived as elements of a lifestyle package of which music is one constituent; pills for personality and aids to better living.

One can see this ironically signified in various commodities in contemporary culture. For example, the group Spiritualized, known for its druggy psychedelic postrock ambient drones, in its very name suggests that even spirituality is something technologically or artificially achieved, through "medication." The group released its *Ladies and Gentlemen We Are Floating in Space* (1997) album CD in a "pill box format," the packaging of prescription medicine from a pharmacy. Instructions for the proper use and potential side effects of specific tracks were included on the inside sleeve. T-shirts worn in clubs and on campuses reflect the normalization of drugs. One features the word "Prozac" inside the Pepsi logo; another simply bears the slogan, "Only Users Lose Drugs."

According to a number of critics, musical genres and the listening experience seem increasingly pharmacologically defined, extending the genealogy of drug-music associations: jazz and heroin, psychedelic rock and LSD, reggae and gan-ja, punk and speed, ragga and cocaine. As Ecstasy culture and the rave scene developed in the late 80s and early 90s, the music at rave and club events changed to accommodate the new variation in the all-night dance-floor experience of drugs, moving bodies, electronic rhythms and textures. The DJs on the decks paced proceedings so that the up-tempo beats and psychedelic riffing of the midnight hour, when the Ecstasy hit the dancers, had gradually segued seamlessly into down-tempo, more languid tracks for an easy come-down by dawn. This did owe something to the older ritual of the night out at the disco that ended with the slow dance and the lights being turned on.

In January 1990, the Chill Out room opened at London's Land of Oz with Alex Patterson of the Orb spinning almost beatless tracks for sedentary (and some-times supine) punters. This "ambient" house, including the Orb's own *Adventures in the Ultraworld* and the KLF's *Chill Out,* featured sheep baa-ing, trains, samples of Elvis, Tuvan throat singing, Acker Bilk, other easy listening, and sound fragments from British children's television. These artists were influenced by Brian Eno's ambient music, sounds designed for particular environments, to serve specific functions—*Music for Films, Ambient 1: Music for Airports,* now Music for Not Dancing in a Club. This was an updating of Erik Satie's ambition to make "furniture music."

DJ culture's raison d'être—the production of music for dancing—can be seen as an indication that the function or use-value of music was becoming as impor-tant as any notion of aesthetic value grounded in meaning. Rather than going to a concert to hear a singer and band tell us something autobiographical, many of us want music to produce an experience of listening defined by our own con-sumer desires. We wish to simulate quite specific leisure environments with our musical choices. Music provides a functional accompaniment for working in the office and working out in the gym.

This may be related to the current vogue for various forms of "mood music," music for lifestyle options, that can be placed under the rubric of "easy listen-ing." The market is full of reissues and reappraisals of bachelor-pad space-age music, lounge music, film soundtracks, new-age trance music, exotica, the sounds of rain forests and oceans. These are musical simulacra, appropriate for narrow-ly defined consumer purposes. The recent success and current hipness of these musical forms that were once despised (by rock musicians and critics) suggests rock's waning power to define the mainstream of popular music culture and limit its range of sounds.[30] As the dance generation gets older, these laid-back sounds fit lifestyles more attuned to the wine bar, the café, the restaurant, and home than the late night dance club. In *Elevator Music,* Joseph Lanza suggests that modern life has evolved into "a megapolis of air-conditioned and sonically monitored atria."

> As restaurants, elevators, malls, supermarkets, office complexes, airports, lobbies, hotels, and theme parks proliferate, the background, mood, or easy-listening music needed to fill these spaces becomes more and more a staple in our social diet. Indeed, background music is almost everywhere: avant-garde "sound installations" permeate malls and automobile showrooms, quaint piano recitals comfort us as we wait in bank lines, telephone technotunes keep us complacently on hold, brunch Baroque refines our dining pleasure, and even synthesized "nature" sounds further blur the boundary between our high-tech Platonic caves and "real life." Along with Muzak and elevator music, there is moodsong to accompany our favorite movie scenes, tickle our subconscious fancies on television and radio commercials, alert us to the next network news station break, and lull us in our home entertainment centers.[31]

In this variegated environment of digital auras, music writers and record companies rooting through their archives have turned to previous periods when music seemed to stretch the sonic envelope and fit our carefully conditioned environments. Current preoccupations with the effects of digital technology on music have sent writers and fans back to the 1950s, when many records were made to promote the high fidelity of stereophonic record players, sonically simulate faraway exotic locations, and provide a backdrop for drinking cocktails and flicking through lifestyle magazines like *Playboy.* Some of the camp impulse behind the lounge (and indeed swing) revival may be an attempt to revive *and* modify masculinist lifestyles before the feminist movement of the 1970s, a kind of retromanhood. The resurgence of easy listening since the mid-90s occurs at the same time that everyday life for most people is anything but *Easy!* (as a book about the genre is titled);[32] the labor environment has essentially been restructured so that the vast majority of people are working longer hours for less money. Statistics routinely verify an increase in incidences of work-related ill health and stress. Music provides a palliative to these pressures.

The interest in the wider sonic scapes of non-guitar rock musical forms initiated by the technological revolutions of hip-hop and electronic dance music has also affected critics looking back at the venerable rock pantheon. There has been a greater emphasis on studio techniques, the artifice in the production of rock's classics, and the sonic shape of virtual worlds. The founding myth figure of rock—

the folk icon of the male blues musician sitting on the porch singing with an acoustic guitar—fades from view as rock historians acknowledge technological mediation and studio process that change the very basis of any notion of musical authenticity. For example, much of the critical appraisal of the Smithsonian Institution's 1997 reissue of Harry Smith's *Anthology of American Folk Music* (1952) and other examples of "primitive music" is centered on the technology of these old analog productions and the question of what has been lost in the sound and grain of music recordings since digitization.

The domination of dance music in the mainstream charts and in various subcultures also reflects shifts in consumer capitalism at the (post-)industrial level. The insistence on niche or target marketing and the mantras of ratings and demographics in business culture are echoed in the musical field. The dance sections in retail outlets for recorded music are divided and specialized under a host of categories like Trance, Hardcore, Happy Hardcore, Gabba, Techno, Jungle/Drum'n'Bass, Downbeat, Acid Jazz, House, Ambient, each with its own subgenres and hybrids given a name and institutionalized by record companies and the music press. Small and large record companies aggressively develop market segments for music around such categories.

The experience of a night on the dance floor is now available in commodified form, as common as the live rock album. The mix CD simulates a session on the dance floor, promoted under the name of the DJ, now a star and auteur in his or her own right as much as any "real" musician; DJs are now admitted into the British musician's union. One track released as a single is often remixed into multiple versions for release as different CDs or twelve-inch singles. You can buy the same song again and again in different mixes. These kinds of product differentiation do relate to the creative innovations of musicians and the development of new musical forms, but the fragmentation and practices of DJ culture also highlight the shifts in the political economy of music as commodity.

Jacques Attali has famously asserted, "Music is prophecy. Its styles and economic organization are ahead of the rest of society because it explores, much faster than material reality can, the entire range of possibilities in a given code. It makes audible the new world that will gradually become visible, that will impose itself and regulate the order of things; it is not only the image of things, but the transcending of the everyday, the herald of the future."[33] In this respect, dance-floor music culture might be prophetic of future social, economic, and political developments as it has responded to the violent restructuring of work and leisure in the last twenty years.

Alexei Monroe suggests that the rapid changes in electronic music genres in the 1990s denote the "terrifying pace and proliferating dysfunctionalities of post-

Industrial consumption."[34] The acceleration of aesthetic fragmentation into subgenres, sub-subgenres, and counter subgenres with their increasingly tribal scenes is integral to the specializing or niche-ing of postmodern cultural markets: "the fate of electronic genres is determined by the interface of extremely rapid technologico-creative development (making it a sector of the cultural market that mutates too rapidly to be entirely 'colonisable') and the need of post-modern cultural production to ceaselessly invent and reinvent new niche markets to service. As fast as the mass market can assimilate and commodify 'underground' subgenres, these mutate and negate each other ensuring the brief creation of precommodified zones, constantly one step ahead of the pursuit." However, as Monroe notes, the pursuit of the new in order to escape commodification is part of a market logic that needs to keep selling the new, to stay ahead of the game. This logic operates in both the subcultural industries and their corporate counterparts.[35]

More mundanely, the music industry has adapted its marketing strategies to a youth culture in which clusters of consumer goods are offered around the same constellations of meaning. The fashion industry designs highly priced, bright but functional club wear for the dance floor. Collectives that may have once organized free parties and cheap raves now present raves sponsored by multinational corporations. Breweries, concerned that consumers might desert alcohol for other drugs, sponsor nights at huge superclubs. DJs are paid colossal fees for a few hours' work on the decks. A score of dance magazines document the best nights at the trendiest spots, catalog the latest releases, and offer trips to dance events abroad through tie-ins with record companies and travel agents.

In this sense, dance-floor culture continues to provide forms of consumer training for young people, the skills needed for a life of adult consumption. Sarah Thornton argues that dance subcultures are involved in processes of creating distinctions (after Pierre Bourdieu). Her work primarily questions some of the truisms of 1970s subcultural theory. Subcultures do not develop and exist independently from the mainstream but are created through their relationship with it. Both the mass media and niche dance press construct the subculture rather than report some preformed field of activity. According to Thornton, participants are still concerned with a discourse of authenticity, for example, maintaining "underground" status and "not selling out," values that are posited against a commercial mainstream. At the same time, the drive to distinguish one musical scene from another, to develop hierarchies of listening taste and consumption, is part of the process of distinction and accumulation of subcultural capital.[36]

Drew Hemment acknowledges the corporatization of dance music but is keen to stress the deterritorializing powers of the dance virus. He considers the many variations of house music a "minor music" (after Deleuze and Guattari's essay on "minor literature"). Electronic dance music has transformed the way music sounds and functions. Hemment stresses the digitized play with repetition, the breaks and sound logic of various dance genres such as drum'n'bass, but also argues that dance music's influence has permeated other aspects of popular music, transforming its production, consumption, and meaning.

> A minor music isn't something set over and against a people, but is something that is essential to their collective existence and public life. It is not that music is tied to a specific community or group so much as that it itself can create (articulate, unite) a community or group: it is through a minor usage that the house is turned into a home. But neither is it about building a wall round a certain location and declaring it your own. A minor music can come from the ghetto, but it is not about reproducing or creating ghettos within music—which would just be to instantiate a major music on a smaller scale. It is rather to subvert the major music from within by making it a stranger to itself. A minor usage is like the secret strategies used by a foreigner, who uses linguistic terms for purposes for which they were not designed. A foreigner does not create a separate domain or dialect within language, but turns all language into something secret and strange.[37]

Hemment's foreigner signifies the potentially disruptive force of a minor music to the body politic, though his reference to language made "secret and strange" is rather romantic and mysterious.

The trope of the nomadic, particularly as articulated by Deleuze and Guattari, has proved a popular theoretical basis for the analysis of space and power. Some cautionary notes: the use of nomadism sometimes tends toward poetic abstraction, may provide the romantic buzz of the transgressive Other, but often isn't anchored in historical specificities. There is a danger that the nomad, rooted in an orientalist romanticism, can become a dehistoricized figure who has left behind the infinite traces of gender, sexuality, race, class, and any sense of location as she or he takes off on a never-ending journey. While traveling theory should be open to the constant fluidity of identities, in its desire to discard "essentialism" in favor of the continual fluctuating performance of identity and space, theorists should not dispense with notions of identity and subjectivity grounded in the material and embodied realities of gender, race, sexuality, class, and so on located in particular spaces.

Hemment is specific about some of the industrial processes that distinguish the new dance music's mobility from a static mainstream recording industry. Dance music has resisted the cult of personality vis-à-vis the pop star with its anonymous DJ mix. It has challenged the hegemony of the song. The codes of the musical event and performance have changed as the dancing audience has become the star of the scene in underground and often mobile circuits of festivals, parties, and raves. DJ culture has created distribution networks for product that bypass mainstream channels. It has fostered the near mythical anticommodity status of the white-label twelve-inch single and the dub plate—the one-off acetate or vinyl disc of a track exclusive to certain DJs, unavailable in the marketplace. These techniques of distinction foster subcultural capital that circulates along with the music in a rhizomatic transnational network of music institutions.

While this has been a challenge to the existing structure of the music industry, Hemment cautions against too much optimism. The major record labels have adapted to this nomadic dance-floor logic.[38] The large companies license the product of dance independents; the cult of personality has been developed around the star DJ; mix CDs sit happily alongside traditional artist-based albums. These corporate adjustments show that nomadism is not only a transgressive strategy, but one of the features of a much more mobile transnational capitalism in which major media corporations foster links to smaller cottage labels and networks in their colonization of capital. Criminal syndicates have also become involved in the profitable economy of night-time leisure.

The Body Politic

What Ien Ang calls the "post-globalised world" has provided the conditions for the emergence of theories of space across the disciplines of anthropology, sociology, geography, urban planning, architecture, and cultural studies. Spatial metaphors proliferate in contemporary cultural theory: position, location, mapping, center-margin, periphery, inside-outside, global-local, liminal space, third space, hybrid space, and so on.[39] Spatial theory has informed arguments about dance-floor politics. Dance music may not subscribe to notions of verbal meaning, but the activities around it have constituted part of the struggle over civic space, rural space, and the landscape of the nation. In the following section, I move from the politics of the dancing, technologized body-subject outward to the body politic.

DJ culture has been examined in regard to the forms of community and association it constructs and how these have been contained, managed, and repressed by the state. Many writers argue that rave fulfills a yearning for community and face-to-face communication against the authoritarian anticollectivist ethos of Thatcherism. DJ culture can be seen against the reduction and fragmentation of the public sphere as government has increasingly regulated assembly and movement in the nation's spaces. At the same time, large business interests have turned tracts of civic space into private property. Dance culture has forcefully articulated the desire for Britons to assemble in large numbers in public against this control of space.

The 1980s witnessed a number of conflicts in which the state authorities battled the so-called "enemy within" with new legislation, weapons, media manipulation, and surveillance technologies: the policing that led to inner-city uprisings against police in Brixton (London), St. Paul's (Bristol), Southall (London), Toxteth (Liverpool), Moss Side (Manchester), Chapeltown (Leeds), and Handsworth (Birmingham); the press and government propaganda against women who protested the stationing of U.S. Cruise missiles at the Greenham Common air force base; the pitched battles between mounted police and striking miners on picket lines; the short, sharp, shock treatment meted out to youth offenders; police attacks on members of Britain's nomadic class—the travelers; the struggle against the poll tax; and the increasingly rigid policing of soccer fans, required by many soccer clubs to carry ID cards.

The Hillsborough soccer disaster in April 1989, when ninety-six Liverpool fans were killed because police kept them caged in pens, coincides with the rise of the rave movement. Simon Reynolds suggests that "like football fandom, rave is a remnant of working-class consciousness, the vague sense of collectivity that abides after the death of organized labour with all its myths of fraternity and shared destiny." And Irvine Welsh has remarked in a television interview that the rave is "one of the only places that working class people can get together."[40]

During the 1980s, a combination of Britain's strict licensing laws, legal limitations on the right to public assembly, and the elitist door policies of many metropolitan dance clubs led to the spread of private and often illegal warehouse parties in unused city buildings. The desire for a massive collective public experience centered on dancing was seized on by entrepreneurs who exploited a legal loophole that allowed a private gentlemen's club to have an unlimited number of members. In the late 1980s, the "rave" era was heralded in airplane hangars in the countryside outside London on the M25 "orbital" motorway encircling the capital. Revelers were informed of the venue and directions on pirate radio. When the police got wind of these gatherings, mobile phones were used to pass on the necessary information to raver convoys at the last minute.

In June 1989 the rave phenomenon went mainstream with *The Sun*'s sensational headline, "Spaced Out! 11,000 Youngsters Go Drug Crazy at Britain's Biggest Ever Acid Party." The tabloid reported orgies at the event and even claimed that a raving teenage girl on drugs had bitten the head off a chicken while dancing. An impressive feat. The end of the 80s saw big all-night raves like Sunrise, Biology, and Eclipse entertain thousands of dancers at a time.

A hardcore techno track of the moment sums up the moral panic of the media and government. Mista E's "Don't Believe the Hype" appropriated the title of Public Enemy's rap hit for a beat-driven collage of media sound-bites, sampling Independent Television News at Ten's chimes of Big Ben and its reportage about "the acid house, a new culture of youth sweeping the country's nightclubs" made up of "advertising executives, firemen, air hostesses, Oxbridge graduates and the unemployed." The Establishment was threatened by the cross-class constituency of this new subculture as much as by anything else. A repeated motif included two samples, a young man's voice saying, "I just want to dance and have a good time," followed by a schoolma'am voice that firmly states, "Stop it." The track repeats the mythological tension between authoritative parents and youngsters who just want to have fun, but there was something more serious behind the conflict than merely a replay of the familiar pop generation gap. The Conservative government introduced policies designed to curb public assembly and movement. Much of this focused on dance-related events. The Metropolitan Police's Pay Party Unit was formed and Graham Bright's Entertainments Increased Penalties Bill of 1990 raised fines and extended prison sentences for those caught putting on illegal events.

In the early 90s, annual rock festivals like those at Glastonbury were joined by open-air events organized primarily around dance music. Travelers who had traditionally attended Glastonbury and Stonehenge gatherings were now drawn to the dance sound-systems, together with urbanites out for a good time in the countryside. DJ collectives like Tonka, Spiral Tribe, Circus Warp, and DiY brought together these different constituencies through cheap outdoor events and free parties networked across the country. Ten thousand people attended the Chipping Sodbury festival. When thirty thousand turned up at Castlemorton in western England in May 1992, the government concertedly drafted further legislation.

The Criminal Justice and Public Order Act of 1994 gave police the power to terminate any event outdoors that disturbed residents with music "wholly or predominantly characterized by the emission of a succession of repetitive beats." The act's explicit attack on dance music in public space was part of a legislative crackdown on other civil liberties. Police were awarded discretionary powers to curb the right to public assembly. A gathering or demonstration of twenty or more persons could be banned if deemed disruptive to community life. If demonstrators were found on private property and attempted to disrupt some lawful activity, they could be charged with "aggravated trespass." Police powers to stop and search and to arrest people on the grounds of antiterrorism were also expanded.[41] If dance music culture had not been political before, the struggle against the bill and then the act politicized many of its participants.

Jeremy Gilbert argues that the Criminal Justice Act has provoked a new politics of direct action, which has had greater credibility for young people than a more traditional politics of the Left and Right. In popular music culture, this has been signaled by the abandonment of what Gilbert calls the "politics of representation," embodied by the voice of community in rock ideology. He sees the rock singer's voice as analogous to traditional representative politics in Britain. In contrast, pleasure for pleasure's sake and immediate gratification are the central features of dance music culture: "the valorisation of the moment . . . is the organising logic of rave culture and of the various political movements which have come to be associated with it in recent years."[42]

The rave phenomenon can be seen as one element in an emergent politics outside the structures and processes of traditional parliamentary politics. Examples of this direct action or do-it-yourself politics include the free rave and party movement, anti-foxhunting campaigns, and land protests against the construction of major roads through rural areas. These new movements bring together different groups in coalition. They are not defined by the class-based institutions of the Left or Right, but informed by the techniques of new social movements and identity politics, incorporating a measure of media savvy in their spectacular style. Rave highlights the diminishing role of institutions like schools, community organizations, trade unions, political parties, and churches in fostering a political consciousness among young people.

George McKay places the rave in a tradition of nonconformism that goes back to hippie festivals, anarchist and situationist temporary occupations of the city's financial zones, and the antiracist carnivals of Rock against Racism and the Anti-Nazi League. In turn, these activities can be linked back further to the protests of the Levellers, the Ranters, and those who dreamed of turning "the world upside down" during the English Revolution.[43] The raves as "temporary autonomous zones" (in Hakim Bey's oft quoted term) echo the spirit of carnival, a revolt against state power along the continuum of an old English tradition of dissidence.[44] In an April 1993 column, the critic Kodwo Eshun went as far as to claim that "ravers saw themselves as the first ever trans-youth unity movement, reclaiming (almost without intent) some Deep-structure Albion inside Merrie England which all their predecessors had been too busy defying the police to notice."[45] Even if the ravers' initial desire had been hedonism, the state's response to public dancing has politicized them.

Hemment contends that the dance culture's methods and practices inherently subvert the state-machine. House music has been mobile and nomadic in its occupation of local and regional spaces with its illegal raves, warehouse parties, and other events. If the state is determined to territorialize space and control the movement of its subjects, rave culture has offered paths and "lines of flight," forms of micropolitics that deterritorialize localities and resist the centralizing power of the state's spatial regimes.[46] These skills and techniques have also been translated into the organization of more stable institutions like dance venues, art spaces, and record labels.

Direct action politics may involve the emergence of new progressive political groupings and reject the conservatism of institutional bureaucratic politics; and dance music culture does exhibit some of the features of new social movements and "radical democracy," incorporating coalitions and alliances not primarily based on class.[47] However, according to Gilbert, it has several limitations:

> These developments might be said to take part in Radical Democracy's abandonment of revolutionary politics (predicated as it was on a historical teleology and a simplistic model of power) for a politics concerned with "the multiplication of public spaces." But they are also in danger of collapsing into what we term a radical *spatialization* of politics; a search for immediacy and an abandonment of any real orientation to the future. Where the politics of representation is about speaking vicariously—through a singer, through an MP—the new politics of the present is about trying to make something happen *now*. Get a house *now* (by squatting), stop the road *now*, dance *now*, rush your little head off *now*. The future, as an abstract point to be waited on and hoped for, has no purchase here; this is a politics which occurs in space—the space of raves, of squats, of roads—but which doesn't have time to occupy itself *with* time. We hear this in the music; techno, trance, jungle and garage are all about creating a pleasurable moment rather than telling a story. They are not to make us feel that we are like (or different from) the performer, or to give us hope, or to make us angry. They are to be used rather than to be *understood*.[48]

A politics of space that doesn't offer a direction for the future has too readily embraced the immediacy of political action. Like Gilbert, McKay also warns that Do-It-Yourself (DiY) or direct action politics often valorizes experience at the expense of thought, action against intellectual consideration. This begs the question that if practice should accompany theory, then where's the theory in practice? This move has been underpinned by a millenarianism and to some extent, in the free-rave movement, a turn to new-age philosophy, which offers conservative notions of the individual.[49] Direct Action is also often a strictly local form of politics that may betray a Little Englandism and simply not deal with the complexities of local/national/global relationships. In its desire to get in touch with a "deep-structure Albion" it celebrates a rural vision of England.

Peter Gartside acknowledges DiY/NVDA (Non-Violent Direct Action) culture's "post-industrial, non-class based collectivism" and that its "affective and mystical aspects point up the bankruptcy of narrowly 'rational' conceptions of politics and the political subject." However, he recognizes a nostalgia for an arcadian vision of England in much of the DiY/NVDA discourse. The countryside is deemed to represent the real England. Such visions of the nation carry "ethocentric notions of pastoral arcadia." The move to the countryside is a move away from the multicultural city to a white place.[50] New-age ideology, ideas of Mother Earth, and a discourse of the folk body and blood of the land suggest that people tap into a tradition embedded in the soil and stones of England centuries past.

In contrast to Gartside, Kevin Hetherington argues that for new-age travelers the countryside is not conceived as rural arcadia, not the green and pleasant lands of English pastoralism and the country garden, but is imbued with the romantic idea of a landscape invested with sacred qualities associated with paganism. Much of the DiY ethos is about reclaiming unused land and property for communal farming and utopian communities, against the interests of government and wealthy farmers.[51]

Gartside concedes that some examples of DiY/NVDA politics, such as the Critical Mass cycling traffic disruptions and the campaigns for housing and community facilities do construct a politics of *urban* space: "They engage with modernity rather than adopting a 'fugitive' stance which would wish modernity away in the hope of a return to a 'simple,' 'natural' or 'traditional' life."[52] However, a strong undercurrent of direct action politics is its regression into apparently self-evident categories like "nature" and "community," which sound warm and fuzzy but inadequately theorize a politics for (post-) industrial Britain in a global economy.

The conservatism of some elements of DiY politics—its appeal to a nation "already there"—manifests itself in the whitest and most conservative of English television programs, *Coronation Street,* which regularly features a sympathetic DiY activist character, Spider, keen to take direct action for the benefit of the street's inhabitants, whatever the issue. *Coronation Street*'s brand of old-fashioned common-sense liberalism—a version of Tony Blair and New Labour's Communitarianism—is represented by the characters Ken Barlow and Emily Bishop and sits easily beside the youthful initiatives taken by Spider, who is Bishop's nephew. This seems to confirm Gartside's observation that DiY culture has a symbiotic relationship with "the dominant political culture's urge for middle-of-the road consensus." In recent episodes, Spider has even taken direct action to remove squatters who acquired tenant rights, a rather confused and incredible ideological move for a DiY activist.

A Les Edwards painting on the inside of the Prodigy's 1994 *Music for the Jilted*

Generation album, released at the height of the campaign against the Criminal Justice Act, captures the energies of this period and some of the contradictory ideological tendencies around direct action politics. A group of ravers is assembled around a sound system with a huge speaker in a rural field. Menacing police approach the gathering but are separated from their prey by a deep chasm, a ravine across which the only access to the ravers is a rope bridge. A single long-haired male raver gives the police an abusive finger gesture as he prepares to cut the rope with a machete. The uniformed boys in blue equipped with riot shields and batons are foiled. The image reproduces the rockist figure of the romantic revolutionary male figure, "giving it" to the authorities. But behind the police on the horizon, on their side, lies the ominous black skyline of the city, its jagged factory chimneys and jutting buildings a contemporary version of those dark satanic mills.

Conclusion

DJ culture, or rave, embodies the contradictions of its historical moment. It incorporates well-worn aspects of the Left's political imaginary as they have been filtered through popular music culture: the romance of rebellion; guerrilla tactics and anarchism used to outwit the state authorities now reconceived as constituting a nomadic war machine, a micropolitics of the rhizomatic network. At the same time, these politics often turn away from the party organization and representative democracy, as they fight the repressive state apparatus.

Feminist and queer analysis has applied the "personal is the political" dictum to dance music culture and claimed that the subjective, embodied experience of music has been ignored by a largely masculinist rock discourse tied to the authenticity of the word and the guitar.

Angela McRobbie suggests that critics concerned with the cultural politics of DJ culture (and music in general) might curb their desire to find the perfect French theory to apply to musical phenomena and instead turn more pragmatically to the "place of employment, livelihoods, and labor markets."[53] At the industrial level, dance music culture has taken up the tactics of Thatcherite small business enterprise. Its entrepreneurship has made smart cash for promoters but has also fostered conditions for communality; we might recall that Thatcher did say there was "no such thing as society." Dance music labels and other institutions are examples of flexible capitalist enterprise, often functioning independently of transnational corporations, but more likely with only relative autonomy. In this regard, they are related to the cottage capitalism of punk institutions. But new technologies have given producers more freedom to develop networks not constrained by corporate capital. On the other hand, in the prophetic mode that Attali suggests, the organization of the dance music industry heralds emerging tendencies in the organization of an increasingly nomadic capitalism. Big labels have altered their practices to accommodate and/or incorporate smaller actors in the industry.

DJ culture has reminded those in popular music studies—a growing and now institutionalized field—of the hermeneutic problem of music. Critics have the tools to analyze the context of musical production and consumption in the light of the regulation of public space and changing organization of the economy. But some methodologies rooted in the analysis of rock music culture have not adequately helped us to understand music that seems to say little and that doesn't sound like it comes from any recognizable place. We have been forced to confront the *materiality* of machine music that circulates through transnational networks and moves bodies and minds subjectively and collectively with its electronic rhythms and textures.

4

Black Whole Styles

Sounds, Technology, and Diaspora Aesthetics

> The sampler is the heartbeat. The desk is the pulse. The processors are the nervous system. The speakers are your soul that pumps out the energy.
> —Roni Size

> Breakbeats have been the missing link connecting the diasporic community to its drum woven past.
> —"Coded Language" by Krust and Saul Williams

The global dimensions of media industries lead to the connection of musicians and listeners in ways that complicate notions of the local, regional, and national "origins" of popular music. Globalization has intensified the sharing of musical sounds across borders. Simon Reynolds believes that these networks result in identifications that make notions of the national redundant: "A noise band in Manchester can have more in common with a peer group in Austin, Texas than with one of its 'neighbours' two blocks away; house music originates in Chicago, but British northern soul fans have responded to it more fervently than almost any US city. The very fact that house is massive over here proves how irrelevant questions of nationality and location are in pop, yet still the media tries to rally an obsolete patriotic allegiance to 'our' bands, a kind of positive discrimination."[1]

While the national may be put in question, does the issue of location really become irrelevant for the analysis of music? In this chapter, I'm concerned with how digital music technologies transform local, national, and transnational media spaces. In a great deal of recent academic and popular writing, new technologies are seen as instrumental in producing music that doesn't *belong* to any geographical location or come from a definable community. According to such a view, digital technology becomes the prime mover in the incorporation of geograph-

ically dispersed sounds into new musical products. Frank Owen and Carlo Mc-
Cormick, for example, suggest that the digital sampler alters our very perception
of time, space, and musical community: "Like postmodern telecommunications
in general, sampling collapses time and space so that pop history enters into both
a sonic one-dimensionality and an eternal music present. A kid in Manchester
sampling a Funkadelic record in his Moss Side bedroom has more in common
with a Brooklyn homeboy sampling that same record than the Mancunian has
with his friend down the street playing in a heavy metal band."[2]

Such digital technologies contribute to the further compression of time and
space that is a central feature of modernity. Music is torn free from its location
to some extent. It becomes harder to talk about "national" music, more problematic to claim that sounds are readable as arising directly from specific identities and localities. This seems most marked in electronic music recordings, many
of which have few if any lyrics.

However, some of the recent assertions that local experience has been squeezed
out of music by new technologies are troubling in their hyperbole. In their claims
to electronic music's rootlessness, these arguments tend to iron out cultural difference and obscure historical specificity in the new global postmodern order.
Here, for example, is Reynolds on house music and the agency of its practitioners: "It's difficult to imagine a genre more place-less or hostile to an infusion of
ethnicity. Although it comes from a place (Chicago) it does not draw anything
from its environment. House departs from the old organic language of music—
roots, cross-pollination, hybridization. Producers like Mantronix and Todd Terry are not authors, but engineers, architects. Their music is not an expression of
the soul, but a product of expertise."[3] And Jon Pareles, on techno's lack of "ethnicity," claims: "The rise of techno represents a recoil against urban, ethnic styles.
Made with rootless synthetic sounds, techno doesn't refer directly to older songs
(as hip-hop sampling does), and its rhythms steer away from the disco memories of house music."[4]

Such musical developments are usually conceptualized in dichotomous terms:
either an older organic and authentic form of musical expression representing a
community has been destroyed by the new technologies, or ethnicity melts away
in this synthesized global mélange. Ross Harley lays out these polarities:

> The question of origins and proper boundaries in house music and its various sub-
> genres—acid house, hip house, techno house, Euro house, Chicago house, etc.—
> blurs into a complex synthesis of musics. To some, this represents the ultimate de-
> struction of locality and cultural particularity, the unfortunate victory of global capital
> over authentic cultural expressions. To others, the phenomenon of house music is a

hyperbolic refraction of what is happening elsewhere in culture: the collapse of boundaries, the end of sequential narrative processes, the repeatability of sounds and genres, the pleasure of synthetic as opposed to organic processes, the elevation of technique over presence, and the construction of an eternal cultural present.[5]

One view suggests a search for authentic "roots," the other emphasizes "routes," the constant movement of culture that transgresses lines of identity defined by place. The former promises fixity, the latter the dissolution of any locatedness. Eschewing the excesses of some postmodern theory, Harley suggests that the new digital technologies still draw on established musical forms and practices. New digitally minded musicians discuss their work, its locatedness, and their subjectivities in often familiar terms. Culture and identity, including musical forms, arise through the intricate flux between "roots and routes," which must be analyzed together to understand the remapping of musical sounds.

This chapter investigates the debate about new technologies in the production of popular music, specifically in relation to black British music in the 1990s. The arguments are largely inspired by the work of Paul Gilroy, which has foregrounded music's role in black culture and politics. Gilroy's *There Ain't No Black in the Union Jack* (1987) and *The Black Atlantic* (1993) and his collection of essays *Small Acts* (1993) argue that black music culture has provided a utopian critique of capitalism and racism. Here I concentrate on his more recent writing, which has been more pessimistic about developments in black Atlantic popular music. Gilroy's comments in an interview on "soul" reveal his qualms about the effects of visual media like film, television, video, and digital music machines like samplers and sequencers on music in the public culture of the African diaspora in the U.K., U.S., and Caribbean. Technological mediation, he believes, has contributed to the decline in black music's political imagination. I agree with much of Gilroy's pessimism about the political shifts in black popular culture, and the "downsizing" and privatization of cultural production are significant developments in black music; however, I think he comes close to technological determinism in his criticisms of image culture and digitization.

Gilroy argues that the desire for redemption and freedom embodied in soul music has shrunk from community to the nuclear family, and then to the singular black body. The politics of the public sphere have been replaced by a celebration of sexuality as the "most intensely felt experience of being in the world." He confesses that he can't hear "soul" in the new music. He blames this on the technology: "most of the funk has gone too. That was killed by the technology and the de-skilling process instituted by digital technologies. I think that soul is only soul in relation to funk and without funk it loses something of its value. As funk is squeezed out of the frame by some of the technological factors at work and some of the de-skilling issues involved in musical production right now, these political changes are paralleled by new kinds of limitations and shrinkage of the creative horizons of musicians and performers."[6] According to Gilroy, the funk comes from the face-to-face communication of the collective musical performance and the antiphonal activity of the live dance hall, now threatened by program-mable technologies that have "de-skilled" black music production.

This chapter considers Gilroy's arguments and other recent writing on tech-nology through an analysis of the work of black British musicians who seem to embrace the new visual and digital technologies. Drum'n'bass musician Roni Size's comment at the head of this chapter implies that technology can be embodied in human terms. Black British electronic music in the 1990s suggests that digital codes have been integrated into the circuits of black subjectivity and memory. I will discuss the work of Massive Attack, Tricky, Barry Adamson, and jungle/drum'n'bass artists A Guy Called Gerald, Goldie, and Roni Size. How do these musicians conceptualize their work with visual and digital technologies? How is their music local and global? What is its relationship to American and Caribbe-an music? What shape does a black British diasporic subjectivity take in the music? What kind of discourse on "blackness" has this music generated in critical writ-ing? And how are the demands of media systems and institutions negotiated by these musicians?

While sympathetic to Gilroy's view, I'm not as pessimistic as he is in his as-sessment that black music and subjectivity have been so weakened and atomized. Musicians have adjusted to the new limits, demands, and possibilities of audi-bility and visibility in new technologies to still create sounds and images that articulate diasporic sensibilities "conscious" of the subjective and collective po-litical realities of black British life. This work reveals strong continuities as well as significant breaks with previous black music practices. In my examination of these questions, I'm also responding, in the British context, to the issues posed by Louis Chude-Sokei at the close of his essay "The Sound of Culture: Dread Discourse and Jamaican Sound Systems": "the question raised most trenchantly by the new sounds is this: how can roots even be contemplated in digital, non-linear space? After all, the history of black cultural resistance and black cultural soundings is a history marked by manipulations of the major technologies of the era. To take this a step further, how can nationalism—race-based or otherwise—exist in the context of multinational corporations where Babylon itself—late capitalism—is increasingly mobile and decentered? Indeed, is the postmodern the end of 'race' as a necessary structure and the beginning of more specific, cul-ture-based articulations of ethnicity?"[7] I argue that digital technology may actually have fostered the conditions in which black musicians have created a uniquely "British" music, which owes much to its black Atlantic forebears and contemporaries, but increasingly sounds the local specificities of the black experience in the metropolitan U.K.

Diaspora Discourse and Music

But first, backtracking a little, turning the record back in an arc before we let the sounds burst in, I want to consider Gilroy's earlier work. A discussion of the concept "diaspora" and its currency and applicability to U.K. musical forms in dialogic relationship with America and the Caribbean helps us to understand the emergence of black British diasporic aesthetics.

Largely denied access to national media outlets, Britain's black communities have nurtured African-American and Jamaican sounds in institutions like sound systems/mobile discos, pirate radio stations, clubs/dance halls, and record shops ever since black settlement began. In his archaeology of black club culture in the postwar years, Gilroy notes that the "town halls and municipal buildings of the inner city in which dances are sometimes held are transformed by the power of these musics to disperse and suspend the temporal and spatial order of the dominant culture."[8] In these venues the sufferation of English racism is suspended for the night.

In the 1980s, sound systems and warehouse parties kept up to date with changes in black music in Jamaica and the U.S. The early part of the decade produced several international hits by black British musicians like Linx, Loose Endz, David Joseph, Imagination, and Junior Giscombe. These records may have been categorized as Brit-funk or soul but were still generally facsimiles of African-American genres.

In the reggae scene, British talkover artists hungered for live tapes of Kingston dance-hall sessions so they could reproduce the chatting styles of the DJs. Things began to change in the mid-1980s. Black Britain forged its own characteristic sounds, still influenced by, but less beholden to, Jamaica and the United States. In *There Ain't No Black in the Union Jack,* Gilroy draws attention to reggae DJ Smiley Culture, whose 1984 release "Cockney Translation" included rhyming in Jamaican patois and English Cockney dialect.[9] "Cockney Translation" and its follow-up, "Police Officer" (a comic riff on the black experience of being stopped and harassed by the police), were to some extent novelty hits, but other DJs on the Fashion label were developing a uniquely British fast style of talkover.

The year 1987 was to prove something of a watershed for black British music with the release of the single "Keep on Moving" by sound system Soul II Soul, a collective of musicians and fashion designers based in London. "Keep on Moving" was a hit in Britain and the U.S., combining a reggae-style bass line, phat hip-hop drums, female soul vocals by Caron Wheeler, and a memorable orchestral strings motif. The track was a Brit-U.S.-Jamaican hybrid, personified by the group's logo of the "Funki Dredd"—funky from America, dread from Jamaica, but now funki dredd in the U.K.

At the cultural studies conference at the University of Illinois at Urbana-Champaign in 1991 (when cultural studies "went big in the USA"), Gilroy used "Keep on Moving" to illustrate the transnational flows of cultural production and consumption that challenge a model of culture and identity based on the nation-state. One of the tracks on the twelve-inch single is a dub remix by Teddy Riley, a U.S. producer of new jack swing. The remix features samples from James Brown's group, the JB's, and the Jamaican DJ-producer Mikey Dread's *African Anthem* dub album. For Gilroy, this is evidence of "diasporic intimacy" that "has created a new topography of loyalty and identity in which the structures and presuppositions of the nation-state have been left behind because they are seen to be outmoded."[10] London is here just one temporal and spatial node in the African diaspora.

Gilroy has been an important figure in the dissemination of the diaspora concept in cultural studies. James Clifford believes that diaspora discourse is to some extent replacing minority discourse because it considers cross-border identifications. The term "diaspora" is also "a signifier not simply of transnationality and movement but of political struggles to define the local, as distinctive community, in historical contexts of displacement."[11] "Diaspora" describes dispersed peoples but also the space that results from this scattering. England becomes diasporic space because of the presence of African-Caribbeans.

If the diaspora concept is used to develop a method of mapping subjectivities and space, Avtar Brah suggests that scholars must be sensitive to the continually shifting differences within the diasporic formation, between diasporic formations, as well as the material distribution of power that allows many histories of displacement to coalesce into one diasporic formation: "the *concept* of diaspora concerns the historically variable forms of *relationality* within and between diasporic formations. It is about relations of power that similarise and differentiate between and across changing diasporic constellations. In other words, the concept of diaspora centres on the *configurations of power which differentiate diasporas internally as well as situate them in relation to one another*."[12] This means that while we can speak of an "African diaspora" its meaning is constantly changing. All diasporas are contested, heterogeneous spaces that are localized. Black cultural forms take their shapes from this condition of displacement and dislocation.

Can we argue that the practices and structures of music manifest a diasporic sense of time and space?

According to Edouard Glissant, African diasporic memory is fundamentally shaped by the Middle Passage. He argues that the Caribbean is a "site of history characterized by ruptures . . . that begin with a brutal dislocation, the slave trade." Therefore, "our historical consciousness could not be deposited gradually and continually and like a sediment." Instead of a linear conception of history, what Walter Benjamin calls "homogeneous empty time," black historical materialism is produced in the "context of shock, contraction, painful negation, and explosive forces."[13]

Drawing on Glissant's work, Barnor Hesse argues that

the diasporic imaginary itself is vitally emergent in the conditions set by the "inability of collective consciousness to absorb" the enormity of the traumas associated with slavery and also the ultimate impossibility of a collective consciousness. Black diasporic imaginaries therefore inscribe a poetics of time and space which is always unimaginable. Paradoxically, Glissant's suggestion that the dislocation of the historical continuum produces a "non-history" complete with the erasing of a collective memory, can be seen as radically productive. It facilitates focus on a system of organizing experiences, space, which is the project of another temporality, not only a different history, but in effect the history of different spaces: the African diaspora.[14]

Gilroy echoes Hesse in his description of diaspora as "a utopian eruption of space into the linear temporal order of modern black politics."[15] Diasporic consciousness seeks to return to a homeland, an impossibility due to the ruptures of history. Home is inaccessible but the desire to be at home is a structure of diasporic subjectivity. Diasporic cultures therefore produce, in Salman Rushdie's phrase, "imaginary homelands." However, it is important to remember, as Vijay Mishra reminds us, that the diasporic imaginary does not mean that the nation-state is dead but that it remains "a complex socio-economic formation with multiple cultural repertoires in which diasporas are always provisionally and problematically inserted."[16] For black theorists and critics, this intercultural positionality provides new modes of analysis that understand culture as an ongoing process between the local and global.

According to Gilroy, music functions within "micro-systems of linguistic and political hybridity" as a "partially hidden public sphere" that draws together "communities of sentiment and interpretation" across the diaspora. Music in the Caribbean, America, and Europe remains a carrier of collective black memory in its drums, bass, and voices. This sound communication transcends language.[17] The dialogic practices of black music in live performance and in the antiphonal (call-and-response) aspects of the dance hall—with musicians, DJs, toasters, and rappers commenting in new lyrical and musical variations on previous cultural productions—sustain black music as, in Leroi Jones's phrase, a "changing same." According to Gilroy, even the reification of commodified music is resisted through this constant dialogic process, manifested in the proliferation of Jamaican reggae "versions" and the multiple remixes of African-American genres. These practices of repetition, cut, and mix in many black music forms reflect a distinctive approach to time and space.

In his discussion of the aesthetics of repetition, James Snead argues that musical practice emerges out of the rupture of the Middle Passage suggested by Glissant: "Repetition is not just a formal ploy, but often the willed grafting onto culture of an essentially philosophical insight about the shape of time and history." He describes the implications of different time-space relations in African and European musical forms: "In black culture, repetition means that the thing circulates in an equilibrium. In European culture, repetition must be seen to not be just circulation and flow but accumulation and growth. In black culture, the thing (the ritual, the dance, the beat) is 'there for you to pick it up when you come back to get it.' If there is a goal in such a culture, it is always deferred; it continually 'cuts' back to the start, in the musical meaning of the 'cut' as an abrupt, seemingly unmotivated break (an accidental *da capo*) with a series already in progress and a willed return to a prior series."[18]

Snead cites James Brown's funk as an example of this repetition-and-cut practice. Brown and his band establish a groove that includes vocal interjections and the call and response of his squeals, yelps, and exhortations with instrumental solos. There are interruptions in the rhythm that do not disrupt so much as play off it, so that when the listener returns to the repetitive, cyclical beat—"the one," as funkmasters like Bootsy Collins and George Clinton theorize it—its plenitude is all the more apparent. Such an approach to musical time and space, according to Snead, "builds 'accidents' into its coverage, almost as if to control their unpredictability. Itself a kind of cultural coverage, this magic of the 'cut' attempts to confront accident and rupture not by covering them over but by making room for them inside the system."[19]

Snead's theory could just as well apply to other black music strategies, from versioning in reggae, cutting and scratching in hip-hop "turntablism," to British jungle's break-beat science.[20] Such techniques of music production and reproduction have traveled across the black Atlantic between, for example, London, Bristol, Manchester, Kingston, New York, Miami, Chicago, and Detroit.

I want to consider briefly the technological basis of some of the Jamaican and U.S. music formative in the development of black British sound systems and recording artists. By expanding on these connections, it will be clear that the break between digital and older music technologies is not as great as Gilroy suggests. The musicians I discuss later in this chapter are in fact translating many of the older techniques into the new digital environment. They remain in dialogue with previous and current forms of Jamaican and African-American music. For example, today's groups like Massive Attack and Reprazent owe much of their initial production to the institution of the Jamaican sound system.

In the early 1960s the sound system, or mobile disco, became "the preeminent media structure in newly independent Jamaica."[21] Entrepreneurs like Clement Coxsone Dodd, Duke Reid, and Prince Buster competed to play the hottest American rhythm-and-blues imports, then turned to studio production to fuel the homegrown ska boom. Dodd's Studio One label and Reid's Treasure Isle imprint produced "specials," unique recordings for exclusive play at their sound system dance events. Tracks that were popular on the dance floor were then released for the broader market. The island's economy could not support live music so recorded music was paramount. Rival sound systems engaged in technological one-upmanship, attempting to provide the loudest bass amplification, highest quality sound, and most arresting audio special effects, as well as the latest and most exclusive records.

By the late 1960s, sound systems were largely playing Kingston-produced 45 rpm seven-inch singles with the main song on the A-side coupled with an instrumental version on the B-side. This practice emerged from American rhythm-and-blues and soul music recordings, which often had a vocal part 1 on the A-side with an extended instrumental part 2 on the flip. With two copies of the same single, the person on the turntable decks, known as the "selector," could segue from the A- to the B-side "version," providing a longer rhythmic groove for the dance hall patrons. This musical structure also provided a backdrop for anyone who wanted to step up to the microphone and talk over the instrumental part of the record. The talkover artist (or DJ, in Jamaican parlance) would often comment on the sentiments expressed in the vocal or digress in his own inimitable style on any subject, from love and the latest fads to religion, local news, and international politics. The DJ version became commodified in record form and often dozens of different versions cut on the same infectious rhythm track would be available on the market.[22] This was an example of Leroi Jones's "changing same," where repetition produces many variations on the same theme, and recorded rhythms become the carriers of an ongoing dialogic conversation and accumulated collective memory.

As Paul Willis notes, the sound system (now an element of many dance music subcultures) is an institution "where the activities of consumption merge into and become intertwined with more conventional forms of production."[23] Through work on sound amplification, the use of electronic skills, DJ-ing, and rap/talkover, records are played and transformed in performance, and consumption becomes a form of production. By the end of the 1960s, the first major DJ star, U-Roy, was toasting for King Tubby's Hi Fi system. Tubby was Osbourne Ruddock, an inventive engineer who was the first to introduce a reverb unit and separate tweeter boxes to the sound system. He also operated a studio where he could cut one-off acetate discs/specials for the sound. Four-track analog tape-recording equipment enabled him to break up a recording into its constituent parts. According to reggae lore, at one particular live sound-system session Tubby took the vocals out of the mix, leaving the skeleton of drum and bass pumping out of the speakers and thus driving the crowd wild.

This live performance engineering was translated into the studio technique known as dub, named after the process of copying dubs (or doubles) on tape. At the console of the sound system and in the studio, the basic drum-and-bass backbone of a reggae tune could be almost infinitely manipulated by engineers and producers like Errol Thompson, Lee "Scratch" Perry, or Tubby and his protégés Prince Jammy and Scientist. In the mid-1970s, King Tubby's was one of the most prolific studios, with the engineer mixing up dubs from recordings by major Kingston producers such as Augustus Pablo and Bunny Lee. These producers usually owned the rights to the original song and recording, so versions, even if they were mixed by someone else, usually generated more income.

Dub expanded and multiplied the possibilities of "versioning." Different elements of the sound mix could be isolated, certain instruments foregrounded. Sometimes every sound was "cut," a wisp of the vocal would then float in after a pause, and the bass and then drums would burst back into the fullness of the mix. Tracks were embellished with special effects like echo, reverb, and flange. Whistles, babies crying, lions growling, and dogs barking were dropped into the mix to create more novel and surreal soundscapes. Tubby even incorporated the sounds of gunfire and police sirens, which caused quite a scare at some of the dances during times of political turmoil in 1970s Kingston. Dub could transform a conventional reggae song into a spacious, cavernous sound in which musical pieces were moved around and vocal utterances were clipped and stretched out, pulling fragments in different directions. The technique foregrounded the multiple spatialities of sound for the listener, who became aware of the "depth" of the sound mix as well as its stereophonic dimensions.

By the mid-1970s, the dub version predominated on the B-side of any vocal recording whether it was a song or a DJ chat. Dub versions were as popular as, if not more in demand than, their vocal originals. From its emergence as a studio and sound system technique, dub achieved the status of a genre. Whole albums of dub tracks were released, one of the first and most influential being Lee Perry and the Upsetters' *Blackboard Jungle* in 1973. When King Tubby's name appeared on the B-side dub version of a single in 1974, the era of the dub auteur had arrived.

The introduction of the twelve-inch single, a format first exploited in the underground black, gay, and Latino disco clubs of New York, provided a wider vinyl groove in the record, which gave a louder and "fatter" drum-and-bass response. This "disco" single, as it was called on the reggae scene, also allowed a track to be much longer, providing more sonic time and space for experimentation. Sometimes the dub mix was almost unrecognizable from the original, though the trademark bass line would usually remain intact. A popular rhythm was often "versioned" on scores of different records. Such musical-technological practices in 1970s Kingston are now taken for granted in dance music culture and its many genres.[24]

In a 1982 essay, Luke Ehrlich describes dub as X-ray music:

> With dub, Jamaican music spaced out completely. If reggae is Africa in the New World, then dub must be Africa on the moon; it's the psychedelic music I expected to hear in the '60s and didn't. The bass and drums conjure up a dark, vast space, a musical portrait of outer space, with sounds suspended like glowing planets or the fragments of instruments careening by, leaving trails like comets and meteors. Dub is a kaleidoscopic musical montage which takes sounds originally intended as interlocking parts of another arrangement and using them as raw material, converts them into new and different sounds; then, in its own rhythm and format, it continually reshuffles these new sounds into unusual juxtapositions.[25]

This outer-space, sci-fi aspect to dub is drawn upon by William Gibson in his cyberpunk hit novel *Neuromancer,* in which the central characters Case and Molly are supported by the dreadlocked and alienated Rastas who have given up on the Babylonian world of the Sprawl for their own settlement. Out in Zion cluster, they are surrounded by music: "As they worked, Case gradually became aware of the music that pulsed constantly through the cluster. It was called dub, a sensuous mosaic cooked from vast libraries of digitalized pop; it was worship, Molly said, and a sense of community."[26]

Notwithstanding the novel's certain romanticization of the black outsider, Gibson's point about worship, community, and technologically mediated cultural memory is central to dub in the 1970s. The rise of dub is tied to the impact of Rastafarianism in black popular culture. Chude-Sokei argues that Rasta's Garveyite rhetoric of "roots and culture" projected a utopian idea of racial

authenticity through the idea of repatriation to Africa. A symbolic and meta-
phorical return to Africa was a way of constructing a diasporic black consciousness against official national discourse in Jamaica (and for that matter, Britain).
Race was more important than nation, or rather, race offered a kind of national
identity with ethnicity *as* geography: "For the Rastafari, as with Du Bois, Garvey,
and many others of their generation, diaspora was the problem and race the
solution. Race allowed the diaspora to be transcended for a discourse of ethnic
and cultural similarity."[27] The mystical spiritual aspect of dread was present not
simply in words but in drum-speak and bass-talk. Sound conjured up this transnational community.

Similar technological-aesthetic strategies are present in U.S. rap music. An
emergent hip-hop culture in Brooklyn and the South Bronx in the mid-1970s
had the input of Jamaican migrants as well as Puerto Rican and African-American influences. DJ Kool Herc Campbell, originally from Jamaica, is one of the
pioneers of South Bronx hip-hop. Rappers or MCs are akin to Jamaican DJs
rhyming over rhythms. In hip-hop, the DJ is equivalent to the reggae selector
on the turntable decks. Hip-hop relies on the DJ's cutting, scratching, and splicing
pieces of previously recorded music on two turntables. These techniques use the
technology of the turntable rather like the Kingston engineering wizards used the
studio console. DJs like Grandmaster Flash could dexterously splice several old
records to create a new musical composition. A particularly pleasurable (and
danceable) part of the record, usually the isolated drum-and-bass pattern at the
core of a track known as a "break," could be repeated to form an endless groove
created from a single fragment, if the DJ had two copies of the record. This break
beat could form the foundation of a new musical performance as part of a live
DJ set and also on a studio recording.

The introduction of digital samplers in the 1980s allowed one to isolate and
record the required part or break from a vinyl album, single, or compact disc and
to reproduce it in a new track by looping it end to end ad infinitum to form the
basic rhythm. David Toop explains the expanded sonic possibilities for hip-hop
created by cheap samplers like the AKAI S900 in the mid-1980s: "Now layers
could be built up, using a rhythm loop from, say, 'Funky Drummer' by James
Brown, augmented by new drum beats from a drum machine, a bass line from a
Funkadelic record, some atmospheric strings from a blaxploitation soundtrack
like Cotton Comes to Harlem and synthesiser squirts from J.B.'s funk track. The
emphasis on early 80s sampling with expensive machines like the Fairlight was.
high quality, but rap demands a raw, xerox feel. . . . painstaking hours could be
spent, using state of the art technology, to make a new track sound authentically
old."[28] New technology was ironically used and abused not to make pristine digital

copies with no degradation of sound but tracks that sounded old and rough enough to have the authenticity of "the street" or "underground" scene.

One DJ, Mark the 45 King, had a hit with a track named "The 900 Number." This consisted of one sample from an old funk record looped continuously for over two minutes on the AKAI S900 sampler. AKAI's S1000, introduced on the market in 1989, featured 16-bit sampling, which meant that a sample of a recording could be recorded and played back in stereo with virtually no degeneration in the sound quality. A sample could be manipulated in multiple ways—chopped up and spliced together in a completely new shape to make a third sample. The availability of the digital sequencer allowed a number of synthesizers and drum machines to be played automatically, without any human performance necessary, by recording electronic signals in a sequence into the memory. These can be played back in the same order at the push of a button.

Soul II Soul's "Keep on Moving" (beloved of Gilroy) uses some of the same sampler and sequencer technologies. Gilroy doesn't seem to be against the sampler in principle because it is responsible for bringing British production, Jamaican music, and American remixing together in its studio-designed diaspora aesthetics. Another of Gilroy's essays, "It Ain't Where You're From, It's Where You're At," takes its title from a line in Eric B. and Rakim's 1987 old skool rap classic "I Know You Got Soul."[29] The track samples a James Brown/Bobby Byrd funk composition of the same name from the early 70s. Gilroy isn't against technological mediation per se. He has written of the vinyl record's importance as akin to that of ships carrying people and histories across the black Atlantic. He argues that we need "an enhanced understanding of 'consumption' that can illuminate its inner workings and the relationships between rootedness and displacement, locality and dissemination that lend them vitality in the countercultural setting."[30] Gilroy uses the example of the twelve-inch single, which developed out of record companies' attempts to cash in on the success of black musical genres. The new musical commodity satisfied the industry's need for more formats to sell to the consumer, but it also facilitated new practices such as scratching, cutting, dub, talkover, and remixing.

However, what had significantly changed for Gilroy by the mid-90s was music's ability to offer a vital public sphere for black cultural politics. This capacity was imperiled by visual media and the increasingly privatized activity of digital music composition. Technological mediation may be productive, but only if it is activated in public performance. Also at the root of Gilroy's worries is the fear that the image culture of the United States is providing the (global) models for vernacular black arts, displacing other geographical nodes and cultural practices in the black Atlantic.

Who Stole the Soul? The Uses and Abuses
of Black Images

According to Gilroy, collective memory in the new sounds is moving away from
the remembrance of slavery, though its ineffable suffering still surfaces in sonic
traces. In his work since the mid-90s, Gilroy is critical of the Afrocentric trend
in U.S. rap, with its myth of origins and tales of black kings and queens in Egypt;
the pharaohs rather than the slaves are invoked as a point of pride. The loss of
slave memory has disabled a black cultural politics across the diaspora. This Afro-
centrism is in fact Americocentric. Gilroy laments that black Britain has made a
"sharp turn away from the Caribbean as its major source of inspiration. Black
political culture in this country now looks to African-American history for guidance, pleasure and raw material for its own distinct definitions of blackness."[31]

After Bob Marley's death in 1981, Jamaican music itself had, according to Gilroy, descended into apolitical concerns with "slackness" (sexually explicit material). In *The Darker Side of Black,* a 1992 documentary made with the director
Isaac Julien, Gilroy on voice-over states that "eleven years after the death of Bob
Marley, the desire to change the world nurtured in the fateful meeting of reggae
music and Rastafari belief has been abandoned." The film credits Julien with
writing Gilroy's voice-over, but in any case, many of its sentiments echo the arguments in the latter's writing. The documentary examines the early 90s currents
of gun talk, homophobia, and heterosexism in Jamaican dance-hall/ragga and
U.S. hip-hop. It covers the transnational success of the Kingston DJ Shabba
Ranks, who on Channel Four's program *The Word* stated that homosexuals should
be crucified. The filmmakers interview another Kingston DJ, Buju Banton, whose
hit "Boom Bye Bye" suggests through onomatopoeia that people should shoot
gay men ("batty bwoy") dead. The film also examines some of rap's misogyny
and the patriarchal and homophobic sentiments of the Nation of Islam's Five Per
Cent group, represented in the film by the rap group Brand Nubian.

Gilroy claims that the transnational currency of a largely North American
commodified black popular culture, in the form of rap, sport, Hollywood films,
and television, relies on the circulation of racially authentic images that often claim
the last word on blackness. These images sell to consumers and are embedded in
racialized discourses of black sexuality, athleticism, and cool.

Corporations put designer clothes and sports shoes made by sweatshop labor
in Asia on public black bodies. Many rap songs present orgies of "high-class"
consumption—gold jewelry, Möet champagne, expensive cars, and designer label clothes. In the late 90s, the producer-entrepreneur Puff Daddy raps "It's all
about the Benjamins" and the Wu-Tang Clan urge consumers to buy their brand-

ed clothing label, Wu Wear. This marks a shift from the economic self-determi-
nation advocated in Eric B and Rakim's "Paid in Full" (1987) to conspicuous
consumption and a mini-corporate black economic nationalism.

Middle-class, suburban film makers bring their images of the ghetto to screens
and represent a return to the patriarchal nuclear family as the solution to chronic problems (unemployment, crime, drugs) faced by a black underclass assaulted by neo-liberal economic and social policies. In films like *Boyz in the Hood* and
Deep Cover, mothers who are either bourgie wannabes, prostitutes, or crack ad-
dicts are held responsible for the dissolution of family values that can be rein-
stated only by strong father figures. As homicide becomes the major cause of death
for young urban African-American men, gun culture is celebrated. Rap discusses Glocks and nine-millimeter handguns as charged elements of urban reality but
also fetishizes these weapons in its rhymes and the images on record sleeves.

Gilroy's main criticism of the new rap, R&B, and reggae is that they transform
black music's "yearning for freedom into a different mode . . . signalled by the
growing centrality of what might be called a racialised bio-politics of fucking: a
means of bonding freedom and life."[32] He believes this biological politics of blackness is a regressive form of identity politics. Citing the American singers Mary J.
Blige and R. Kelly, Gilroy argues that even though generically their music may
be part of the soul tradition, its yearning is defined by the immediate needs of
the body. He mourns what he believes to be the loss of a deeper notion of *soul.*
Soul in the 1960s, 70s, and 80s was "the site of a kind of ambivalence about the
memory of slavery and the desirability and the obligation to forget things which
are difficult."[33] Soul is a sign of the impossibility of redemption from a history
of suffering. The new "soulless" black music suffers from its departure from the
live-and-direct arena. The performative and collective aspects of black popular
music culture are being eroded by technological mediation: "These hip hop users are screenies. They connect with it through video, not audio. Where do they
listen to the music? Certainly not socially and collectively in real time, but in a
privatized mode. Cars, not dance halls, are the primary context for listening to
that stuff; perhaps that might be where that primal moment of consuming takes
place."[34]

Gilroy concentrates his criticisms about this "regression of performance" on
some of the recent African-American and Jamaican music, but suggests that such
tendencies permeate British popular culture. While black British music came into
its own in the 90s, it was still influenced by U.S. and Caribbean sounds and
images, and depended on the same mediating technologies. However, black British music does have different institutional pressures exerted on it from the music press, record labels, club networks, and television.

In the last fifteen years, black bodies have become more visible on television, and this has depended to a great extent on the wide success of black music culture. Stuart Hall argues that this brings mixed dividends:

> One parameter underlying this shift in visibility is the vigour, vitality and diversity of the black cultural revolution which has exploded across the British scene in the last fifteen years, especially from Asian and Afro-Caribbean (Black British) urban cultures. Its effects can be seen, at one level in the vitality of black music, dance, theatre, and the visual arts (with their inevitable spin-offs into television, film and video). However, its principal space of representation in television is the highly ambiguous pop music/"youth TV" sector, where black street styles and black bodies have become the universal signifiers of modernity and "difference."[35]

Television exploits the commercial popularity of black music and fashion, which have moved closer to the center of British youth culture. Soul, funk, reggae, hip-hop, house, drum'n'bass, garage, and a score of other "black" music genres have multiplied and thrived. Black style has found its way to main street.

Black visibility and the selling of blackness also have been integral to developments in the youth market for a host of commodities. The late 1980s saw the explosion of youth television with music video and magazine programs televisually reproducing the format of lifestyle magazines like *The Face* and *I-D* that reported on black music and club culture in Britain's cities. According to Frith, youth television was the focus for broader debates about television and the viewer in the emerging satellite economy. He suggests that "youth" functioned as "a metaphor in the much more general attempt to redefine the TV viewer to match the new TV landscape. . . . In 1988, when 'youth' became a resonant term for arguments about the future of television, the implication was that everything in broadcasting was changing, that young people were, somehow, the 'different' viewers of the future. To get youth programming right was, therefore, to provide a blueprint for the general transformation of viewing behaviour."[36] Though Frith doesn't mention black culture in his discussion, the notion of British youth culture in this period is closely linked to black images and sounds.

Gilroy believes that this visualization of black music is having deleterious effects: "The longstanding power of a dissident culture based on the manipulation of sound is at risk of being repudiated in the uncritical dash towards an alien regime of signification dominated by images."[37] He concedes that sound will lose its battle with vision: "The protracted competition between sound and vision to define the conceptual co-ordinates and axiological priorities involved in black subculture and its overground offshoots cannot be won by sound."[38]

This suspicion of the image is a recurrent theme in many recent critical writings, which suggest that images fix meaning whereas sound manages to evade such regimes of power and knowledge. For example, Iain Chambers argues that the "surveillance of ocular sense" and a belief in the truth-value of the visual tend to limit the flexibility of the image. In contrast, sound is nomadic. Though the body is still part of the visual economy, it "continually exits from this daily frame through the migrations of sound," and so resists "ocular hegemony."[39] Gilroy also speculates on the visual's implications for the formation of black subjectivities in a racist economy of images. Different technologies organize space and time in particular ways. Visual technologies objectify black bodies, fixing and commodifying images of racial alterity. The visual values the symbolic, whereas sound facilitates the imaginary.[40]

However, this ontological distinction between sound and vision seems problematic, given the ongoing convergence of media and the integration of media industries. One must also be wary of what sometimes border on technologically determinist claims about subject formation produced by sound rather than vision, or about immutable distinctions between the effects and affect of different technologies. Technologies of sound and vision are themselves products of representation. They make sense through discourse. As Steve Wurtzler argues, "the ideological effect of any technology also involves the way that technology and its practice are 'known' by consumers, the way it is itself represented and discursively produced as a science and/or commodity."[41]

Sound (Re)production and Being Digital

In the digital age, production and reception of music are often mediated by the same reproductive technologies. Models of communication that still insist on a clear division between production and reception must be modified in light of these shifts in mediation.

Paul Théberge has examined the implications of the convergence of music production and consumption. He believes that this limits the possibilities for composition. The electronic instrument manufacturing industry regulates the emergence and availability of new sound possibilities through the invention and dissemination of new keyboards, sequencers, and samplers on the market. Musicians' magazines generate this consumer demand. The new instruments define the range and quality of musical sounds. This encourages a standardization and universalization of sound. Since the traditional separation of sound and performance is no longer applicable, the variety of potential musical sounds is diminished. However, Théberge believes that new technologies have led to an intensification of discourse on music's "sound," with musicians developing a language to articulate the kind of music possible with machinery, "a wealth of concepts, slang, and metaphor that describe the qualities of musical sounds and their importance in the musical texture."[42]

Théberge could be describing the typical house, techno, rap, or drum'n'bass tune when he writes: "When confronted with such a work, the listener is immediately struck by a feeling of fluctuating, multiple temporality; a difference in the perceived relationship between past and present; the nature of one's own subject position as a listener; and the apparent dispersal of the unified subject, or persona, of the composer/songwriter embodied in the work itself."[43] Théberge suggests the development of a new kind of listening, one more keenly aware of musical space and the strange new juxtapositions of sound elements possible in this loosening of traditional pop song structure. When music is created by reproductive technologies, the practice of listening to recorded sound also becomes more closely allied to production.

Digital technologies accentuate and develop the analog possibilities explored in Jamaican dub and hip-hop turntable techniques. The increased potential for storage and juxtaposition allows incredibly varied recorded sounds from different times and places to be endlessly manipulated. Andrew Goodwin also suggests that the making of electronic nonmusical sounds into music has highlighted the illusionistic qualities of sound. Samples and never-heard-before sound effects make the listener more aware of the construction of musical space and time, and the synthetic mutations of the studio. Recorded music is unmoored from its supposedly authentic expression in live performance.

Goodwin tempers Théberge's pessimism about the rationalization of the sonic arts, arguing that digital technologies have democratized musical production. Musicians can buy relatively cheap electronic equipment and potentially record material in their bedrooms without traditional musical skills. The difference between the demo and the "proper" studio recording has narrowed. However, Goodwin warns against a techno-utopian assessment of these possibilities. For example, techno music production is dominated by men.[44] Iara Lee's documentary *Modulations* (1998), an overview of the history of electronic music, reminds us that dance music culture is no more female-friendly than rock. The film presents only men in its gallery of interviewees. The only rupture in this boy's-own celebration of techno-musics is a telling shot of the women workers as they assemble Roland machines in an Asian factory.

Neither Goodwin nor Théberge deals specifically with the use of these technologies by black musicians. The question of race/ethnicity in relation to technology is absent. Histories of black music have tended to "naturalize" the black arts. Gilroy notes that in early discourse on jazz, "the mediation of racial creativity by technology was minimised just as the long hours of practice and study that lay behind the stylised simulation of spontaneity were systematically concealed. This music had to be apprehended as an organic feature of black life that could be conjured up without effort. It was to be as resistant to regulation and self-conscious thought as the teeming jungle that supplied its governing trope."[45]

This ideology has been applied to writing about other black music forms in the twentieth century. Tricia Rose argues that rap cannot simply be inserted into a tradition of African-American orality without considering its technological practice: "Rap is a complex fusion of orality and postmodern technology. To suggest that rap follows in a long line from the blues, boasts and dozens of the past is to romanticize its communal and traditional origins and assume that a notion of community is pretechnological."[46]

Practices such as digital sampling imagine community in their affirmation of black musical history. The quotation of instrumental riffs, vocal snatches, and recorded speeches by black figures such as Malcolm X and Martin Luther King Jr. contributes to a collective repository of sounds. This is homage to black heritage and a recontextualization of the past. But as Greg Tate notes, hip-hop's approach to the past is irreverent and iconoclastic, and "the trappings of tradition are never allowed to stand in the way of innovation and improvisation."[47] The science-fiction author Samuel Delaney Jr. also argues that the attitude toward technology, as well as history, is not reverential, since hip-hop is "a specific *miss-use* [sic] and conscientious *desecration* of the artifacts of technology and the entertainment media."[48]

The machinations of hip-hop work belong to a continuum of black "misuses" of technology from the broken bottleneck applied to the blues guitar, and the oil drum bashed and buffed to create the Trinidad steel sound, to the Roland 808 drum machine. The latter instrument failed to reproduce the sound of "real" drums, was dumped by many musicians, and was picked up secondhand by black producers in Chicago who turned its "unmusical" sounds into the basis for house music. The Roland TB-303 Bass Line, released in the mid-1980s, sounded insufficiently like a bass guitar, but black musicians appropriated this failure of "correct" reproduction to create the characteristically burbly, squelchy sound of acid house rhythms. In the 1960s and 70s, many black musicians took to the Moog synthesizer not as a replacement for acoustic instruments, but for its alien sounds, which could still be made funky and soulful. Black musicians have consistently violated the manufacturers' manuals, which rationalize music consumption and production.

The creation of unheard-of electronic sounds has been part of what Kodwo Eshun calls "AfroDiasporic futurism,"[49] one element in a theater of alienation.

The slave ship from Africa carrying an alien nation forcibly to the New World
has been transfigured in a number of musical vehicles; the jazz band leader Sun
Ra describes his big band as an Arkestra from Saturn: the Jamaican producer Lee
Perry named his studio the Black Ark in the 1970s; and at about the same time,
George Clinton brought the P-Funk down to the stage in Parliament-Funkadel-
ic's Mothership. If "space is the place," as Sun Ra preached, then Afrika Bambaataa
and the Soul Sonic Force took up this invocation in their germinal electro track
"Planet Rock" and thus summoned the imagined community of the Zulu Nation in the South Bronx (with the help of sampled rhythms and melodies from
the German electronic group Kraftwerk). The idea of "organic" community meld-
ed to the technological has not been a contradiction in black sound design.[50]

Ian Penman believes that rock ideology, "with its stress on the single white
saviour, on the unifying spokesman, on some sweat-browed *embodiment* of rock's
principia ethica," has failed to consider "the possibility that there has always been
this entirely Other politico-musical discourse, in which there is no separation
between text and texture, human and technology: a music of eerie *dis*embodiment, far more in keeping with the mood of the times."[51] The body merges with
the music through technological means. Kodwo Eshun suggests that digital sound
machines create music of "hyperembodiment." Following Greg Tate, he argues
that the abduction and terror of the Middle Passage and slavery meant that black
culture was dematerialized and so became "immediately mental." Since that historical moment, black culture has had to be rematerialized. Eshun considers black
culture as a series of *techniques*. Digital sound machines are the latest technology
through which this rematerialization takes place.[52]

According to Eshun, these machinic techniques express the synthesized nature
of the African diaspora. Since African slaves were classed as chattel and animals,
the "human" has been a treacherous category for black people.[53] Eshun calls for
the rejection of a humanist conception of black subjectivity and music. He turns
instead to the *materiality* of recordings, arguing that "far from needing theory's
help, music is already more conceptual than at any point in this century, pregnant with thoughtprobes waiting to be activated, switched on, misused."[54] Pro-
fessing to turn away from theories embedded in "CultStud, TechnoTheory and
CyberCulture" or political, historical, and social interpretations of the organization of sound, Eshun analyzes the intricacies of recorded music's sonic textures.
According to him, the sociological imagination has produced reflectionist conceptions of black music: "Everywhere, the 'street' is considered the ground and
guarantee of all reality, a compulsory logic explaining all Black Music, convenient-
ly mishearing anti-social surrealism as social realism."[55]

While I agree with Eshun that analysis of black music is often couched in the limited, literal terms of its documentary quality, its "realness" with reductive notions of authenticity grounded in this realism, I question how can we desert the social, political, and economic context of its production, circulation and consumption. Eshun's book is full of dazzling insights into the construction of some fabulous tracks, and like any good music book it makes you want to go and listen to the music again. But he tends to get a little dizzy with new-age network computer science vocabulary that is itself quite fashionable in the very CultStud, TechnoTheory and CyberCulture he disparages. One can concede that this techno-lingo might be a form of cyborgian poetics, but *More Brilliant than the Sun* questionably presumes a technological determinism in its arguments. I'm also doubtful that musicians are more artificialized by the new digital technologies than they were by previous technologies such as the electric guitar. While digitization may bring changes in the way subjectivities are articulated through music, as I've argued, there are continuities with previous forms of performance and recording. Some of the metaphors used to describe musical practice and texts may have changed, but musicians often continue to speak in quite familiar terms when they describe their technologically mediated diasporic aesthetics.

We can see these continuities in the following discussion of specific black British musicians and their work. This reminds us that any assessment of technology itself must consider discourse *about* technology. In the discourse of these musicians, we can listen to how they conceptualize their soundings and imaginings of diasporic space through digital sound technologies. This takes us back, as Eshun reminds us, to the materiality of music. However, we should also remember the economic and institutional forces that have an impact on these musicians and musical genres in the recording industry. The music is also mediated by the music press, television, and film. And consumers-listeners-fans bring their experiences to the music's interpretation.

System Echo: Massive Attack

Most of Massive Attack and Tricky's music is recycled, cut up, and reprocessed through computers. It has been branded by the press and record labels as "trip-hop," another dance music genre with its own section in the music retail outlet. The categorization has annoyed its practitioners as yet another limited buzzword. Trip-hop has best been described as "hip-hop in a flotation tank," a leisurely and largely instrumental form that takes in the break beats of hip-hop without its verbal calisthenics. It also incorporates the spatial and psychedelic distortion of dub reggae. Trip-hop's tempo makes it dance music removed from the dance floor, music for home listening, accompaniment for marijuana smokers, or background music for cappuccino drinkers in the hip urban café. The genre has been placed in an African tradition of sounding: "[Trip-hop] acts as if there are no limits to what musical sources can be used to create your mixes. In the process, it inherits the spirit of the first time mixologists—the Jamaican dubmasters, who with the notion of 'the version' created a place for modern music to pass from passively received consumer product (rock) back to the West African notion of sound as a continuous, communal mix where everyone can fuck with the mix."[56] The techniques of the Kingston dubmasters have been translated by their descendants in black Britain. Massive Attack began essentially as a sound system consisting of a number of friends who played records at the Dug Out, a club in the Clifton area of Bristol. The group's bestselling recordings are composed largely from computer floppy discs with their riff banks. However, their brand of machine music still emerges in a specific location, the western English port city of Bristol.

According to Phil Johnson in *Straight outa Bristol,* the city's burst of musical creativity in the 1980s resulted from the fallout of the April 1980 uprising. After a club in the St. Paul's area was raided for drugs, residents fought the police for several days. In the wake of this event and international media attention, the authorities toned down the police presence in the area. This created a space where clubs could operate without quite the same level of surveillance. The Dug Out's location attracted students and would-be bohemian types from Clifton, residents of the white working-class tower blocks in Barton Hill, and young African-Caribbeans from St. Paul's. Bristol has one of the oldest Caribbean communities in Britain. It is a city built on the profits of slavery; as one major node in the African diaspora, it is what George Lipsitz refers to as a "dangerous crossroads."[57]

The biographies of Massive Attack's three core members reveal a rich history of migrations and settlement. Grant "Daddy G" Marshall is the son of settlers from Barbados. Andrew "Mushroom" Vowles has a Dominican father and an English mother, was born in New York, and moved to England when he was three years old. Robert "3-D" Del Naja is the son of a Neapolitan father and an English mother.

In 1982, Daddy G and his friend Nellee Hooper went to their first rap show in Bristol. The New York rap star Kurtis Blow rhymed while DJ Davy D cut and scratched the beats. Charlie Ahearn's *Wild Style* (1982), a film influential in the transnational dispersal of New York hip-hop culture's DJ-ing, rapping, breakdancing and graffiti styles, was screened in Bristol. The Bristolians avariciously collected imported twelve-inch rap singles. Inspired by these recordings, they assembled a posse of like-minded people and dubbed themselves the Wild Bunch crew.

This included 3-D, who had developed into one of the most well-known graffiti artists or taggers in Bristol. On weekends Daddy G, Hooper, and their friend Miles Johnson, often supported by the younger Mushroom and 3-D, would play the Dug Out as well as private parties, mixing soul, funk, rap, dub, and reggae. The Wild Bunch acquired a city-wide reputation for playing the sharpest blend of tunes.

Through contacts at the style magazine *The Face* and the help of another friend, Neneh Cherry, a successful solo recording artist who had sung with the Bristol-based free-jazz-funk group Rip, Rig, and Panic, the Wild Bunch received some industry attention. The sound system toured Japan in 1987. Del Naja came back early and was kicked out of the group. Johnson and Hooper independently signed a deal with Island and released a couple of singles as the Wild Bunch, including a hip-hop-influenced version of Bacharach and David's 1960s chestnut "The Look of Love." The record was a commercial failure; Johnson and Hooper fell out, and the Wild Bunch was disbanded. Johnson returned to Japan, then settled in New York City, while Hooper, who had moved to London, formed Soul II Soul with Jazzie B. Back in Bristol, Del Naja, Marshall, and Vowles formed Massive Attack, which was conceived as a Soul II Soul collective that would be produced by Hooper as an offshoot from his work with the London group. Massive Attack negotiated a management deal and then signed to Virgin.[58]

Many of the group's recordings highlight the translation of the rap format from the United States to Britain. This is not just a matter of appropriation but the formation of a recognizably different genre through local mutation. Though hip-hop culture has been popular in Britain, the local vernacular and subject matter of New York rap have not always seemed applicable to the U.K. situation. The politics of race, neighborhoods, and the mediascape are clearly quite different in British cities. Within rap-inspired British music, there has been a struggle to draw on, yet not mimic, the American accent of beats and rhyming styles. Back in the 1980s, as William Shaw notes, "no one was sure what British people should rap about."[59]

Massive Attack's distinctive rapping style emerged from the particular environment of music consumption in Bristol. If the style of U.S. rappers comes largely out of clubs in which a rapper has to be assertive and aggressively loud, often bragging about his or her prowess in freestyle rhyming competitions, in contrast, Massive Attack's intimate whispers and mumbling seem less public, more domestic, sometimes even private, in the case of 3-D's musings. In Channel Four's 1994 documentary *New Soul Nation*, 3-D explained that the group's low-key rapping style (which often sounds like a conversation over a pint of cider and a joint) came from the run-of-the-mill activity of sitting around and chatting while music played in the background at home or at the Dug Out, which was more of a hangout than a discotheque. The almost conspiratorial, secretive aspect of Massive Attack's rapping is exaggerated in its recordings, which often seem hermetically sealed in the studio's sonic "womb."[60]

"Five Man Army," from the group's debut album, *Blue Lines* (1991), exemplifies these vocal phonetics and illustrates how sampling can construct a diasporic perspective from the specificities of British life. The six-minute track slows down the bass line from a 1970s Rastafarian track of the same name by some of Jamaica's premier DJs, singers, and players of instruments. The bass line has been replayed on a guitar in the studio rather than directly sampled from the original. However, an almost subliminal vocal and harmonica from the original is sampled as a repeated echo in the depths of the mix. Horace Andy, a veteran reggae vocalist, guests on the recording. He sings fragments from his well-known early 1970s hits "Skylarking" and "Money Is the Root of All Evil." Andy's voice takes precedence in the second half of the track like a "version" of Massive Attack's languid raps at the beginning of the track. His contributions are not samples but re-recorded moments added to the track. Even though this is "real singing," the recording incorporates the logic of the sample and the loop; Andy sings only vocal riffs from these songs; both are dread missives of warning to the youth. Despite the playfulness of some of the group's rhymes, Andy's singing and the heavy bass line give the track a gravity. The recording becomes a kind of vessel, as described by Théberge, in which scattered moments of music history from Jamaica come together in new form in Britain.

"Five Man Army" is modeled after the rap and reggae technique in which MCs and DJs step up to the microphone on stage and in the studio to distinguish themselves from the rest of the pack. Such a message functions as a kind of hallmark, designed to stamp the performer's persona, presence, and unique skills in the listener's mind. Following the slow shuffle of a break beat and the introduction of the catchy bass line, "Five Man Army" opens with Daddy G rhyming in an English accent. He describes an encounter with a young woman and the need to maintain the secrecy of what may be an illegal warehouse party or a pirate radio station's location. He compares his rhyming skills to those of a West Indies fast bowler in cricket.

Part-time member Tricky loquaciously announces his presence as Tricky Kid, like a legend in the neighborhood. Daddy G returns, this time rhyming in Caribbean Patois when describing the group's tour to Japan with their Technics turntables and mixing deck.

The oral signature of 3-D includes his fascination with Subbuteo table soccer and the Jamaican Studio One label. He also mentions his prestigious Sony Budokan Walkman.

After a couple more indecipherable rhymes from him, Daddy G interjects with a message of racial unity to the listener in his "English" accent.

Then, 3-D interrupts with a statement that these unity sounds come through your wireless, invented by fellow Italian Marconi, and then through the mediation of Sony. Massive Attack's sounds might be coming through these technologies but they're exclusive, or "exclusione," as he says in fake Italian.

Mushroom is responsible for the combination of bass line, sampled snare drums, and electronic loops. This track invokes the original song through a replaying of the structurally vital bass line and a sampled loop from the original recording. Through sampling technology, we can hear the grain of the original recording of "Five Man Army."

The Massive Attack *version* transforms a Rasta hymn into a very local document on things English. The rhyming owes something to both Jamaican toasting and American rapping, but at times also takes on the cadences of English accents. Playful raps about growing up with table soccer, Jamaican records, advertising slogans for razor blades, West Indian cricket, the rhythms of spoken English, Patois, and Italian are elements of a hybridized language. This cut-and-paste soundscape invokes Jamaica and a history of black orality, as well as consumer culture in the U.K.

The fetishization of sonic gadgetry by 3-D seems appropriate in a "song" that sounds like it could have been created only in a studio. Mushroom describes the process of construction as "piecing it together like a jigsaw, with loads of bits missing, which is what gives it the space. . . . Five man army is a total system echo, it's like here's the instrumental, here's the bass line, everyone take it in turns, which was very freestyle."[61]

The promo videos for the group's first three singles, "Daydreaming," "Safe from Harm," and "Unfinished Sympathy," all directed by Baillee Walsh, also foreground the group's associations with the Caribbean and America. All three tracks feature Shara Nelson on vocals. Shot in black and white, "Daydreaming" appears to be set in a Caribbean location. We hear the sounds of crickets, then fade in to a closeup of a lizard. The camera tilts up to reveal a shack, then tracks in through the window into a dark room where the members of Massive sit at a large dining table or lounge in a sofa. The scene reinforces this music as one of domestic interiors. Set apart from the men, Nelson stares out of a window at the sky as she sings the yearning recurring motif of the song. The men seem content just chilling, amused to pass the time puttering about the place, offering their raps in an almost disinterested fashion. The rhymes quote from *Fiddler on the Roof* ("If I Were a Rich Man"), Bob Marley/the Specials ("Concrete Jungle"), and the Beatles ("Here Comes the Sun"). This is rapping as conversing in free association, unconcerned if anyone is listening. The men's daydreams are wisps of pop culture citation, like bits of "trainspotting," while Nelson's daydreaming coheres into song.

In contrast to these Caribbean climes, the architecture of decrepit state housing in the U.K. is the setting for Walsh's video for "Safe from Harm." The location resembles a block of flats in Camberwell, London. The promo echoes the beginning of the tropical "Daydreaming" video; instead of focusing on a lizard and shack, it opens with a closeup of a dead pigeon. The camera tilts up to reveal the forbidding gray exterior of the tower block at night. The howling wind at the beginning of the track adds to the sense of foreboding. The bubbling bass line, looped from an early 70s track by the jazz-funk musician Bob James, kicks the music forward as the camera follows Shara Nelson into the building. She wears a winter coat and carries a bag of groceries. Mushroom, 3-D, and Daddy G lurk around the elevators, hassling Nelson with their overbearing in-your-face presence. One elevator is kaput. The men block her entry into the other one, so Nelson is forced to take the stairs. A steadicam precedes her as she walks laboriously up several flights, singing about the many dangers she faces in the city from "midnight rockers, city slickers and gunmen." She insists that she will protect her child at all costs. Nelson's long ascent is intercut with claustrophobic shots of the elevator's interior as it climbs through the hollow core of the building with 3-D inside it. His paranoid whispers interrupt Nelson's singing with words that suggest that everyone is watching everybody else, primed for anything dangerous that might disrupt the uneasy status quo. His words suggest the layers of looking and surveillance in the building. He has been watching Nelson, she has anxiously returned his look, but the closed-circuit cameras are watching them both. In the murky corridors of the building, a kid appears at the door of a flat donning the mask of Freddy from *Nightmare on Elm Street*. A man's gaunt bug-eyed features take form from the darkness around a corner. The music and video evoke the atomized lives in some of these inner-city tower blocks.

The color video for "Unfinished Sympathy" is set in Los Angeles. Walsh's video both quotes and transforms some of the conventions through which the urban neighborhood is represented in rap videos. Promotional video images have often shown the city block and the sociality of the (mainly male) posse or crew as a tactic to reclaim urban space from its official surveillance and policing. Rap recordings, record sleeve design, and videos often feature aural and visual references to specific locales and street signs that mark communities. Representing

the place where musicians come from also fights the demonizing discursive regime of the television network's nightly news and the press, which repeatedly
describe the "ghettoes" as no-go areas rife with drugs, gang-banging, poverty, and
violence.[62]

Walsh's video is shot in a multicultural neighborhood. "Unfinished Sympathy"
doesn't feature any rhyming, only Shara Nelson's lovelorn lyrics. It's a song about
a failed yet unfinished affair, sung over a driving beat and a lush string/orches-
tral break reminiscent of Soul II Soul's early recordings. The video consists largely
of a single tracking shot of almost five minutes, beginning with a closeup of two
metal balls (signifying testicles?) rolled and clinked together in the palms of a dead-
hard-looking Latino body builder in shades. The music begins. The camera moves
down his body to the ground where a puggish, vicious-looking dog wearing sun-
glasses strains at the leash. The camera swoops up on a crane into a long shot of
the man and a group of young men in shades, bandanas, t-shirts, and jeans; then
it moves away from them, up and over telephone wires and down to another part
of the street where a young black boy rat-a-tats away at the camera with a toy
machine gun as we hear the *zigazigazig* scratch of hip-hop turntablism on the
track. This visual pastiche of gangsta style is soon left behind as the camera moves
up the street. Shara Nelson in a simple black dress walks along the sidewalk, and
the orchestral string arrangement becomes more prominent. The camera remains
a few steps ahead of her just as in the "Safe from Harm" video. She sings/lipsynchs
the lyrics, while walking, oblivious to her environment, lost in the soulful melancholy of the song. Daddy G and 3-D appear at different points along her stroll,
walking some feet behind her, silent and relatively unobtrusive. Daddy G push-
es a shopping cart as 3-D gets off a pay phone and follows the same route. They
remain in the background, never in closeup. The viewer's attention focuses on
Nelson, then shifts to the "ambient" features of this urban landscape. A disabled
white man rolls across the sidewalk on a large skateboard. We pass white bikers,
Latinas walking out of a hairdresser's to observe the filming, and two black teenage girls having a food fight with vegetables outside a grocery store. They all look
at the camera as it slowly glides past them.

The remarkable feature of the video is its documentary quality; after its opening moments it's quite hard to tell which parts of the video occur "naturally"
during the shoot and which have been recreated. The images of the man rolling
the ball bearings in his hand and the little boy with the machine gun seem staged,
possibly as an ironic commentary on the glorification of machismo and violence
in many rap videos of the period.

Though they enact a spatial resistance, rap videos still show the neighborhood
primarily as a place of masculine activity. East Coast rap videos feature posses

on foot in their milieu. West Coast hip-hop images tend to foreground young men cruising through the neighborhood in their cars. For example, both Ice Cube's "It Was a Good Day" and Dre Dre's "Nothing but a G Thang" from this period show the rappers in their customized low-rider convertibles with shiny wheels, gliding through neighborhoods to chilled-out "G-Funk" beats and electronic keyboards. In contrast, the video for "Unfinished Sympathy" shows a woman at the center of the narrative as she cuts a physical and sonic path through the neighborhood.

I do not claim that heterosexism is absent from black British music, but racial authenticity centered on a patriarchal masculinity is not as strong a current in U.K. sounds as in U.S. rap. Gilroy's comments about the black body's sexualization in 90s R&B and hip-hop apply to the way female performers like Mariah Carey and Janet Jackson have increasingly represented themselves. These tendencies have been resisted by black British women performers like Nelson and the Nigerian-born Nicolette, with whom Massive Attack has also worked.

Massive Attack does not represent an ideal situation for male and female performers to work together. The three core members define the sound, with guest vocals from female singers. And Nelson did leave to pursue a solo career. But the sound system ethos has offered a relatively flexible structure. Horace Andy has come into the setup to record some of his old Jamaican tunes in a new arena; and women have written and sung on the group's albums. Apart from Shara Nelson and Nicolette, the group has worked with Tracey Thorn of Everything But the Girl and Elizabeth Fraser of the Cocteau Twins. This has displaced the centrality of the men, as well as bringing creative input from other sources into the orbit of the group's sound. After four albums in a recording career that spans most of the 90s, the group has established a recognizable Massive Attack sound, but this sound has still been open to other voices.

The sound system offers an alternative model of musical organization and practice from the traditional rock group. Its method is more directly adapted and commodified in the album *No Protection,* a dub album of the tracks on *Protection,* remixed by the Mad Professor, the producer responsible for the Ariwa reggae label in Peckham, South London. *No Protection* is billed as by Massive Attack vs. Mad Professor, in homage to the reggae sound system competition or sound clash. The painting on the record sleeve shows a threatening Mad Professor and multicolored ninjas and creatures firing laser shots at the shocked members of Massive Attack against a high-tech Japanese anime city skyline. The image updates the legendary comic book images on Jamaican dub albums from the late 70s and early 80s, such as *Scientist vs. Prince Jammy in Heavyweight Dub Competition* and *Scientist Wins the World Cup.* In mid-70s Kingston, King Tubby remixed the analog studio recordings of Augustus Pablo's Rockers sound system to create the famous dub album "King Tubby Meets the Rockers Uptown," and twenty years later the Mad Professor was essentially applying the same concept to Massive Attack's recordings, using digital technology. Many critics lauded his dub version of *Protection* as superior to Massive Attack's original.

In the contemporary music industry, sound-system practice has been adapted to studio production and the requirements of disc product for the market. However, some of the industry's institutionalized practices remain quite durable. After the release of an album, an artist still usually goes on the road to promote the new release. This presents the sound-system-styled group with a problem since it doesn't offer the traditional concert spectacle. Mushroom explains: "The last time we went out live on the East Coast of America, it was a big mistake. . . . We just jammed on the mic like an old-fashioned sound system but they put us up on a bright stage right after a ten-piece jazz band and the whole atmosphere was wrong. This time we're going to create an environment where the raw sound attitude works. We'd rather just rock a crowd with sound, maybe have a few visuals and the singers and DJs stepping up to the mic, Jamaican-style, with one red light above the decks."[63] The American tour was a failure because "no one understood the sound system thing there."[64]

The group faces the dilemma of many artists in dance floor and sound system culture who have to adjust their performance style according to the dictates of the concert hall. In 1994, 3-D told *The Face*: "Because we're not a pop group who get up on stage and play, we've got to create suitable environments for people to come and interact with the music. . . . We've got this whole installation/exhibition/animation project underway using computer graphics and virtual reality. The thing is, people are baffled by it 'cause they've seen *The Lawnmower Man* and they think that's it—you blast off into cyberspace, go mental, have a wank and everything's happening."[65]

Many fundamentally digital musicians share 3-D's desire to create a complete audiovisual experience that goes beyond the basics of the sound system yet avoids the clichés of the rock concert. Music made by machines and aimed for the club dance floor does not offer the display of musical virtuosity seen at rock shows. The new musicians have overcome this with a variety of strategies for live performance. As I noted earlier, the Pet Shop Boys consigned most of their computers and drum machines backstage and presented a show influenced by theater, opera, and West End musicals. Their program booklet made their machines the stars of *Performance* as much as the duo itself; a huge photograph of all the sequencers, samplers, and other computers used in the show constituted the program's center spread. The Prodigy, which began as a faceless techno outfit led by

Liam Howlett, increasingly emphasized the punky image of the spiky-green-haired vocalist Keith (a Johnny Rotten for the digital generation) to personify the aggressive techno sound of their 1997 album *The Fat of the Land.* The DJ/production duo Coldcut produces computer-generated imagery for projection with its sounds, along the lines suggested by 3-D.

The complaints just a few years ago about the use of "performance-enhancing" technology at live concerts have been brushed aside as acts from Whitney Houston and Madonna to more obscure drum'n'bass DJs combine computer-programmed sound reproduction with on-the-spot "live" performance. Sooner or later, most studio-bound musicians tread the boards of the live stage in some form or other. Even the star DJ who merely appears over the turntable, spinning records, fiddling with mixer levels, and twiddling some knobs is now supported by lasers and lighting effects to boost the visual spectacle. Live musicians and singers with a more traditional address to a big concert crowd remain important for the internationally successful "name" act.

By the time Massive Attack toured in 1998 with its heavily promoted fourth album, *Mezzanine,* it was playing large venues, looking and sounding more like an old-fashioned pop group. A band was put together to reproduce the studio sound. The show combined turntables and computers with live guitars and voices. In fact, like many electronic musicians, Massive Attack now uses a combination of machines and nondigital instrumentation in the studio. Even though the "feel" of *Mezzanine*'s sound, with its echo, reverb, and sub-bass frequencies, nakedly flaunts its design as music made for "living in your headphones" (as 3-D once rapped in "Daydreaming"), and the videos stress Massive Attack as a music of *interiors,* this sound can now be simulated in big stadium concerts.

In a similar vein, Tricky, whose debut album after he left Massive Attack was sculpted with samplers, sequencers, and programmed voices at the studio console, found out that once the music was a hit, it needed to be taken on the road:

> I never ever thought we'd do *Maxinquaye* live. As far as I was concerned, it was a studio album, and it never even occurred to me. Then one of my managers suggested doing a live show. I wasn't not into it, but I wasn't into it; I never thought of doing it. So I went down to a rehearsal, and these guys played "Overcome," and they fucking rocked my album. I couldn't believe it. I could not imagine how that could be played live, and there they were, playing it live. And it still had the emotion. So we had a live gig; it was just lucky. . . . Now all these producers have live bands. All these well-known producers and posses. . . . Man, even Massive Attack have a live band now. Now I've got a keyboard with sounds and all my samples in it, and I can freak out. I can smash things up and make shit up when I get bored in the middle of "Overcome," which I've played a million times. I'll say, "Give me a drum beat," and grab

a mic and talk about any old shit, 'cause I'm doing it for me as well. But in the beginning I was shy and scared.[66]

Here the engineer-programmer-musician discovers with pleasant surprise that his music can also be played by musicians on stage. Like Massive Attack, Tricky has moved on to record with a more conventional band in the studio. Digital electronics have been integrated into a familiar discourse on musicianship and live performance.

On the 1996 album *Pre-Millennium Tension,* the processing of samplers and sequencers is supplemented with bass guitar, guitars, and real drums. Even electronic musicians feel the need to justify the fact that they are making "real music." Music made with the new technologies must be humanized. The official website for Tricky's album explains:

> Musically, all eleven cuts are imbued with a raw organic and passionate quality often missed in technologically based music. Instead of gluing together found sounds and loops, Tricky came up with his own on his shoe-box sized [Yamaha] QY20 sequencer. Like a road paved with hundreds of different oddly sized bricks that somehow interlock, these homespun bits and pieces were then sampled and pasted together. . . . "That's why a lot of it speeds up and slows down, 'cuz I'm playing little melodies, riffs, drum patterns, strings straight from the sequencer. It's live music." He's emphatic: "when people say I don't write music, I say that's exactly what I do." . . . Obscured, "low-fi" vocals were often cut at the production console instead of in the recording booth "because when I get a vibe, I can't wait 20 minutes for someone to set up a mic and move all that shit in there."[67]

The goal posts of authenticity have been moved; Tricky is a spontaneous musician because he's recording at the console whenever he gets the right vibe. Tricky proves the case that while he might produce, as Ian Penman suggests, a studio music of "eerie *dis*embodiment," his musicianship and authorial presence are marked in a number of fairly conventional ways.[68]

The music industry is still hooked on the cult of personality to sell its products and so Tricky has had to negotiate the way he presents his persona and the way it has been marketed by the record companies and by the media that contribute to popular music discourse. His career also illustrates the ongoing diasporic dialogue between black British and African-American musicians.

Red Zones inside My Headphones: Tricky

Tricky is the tag of both Adrian Thaws and his group. Thaws grew up in Bristol. His half-African, half-Welsh mother committed suicide when he was four. The

1995 album *Maxinquaye* is named for her. His Jamaican father had abandoned them earlier. Thaws was brought up by his grandmother in the "white ghetto" of Knowle West, and then by his aunt and uncle in suburban Arncliffe, where he spent most of his time in his bedroom writing raps. He suffered from asthma and eczema. He was repeatedly in trouble with the law as a teenager, once caught stealing from a game machine at the YMCA; as a seventeen-year-old, he spent four days in prison for passing forged fifty-pound banknotes. His asthma inhaler was confiscated by the police and he was attacked in his cell. When he rang the alarm button, gasping for air, no one answered, and he almost died. On the tracks "Vent" and "Anti-histamine," he has sung about how hard it is to breathe. The throatiness of some of his vocals exaggerates this disability.

On Massive Attack's "Blue Lines," Tricky's most interesting contribution was the lines about his "English upbringing, background Caribbean." In a number of interviews he has drawn attention to this bifocality or what poststructuralists might call "multiple subject positions": "I would hang around with a posse of pure black guys, and then with a posse of beer guys, all white; you've got to play both sides of the game, to have a few personalities so you can talk and chill with anybody. Both of them are still in me: the white guy making black music and the black guy making white music—it was all integrated from way back."[69] But Tricky also told another interviewer that these multiple personalities did not easily exist beside each other: "I grew up with a half-white family, so I was hanging around with black kids one night and white kids the other night. None of them really liked each other, so I wondered where I was supposed to be. Then I saw the Specials on TV. Here was a band with black and white kids, and it was obvious: I'd be a chameleon and do both. I've seen both lives. I've hung out with white kids drinking beer, I've hung out with black kids smoking weed. I've lived both lives, and they're both as stupid as the other, and it's because they both don't know anything about each other."[70]

In feeling popular music and understanding it as listeners and fans, we are hailed by the song and the recording. This forms part of that magic, the ineffable, the sublime that modernists and postmodernists alike believe is the most important thing about an encounter with the aesthetic. We give ourselves up to the music. However, we may be drawn in by an accumulation of other effects too. As a fan of Tricky's music, I also situate his voice, identify where he's coming from, interpret intent, based on the recording, but also the star-image circulating in the media. Some fans seek correspondences. Though I'm not a mixed-race Britisher, as a Pakistani-English who occupied both brown and white worlds, often quite distinct from each other, I find Tricky's double vision familiar. This colors my reading of the work. I can imagine Tricky walking home from school to his grandmother's house, alone in his thoughts, somewhat out of place, and dreaming of music. I can feel the breath-quickening anticipation as he makes his way to the local record store to buy a record that makes perfect sense of his situation and keeps the blues at bay. Like Tricky, I remember "going to town on the bus the day the Specials' first album came out, buying it, staring at the black-and-white sleeve the whole way home, then listening to it over and over again for hours, thinking, this is it, this is a record about my life."[71]

This interpretation of Tricky's music is necessarily imperfect and incomplete, a deformation of his history as it comes into dialogue with my experience. Reading and compiling biographical details gives shape to hunches about *Maxinquaye*'s elliptical meanings, puts the sounds into relief. Even though the album is a digital construction in which Tricky's voice melts into the intricately woven samples, clicks, riffs, and distortions, Tricky and his fellow vocalist, Martina Toppley-Bird, seem to sound a piece of black Britain.

Antihumanist approaches to the construction of self can still contain a notion of the self and identity as a necessary discourse in making sense of popular music. Subjectivity for those of us who have grown up in audiovisual, media-saturated environments often seems like one vast compilation album or ongoing DJ mix of samples, many of which originate in pop music, film, and television. Minds may have been technologized, but the desire for the authenticity of authorship on the part of musician and listener remains strong, even when the music is machine made.

The *Bladerunner* sample on the track "Aftermath" indicates that we may all be programmed beings, our memories and selves subject to determining forces beyond our control, yet internalized in consciousness. "Let me tell you about my mother," the replicant says as he is interrogated. What distinguishes the false memory from the real one? Tricky uses the sample as a memory machine to invoke his dead mother. "Aftermath" places Martina's childlike sing-song voice beside Tricky's hoarse mumblings and Mark Stewart's groaning quotation of 70s teenybop success David Cassidy's "How Can I Be Sure in a World That's Constantly Changing?" A slowed-down hip-hop snare drum pattern and dub bass line promise to take the listener nowhere except the black hole of its ceaseless grinding repetition.

A dread apocalyptic tone suffuses *Maxinquaye*'s bytes of hip-hop, dub, funk, soul, gamelan. Tricky grunts, mumbles, slurs sentences and gnostic phrases, slipping in between the categorizations of musical voice: "It's not rap, it's not poetry. I don't know what it is, it's more like talking, communicating. I always use the first stuff I put down in the studio and leave in all the mistakes."[72]

The darkness of Tricky's vision is palpable in the static of "Hell Is Round the

Corner," a haunting collection of crisis-laden and cryptic epigrams croaked over a scratchy, slowed-down string loop from one of Isaac Hayes's languid orchestral soul tracks, "Ike's Rap II." Precisely the same brooding groove on which Hayes apologizes for the way he's mistreated and abused his lover was used by the Bristolians Portishead on "Glory Box," a track from the group's cinematic trip-hop album *Dummy* (1994). Tricky splutters vocal shrapnel as he compares his brain to a bomb. His request to be dressed in Stussy seems as much an ironic comment on the way black men are *fashioned* and commodified as it does a desire to wear snazzy designer gear. Tricky refers to "isms and schisms," the Rasta denunciation of ideologies and discourses that perpetuate Babylon system. "Imperial passages" and drums that sounded out a kill hint at African colonial memory and the violence of the landscape. Other phrases suggest places nearer home; Tricky seems to need a reference to get residence, to prove that he's a decent neighbor. This suggests the stark alienation of Tricky's youth and the spatial/territorial politics of British racism. On "Hell Is Round the Corner," when Tricky grows, he grows collectively.

The commercial and critical success of *Maxinquaye* provided impetus for the cultivation of Tricky's "personality" in the pop media. Magazines have often photographed him in a black-and-white smoky haze, marijuana joint in hand. He is open about his marijuana use, leading to a reputation as a paranoid young man prone to the odd verbal and physical scrape with his fellow celebrities. The press's construction of Tricky again testifies to the power of romantic ideology in the creation of popular music stars. The negotiation with fame and his public image have forced Tricky to live up to and beyond his name. He takes on the role of trickster, donning masks to work through the projections of his self in all their various packages. "Tricky Kid," his own signature tune from *Pre-Millennium Tension,* voices his slipping identities and the demands of the industry, as he invites us to look at his "mongrel eyes."

Tricky's work has consistently examined rap music as a technology of self. He has absorbed the tropes of U.S. rap while critiquing some of its masculinist tendencies; instead of braggadocio, Tricky projects masculine angst. To Americocentric critics who see him as racially inauthentic and not true to the rap (genre) game, he counters with a diss missive, the noisy assault of "Brand New, You're Retro." The critics' melanin myopia is denounced with a dare to check his chromosomes, a rejoinder to the racialized reduction of blackness to the epidermis, which Gilroy identifies as a current in the contemporary black public sphere.

The group Tricky's gender-bending confounds expectations of the typical rap act. Photographs on CD and record sleeves present Martina in an oversized suit and top hat, Tricky in a white dress with lipstick smeared over his mouth. It's difficult to imagine many American rappers performing this kind of drag. As one critic notes: "This isn't the gangster posturing of South Central Los Angeles, but something much more ambiguous."[73] While Tricky indulges in a fair amount of boasting on recordings, he also consistently undermines his claims to power and omnipotence, the dead end of rap's competition. Again and again, he tells us he has nothing much to offer in intense emotional and sexual relationships.

The group Tricky gender-switches in many of its rap covers. In the punked-up versioning of Public Enemy's angry prison narrative "Black Steel," Martina takes Chuck D's perspective as a black man wanted by the government for military service. Martina also chats up Eric B and Rakim's boastful rap, "Lyrics of Fury," in homage to Rakim's abstract rhyming skills. She also covers two old skool classics, "The Moment I Feared" and "Children's Story," by Slick Rick, a displaced English rapper known for his urban fables. Martina's bland telling of "Children's Story" amplifies the dread of a bedtime tale about a kiddie who goes on a shooting spree and is finally shot and killed by the police.

Tricky consistently mines hip-hop's fictional and real territories of violence. *Angels with Dirty Faces* (1998) examines the public discourse on blackness, particularly black masculinity in the context of the O. J. Simpson case and the murders of the rappers Tupac Shakur and Biggie Smalls AKA the Notorious B.I.G. "Broken Homes," a duet with PJ Harvey and a gospel chorus, comments on how black violence becomes magnified in the United States when the media and a murderer sit side by side in court. The album's final track, "Record Companies," alludes to the East Coast–West Coast rap rivalry, gang gun culture, and business profits from the deaths of rap stars.

Like many stars, Tricky's own stardom has become a subject for his songwriting. In "Tear Out My Eyes," he wants to blow his head off like Kurt Cobain. In "Demise," Tricky compares the media's characterization of himself and Martina to their focus on black pop's most famous dysfunctional couple, Ike and Tina Turner. Tricky professes that he cannot and will not live up to the macho gangster archetype. In "Analyze Me," Tricky continues to write aggressively about the media's construction of him with a dare. On his 1999 album *Juxtapose*, the opening track and single "For Real" has Tricky meditating on the extent of his "realness," doubting it because he watches too many films.

For those who might dismiss all these songs about being watched and defined by the media as only pop narcissism, the "fact of blackness" makes the commodification of the performer's self a vexed issue. Tricky explores this problem through an ongoing dialogue with U.S. rap.

Fade to Black: Barry Adamson

The screening of the black subject caught in the racist gaze is also theatricalized in the work of Barry Adamson. As Michael Bracewell writes in his sleeve notes for the album *As Above So Below* (1998), "Adamson's artistic project is fixated on the casting of his various selves into a single role of multiple identity."

Adamson began his music career as bass player with the Manchester punk-era group Magazine in the late 1970s. He went on to play bass with the Birthday Party and then with Nick Cave's other group, the Bad Seeds. In the late 1980s he took to solo recording, cutting a funked-up version of Elmer Bernstein's brassy, raunchy theme tune for Otto Preminger's film *The Man with the Golden Arm,* which starred Frank Sinatra as a junkie. He also recorded a version of the television theme for *Alfred Hitchcock Presents.* He has since composed a number of soundtrack albums for movies that don't exist on celluloid, as well as the odd real feature film. Adamson has used the genre narratives and music of thrillers and films noir to work through his black British identity. Since Gilroy is worried about how black music is threatened by its increasing visuality, Adamson is an arresting case for interrogation.

The inner and outer sleeves of the 1988 album *Moss Side Story* suggest a seedy thriller set in the Manchester neighborhood. The gloomy black-and-white photographs of this inner-city landscape show the exterior of an undertaker's place, and a streetcorner building with flyers promising live appearances by Burning Spear, Sugar Minott, and other reggae stars. This is a black Manchester Morrissey doesn't represent.

Another photograph seems to come from the mythic stock of cinematic clichés found in the gangster film. The hood of a Mercedes stretches out before the camera, which looks down a typical working-class street of row houses in (presumably) Moss Side. The classic black outline of a factory throws out smoke into the dark sky. The image has all the hallmarks of the working-class prodigal returning to his old haunts once he's made it good. It's reminiscent of the scene in the 1979 gangster film *The Long Good Friday,* in which a Cockney gangster played by Bob Hoskins drives down the street where he grew up, moaning about how it's now "full of coons."

On the front cover of *Moss Side Story,* a tense Adamson stands in a dark suit with an umbrella, in attendance at a friend or associate's cinematic funeral. The caption reads, "In a black and white world, murder brings a touch of colour."

The predominantly instrumental music on the album sounds like the jagged, prickly soundtrack of a 1970s thriller in the vein of *Get Carter.* Adamson plays bass and computer programs and writes all the music but has the support of strings and brass, drums, and percussion. In this imaginative mapping of a black Moss Side, the air is thick with tension, its activities monitored by the police. The *Casablanca*-inspired title "The Usual Suspects" samples a police officer from a news broadcast bemoaning the influx of Jamaican "yardies," apparently responsible for the rise of crack cocaine and drug crime in Manchester: "We see it in the nature of a cancerous growth," the copper tells the reporter.

The Taming of the Shrewd EP (1989) features two parts. Part 1, billed as "Samplers against Apartheid," contains "Diamonds," a track with a twangy electric guitar that sounds like Ennio Morricone's spaghetti-western music crossed with Duane Eddy's theme to *Peter Gunn*. Part 2, "Half Cast in the Movie of Life," features jazzy number "Splat the Cat" with a 1960s John Barry pastiche called "From Rusholme with Love."

The flash, brassy erotics of the thriller genre are expanded on another EP, *The Negro inside Me*. Adamson covers the Serge Gainsbourg and Jane Birkin breathy orgasmic 1970 hit "Je t'aime . . . moi, ne plus" with more emphasis on the drum beat. "Busted" sounds like a Lalo Schifrin theme for any of a half dozen U.S. television cop shows. Flashes of Blaxploitation wah-wah pedal pepper the track.

Over the course of his career, Adamson increasingly has identified himself as the central protagonist in these make-believe film soundtracks, developing a persona to investigate some of the troubling ironies of racial identity in Britain. *Soul Murder* (1992), nominated for a Mercury Prize, contains orchestrations that break down into scenes, romantic interludes, thriller suspense, and action sequences. The track "007—A Fantasy Bond theme" interrupts a pastiche of John Barry's famous brassy opening riff with a Jamaican-accented male voice telling the story of a kid who dreamt of being the special agent. He says that "Bond was black" before a bouncy skittering ska version of the tune by the Jamaican group the Skatalites is superimposed over a more familiar rendition of Barry's theme. Adamson's *versioning*, as Mark Sinker suggests, "relocates Bond to the culture his creator Ian Fleming lived in and never noticed, the Caribbean."[74]

The complexities and fragmentation of black subjectivity in Adamson's work ironically echo Frantz Fanon's angst in *Black Skin, White Masks* when he encounters the French child's frightened utterance, "Look, a Negro!": "Then, assailed at various points, the corporeal schema crumbled, its place taken by a racial epidermal schema. In the train it was no longer a question of being aware of my body in the third person but in a triple person. In the train I was given not one but two, three places. I had already stopped being amused. It was not that I was finding febrile coordinates in the world. I existed triply: I occupied space. I moved toward the other . . . and the evanescent other, hostile but not opaque, transparent, not there, disappeared. Nausea."[75]

On *Soul Murder,* Adamson adopts the laconic American accent voice-over of a film noir hero. In "Split" he collects some of the masks he wears, "Oscar de la soundtrack, Mr. Moss Side Gory, From Rusholme with Love, Harry Pendulum, the Last of the Big Time Swingers, The Man with the Golden American Express Card." The many (black) selves do not exist alongside each other comfortably. In the voice-over, Adamson makes it clear that there's no easy way to return to some idea of black authenticity represented by "Ethiopia." He uses the notion of black athleticism to examine this impossibility and the potential implosion of the soul. The narrator has no passport. He's a mixed-race person, a series of nationalities competing in an athletic event. None of these nationalities is on the same team, which means he'll be split, cut to pieces, no longer whole, a shattered soul.

The noir persona has continued to thrive in the rest of his work. The oedipal drama of the film noir has been appropriated by Adamson to work a droll commentary on blackness. With a black father and white mother, Adamson riffs on the oedipal myth in his album *Oedipus Schmoedipus* (1996), but he also undermines that myth with Yiddish slang. The joke behind the title—"Oedipus Schmoedipus! What does it matter so long as he loves his mother"—suggests the binding of the two. The inner sleeve includes a tinted photograph of a white woman who, as a fan, I want to believe is Adamson's mother.

The track "The Vibes Ain't Nothin' but the Vibes" enacts an encounter between a white woman and black man over cocktail piano and the sounds of clinking glasses. Adamson's noir antihero delights in his account of the couple spotting each other across a crowded room, then leaving together to consummate their desire. The black-and-white sex encounter is described in a world-weary manner, but the hail of spit around them and their urges to violence are powerful images of the exterior social and interior psychic manifestations of racism.

Adamson continues to record an edgy, discomforting vision of black subjectivity through his American film personae. His screening of the black male, like Tricky's, shows that Gilroy's worries about "screenies" need not result in an uncritical meditation on the politics of being black (and British).

Digital Diaspora: Jungle, AKA Drum'n'Bass

Returning more directly to the status of sonic, rather than the visual, the music known once as "jungle" and now bearing the more "respectable" tag "drum'n'bass" is grounded in digital technology. According to Martin James in his history of the genre, *State of Bass,* "the sound of drum 'n' bass is the hybridisation of the last thirty years of technology based black music." Kodwo Eshun calls it a "mix-ological music," a technological hybrid. If house music needed the sound-engineering capabilities of the sequencer to happen, then jungle is the product of the digital sampler's creative possibilities.[76]

The following brief discussion shows that this British music continues to draw on the Caribbean and America and puts together these influences in a distinctly localized flavor. I also consider how musicians themselves conceive of their digital musical production. As I've described with Tricky, this is usually not a question of giving up "humanness" to accept the machine and a cyborgian future, but the integration of technology into existing discourses of musical creativity. I also return to the important economic realities for black musicians, who operate within the recording industry's mode of cultural production and attempt to create relatively autonomous spaces and institutions for their work. In its form and rapid institutionalization as a recognizable musical genre, jungle exemplifies the increasing speed and mixing of technologically driven sounds in a transnational electronic economy. The success of drum'n'bass also suggests that the critical discourse about blackness in relation to the digital age is not particularly new but framed in familiar and often hackneyed terms.

Jungle emerged in 1990–91 when the very rapid electronic beats of hardcore rave music began using speeded-up break beats from hip-hop and vocal samples from Jamaican DJ music. Though open to mutation, the basic elements of jungle are a reggae-style bass line of about 90 beats per minute over which are laid break beats, sometimes as fast as 180 bpm. These are drum patterns sampled from other recordings. Often these samples have their tempo changed by adjustments in the pitch control on the turntable or they are modified through the sampler itself. The sampler allows two or more breaks to be electronically stitched together and transformed into an unrecognizable new percussive fragment. It is fitting in an era of digitally transcribed diasporic identifications that the origin of the name of this British music might be an audio sample from Jamaica. According to one myth of origin, a sound system tape was sampled for its cry of "Alla the Junglists," a term derived from a gang in the "Jungle," the nickname for a neighborhood in Tivoli Gardens, Kingston.

Jungle, taking its cue from hardcore techno, departed further from song structure in its horn/guitar/keyboard/drum riff samples and vocal snatches from funk, soul, hip-hop, film soundtracks, and reggae and its digital descendant, ragga. The psychedelic sound effects of Jamaican dub were updated with digital technology. The currency of the generic tag "jungle" inverted the racist history of the term "jungle music." Some of its scenemakers thought this was an empowering way

to assert the blackness of the music and subculture, while other musicians considered the term a racist one. By 1993, the new music was being played on London's illegal pirate radio stations and attracting mixed crowds to clubs.[77]

The various responses to jungle's rise in prominence were informed by the
context of British racism. Grooverider, a premier DJ and recording artist, described jungle as "England's answer to hip-hop." He claimed that "unlike hip-
hop battling, jungle's about unification. The whole point of the music was to
break down racial boundaries."[78] Rob Playford, a producer with Moving Shadow Records, supported this view:

> The whole Jungle thing is more than just a sound, it's a scene as well. . . . It's a cul-
> ture. There's an attitude that goes along with that as well which is pretty free and
> easy going. We're not narrow-minded. There's so many different cultures wrapped
> up in it, and the music and attitude of everyone has reflected that. It's a multi-racial,
> multi-political society; no one in the Jungle movement has any extreme views. It's
> like whatever you think, you think. The music has its base elements, but it draws
> on loads of different cultures to flavor it and give it its spice. Those flavors change
> every few months, but the core of the music is drum and bass. After that there's
> sprinklings of all other sorts of cultures and sounds.[79]

Grooverider's and Playford's stress on jungle's positive multiculturalism might be
a rejoinder to some of the negative press associated with jungle in its early years.
In June 1994, Gwen Lawford, an editor of the RaveScene fanzine, told Matthew
Collin that jungle had killed the spirit of the rave movement with its aggression.
It had expunged the good vibes from the music.[80]

Jungle's early period was marked by the "dark" sound, full of ominous sub-bass
frequencies and samples from gangsta rap and ragga. The music was preoccupied
with the representation of crime in music, film, and television. Early jungle appeared
to have many of the same nihilistic aspects of U.S. rap and Jamaican ragga in the
period documented by Isaac Julien's film *The Darker Side of Black*. The drugs on
the rave scene had also changed. Ecstasy overuse had dulled its blissed-out effects,
and pills often contained amphetamines. Crack cocaine had a greater presence, and
drug-dealing syndicates increasingly exploited the dance-floor scene for business.

But racist attitudes were often behind the criticisms that jungle brought crime
and violence to the techno/rave scene. If, in the late 1980s, the yellow smiley face
had been the symbol of the acid house generation on Ecstasy, the smile had now
gone, and the face was now brown, or as Eshun put it in *The Wire* magazine: "All
too often, the dislike of Jungle translates into a fear of the Alien Ruffneck, of the
Rudeboy from the council estate who's supposedly spoilt the peace-and-love vibe

and the dream of trans-tribal unity. Jungle, so this racist myth goes, is what killed Smiley, turned every raver's little Woodstock into an Altamont with bassbins."[81]

Jungle developed in London dance clubs with multiracial clienteles. The large volume of hurriedly and independently produced twelve-inch singles constituted the genre's primary format. Most of its star names were anonymous studio musicians hiding behind monikers modeled after the techno-media cultures of rap, rave, reggae, animation, and video games: for example, Nasty Habits, Tek 9, Manix, Dillinja, 4 Hero, Dropping Science, Boogie Times Tribe. Blank white labels and one-off acetates continued the underground practice of the Jamaican dub plate, made each DJ's session at a club more unusual, and fostered subcultural capital within the scene. Formative DJs like Fabio and Grooverider, and the female deck duo Kemistry and Storm, relied on this practice to stay ahead of the game. New tracks were tested out on the dance floor as acetates before being released on vinyl or dumped with the delete button. Independent labels like Suburban Base, Reinforced, V, and Moving Shadow released scene-altering twelve-inch singles, which were rapidly assembled on vinyl and CD compilations in a kind of accelerated version of the institutionalization of a musical genre and its gallery of goldplated classics.

Jungle faced a turning point in 1994. Shy FX and UK Apachi had a hit with "Original Nuttah," a fast Jamaican-style rap by a British-Asian DJ, and British ragga DJ General Levy reached the Top 40 with "Incredible," a track made with producer M-Beat. Jungle had gone overground. Levy claimed to be the main player in the scene, to the disgruntlement of many of its participants. Club DJs and the engineer-producers behind the records were locked in conflict to determine who would profit from an emerging jungle economy. Different actors vied to shape and control the development of jungle. DJs were worried that their spinning of tracks at clubs would become less integral to the scene than the musician-producers' creation of new tracks in the studio. The latter were cautious about the major recording companies' interest, anxious that economic control of the music's development and its organizations would be wrested away from them.

By the mid-90s, a generic sound with reggae bass lines and crime samples had become codified; there were scores of cash-in bandwagon recordings. Compilations bearing the phrases "Ambient Jungle," "Jazzy Jungle," "Artcore," and "Intelligent Jungle" began to appear in the racks of specialist record stores, indicating the fragmentation of the genre, differentiating the product, and distancing it from the pack. The music took on different tempos, captured various moods. Many musicians now tended to sample old jazz and jazz funk records rather than gangsta rap and ragga. "Drum'n'bass" was established as a catch-all term by the genre's pioneers. This generic label gained currency in press, record labels, and musician-speak.

In the studio, musicians pursued new creative directions for a number of reasons. Some wanted to be rid of the criminal taint of jungle's hardcore past. Others hoped the music would be taken seriously as home-listening music and "art," not just functional stuff for the groover on the dance floor. Some believed that the spirit of invention and experiments in sonic engineering had been curtailed and regimented in commercial ragga-style jungle. Many musicians signed deals with major record companies. Some of these agreements gave recording artists the opportunity to start their own label imprints with distribution support from the majors.

The critical discourse on jungle in this period reveals the anxieties about its institutionalization. In a 1995 article in *The Wire,* Simon Reynolds betrays the soundings of a well-worn critical debate about music, authenticity, and blackness. He argues that the move toward "deep," "cool," and "jazz" categories for drum'n'bass is an attempt to assign it the value of "musicality." For Reynolds, music is a sign of class position and mobility. These market categories and their musicality signify the desire for status in black music. This is jungle or drum'n'bass turning its back on its roots in ragga and rave culture. According to Reynolds, jungle is a site for a battle between contesting notions of blackness. He argues that, for example, the work of Roni Size and Dillinja is "an aesthetic strategy of alienation analogous to bebop or free jazz, an attempt to discover who's really down with the programme by venturing deeper into the heart of blackness. . . . What's going on in drum'n'bass right now is a productive conflict between two rival models of blackness, one American, the other ultimately derived from Africa, via the Bronx and Jamaica; elegant urbanity (jazzlite, smooth soul) versus ruffneck tribalism (Hip Hop, ragga, dub—all based on African music principles like bass frequencies, polyrhythms, repetition)."[82]

Reynolds's mapping of black Atlantic music is rather schematic, as well as confused—isn't the Bronx American? Many of his writings on black music reveal a disdain for what he considers softer, gentler strains of music. The sonic architecture of music is simplistically attached to a notion of class identity. Rough, hard music is apparently more working-class than the middle-class sounds of soft soul and jazz. Reynolds has confessed that he has "a bias towards extremity in music."[83] The best music is a search for the abject, the most hardcore, the revolt against the symbolic, the music of abandon and jouissance, the noise of destruction rather than social construction. Reynolds is worried about musicians "diluting the renegade essence of drum'n'bass" and celebrates those "impelled to plunge ever deeper into the anti-populist imperatives of the art's core, which means intensifying all the stuff that happens beneath/beyond the non-initiate's perceptual thresholds."[84] Reynolds defines the value and pleasures of black (dance) music in rockist terms.[85] In the same issue of the magazine *The Wire,* the editor, Tony Herrington, argues that Reynolds's position is typical of a white critical desire for a certain brand of blackness.[86]

Reynolds's desire for a certain blackness is similar to the fantasy of unity between the white working-class and blacks promulgated by British (sub)cultural studies in the 1970s. White boys just wanna get down with the black boys. Such critical projections have often been part of a discourse (by white *and* some black nationalist critics) that has vilified musicians like Duke Ellington and Charles Mingus for not being "black enough." These arguments have also depended on a strict correspondence between particular aesthetics and racial/cultural identity. While Reynolds might find the admittedly awesome pounding sub-bass and headlong aggressive funk of a Dillinja record more pleasurable and aesthetically revolutionary than the gentler strains of LTJ Bukem's jazzy fusion sounds or the soul of Luther Vandross, the definition of an aesthetic cannot be a measure of racial authenticity. In any case, who are white critics to say whether one musician is more or less black than any other? And jungle is not just *black* music in any racially essentialist sense, but a multiracial space with Asians, whites, and African-Caribbeans contributing to the scene as producers and participants.

Critics keen to define narrowly a black aesthetic, demarcate genres, and pronounce upon the next great record have tended to neglect the unromantic, nuts-and-bolts issues of the economic independence, creative control, and institutional autonomy of drum'n'bass. What they might assess is not just sound aesthetics but the production process and institutions created by black musicians who must deal with a recording industry and its ancillary businesses keen to sell blackness defined by old methods and terms. Many musicians have achieved a degree of creative and economic autonomy by signing to major labels. They have negotiated deals to set up their own labels with distribution and promotion provided by the major; for example, Massive Attack (Melancholik), Tricky (Durban Poison), and drum'n'bass musicians Roni Size (Full Cycle) and Goldie (Metalheadz). An institutional space is thus cleared within which other performers can record and release their work. This seems rather more important than an argument over who's blacker than who, what black is and what black isn't, a racial identity interpreted purely from the surfaces of the music. And what musicians say about their "black music" can be instructive.

In conclusion, I want to examine how some prominent drum'n'bass musicians have articulated their techno-aesthetics and methods of work in relation to a nonessentialist Anglo-located black cultural identity.

One of the records that brought "artistic" merit to drum'n'bass and established it as a genre to be taken "seriously," because it could be sustained on an entire album-length recording, was A Guy Called Gerald's *Black Secret Technology* (1995). Hailing from Manchester, Gerald Simpson had one of the early British techno hits "Voodoo Ray," in 1989. He was then signed by CBS, which wanted him to record facsimile hits. After failing to achieve these corporate goals, he was dropped by the major. *Black Secret Technology* was released on the independent Juice Box label after a period of experimentation with programming techniques.

Gerald Simpson is among many musicians who explore their Afro-diasporic heritage through digital technology. He appears in John Akomfrah and Black Audio Collective's *The Last Angel of History* (1995), a film that suggests that though the diasporic subject's return to Africa is impossible, the black artist has pieced together, juxtaposed, and digitally mixed up the fragments from the past—rummaged through the rubble, the documents of barbarism, in Benjaminian fashion—to create something that bears the traces of a history of ruptures. Through these processes of looking backward to the future, the "data thief" assembles fragments, techno-fossils, making connections to "Africa."

Gerald describes his programming of drum machines and mixing as incorporating the logic of African drumming, which he studied with a friend from Detroit. The artist makes an imaginative leap to some notion of Africa through digital technology. On the album, the track "The Nile" is a polyrhythmic drum workout, with machine-like rhythms layered and bouncing over each other and a black female voice adding some "oo-ooh-oo-ooh" vocal oscillations. There are traces of African music in the polyrhythms, in the timbre of some of the drum sounds; the "Africanness" is explicitly articulated in the track's title. To African ears, this music might not sound like any African music, but the African diasporic approach to sound is in the process as much as the final product. Gerald's Africa is also a necessary misreading of the continent. The Nile is also the name of a bar in Moss Side, located above the Reno, a music club frequented by Gerald and many other black patrons. The tracks "The Nile" and "Reno" are Gerald's homages to two black Manchester locations.

The language Gerald uses to describe his digital musicianship testifies to the domestication of technology through recognizable metaphors:

> You just pick up on certain things, like "why does this rhythm work and this one doesn't?" Or tones that make certain things vibrate. How can you make a purer sound? What sounds move you? I can actually pinpoint high frequencies moving while low frequencies stay more stable. You build up a little graph in your head. I keep low frequencies centred like a strong bass, while the high frequencies sometimes

go nuts. It's like water, earth and air. People think the earth's solid but water's a much stronger force. I had that core for most of the tracks on the album. It was like you have a bass track, mid and then high points. On another level, you have rhythms and polyrhythms.[87]

Here Gerald combines the cyborgian metaphor of a graph in the head with the organic metaphors of water, earth, and air to describe his composition technique.

Another prominent drum'n'bass musician, Goldie, treats technology like an archaeologist, excavating the detritus of old sounds and using it to create new sonic structures. In a description of his early forays into the studio, he says:

I started to get into the more technical stuff—I was thinking a lot about various theories and this idea of dimensional sound but it was still quite a barbaric process. I just went in there and tried throwing nu-skool samples against old-skool stuff and then pulled other things in. It was just experimenting and trying things out. The name I came up with was Rufige Kru: "rufige" was the way you described things that were left lying around on the surface—more or less scum—which you collected together and turned into something new. I was using fourth or fifth generation samples, just trash sounds, but they had a grittiness and a roughness which identified with the feel of the street. So it was the perfect name to go with the kinds of records I was doing.[88]

In his description of the *Timeless* (1995) and *Saturnz Return* (1997) albums, produced on Pro Tools and Logic software, Goldie describes his sound composition as if he's collecting debris and reshaping it with his Macintosh into future sounds.[89] He has also likened his use and misuse of technology as akin to joyriding a car or overriding the proper use of the car's features: "In my car I've got this built-in computer which tells me the best way to get to my destination . . . but sometimes I decide I want to go in a different direction and I override it. That's me placing my own sense of aristocracy over the original designer's aristocracy. The computer says turn left, it's pre-ordained, but I'll turn right whenever I want to. Which is how I view machinery. The program might say I've got to take the track in one direction but we just override it and go down another street."[90]

Goldie's most famous track, "Timeless," is a twenty-one-minute epic in three related sections—"Inner City Life," "Jah," and "Timeless." It incorporates a "shift in gear" from the languid soul of Diane Charlemagne's singing about inner-city pressure through break beats reminiscent of the militant drumming of roots reggae's Leroy "Horsemouth" Wallace in the mid-1970s, to Goldie's distorted voice intoning "Jah" and the ambient synthetic textures that bring the thundering track to a glacial close. "Timeless" is an archive of overlapping sounds from Goldie's past—Jamaican dub, Brit-soul, rave, Detroit techno, hip-hop, and developments in jungle/drum'n'bass. In interview after interview, Goldie has explained that "Timeless" was the aural equivalent of a huge wall covered with the graffiti art he has worked on for years. His whole experience growing up in England has gone into the composition.[91] Though the lyrics don't explicitly say all of this in any literal way, the life narrative given by Goldie in interviews and interpreted by journalists sends the listener/fan down certain interpretive roads.

Goldie was born in the Wolverhampton area of the West Midlands in 1965, the son of an English mother and a Jamaican father. His father soon left the family for the United States. Goldie grew up in foster care, living with a series of families. His early years coincided with Enoch Powell's speeches against immigration from the Caribbean and the Asian subcontinent, in the same West Midlands area where Powell was an MP and Goldie and I lived in the late 1960s and early 70s: "I was half-caste in a school that was all white with a few black people, I had to try and be a bit more than everybody else because I was a fucking nigger. They used to say 'Goldie, you're a fucking Paki' or 'you're a nigger,' I had it for years."[92]

When hip-hop took off in Britain in the early 1980s, Goldie began breakdancing seriously for local crews that would compete across the Midlands. Like 3-D of Massive Attack, he saw *Wild Style* on video and then took up graffiti art. In fact, 3-D and Goldie painted walls together in Wolverhampton. When the South Bronx electro/hip-hop pioneer Afrika Bambaataa did a show in London, Goldie met some of the Zulu Nation and went to New York to take part in a gallery exhibition of graffiti. Goldie often compares his musical productions to graffiti pieces. He lived in Miami with his father for a brief time, then came back to Britain, went through a period of petty crime, followed by a Rastafarian hiatus. He was introduced to the rave scene by DJ Kemistry in 1991 and encountered Ecstasy and the DJ skills of Fabio and Grooverider.

Matthew Collin, who has interviewed Goldie a number of times, points out that this experience, biography, and history have become part of a Goldie myth. With his trademark gold teeth and often aggressive persona evident in photographs and press reportage, Goldie has become a recognizable star commodity—in effect, the first star of jungle. Goldie's response to the fixing of his star-image echoes Tricky's and Barry Adamson's use of many masks and personae: "I'm a chameleon. I can change shape any time I want. I'm a complicated character. Shapeshifting all the time."[93]

On the other hand, a high media profile has helped Goldie achieve a measure of power and creative control in the industry. Metalheadz, his almost boutique recording label, develops new talent, and Metalheadz club nights in London provide an influential space for new music, DJs, and producers to be heard. More generally, this also reflects the importance of dance clubs, now often the engines driving the release of CDs, compiled and/or mixed by well-known DJs. A compilation or mix will often have the club's name in its title, indicating that it is a simulation of the "live" experience of that particular club event.

Roni Size is another prominent jungle producer. His Bristol-based collective or crew, Reprazent (including producers Suv, Die, Krust, and the singer Onallee), is modeled on the reggae sound system. In the late 80s, as a teenager who left school, Size went to the Basement Project, a music technology workshop in the Sefton Park area. He acquired the skills needed to master drum machines, AKAI samplers, and Cubase software. In 1992, he began to release twelve-inch singles on V Recordings, a label set up by a local DJ, Bryan Gee. With Krust and the free-party organizer Chris Lewis, Size set up the Full Cycle label and released a succession of twelve-inch singles.

These influential jungle hits often involved the play of heavy bass and sub-bass frequencies, complex overlapping drum patterns and jazz samples. The pummeling "Music Box" (with DJ Die) sounds like several drummers playing at the same time but a beat behind each other. The single "11:55" fires fragments of blaxploitation strings, jazz keyboard ripples, dueling cymbals and snares, and a sinuous heavy bass, along with an African-American voice exhorting the listener to "Come On." This jungle/drum'n'bass is a music of samples—sound effects, riffs, and vocals used like the chorus and verses of a song.

Major labels approached Size and in 1995 he signed with the DJ Gilles Peterson's Talkin' Loud, with distribution through Warner's. Reprazent's first album release, *New Forms,* was a critical and commercial success, winning the Mercury Prize in 1997. The double album, described by Forrest Green III as "lindy-hopping music for Mossimo-fitted B-people," collected tracks that owed much to jazz, dub, dance hall, soul, funk, and rap.[94] Like Massive Attack's *Blue Lines* and Goldie's *Timeless, New Forms* brings together in a digital package many genres of black Atlantic music from the last quarter century.

The videos for the singles from the albums also emphasize the human-technology interface. In the promo for "Brown Paper Bag," Size rotates an egg-like contraption to lock time into an oscillation as the Reprazent crew negotiate a North American cityscape to get to the airport in time for their flight home. In "Share the Fall," a technological duplication machine produces doubles of the crew. These doppelgangers or bio-digital clones chase their human counterparts through a warehouse. One promotional photo printed in *The Guardian* when *New Forms* was released shows Size in shades, his dreadlocks transformed into electronic cords; he has become a dread cyborg, a natural man-machine.

This combination of human agency and technology extends to Size's discussion of his own music production. He works in the studio and his office, where he records "live" instruments that are then sampled and filtered through computers. As with Tricky and Massive Attack, there is no contradiction between the machine and the live in the musician's discourse. The "originality" of the music and the authorial stamp happen in the processing of sound as well as the playing of instruments. Performance and processing are integrated: "I base a whole tune on live performances, I just don't want anyone to have the sounds I get, I feel sick if I hear someone using the same sample as me. I feel embarrassed. No one can have identical sounds as me because I record them live and sample them—it's a vision! I take it back and sample it and put it back into the computer."[95]

The "raw" feel of the music for Roni Size, Goldie, and A Guy Called Gerald is often achieved by the use of samples that have degenerated through repeated sampling and doctoring in the technological process. Productions often keep the hiss, hum, and crackle of old records and tape in the final composition, so that the sound is not pristine. In such a fabrication of authenticity, new technology is manipulated to reproduce the sonic "feel" of old recordings. Musicians routinely talk about trying to capture the "warmer" sound of analog instruments with their digital counterparts or by using a combination of analog and digital machines.

These black British musicians justify their digital music production in terms of established notions of authorship and musical creativity. They also conceive of their composing with samplers and sequencers in a continuum of black Atlantic music production. New technologies have facilitated these diasporic links and created new syncretic possibilities. The Caribbean, Europe, and North America share sounds and images in a transnational popular culture. The sonic and visual signs of blackness are dispersed and appropriated differently in particular places. Of course, these signs can be exploited as they have been in the past, but cultural analysis should be grounded in a nuanced understanding of the uses, abuses, and transformations of these forms in specific contexts. We cannot prescribe the shape and meaning of black vernacular forms. "Black music" has a history and culture that should not be defined by recourse to a biological notion of racial authenticity. Many of the "black music" artists discussed in this chapter are of mixed-race parentage or white.

In the appropriation, translation, and hybridization of black musical styles, there are politico-cultural gains and losses. Bristol and London are sites for certain developments of local vernaculars related to but distinct from U.S. rap and Jamaican reggae; for example, Massive Attack's whispered raps and Tricky's croaking style. Studio effects from the analog universe of Kingston dub are rearticulated by the junglists in Britain. American hip-hop and Jamaican reggae themselves drew on multiple influences. While hip-hop and its sibling musical forms may be international, they can never become completely homogenized. Advocates of the cultural imperialism theory and U.S. writers from *The Source* who celebrate rap's global spread as evidence of U.S. hip-hop hegemony may need to be reminded that Bristol is not the Bronx, London isn't L.A. Though these places increasingly share images and sounds, heterogeneity never disappears, and new sets of distinctions, musical forms, and practices are generated by producers, mediators, and consumers.

Technology is used for recording experiences and articulating a sense of location and identification with a black past in many places. The realities of that past are not simply deleted but unevenly distributed through black networks. As U.S. rapper KRS1 says on his transatlantic collaboration with Goldie—the 1997 single "Digital"—black people are "representin' like the Internet." Digital resources testify to both sufferation and joy under Babylon system. The days of Gilroy's dance hall as the *primary* site for black music culture may be numbered. But there's no reason why the black public sphere cannot incorporate the digital communication media. The technological futurism of dance music is often dazzling—completely novel sounds put together in unforeseen ways. But the digital age has not brought about quite the *rupture* some critics contend. The era of the break beat hasn't necessarily resulted in a break with the past. Rather it has accentuated tendencies already present in popular music recording. The Roland 808 drum machine and AKAI S-950 sampler should not be seen in terms of dance vs. rock, digital beats vs. electric guitar, global vs. local, black vs. white, but as connected to other technological changes in the history of twentieth-century popular music. Digital machinery continues the technological/studio mediation of music performance with recording artists negotiating old and new practices to maintain a sense of human agency in musical composition, though this "human" may be a shifting category in terms of its "authenticity." While Gilroy rightly points out the increasing privatization of performance in the digital modes of music production, his "mourning of the analog" claims that recycling in today's black music forms promotes a "pseudo-memory . . . an uncomplicated variety of *pastness*."[96] This, I believe, fails to engage with the multiplicity of memorial work going on in the post-soul present and is marked by what Gilroy confesses is "a sense of loss that is my demographic, geographical, and generational affliction," a nostalgia for the golden age of Bob Marley and sweet soul music.[97]

However, as Gilroy reminds us, the selling of an apparently authentic commodified black image and black body goes on apace in the media industries. Certain representational regimes will not disappear in the so-called digital age. The facts of racism do not disappear. The notion of "race" still has descriptive

and analytical currency, but "blackness" is fragmented and specifically articulated. Black Atlantic collective memory is still vital, but it is constructed from various perspectives *rooted* in particular places cut through with *routes* to and from
points elsewhere. The memory of slavery may still be registered in cultural forms
but will not be "the overdetermining instance of black Atlantic sociality."[98] As
Chude-Sokei writes:

> From hip-hop to black British junglism, from roots reggae to ragga, cultural-histor-
> ical specificity crashes against global dispersal and the attendant myths of racial sol-
> idarity. For the Rastafari, sound was culture and culture was "race." With today's black
> underground media complex, sound is closer to culture than "race" ever was. "Race,"
> of course, is not out of the picture; it has not been banished from the discursive
> mechanisms of Jamaican sound culture. What has happened is that without the use
> of "Africa" as a centralizing logos, as a focal point for postmodern black destiny, "race"
> is deconstructed as a universal principle and is fragmented by culture and the dif-
> ferential histories of colonialism. This transformation features instead the reification
> of separate and distinct historical blacknesses, each migrating around each other,
> trapped in an orbit like planets around the dim memory of the sun.[99]

As black musical styles and genres scatter, disperse, and travel in their various-
ly commodified forms, they are also taken up, reinterpreted, and sometimes
unrecognizably mutated by other diasporic populations in local contexts. Can
"black music" then continue to be circumscribed only by the imaginative geography of the black Atlantic? As a British Asian I've been drawn to the work of
many of the musicians discussed in this chapter because I've recognized aspects
of their alienation, their double consciousness or multiple selves. Their music has
provided dread and funky resources in the fight against English racism. The
dominant interpretations of black music in Britain have been made by white
critics burnishing their fantasies of blackness. White and black critics have largely
kept the debate about music as a closed dialogue between themselves. Britain's
South Asians also have their own problematic relationship to the African diaspora,
but our marginalization and Englishness have been spoken to and then spoken
through soul, reggae, funk, hip-hop, drum'n'bass—the sounds and images of
commercially mediated black popular culture.[100]

5

Asia Massive
Home Abroad with Brit-Asian Tracks

The world is sound.
—Talvin Singh, "Traveller"

The British Asian musician Nitin Sawhney suggests the sense of displacement felt by many South Asians who have grown up in Britain: "You talk to any Asian person, and there's a romantic yearning for either Pakistan or India because basically, that's the homeland—that's the escape from a world that they don't quite fit in or belong. No young Asian really feels that they are truly British. Not when you still see marches from the BNP and fascist movements all over Europe. You can't possibly feel that you are indigenous to this country. We're constantly thinking that there's always India or Pakistan, yet when we go, we don't fit in any more than we do here."[1] Sawhney expresses a double bind, a fundamental ambivalence: neither England nor the Asian subcontinent can fully become "home" for Britain's South Asians. Even though some of us have only a halting or partial command of our many "mother tongues," we still *feel* Punjabi, Kashmiri, Gujarati, Bengali, Tamil, Indian, Pakistani, Bangladeshi, Sri Lankan. We are local and global at the same time, occupying both here and there, home and abroad. England *and* South Asia are both home, yet they are also both abroad. This Brit-Asian double (dis)location, an awareness of multilocality, is one of the features of a "diaspora consciousness."[2]

The meeting of different peoples through migration and settlement and the technological channels for rapid musical communication have created new syncretic processes and forms in the movement between *here* and *there*. Popular music is used to make sense of our place(s) in the world—how we belong in the neighborhood, city, nation, and beyond the borders. In this chapter, I'm concerned with how Brit-Asian music imagines both home and abroad together.

Dr. Das of the group Asian Dub Foundation describes how a very Indian practice of appropriation and indigenization becomes a strategy that emerges from the specifically British and *local* experience of South Asians:

Culture constantly moves very fast. It doesn't have to dilute anything. We see our music as a natural outcome of having been brought up in this country. Culture does not stay stationary, there's no such thing as pure culture but certain people like to draw lines around it and solidify it. In India people are very aware of diverse elements coming in all the time. What we are doing is in some respects part of an Indian tradition of assimilating ideas and taking the best. It's not part of a fusion it's just normal. It's taking in everything that I hear. When I lived with my parents I'd listen to Indian classical music, watch Hindi musicals and listen to Sunrise radio; at the same time I was listening to dub, Hendrix and techno. There is no contradiction in putting all these sounds together. It's normal and natural. Our music is the sound of urban London today. It's like a soundtrack. It's real Britpop—not revivalist or nostalgic.[3]

On the other hand, Talvin Singh imagines sound in more broadly dispersed, global terms. The words "The world is sound" are repeated several times on "Traveller," the opening track of his Mercury Prize–winning album *OK* (1998). Singh named the album *OK* because "anywhere you go in the world, people know what OK is. Music shouldn't have boundaries. That's the most valuable thing in music today. We're living in a time when things have got to unite." This point of view, quoted, appropriately, in the November 1999 Singapore Airlines in-flight magazine, reflects a popular affirmative discourse on globalization. Singh's vision is more universalistic than Das's more local focus, though both men grew up in London's East End and draw on South Asian elements in their music.

In this chapter I explore the different local, national, transnational, and "global" imaginaries produced by Brit-Asian musicians. How was *here, there, in-between* constructed in the musical sounds of a generation of Brit-Asian musicians in the 1980s and 90s? This wide range of artists includes Apache Indian, Bally Sagoo, Fun^da^mental, Hustlers HC, Asian Dub Foundation, Talvin Singh, Echobelly, Cornershop, Black Star Liner, and White Town.

The imaginaries offered by popular music culture are structured to a great extent by economic and political forces. The discursive regulation and institutionalization of music are part of the broader social construction of the "British Asian" subject. Postmodernism may have told us that identities are fluid, open, always becoming rather than being, perennially incomplete, but regimes of representation in commodity capitalism attempt to fix what it means to be a British Asian in order to better manage and promote an identity for political and commercial ends. The discourses of cultural racism, identity politics, orientalism, notions of multiculturalism, and the contemporary vogue for hybridity-talk inform and shape Brit-Asian audibility and visibility.

This music must be considered in the context of the "worlding" of popular music in recent years. The emergence of a recognizable broad field we might call Brit-Asian music is contemporaneous with the appearance of "world music" and "world beat." The term "world music" was introduced in 1987 as a marketing device in the U.K. and the U.S. by small record companies who believed that a new category would help sell music from Africa, Ireland, Latin America, and other places that might have been lost in the existing genre sections of retail outlets. World music is now an expanding niche in the Western record store, which is generally classified according to continental and national origin. Certain musical forms, wherever they are actually produced, are seen to "represent" their local and national communities; so that Punjabi bhangra, for example, is often found in world music sections under "India," even though it may have been produced in London or Birmingham by British citizens.

There have been a number of related criticisms of world music from musicologists and cultural studies scholars. The category is seen to reproduce the power relations of colonialism, imperialism, and Western tourism, and the attendant discourses of anthropology and the museum system. Record-company marketing often includes *National Geographic*–style visuals of exotic foreign locations with stoic natives or happy-go-lucky primitives. Travel and boutique multiculturalism often overlap when the world is presented as a department store with other cultures commodified in images and sounds. For example, Najma Akhtar, a ghazal and jazz singer from Britain, was requested to refrain from cutting her hair by executives at her record company because they "liked the Indian image of long hair and sari."[4]

The "worlding" of music also caters to a left-liberal disaffection with modern life. Cosmopolitan consumers desire cultural alternatives to the apparent alienation of Western society. The myth of world music offers older forms of folk spirituality in CD packages. This music takes the listener back to a more acoustic, human, and soulful authenticity, away from the technologically rationalized and commercial synthetic pop of North America and Europe.

Like "world music," "world beat" satiates the desire for the exotic, but a more familiar, "other." The "beat" denotes the danceability of much of this music. A term coined by an Austin, Texas, DJ, Dan Del Santo, in the late 1980s, "world beat" is sometimes used to pigeonhole Brit-Asian music. The category carries with it notions of musical fusion, cross-cultural mixing, East meeting West, the violation of boundaries; it celebrates musical hybridity, the melting pot, the quirky global mélange that produces surreal, idiosyncratic juxtapositions for the entertainment of the ironic consumer.[5]

Record companies and media organizations in the "developed" world dominate the regulation of this musical traffic between the West and the rest. The
musical *imagination* is structured and sold through such institutions and their
various practices. The imagination is, as Appadurai reminds us, "an organized
field of social practices, a form of work (both in the sense of labor and a cultur-
ally organized practice) and a form of negotiation between sites of agency ('individuals') and globally defined fields of possibility."[6]

But while economic and institutional forces are important regulatory factors,
we should also examine the psychic dimensions of music production, as well as
its consumption. The imaginary created by musicians cannot simply be reduced
to what Georgina Born calls the "institutional technology of market maximiza-
tion."[7] The Marxist consideration of production should be aware of it as a negotiated set of practices in which the artist has some agency. Brit-Asian musicians
imagine their connections to the subcontinent and other places and histories in
their mixed-up sounds, which are recorded, distributed, sold, and performed
through a complex web of institutions. In this chapter I'm interested in what
animates these "homing desires." How are they structured and regulated? What
kind of cultural politics are manifested in these recorded tracks and the way
musicians talk about their work?

These musicians and their music enact aspects of the diasporic imagination.
As Avtar Brah suggests, "'home' is a mythic place of desire in the diasporic imagination. In this sense it is a place of no return. . . . The concept of diaspora places
the discourse of 'home' and 'dispersion' in creative tension, inscribing a homing
desire while simultaneously critiquing discourses of fixed origins."[8] Diaspora
functions as a critical concept, yet a yearning for "home," for a place of plenitude and security—the motherland or fatherland of psychic wholeness—is likely to be as politically reactionary as it is progressive; ethnic, nationalist, and religious fundamentalisms also emerge in diasporic formations.

One of the weaknesses of the diaspora concept is its encouragement of a cultural studies that sets up lines of affiliation and identification that stretch almost
exclusively from globally dispersed nodes of South Asian populations back to a
point of *origin* in the South Asian homeland. We must also be aware of other
vectors in the formation of South Asian diasporic identities. Families may not
be in South Asia but dispersed in different locations—the Gulf, Canada, the
United States, Australia, and New Zealand. For example, a Pakistani Muslim in
Britain may think of Pakistan or its regions and even a pre-partition Muslim India
as "home," but transnational identifications extend beyond this return. A pan-
Islamic consciousness can include links to Saudi Arabia, Iran, Afghanistan, Bos-

nia, and Kosovo. Some young British Muslims, for example, fought as *Mujahideen* in the Bosnian war.

To take a music-based example of an identity that transnationally juxtaposes aspects from many places and histories, *The Face* magazine once interviewed a ragga fan, DJ, and young Punjabi Muslim from Birmingham who calls himself Homeboy E: "But things like alcohol, I'm not into, basically because it's against my religion. I'm Muslim and I like to keep to my religion. I'm a roots man. Of course you're not meant to do spliff [marijuana] and get high but that's part of life. It's only really when I'm playing out that I puff and when I'm in the studio. People like Malcolm X, he's a hero, a brother, part of the Nation of Islam, and I'm Islamic."⁹ Homeboy E is a South Asian Muslim but in Britain he draws on the Nation of Islam's African-American style and on the Rastafarian notion of the "roots man" in a local vernacular that is itself a translation of U.S. and Caribbean talk. These examples suggest that when we think through the concept of diaspora we should be open to the multiple cultural vectors in an ongoing politics of location. A sense of orientation, of place in Britain, is constructed through many transnational identifications.

Given the rhizomatic circuits of mediated popular culture, Raminder Kaur and Virinder S. Kalra argue that the notion of diaspora is limited, for global media, telecommunications, and "the flow of sound structures divorced from their place of manufacture, have provided for a greater interconnectedness and interdependency for minority groups." In place of the "South Asian diaspora" they offer the "imagined spatial arena of Transl-Asia not as a fixed area of the world but rather a continuous movement of imagined and actual arenas. To a greater or lesser extent, South Asia is one of the many reference points of Transl-Asia, but not necessarily its originary location. . . . Transl-Asia describes an arena of cultural flows, not entirely geographically grounded nor always nationally bounded, but constantly on the move charting out new spatial configurations."¹⁰ Whether the term "Transl-Asia" will have an academic shelf life is not as important as its use in remapping transnational identifications as a constellation of points, joined by multiple lines or vectors that are continually shifting. The term emphasizes the transnational quality of these connections and the activity of translation as crucial in making sense of the other nodes in a particular location. This notion of "roots and routes," which Paul Gilroy, Kobena Mercer, and many other critics have drawn upon, is an appropriate means to think about the way culture functions in a world of cellular phones, e-mail, the internet, videotapes, audiocassettes, satellite television, and other mobile technologies. In the computer age, the *network* has become one of our dominant cultural metaphors.

Some of the strongest links made by second-generation Brit Asians have been with black popular culture. We have drawn on black images and sounds as fortification against racism. Some of these interdiasporic and cross-cultural identifications and fantasies of blackness have been as unstable and contradictory as white identifications with black culture. Solidarity has not always been an easy thing to construct, but a shared sense of racial grievance and displacement has created some commonalities. Communities have not always interacted on the best of terms, but the everyday practicalities of neighborhoods in which African-Caribbeans and South Asians live together have produced positive political effects.

Alongside the identifications developed through living together in neighborhoods and schools, black America, the Caribbean, and black British popular culture have been imbibed through media images and sounds and then worked upon in the Brit-Asian imagination. This saturation in black media has fostered affiliations of affect. Living in white neighborhoods, I first saw and heard black people in the media. One of my earliest memories is the sight of the American sprinters Tommy Smith and John Carlos raising their fists in the black power salute on the podium at the 1968 Mexico Olympics. In the early 1970s, a Muhammad Ali fight on television was an excuse for a Pakistani function; he was one of us—a Muslim—whupping whitey with fists, the shuffle, and the rhymes. In the same decade, Bob Marley became a postcolonial icon, a spokesperson against white supremacist Babylon. In the 1980s and 90s, soul, funk, hip-hop, and ragga belonged to Asians as much as to white Britishers. The cultural politics of these many associations have not always been agreed upon, but the black-Asian relationship has crucially shaped a Brit-Asian political and cultural presence since the 1960s.

Are Asians Black?: Antiracism, New Ethnicities, and Hybridity

Before moving on to a detailed discussion of Brit-Asian music, I'll briefly lay out a contingent history that charts the emergence of a "British Asian identity." This contextualizes the work of this generation of musicians in some of the important political and cultural debates about Asians and their national identity in the U.K.

A political rather than biological notion of "black" emerged in the late 1960s and 1970s as a response to the rise of populist racism, marked by Enoch Powell's 1968 "rivers of blood" speech. This black movement incorporated an antiracist coalition that stressed the common experience of African-Caribbeans and Asian settlers. As Kobena Mercer notes, *Black* became "an empowering signifier of Afro-

Asian alliances."[11] These alliances were fostered by black and Asian workers' organizations. Many of us growing up in Britain during this period and shaped by racism accepted that we were black quite easily, though South Asian parents sometimes had a racist suspicion of "lazy, criminal, promiscuous West Indians" and feared that Asian communities would be tainted by association, "tarred with the same brush."

In the late 1970s, workers' organizations, the Anti-Nazi League (ANL), and Rock against Racism (RAR) formed a social movement mobilized against the rise of populist racism, which took its most extreme forms in the National Front and other far-right political acts. Popular music was one terrain on which this struggle took place. RAR was initiated after the guitarist-singer Eric Clapton made some anti-immigration remarks. With the ANL, RAR adopted the carnival model in public demonstrations against fascism. Political speeches were supported by live music in parks, small clubs, and student-union buildings. As Virinder Kalra, John Hutnyk, and Sanjay Sharma argue, the music itself was largely "white boy adventure rock," punk/new wave, and reggae. Asian musicians were rarely part of these events. Gilroy has described another limitation of the movement: the ANL adopted a nationalist rhetoric in its antifascist message; the National Front was akin to German Nazis and anathema to British life. Fascism was constructed as something foreign. Apart from an emphasis on racist policing, the structural, institutional racism of the British state was obscured in ANL/RAR rhetoric as it singled out the alien, un-British qualities of fascism.[12]

The peak of late-70s RAR and ANL activism coincided with the last few years of my secondary education. My lefty white school mates and I attended RAR concerts, went on marches, sold newspapers, and distributed pamphlets. We wore a multitude of badges with slogans and went along to demonstrations organized by the Campaign for Nuclear Disarmament (CND) and Troops Out movement, where an array of leftist groups would try to solicit our support and membership. The politics were immediate, tied to music and the hip aspects of youth culture.

In late 1979, tens of thousands marched in London against the Thatcher government's decision to allow the U.S. to station Cruise missiles at air force bases in the U.K. At a rally in Trafalgar Square, the historian E. P. Thompson, the actor Susannah York, Labour MP Tony Benn, and officials from some of Britain's churches gave speeches against nuclear weapons. The political rhetoric was powerful, but the promise of a music concert in Trafalgar Square had really helped me climb out of bed very early on a chilly West Yorkshire morning and get on a bus bound for London.

The Pop Group from Bristol performed under Nelson's Column, framed by the statues of Britain's lions. Those lions could have been the Lions of Judah once the band's booming bass pumped out its funked-up version of William Blake's "Jerusalem." Mark Stewart screeched out the words, trying to reclaim the spirit of a dissident English nativism, which the Pop Group now colored with postcolonial sonic warfare. This sound fueled my festering grudge against Britain. Punk had given voice to my disgust with white racism, English nationalism, and all that Jubilee bollocks. Participation in RAR, ANL, and CND gave this rage a structure that wasn't strictly defined by party politics and the parliamentary system. Music was integral to this participation in the public sphere and the formation of something called a "political consciousness." Musical culture provided the models for multiracial alliance.

One Saturday in early July 1981, my friends and I went into Leeds on the bus from Ilkley. The city center held three political events: a demonstration by Troops Out in support of the IRA hunger strikers in the Maze prison, a British Movement rally, and an antiracist march. We took part in the latter, chanting the anthemic chorus of Heaven 17's recent electro dance hit "Brothers, Sisters, We Don't Need that Fascist Groove Thang!" as several thousand marchers wove their way from Leeds city center to Potternewton Park in Chapeltown, an area with a significant black population. The march culminated in what was billed as "a Carnival against Racism." The outdoor venue was dotted with food stands, political stalls, a reggae sound system, and a large stage on which a long line of musical acts played for half the day. Among these was Misty in Roots, a reggae band from Southall in West London, who informed the crowd that there had been rioting in their home town the previous night. We later found out that Asians in Southall had burned down a pub hosting some right-wing skinhead punk bands.

The carnival headliners were the Specials, recording artists on the Two-Tone label. Their single "Ghost Town" was number one on the British charts, a lilting but eerie song with a reggae undertone about the despair of cities up and down the country faced with high unemployment and the breakdown of their civic infrastructures. The Specials told us that the clubs had been closed down because there had been too much fighting on their dance floors. The nation's cities were transformed into the ghost towns of a Wild West landscape, stressed by the sounds of swirling wind and tumbling tumbleweed on the recording. In a lineage of reggae songs that draw on spaghetti westerns, "Ghost Town" features a melancholic harmonica arrangement reminiscent of Ennio Morricone's work. The trombone solo by the veteran Jamaican session musician Rico Rodriguez gives the track a dread gravity. As emotional counterpoint, the "ya, ya, ya, ya, ya" chorus of pantomime spooks and songwriter Jerry Dammers's Hammer horror-movie organ riff and Terry Hall's vocals ironically invoke a cheery English music hall nostalgia about the good old days of prosperity before the boom was over.

At the end of the show, the Specials invited members of the audience to join them on stage as they played and danced through one of their faster encore numbers. This event marked me significantly. In his epilogue to *Lipstick Traces,* Greil Marcus writes that the Free Speech movement in Berkeley during late 1964 left him with "an incomplete but indelible image of good public life."[13] He looked for traces of this moment's energies in the past and the present. For me, the memory of the Specials at Potternewton Park at the culmination of the day's activities in July 1981 embodies, however fleeting, a fusion of politics, pleasure, and public life. The broad left alliance of various groups and the music organized around antiracism offered hopeful if flawed models for a multiracial community.

In hindsight, the day seemed to bring the forces of that historical moment—the early Thatcherite conjuncture—to a head. No wonder that Gramsci's notion of "crisis" was rigorously applied by cultural studies scholars at the time. That same summer in West Yorkshire, twelve Asians from the United Black Youth League, a splinter group from the Asian Youth Movement, were arrested and charged with conspiracy after police discovered two milk crates of petrol bombs on some wasteland in Bradford. The Bradford Twelve were acquitted the following year.[14] The urban uprisings or "riots" up and down Britain in the summer of 1981, which seemed to occur once a week, radicalized many black British citizens. As Kobena Mercer points out, this civil disorder "encoded militant demands for black representation within public institutions as a basic right."[15] Authorities were forced to recognize the demands of "minorities" in legislation and funding. Government was motivated by a mixture of good sense and the need for crisis management. The Thatcher regime's attacks on local government, particularly the left-wing leadership in Greater London and Liverpool, curbed funding to black and other minority groups. This was part of Thatcherism's crackdown on the "enemy within," including the miners, the unemployed, the blacks, Pakis, and queers who were regularly attacked by Conservative ideologues, think-tanks, and a Tory-dominated press.

Given declining public funding in the 1980s, Channel Four became an important institution for black cultural politics. Established by government charter as a potential model for an independent, commercially driven television network, it was also meant to cater to minority tastes. For example, the channel provided an economic resource and media outlet for black British film collectives that were moving from simply battling stereotypes and offering positive images toward a "politics of representation" that explored the gap between the apparently separate categories of blackness" and Britishness. The work of the film collectives, black photographers, and the Asian Women Writers Collective encouraged a redefinition of Englishness and Britishness. These groups shared a resistance to the notion that black British communities should be conceived under the ghetto- ized rubric of race relations policy.

Black media and arts activism focused on differences within the black com- munities, partly emboldened by the increasing currency of "difference" in the de- constructive turn in cultural theory. Many black academics wrote and spoke in public forums, so maintaining a dialogue with media practitioners and political organizations. Academic discourse also responded to the demarcation of cultur- al difference in identity politics. Stuart Hall argued for working through the prob- lematic of cultural difference—not the kind of difference that "makes a radical and unbridgeable separation," but a difference that is "positional, conditional and conjunctural."[16] Such an approach would explore the plural nature of blackness and the differences within communities in terms of previously silenced issues and identities constituted around, for example, gender and sexuality.

At the Black Film/British Cinema conference at London's Institute for Con- temporary Arts (ICA) in February 1988, Hall argued that regimes of representa- tion play "a constitutive, and not merely a reflexive, after-the-event role" in the construction of black identities. He attempted to reclaim the notion of ethnici- ty: "the term ethnicity acknowledges the place of history, language and culture in the construction of subjectivity and identity, as well as the fact that all discourse is placed, positioned, situated, and all knowledge is contextual." According to Hall, an acknowledgment of "new ethnicities" would engage rather than suppress difference, would reveal multiple identities and identifications within the black communities, as well as draw attention to the constructedness of whiteness as an ethnicity. This was, according to him, the "end of the innocent notion of the black subject."[17]

The emphasis on difference made by feminist and queer politics had a posi- tive impact on the narrowly class-based conceptions of left-wing activism. How- ever, cultural difference was also emphasized by Thatcherite rhetoric and cement- ed in communal differences. The notion of "culture" was increasingly invoked on both sides of the political divide. Thatcherism vilified African-Caribbean populations and Asian working-class youth but celebrated the small-enterprise culture of Asian business people. Asians were encouraged to see themselves apart from African-Caribbeans. The result of these contradictory forces freed the epi- thet "black" from some of its earlier meanings. The notion of "political black- ness" rooted in the late 1960s has since almost disappeared as its various constituencies have argued for their respective spaces. National origin, religion, gender, and sexuality have come into relief. Blackness has broken apart to reveal differences within African-Caribbean communities, and the relationship of Asians to blackness has also been exposed.

The 1990s witnessed the widening gulf between the terms *black* and *Asian*. Brit Asians may still be referred to (and refer to themselves) as "black," but, broadly speaking, "Asian" now has greater currency in popular and critical discourse. In the 90s, Hall acknowledged that the notion of the black British subject "had a certain way of silencing the very specific experiences of Asian people."[18] This muting had been a weakness of a great deal of white-left cultural analysis (as I discussed in chapter 1), which awkwardly positioned Asians in the class struggle.

Some Asian scholars have welcomed the end of the hegemony of "political blackness." Tariq Modood believes that Asian identities have been ignored in antiracist identity politics dominated by African-Caribbeans. He argues that we should give up "the corrupting ideal of a solidaristic monism," replacing it with the category of "Asian." But Asian identity according to Modood is defined by an affinity to a Mughal and North Indian Muslim version of the Asian subcontinent: "What I mean by 'Asian' identity is some share in the heritage of the civilizations of old Hindustan prior to British conquest. Roughly, it is those people who believe that the Taj Mahal is an object of their history."[19] This reminds me of those tacky marble Taj Mahals many Brit Pakistani households had on their living room coffee tables when we were children. But more seriously, as Sanjay Sharma observes, Modood's nostalgic version of history and identity "fails to acknowledge the huge internal diversities and cleavages of the multiple histories of South Asian people."[20]

The end of political blackness has also caused fragile coalitions to splinter into discrete groups, now replaced with increasingly reified identity politics. While differences in Britain's black communities have been important to articulate, many have retreated into politically limited and regressive forms of culturalism. If for many years the common Brit Asian statement "this is our culture" had a ring of innocence as an apology/explanation of something different from the English *norm,* the notion of "our culture" is now often hailed as immutable tradition: you do it your way, we do it ours; cultures exist alongside each other, equal but separate. This apartheid is encouraged by the state's official multiculturalism, and Asian "community leaders" often agreed on the boundaries of Pakistani Muslim, Bangla, Hindu, Jamaican, Trinidadian, and white English cultural identities.

Aziz Al-Azmeh identifies one such response in the wake of the 1989 Rushdie affair: "Muslim differentialist discourse, a counter racism or a racism in reverse, would seem appropriate in a Britain where culturalist differentialism has . . . fully internalized the Powellite conception of history as the savage play of ascriptive sympathies and antipathies, in which the 'natural' condition of groups of different origins is one in which they are wholly apart, and in which any attempt to mix them would render conflict inevitable. Such is perhaps natural in a Europe that regards itself as tribal territory with precise border controls, in which nations (for some sections of their members) regard themselves as tribes, all ranged above one another according to a tributary model of subalternity." This cultural differentialism manifests itself in, for example, the Yummies, young upwardly mobile Muslims, "who stand against non-liberal liberalism, who dress sharply in clothes to pray and play in, who cloister together in home-centred communities, immune from the vices of the ambient society, but nevertheless sharing the housework."[21] Another troubling form of this phenomenon is the self-appointed "Muslim Parliament," which purports to represent the interests of British Muslims in a pastiche of Westminster. This patriarchal parliament calls for separate Muslim schools and, almost in the magic realist mode of a Rushdie novel, churns out reams of literature cataloging the perfumes, chocolate bars, and other commodities that contain any minuscule trace of alcohol.[22]

If the Rushdie affair spectacularly demonstrated the failure of both an ethnicized religious fundamentalism and a liberal multiculturalism with white Englishness at its core, surrounded by discrete cultures, the re-emergence of the "hybridity" concept seemed to offer a theoretical clearing exercise, one that opened up a space between national monoculture and its mirror-image, ethnic absolutisms.

In his work on the nation and hybridity, Homi Bhabha explains the instability of any single construction of the Nation. "Performative time," the continual present in which national culture/the national is being performed, breaks down unity, refusing the ordering discourse of a reifying history or a collective future. Drawing upon Fanon, Bhabha refers to the people's culture as the "fluctuating moment that the people are just giving shape to." National culture is always liminal, on the threshold of enunciation, its shape never grasped in a single gesture: "The present of the people's history is a practice that destroys the constant principles of the national culture that attempt to hark back to a 'true' national past, which is often represented in the reified forms of realism and stereotype. Such pedagogical knowledges and continuist national narratives miss the 'zone of occult instability where the people dwell' (Fanon's phrase). It is from this instability of cultural signification that the national culture comes to be articulated as a dialectic of various temporalities—modern, colonial, post-colonial, 'native'—that cannot be a knowledge that is stabilized in its enunciation."[23]

According to Bhabha, the ambivalence of the sign of the nation opens up "a supplementary space for the articulation of cultural knowledges that are adjacent and adjunct but not necessarily accumulative, teleological, or dialectical." It is in this gap or (third) space that hybridization occurs, leaving all forms of cultural meaning open to translation "because their enunciation resists totalization."[24] In this hybrid space, "denied knowledges enter upon the dominant discourse and estrange the basis of its authority—its rules of recognition."[25] Bhabha's political hope is that "a willingness to descend into that alien territory . . . may reveal that the theoretical recognition of the split-space may open up the way to conceptualizing an international culture, based not on the exoticism or multi-culturalism of the diversity of cultures, but on the inscription and articulation of culture's hybridity."[26] In an interview with Jonathan Rutherford, Bhabha says that "the importance of hybridity is that it bears the traces of those feelings and practices which inform it, just like a translation, so that hybridity puts together the traces of certain other meanings or discourses. It does not give them the authority of being prior in the sense of being original: they are prior only in the sense of being anterior. The process of cultural hybridity gives rise to something different, something new and unrecognisable, a new area of negotiation of meaning and representation."[27]

Hybridity now enjoys a popular currency, often as a rather sweeping metaphor used to explain the acceleration of cultural mixing in the "global postmodern." Several criticisms have been leveled against its use. Since all cultural processes involve the dynamics of hybridity, the term often lacks any analytical specificity. After all, if everything is hybrid, what's the point of defining the particular as hybrid? For example, the Smiths and almost all English pop is in some ways a hybrid, a translation, a mimicry of North American and Caribbean forms. In his history of the concept, Robert Young suggests that hybridity is rooted in nineteenth-century racialist discourse. The hybrid was considered a biological and cultural mutation with negative consequences.[28] However, one could argue that the term may be reclaimed for other political goals along the lines that *black* and *queer* have been mobilized.

The valorization of cultural hybridity may also be a contemporary form of orientalism and economic domination. According to Aijaz Ahmed, from the vantage point of India, the economic-power relations in the formation of hybrid culture are repressed in the work of Bhabha:

> Into whose culture is one to be hybridised and on whose terms? The wilful [*sic*] relegation of this question to obscurity reveals nonetheless that the underlying logic of this celebratory mode is that of the limitless freedom of a globalised marketplace

which pretends that all consumers are equally resourceful and in which all cultures
are equally available for consumption, in any combination that the consumer desires. Only to the extent that all cultures are encountered in commodified forms does
it become possible to claim that none commands more power than any other or that
the consumer alone is the sovereign of all hybridization. This playful "hybridity"
conceals the fact that commodified cultures are equal only to the extent of their
commodification.[29]

Hybridity does tend to be invoked in the celebration of a largely *Western* cosmopolitan multiculturalism, which is defined against the essentialist identity politics and nationalisms elsewhere, or, closer to home, the diasporic fundamentalisms in the Western metropolis.

Jonathan Friedman contends that hybridity is a normative discourse constructed by postmodern cosmopolitans to rationalize their own praxis in a globalized
world. The fragmentation of the national body politic involves indigenization,
regionalization, and the ethnification of both migrants and nationals. According to Friedman, cultural theorists like Bhabha, Hall, and Gilroy are part of an
intellectual elite that positions itself above the so-called essentialisms and makes
sense of this fragmented global condition for the rest of us: "Hybridisation is a
politically correct solution for this group. It is antiracist, anti-ethnic, and sup-
plies an objective alternative identity."[30] This echoes Ulf Hannerz's view that such
critical discourse is a form of cosmopolitanism claiming mastery over a rapidly
changing world.[31] Clearly, if hybridity is used as a normative model for postmodern subjectivity then it is questionable, particularly when placed in opposition
to some notion of nonhybrid identity. The "reverted" Muslim youth engaged in
hassling women sex workers in Bradford, fictionalized in Hanif Kureishi's *My Son,
The Fanatic,* is, after all, as hybrid in his Islamist beliefs and actions as Kureishi
and his cosmopolitan London literati buddies.

Despite these problems with the hybridity concept, it can have some value for
the analysis of new subjectivities in a world of increased migrations and global
telecommunications. In terms of the specificities of Brit-Asian life, the turn to
the hybrid does make some sense of our in-betweenness and offers a way to represent our experiences after we failed to fit fully into the normative models of
both white English and traditional South Asian identity formations. At the same
time, we should remember that hybridity is not some kind of identity achieved,
a final state. The "hybrid" is a term more constructively adopted to analyze cultural production as process rather than identities. Bhabha himself argues that he
does not seek to answer the question, "What *is* a hybrid?":

The problem is not of an ontological cast, where differences are effects of some more totalizing transcendent identity to be found in the past or the future. Hybrid hy-phenations emphasize the incommensurable elements—the stubborn chunks—as the basis of cultural identifications. What is at issue is the performative nature of differential identities: the regulation and negotiation of those spaces, that are con-tinually, *contingently,* "opening out," remaking the boundaries, exposing the limits of any claim to a singular or autonomous sign of difference—be it class, gender or race. Such assignations of social differences—where difference is neither One nor the Other, but *something else besides, in-between*—find their agency in a form of the "future" where the past is not originary, where the present is not simply transitory. It is, if I may stretch a point, an interstitial future, that emerges *in-between* the claims of the past and the needs of the present.[32]

Smadar Lavie has argued that Bhabha's psychoanalytic model of hybridity as "mimicry in the form of hegemonized rewriting of the Eurocentre" is a "response-oriented model" that "lacks agency." In Bhabha's model, the fragmented Other-ness of the hybrid "can be mended together, forming seams, so that they can be narrated in a Cartesian linear manner." In contrast, Lavie suggests that Gloria Anzaldua's model, outlined in *Borderlands,* gives the hybrid more agency and is collective rather than individual. When hybrids perform an archaeology of their past, they do not recover an uncontaminated precolonial past but one that rec-ognizes the hybridity of the past. According to Lavie, this empowers the self and aims toward collective agency:

> Hybridity is a self that fractures into multiple subjectivities which are unable to mend by forming seams, so the hybrids refuse a Cartesian linear narration. The hybrid's refusal of individuation empowers them to agency as a group, to resist the hegemo-ny of the Eurocentre, not only reacting to it but by opening up a new creative space in the borderzone. The group's creative action can implode the USA-Eurocentre. Therefore the borderzone is not just a dangerous space, but a festive one, because of the creative energy liberated by the common struggle for resistance.[33]

Bhabha's concept of hybridity is also primarily applied to literary sources. Its emphasis on narration has some application to music, but music's extra-linguis-tic qualities may not be adequately accounted for by his theory. To what extent can we apply a general notion of hybridity to Brit-Asian music? Bhabha's em-phasis on creating a narrative is quite different from the continuing fractured subjectivity that seems apparent in Brit-Asian music production. Music cannot be contained simply by narrativization. A sound mix does create seams but is nonlinear, even more so in the digital age. Commodities like recordings, videos, films, and record sleeves do not reflect Asian identities, social types, or archetypes. Music stages identifications, imagines subjectivities, and performs community;

it has a force in its techniques that doesn't simply reflect sociopolitical and cultural conditions. The critical shift away from the relatively static term "identity" to "identification" might offer a better way to suggest the open-endedness of fantasy, imagination, and transdiasporic appropriation in these processes. Such identifications may be fleeting or continuous, reactionary or progressive.

In the music press, hybridity is often invoked with musical "fusion." But fragmented subjectivities with different subject positions in juxtaposition may be considered distinct from the "fusion" in which two separate musical traditions come together seamlessly. Prasad Bidaye writes:

> For musicians, the only alternative is to tune into these frustrations and improvise on them. So they navigate through their musical headspace, finding fragments of chords and raags, beats and taals, and orchestrate them to make sense of the confusion. But be it personal or musical, it still isn't fusion. It isn't easily resolved, like the utopias of an "East meets West" record by the Beatles, Alice Coltrane or the Mahavishnu Orchestra. For the new generation of South Asian artists, East and West have already met, in the bloodstream and the ear. . . . The identities of South Asian people in the West are no different, except for many of us, there is no cohesion— just tension, leaving our minds in a cultural disarray. We are encouraged on one hand by our parents to maintain static notions of tradition; or on the other hand to assimilate our sounds, smells, thoughts and behaviour into the white, Euro-centric, Christian fold. In the new music of our peers, those forces are being refuted and the elements are re-fused. . . . South Asia and the West "talk" through each other's instruments. It doesn't sound pretentiously academic, or like music being made for a lab experiment, a cultural test tube. Each of these translations is an expression of a fused identity. And they're happening naturally in the living experiences of the musicians before they are even played out.[34]

This is a fusion of sorts, but not one where two readily formed "cultures" come together; this fusion is partly a re-fusal. Its musical articulation is the sound mix. The discourse of the music press is forever groping for a language to describe the mixed-up hybrid sounds of the new music. The metaphors are varied; culinary ones are among the laziest and most popular, comparing the mix of sounds to the blend of ingredients in a masala. This seems the easiest way to assimilate the foreign into the national body politic, to cannibalize the other. Therefore, when I use the headings "Hotter Than a Vindaloo Curry" and "Bombay Mix" in this chapter's sections on Apache Indian and Bally Sagoo, respectively, I'm ironically signaling the orientalist practice perpetuated by the music press and sometimes the musicians themselves.

For some critics, the "culture clashes" and restless dialogics in popular musical culture have provided glimmers of hope for a multicultural Britain. In the late

80s, Hebdige suggested that instances of cutting and mixing musical genres across racial-ethnic lines help to redefine national identity: "Through the patterns of belonging and distancing established in these forms of cultural production, new forms of 'British' identity become available which circulate along with the records themselves in the clubs and cassette players and on the pirate radio stations. At a time when the integrity of the national culture is asserted against a common European identity, a genuinely cosmopolitan post-colonial space is opened up within and against 'Englishness'—a set of identities available to all irrespective of their skin colour, 'rooted' in the airwaves."[35] These technologically mediated musical exchanges do often suggest a more open version of the national but their hybridity quotient doesn't indicate their political value. Reactionary and progressive impulses are present in these forms. As we track these sounds, we need to listen to the multiple ways in which their aesthetics and politics might be smart and/or simplistic.

Pump Up the Bhangra

Hebdige was responding in part to the emergence of bhangra-based music in Brit-Asian communities in the 1980s. Bhangra was the first Brit-Asian popular music to be written about extensively by the white English press and has been linked to the emergence of a specifically *British* Asian identity.

Bhangra has its origins as a rhythmic folk music played to celebrate the Punjabi new year, Dhasaki, the festival of the harvest, and weddings in the Punjab. The characteristic rhythms of the dhol drum encouraged dancing. In the early 1980s, bands like Heera and Alaap in Punjabi West London, who had once performed in temples, took their sets to weddings and other social functions. With growing reputations as live acts, these artists began playing larger concert venues. Mikha K of the KK Kings believes that bhangra culture took hold during the ascendancy of the video cassette recorder in Asian communities: "In the 1970s, the only chance to meet the opposite sex was at the local Rex cinemas, which we used to go to every Sunday after temple. But once the VCR came out, parents could say to their daughters, 'Oh, we'll just get those movies out on video.' Who wanted to go to the Rex and sit with a hundred other boys? Eventually, they all closed down. Suddenly, there was nothing for us."[36]

With the demise of Indian movie theaters as public meeting places, weddings and concerts were promoted as bigger and more elaborate social occasions. Musicians from the Punjab and Britain would play these events, often supported by a DJ spinning dance records from the U.S. and the U.K. Initially in the early 1980s, very little U.K. bhangra was available on vinyl. This limited DJ-ing. Busi-

nesses and specialist shops in Asian neighborhoods could afford only to release
the cheaper cassette format. As the demand in Punjabi neighborhoods grew,
bhangra was eventually released on vinyl in albums and twelve-inch singles. Soon
DJs were mixing reggae, U.S. black music, and bhangra in clubs, followed by
studio mutations based on these techniques. Alaap went into the studio to record
an album with the producer Deepak Khazanchi, using synthesizers and drum
machines to supplement traditional bhangra instruments.

By the mid-1980s, bhangra discos were held in large dance venues. The grand-
children of empire regularly filled the Empire Ballroom in Leicester Square. Several thousand teenagers and young adults would attend these dances, which were
often scheduled in the afternoon to get around the curfews imposed (particularly on girls) by some Asian parents. Girls would duck out of school, change out
of their school uniforms into shiny shalwar-kamiz outfits in the loos, dance,
maybe drink, meet boys, change back into their school uniforms, and be back
home before dinner time. Of course, the English media were quick to latch onto
this aspect of bhangra culture, hungry for stories of tradition-modernity generation clashes so they could remind us that Asians came from "backward" cultures.

Pirate and community radio stations like Sunrise continue to lend support to
bhangra music. Magazines such as *Ghazal and Beat* have helped to shape an audience in a burgeoning Brit-Asian music industry. Cassettes and CDs released
by Asian labels may sell over 100,000 copies in the case of established bands like
Safri Brothers, Alaap, Heera, and Pardesi Music Machine but do not reach the
chart shops because they are still predominantly sold in grocery stores and other
Asian retail outlets rather than mainline music shops and megastores.[37]

By the late 1980s, the discourse on British bhangra considered it a reflection of
the identity of the generation born and/or brought up in Britain. Bhangra allowed
for the assertion of British Asian identity for many Asians who had previously felt
"lost within a scopic economy of black and white."[38] Gurinder Chadha's 1989 short
documentary *I'm British But* used mostly bhangra music to reveal how sonically
and psychically Brit Asians were "in the mix." To illustrate this, in one of the film's
rhythmic montages the brightly colored record sleeve for "Rule Britannia/Bhangra
Lovers," a twelve-inch dance single by D.C.S., spins into frame: Lord Kitchener
points at the viewer in the famous pose of the "Your country needs you" recruitment poster from the First World War. This new version of the patriotic image
features the aristocratic minister wearing a turban with a Union Jack design. The
musical commodity itself, in its images and within the grooves of the record, contains new ways of conceiving of Britishness past and present.

Though bhangra as an indigenous Punjabi form had been transformed by
Punjabi diasporic sensibilities in the U.K., it was seen as emblematic of a

broader "Asian" identity that encompassed other subcontinental descendants in the U.K. While the bhangra scene has proved attractive across ethnic and religious lines, the conflation of the music with Brit-Asianness simplifies its dispersal and overestimates its currency with Brit-Asian youth. Many Brit-Asian musicians not working in this particular musical idiom routinely express annoyance with the white media's perception that if they're British and Asian their music must be bhangra.

Record companies and the music press in the early 90s had high hopes that bhangra would cross over into the pop charts or at least occupy a sizable chunk of the world music market. The West London–based label Multitone was picked up by BMG for international distribution. However, these hopes have not materialized. This may be partly due to the image of the music, which restricts its wide marketability. The bhangra look is often personified as "old men with Elvis suits and beer bellies." The shiny shirts and flared trousers of many of the older bhangra acts were often an embarrassment to Asian youth trying to define themselves as hip and modern against an established image of Asians as thoroughly uncool. Bhangra is also music primarily for dancing, and its lyrical repertoire has mostly remained limited to subjects like romance and the battle of the sexes. But despite its lack of crossover success, many Brit-Asian owned-and-operated labels continue to release bhangra with international distribution. Independent labels like Nachural and Roma Bank, based in Birmingham, have released material that mixes bhangra with ragga, funk, and jungle. Bhangra maintains a transnational network of labels, specialist shops, clubs, and internet websites across the diaspora with important focal points in Southall, the Bay Area in California, Chicago, Toronto, and Punjab.

Hotter Than a Vindaloo Curry: Apache Indian

The moment of bhangra's articulation of "Asian" identity and *I'm British But* at the end of the 1980s was also the moment of *The Satanic Verses.* In the book that Rushdie calls a "love song to hybridity," he documents the importance of black/Asian dance-floor culture. In the deterritorialized, diasporic spaces of the postimperial capital, Ellowen Deeowen, he stages the following cinematic scene, an urban location that exists somewhere between the expressionist milkbar of *A Clockwork Orange* and the subterranean jazz club of *Absolute Beginners:*

> What is to be found here, one mile from the Shandaar [Cafe], here where the beat meets the street, at Club Hot Wax, formerly the Blak-An-Tan? On this star-crossed and moonless night, let us follow the figures—some strutting, decked out, hot to

trot, others surreptitious, shadow-hugging, shy—converging from all quarters of the
neighborhood to dive, abruptly underground, and through this unmarked door.
What's within? Lights, fluids, powders, bodies shaking themselves, singly, in pairs,
in threes, moving towards possibilities. But what, then, are these other figures, obscure in the on-off rainbow brilliance of the *space,* these forms frozen in their attitudes amid the frenzied dancers? What are these that hip-hop and hindi-pop but
never move an inch?—"You looking good, Hot Wax posse!" Our host speaks: rant-
er, toaster, deejay nonpareil—the prancing Pinkwalla, his hair the palest rose, the
whites of his eyes likewise, his features unmistakably Indian, the haughty nose, long
thin lips, a face from a Hamza-nama cloth. An Indian who has never seen India, East-
India-man from the West Indies, white black man. A star.[39]

The hybrid disc jockey presides over the turntables and the microphone, exhorting
the dancers in this Asian underground venue with his "rants toasts raps." The
groovers in Rushdie's imagined club move amidst the waxworks figures of an
alternative Madame Tussaud's—"migrants of the past," forgotten black people
of British history like the Crimean War nurse Mary Seacole, Queen Victoria's aide
Abdul Karim, and Ignatius Sancho, who in 1782 was the first African writer to
be published in England. In another section of the club, other figures stand
motionless in a national chamber of horrors. This waxworks of English villainy
"bathed in evil green light" includes Oswald Mosley, Enoch Powell, and Margaret Thatcher. In a bizarre ritual, the dancers choose a sacrificial figure, which is
placed in a giant microwave and then melted down. This night the crowd's most
popular choice is "Maggie-maggie-maggie," who, after a switch is thrown, melts
into a puddle. The club's clientele heaves a cathartic sigh, as Pinkwalla proclaims,
"The fire this time."

Homi Bhabha praises the scene for its enactment of "the revenge of the migrant hybrid."[40] In contrast, Timothy Brennan argues that Rushdie's parody of
dub poetry in Pinkwalla's rhymes demeans the work of poet performers like Lin-
ton Kwesi Johnson, reducing their work to "a kind of proxy politics or mastur-
batory venting of rage."[41] Admittedly the lyric in question is rather simplistic
verse—"Now-mi-feel-indignation-when-dem-make-insinuation-we-no-part-a-
de-nation-an-mi-make-proclamation-a-de-true-situation-how-we-make-contri-
bution-since-de-Rome-occupation"—and it doesn't measure up to the dread
rhymes of LKJ at his best, but there have been countless "political" rhymes of
this simplicity recorded by Black British and Brit-Asian artists, including Asian
Dub Foundation. Rushdie's mild piss-take of the agitprop toaster shows that
Pinkwalla is not based on the great dub poets LKJ and Michael Smith, but more
likely incorporates elements of many MCs, including the albino DJ Yellowman,
who came to fame in Jamaica during the early 1980s.

But there is also an element of prophecy in this literary scene; for the early 90s almost immediately brought forth a real British Indian toaster chatting on the mic in Jamaican Patois and Punjabi. This was Apache Indian (real name Steve Kapur), Britain's first major South Asian crossover star with big hits in the British pop and reggae charts, as well as in Jamaica and India. Often combining the two musical genres, Apache Indian remains more of a ragga artist than bhangra musician. He takes his nom-de-plume from the Jamaican ragga star Super Cat, who often calls himself Wild Apache and the Don Dada. Apache Indian also goes by the name of the Don Raja, a title favored by fans in India. Kapur was born in Jullander City in Punjab but grew up in Handsworth, Birmingham:

> It's a very multicultural, very close community, strongly Asian and black. Very strong reggae vibes seem [to] come from Handsworth. I went to the same school as Steel Pulse and a lot of bands and sound systems come from there. Again, I went to a very multicultural, very mixed school. I had black friends, white friends, Asian friends, and I got to appreciate and understand other people. . . . When I had dreadlocks, everyone assumed that I was black, not Asian. I once went into an Indian shop on Soho Road in Handsworth and the people in the shop said (in their own language— which was also my own language) "watch out, he's a thief." They thought I was black, but obviously I could understand what they were saying. I didn't say anything. I just left the shop, but I realised that maybe every black person gets that all the time.[42]

Apache's experience reflects the antagonisms as well as the affinities between African-Caribbean and Asian settlers in a neighborhood like Handsworth.

After leaving school Apache worked as a roadie for several reggae sound systems before finally getting a chance on the microphone to voice his own Handsworth songs. He privately financed the pressing of "Movie Over India," a single that combined Jamaican Patois and Punjabi rhymes. After receiving some radio airplay, the single was a local success and then a national hit on the reggae charts. Apache was signed up by the major label Island Records. His 1993 debut album, *No Reservations,* was an international triple-platinum hit and nominated for the Mercury Prize. Tracks like "AIDS Warning" (promoting safe sex) and "Drink Problem" dealt with issues that some thought constituted an unnecessary airing of the Asian community's dirty linen in public.

What kind of diasporic imaginary and vision of India is present on *No Reservations?* How does Apache Indian construct "home" from his Handsworth location? The album sleeve features the Don Raja posing in designer sportswear and heavy gold jewelry, arms folded in macho ragga pose against a gigantic backdrop of the Indian tricolor flag. The Wheel of Dharma in the middle of the flag encircles his head like a halo. On the back of the sleeve, a collage of images juxtaposes Indian and Jamaican maps, bank notes from both countries, and Rasta symbols like the Lion of Judah and the Star of David. In the sleeve's old photographs, Apache is a baby, a toddler on the mic, poised over a soccer ball in a Manchester United outfit as a young lad, and huddled with other reggae musicians as an adult professional musician. Among these pictures lie the portraits of family members from three generations, snapshots that make the connection to a history rooted in Britain and India. The collage is a representation of diasporic time and space.

Apache hails the Bradford, Birmingham, and Southall posses at the beginning of his first single, "Movie Over India," in which he describes a visit to the motherland to make a film. He travels to famous places and meets Indian celebrities. He rhymes in Patois but also translates Punjabi to English in the song. Another hybrid language is created. The different spellings of proper names such as Lata Mangeshkar and Ravi Shankar in the album's printed lyrics show how a creole language combines Punjabi, Hindi, and Patois and makes a new dialect.[43] At one point on the track, he foregrounds the fact that his style is based on translation by introducing the listener to the members of his family in Punjabi, then translating their titles into English. For the Brit-Asian listener these lyrics offer the pleasure of recognition.

"Movie Over India" promises a fantasy of triumphant return. The homeland is represented by the imagined Punjabi state of Khalistan and the magical world of Bombay cinema. The nation is a collection of tourist sites and mega-stars like Amitabh Bachchan and Rekha. Apache imagines himself to be as omnipotent as these icons. The syncopation of a bouncing dance-hall beat with a harmonium motif and the dhol provide the sonic backdrop for this travel.

Another song that incorporates a journey to India is the hit "Arranged Marriage." The dhol, Indian flutes, and a characteristic Punjabi wedding rhythm introduce the rhyming Patois of this song about going to the Punjab to find a bride. "Arranged Marriage" is a humorous miniature describing a common social ritual. Apache in character tells his parents that he wants a Punjabi wife. They send him home to Jullander City where he is introduced to a matchmaker. He meets young women of all shapes and sizes, and lays down his prescription for the perfect mate. She has to be beautiful, sweet like Jalebi (a sticky, syrupy sweet), speak Punjabi, English, *and* Patois, and provide him with excellent cooked food and the finest sensimilla herb. She must respect him and the members of his family. At the end of the song, with his new Indian bride back in Birmingham, he wonders how he is going to tell his girlfriend the news. Many Asian men have (often secret) relationships with women whom they unceremoniously dump when they find an arranged match more in keeping with their parents' requirements.[44]

The sexual politics of the song are ambiguous. Asian listeners will recognize the continuing tradition of sending young men back to the continent to fetch a (virgin) bride. In the song, a young woman's desired qualities serve the needs of a dominant male. The male chorus of "Me Want Gal" resounds hungrily through the song like the lustful male chorus in a Punjabi wedding dance. On the other hand, the female backing singers pose the question, "Is it love or just a lover?" They immediately answer, "I can be one or the other." Does that mean both or only one? The song is such an over-the-top staging of the whole arranged marriage scenario, with its litany of ridiculous demands of this idealized woman, that it undercuts the masculinist rhetoric. We need not take it literally. The banter between men and women recalls the staged musical dialogue about gender relations at many Punjabi and South Asian social events, particularly weddings. Apache's confession that he has a girlfriend at home reveals the duplicity of the man. On the other hand, the musical art of dance-hall rhyming (like rap) is often based on boasting and claiming masculine agency and omnipotence in a white world where black (and Asian) men do not have much social power. The story is told within this structure. The song is a very infectious dance tune that panders to a fantasy of male power and marital bliss defined by patriarchal standards, but it is also a piece of musical theater that allows Asian women and men to laugh at the ludicrous claims of these masculine desires. The video for "Arranged Marriage" presents a multicultural crowd of British good-time groovers locked on to the object of their gaze, a lone exotic and poorly choreographed Indian dancer with the obligatory bindi on her forehead marking her cultural difference. This is the kind of orientalist image of India one expects to see perpetrated in a Michael or Janet Jackson video.

"Arranged Marriage," like "Movie Over India," presents an India of plenitude and infinite promise. The woman is the motherland.[45] "India" has feminized contours here that are similar to those defined by tourist discourse. With its more hip-hop-style beat, "Come Follow Me," another song from the first album, features Apache's Patois-and-Punjabi description of another visit home. Apache goes to Agra to visit the Taj Mahal and to Bombay, the Himalayas, Khalistan, the Ganges. This map of the nation is supported by references to historical figures like Mahatma Gandhi and General Dyer. This is picture-book India, though the names of Gandhi and Dyer immediately have a powerful resonance in collective memory. At the end of the tune, Apache's black British friend Mikey G asks him if he can get a ticket for the next trip to India. Such tourism is rather like the vision of Jamaica in the album's "Magic Carpet," a fantasy for masterful global travel and an exotic view of the Third World. Apache maps out his flight over the Caribbean island, catching all the sights, but he cannot find anywhere to park his carpet. Caught in the tropes and traps of tourism, and despite his vantage point above the clouds, he still has only partial sight of the nation.

Apache Indian's meteoric rise coincided with the opening up of the Indian economy to foreign investment and commodities through the Congress government's policies of "economic liberalization" in the early 1990s. Sales of his recordings benefited from the expansion of MTV-Asia and Rupert Murdoch's Star TV. "Arranged Marriage" was deemed the "biggest Western music hit in the history of the subcontinent. Even bigger than Michael Jackson's 'Beat It' which until then had been the biggest hit in India."[46]

The India imagined in Apache Indian's music was very different from the India he visited for the first time since he was seven years old. The artist toured India in 1993, played to crowds of several thousand people in Delhi and Bombay, met high officials, gave money to charity, and was asked how he would solve political problems in the Punjab. The tour came in the wake of the destruction of the Babri Masjid in Ayodhya in December 1992, communal violence in many of India's cities, and the May bombings in Bombay. A frenetic but successful first Indian tour was followed by a second that was badly organized. A British pop star who had made some "political" points on his recordings was out of his depth in the spotlight of the unfamiliar Indian media. It was also impossible to live up to the U.K. music press's ridiculous tag of the "Gandhi of pop." Apache returned to Birmingham. "Move On" was an attempt to come up with a response to events in Ayodha but Apache's political imagination stretched to naive original lyrics that sounded like they might have been written by Rushdie's Pinkwalla.

In 1994 Apache released his second album, *Make Way for the Indian*. A collection with fewer bhangra influences, the recording marked a return to his Jamaican dance-hall roots with some hip-hop collaborations. Tracks included socially conscious reggae in the cover versions of Willie Williams's "Armagideon Time" with Yami Bolo and Doctor Alimentado's "Born for a Purpose" produced by Kingston's Bobby Digital. The fewer markedly Indian elements in the music may have been a reaction against Apache's "homecoming" experience and the burden of representation this entailed, though the shift in musical style could also be attributed to the rising number of collaborations and musical crossovers between Jamaican ragga/dance-hall and African-American hip-hop. Some critics accused Apache of discarding his Asianness; others argued that he had made the transition from novelty act to more mature performer and recording artist.

Apache had his biggest U.K. hit with "Boom Shack a Lack," a catchy singalong ragga number that had no trace of Indian culture in its lyrics and music. In February 1995 he left Island for Warner Music Sweden AB, which could assure him of wider international distribution. He negotiated a deal for his own label, Sunset Records. *Real People* (1996), re-released as *Wild East* in a slightly different version, returned to Punjabi influences. The album was produced by Harjinder Boparai, the respected producer of the bhangra group the Safri Brothers, and it incorporated Apache's Patois rhyming over Punjabi vocals by Malkit Singh and Hindi singing by Sameera Singh.

If the novelty of Apache Indian has worn off and much of the music is unremarkable, Apache has negotiated a strong position within a transnational market for music made by South Asians. While his difficult return to India might reveal what Tony Mitchell calls the "deracination" of diasporic South Asians and the gap between the fantasy and the reality of the homeland, Apache Indian is now as much a pop commodity in India as in Britain and Jamaica.[47] One way Apache has maintained a relationship with the South Asian homeland has been through the formation of the Apache Indian Foundation, which puts money to work for the disabled in India, particularly the visually disabled.

Bombay Mix: Bally Sagoo

Born in New Delhi, Bally Sagoo also grew up in Birmingham, in the Balsall Heath area. The imaginary in Sagoo's work provides an interesting comparison with Apache Indian's version of the subcontinent. Both Brit-Asian artists emerged in the early 90s and have moved beyond U.K. success to enter the Indian popular music market. Sagoo is a DJ-turned-remix-artist and producer. Like many South Asian musicians and DJs he has absorbed Afrodiasporic musical forms like funk, reggae, soul, house, and hip-hop. Immersed in bass culture, Brit-Asian DJs and mixing engineers like Sagoo and Panjabi MC have developed their own recording identities in the process of remixing other people's works. The account of his youth and early DJ-ing reveals the negotiation of a black-Asian British identity:

> When we moved to England (from Delhi), I was about seven months old, so I was brought up there. My parents are very traditional and so they should be. The struggle I went through in the early years, being brought up in a black area, not having too many Asian friends, losing my identity as a British citizen really, not knowing what India was all about, I mean I was hundred per cent kala [black]. This was when I was probably 15, I was hanging out with those kind of boys. I was listening to what was called "electro" in those days which was Afrika Bambaataa—in the early 80s there was a big boom for that kind of music. I got into remixing with my friends in my bedroom with a couple of turntables. I always dreamt of having a pair of Technics turntables because it was the Rolls Royce of mixers. I couldn't afford them so we were using turntables with no kind of pitch control where you could speed or slow up a

record. That's really how I got my experience. I was getting into so much remixing, that everytime I heard a record, I was instantly doing something different with it and was getting so much credit from the black crowd because I was beating the black boys at their own game. It was a compliment and nobody was doing it. . . . The music scene was very traditional—Indian music was Indian music, Hindi music was Hindi music, Bhangra music was very very Alaap (they were the pioneers). I did not go to Indian parties, I did not hang out with Indian people, I didn't like Asian girls, (smiles) to be honest—I was too much into the hip-hop side of things. I think as the years went on, it worked to my advantage because then I realised, listen, I am Asian when I look in the mirror. My parents are speaking Punjabi, I eat with my hands and not with a knife and fork. Yet, when I walk out the door, I am walking with a little bounce.[48]

Sagoo's blackness is *embodied* in his everyday life; his activities, the way he walks, and his sexual desire reflect his deep identification with black culture. Eventually Sagoo was to explore his own South Asian roots through black musical forms.

In the early 80s Sagoo began mixing British-based Punjabi music, beefing it up with bass lines that owe more to reggae, hip-hop, and house records. These CDs and tapes were released on the Oriental Star Agencies label, a record company operated from an Asian-run music shop in Birmingham. Sagoo's music owes as much to the South Bronx as it does to the Punjab, Bombay, and Birmingham. Its guilt-free global pillage is a common feature of contemporary dance music culture. The crazier the juxtaposition the better, as long as the tracks are danceable. With samples and motifs from the highly self-referential and global economy of dance-floor cultures, Sagoo marshals ragga, house, and sparser techno rhythmic styles on his remixes for Britain's bhangra singer Malkit Singh on the *Golden Star* EP (1991). On the title cut, the Punjabi singer's voice is cut-and-pasted across ragga beats, sometimes interrupted by Jamaican chatting or toasting. Chunky electronic R&B bass tones and the sampled voice of Liberace open the "hardcore mix" of "Gur Nalon Ishq Mitha." The Deff and Dubb mixes of "Hey Jamalo" combine familiar harmonium riffs from Indian folk music genres with the beat-box frenzy of early hip-hop.

On *Magic Touch,* a remix album of the Pakistani qawwali singer Nusrat Fateh Ali Khan, "Kinna Sohna" transforms an Islamic devotional into a soul-style love song. Sagoo's remixes of bhangra and qawwali tracks sold over 100,000 copies each in the South Asian market in India, Britain, and North America.[49] *On the Mix,* a compilation of these remixes, was released in 1993 through a distribution deal with Island Records. With this distribution network and potential crossover appeal, Sagoo caught the attention of talent scouts from other major labels. He signed a lucrative $2.5 million five-album deal with Sony that gives him world-wide distribution.

In the "worlding" of popular music, Sony envisaged that Sagoo could be sold to a transnational South Asian market, a huge demographic constituted in India itself. With that in mind, in his first Sony album he tapped the place of Hindi film and its songs in South Asian popular memory. The Bombay-based Hindi film industry (Bollywood) is the most powerful media institution in India and the diaspora. Hindi films now open almost simultaneously in Bombay, Delhi, Chicago, Auckland, and London. The Odeon at Marble Arch regularly screens Bollywood blockbusters, and Indian film producers have set up offices in London. Middle Eastern, North American, and African territories are also lucrative markets for production companies.

For Brit Asians, Hindi films and their songs are vital links to Indian cultural life. Neighborhood stores across the diaspora rent videotapes of movies that have become integral to a collective image of India and Indianness, an imaginary that often crosses religious and ethnic barriers. Sagoo understood that his move into Bollywood musical territory could be profitable for him and Sony. Instead of continuing to mix Punjabi bhangra or qawwali tracks, he chose to re-record Hindi film songs because Bollywood is the hegemonic South Asian cultural formation. Says Sagoo, "You're conquering a bigger market with Hindi. Bengalis, Sikhs, Muslims all listen to Hindi songs, whereas Punjabi bhangra is more of a specialist scene."[50]

Sagoo's first album for Sony, *Bollywood Flashback* (1994), is a state-of-the-art dance-floor production that sounds as polished as a Madonna or Mariah Carey record. The album's slickness is indicative of the transnational recording process, in which different parts of a track can be recorded in far-flung locations, then pieced together in the studio. Sagoo recorded singers in Bombay and rappers and toasters in the U.K. to reinterpret some famous Hindi film songs. In his Birmingham studio, these recorded voices were mixed with his own rhythms. The family record collection was his archive and the basis for the choice of songs on the album. Sagoo picked the songs his parents had played when he grew up in Balsall Heath. His re-recording is, in part, a recalling of that childhood memory.

Cover-version albums of Hindi film songs are common in India. Famous songs are ubiquitous, and parlor games like Antakshari rely on the public's knowledge of famous song lyrics. However, in the early 1990s, the lyrics and melodies of these film songs were rarely supplemented with the bass-heavy arrangements of ragga, R&B, and hip-hop. Significantly, Sagoo's album is dedicated to the eclectic and prolific musical director R. D. Burman, the composer of Hindi movie soundtracks that themselves were the sites for hemispheric collisions. Like Burman, Sagoo continues a tradition of scavenging. *Bollywood Flashback* repeats the hybrid versioning practices of Hindi film music. Such a mix of East and West is nothing new. Whereas Burman took soundtrack riffs from spaghetti westerns and ripped off the twist, bossa nova pop, samba, blaxploitation, and disco forms, combining them with the melodies and elaborate string orchestrations of Indian folk and classical forms, Sagoo now layers the bass-and-drum rhythms of the African diaspora with baroque Hindi melodies, juxtaposing high-pitched female vocals in Hindi with male toasting in Jamaican Patois or rapping American-style. *Bollywood Flashback* is a specifically British view of Indian national popular memory, filtered through Caribbean and American forms. The songs are stretched out into mood pieces. The album simulates travel as a collection of memories.

The opening and closing tracks of the album provide typical examples of Sagoo's revamping of Hindi film music. "Chura Liya" (You've Stolen My Heart) is a song originally arranged by R. D. Burman with a duet by the prolific playback vocalists Asha Bhosle and Mohammed Rafi, from a 1973 blockbuster, *Yaadon Ki Baraat* (Procession of Memories), that Ashish Rajadhyaksha and Paul Willemen lament brought the disco era to Hindi cinema.[51] In Sagoo's version, the duet is essentially duplicated by Reema and Debashish Das Gupta. Cheshire Cat, a white Birmingham toaster, interrupts their romantic reverie in the second half of the track with some completely unrelated boasts about his skill on the mic and his premier place in the sound mix. This is typical of a reggae love song, where a vocal version is followed by a *dub* or largely instrumental version that allows a DJ to talk over the rhythm. Cheshire Cat takes over, riding the very low frequency bass line, as the lovers melt into the depths of the mix, their voices floating in Bollywood dreamland. His presence accentuates the syncopation of Sagoo's version. This is first and foremost a slow jam/dance record with a reggae bass line. Electronic keyboards, drum machines, and a "deep" sub-bass line translate the catchy R. D. Burman Latin shuffle, acoustic guitar, and strings into a more contemporary though still romantic sound for the dance floor. The track is a sonic challenge in the competitive world of sound-system culture. As Sagoo comments in the black-brown-white vernacular of his (deliberately?) misspelled sleeve notes: "This album is goin out to those who have waited all this time for Bally Sagoo to sit in the hot spot and twist the pots on the mixing desk and produce the most modern Hindi album ever!!! To the pozers who recon their sound system can handle the bee line on 'Chura Liya' . . . Bullshit!!" "Chura Liya" was the first Indian pop song to get daytime rotation on BBC Radio One and also had heavy rotation on Channel V and MTV in India.

"Choli Ke Peeche," the closing track on *Bollywood Flashback,* is a suggestive, even raunchy, rhythmic number originally sung by Alka Yagnik and Chorus for the star Madhuri Dixit in the 1994 film *Khalnayak* (The Villain). The sexually suggestive original had Indian politicians calling for its ban in India; "Choli Ke Peeche" translates as "What's behind your blouse?" In Sagoo's version the oft-sampled keyboard ripple that opens the original is still present, but the rhythm is replaced by a jump hip-hop beat, similar to that used in the international rap hits "Jump" and "Jump Around" by Kriss Kross and House of Pain, respectively. "Bounce, come on, now check it. Bounce, come on, now check it," repeats the rapper MC Chan several times, addressing the listener as well as the women who sing the Hindi verses. He brags of his amorous skills and "giving it to you all night long." Black male bragging meets Indian female coquettishness in a playful flirtatious dialogue. Ironically, Indian masculinity is articulated through *black* popular cultural vernacular form, while Indian femininity is based on representations in Indian films. Like Apache Indian, Bally Sagoo imaginatively returns to India *through* blackness.

Bollywood Flashback initiated a huge "Hindi remix" movement. The term is largely a misnomer since most examples of Hindi remix are not strictly remixes but re-recordings or cover versions of old film songs with new dance beats and nothing of the original sound recording. Since the early 1990s, Hindi film songs have become more "disco-fied," much to the chagrin of most Indian critics, who mourn the decline of the lyric in Hindi film *geet*. Lyrics tend to be catchy and childishly simple rather than poetic. Countless Hindi songs are replicated over the functional dance beats of cheerfully hammering Eurodisco rather than the more complex play with repetition of Jamaican and African-American rhythm styles.

Sagoo's follow-up album, *Rising in the East* (1996), features singers from India and Pakistan on original Sagoo compositions. He describes the record as a contemporary R&B album with Hindi and Punjabi lyrics. The arrangements are slower, more languid, less designed for the up-tempo dance floor. "Dil Cheez," a single from the album, was the first Hindi song to reach the British top five. The success of *Bollywood Flashback* also gave Sagoo a host spot on Club MTV in India. Many of his releases now cater specifically to the Indian market. He recorded an album with the film megastar Amitabh Bachchan under the title *Aby Baby*. The recording features Amitabh talking in his famously dulcet tones over some decidedly insipid backing music composed by Sagoo. The saxophone interludes on the album reproduce the style of Kenny G., another favorite in India. With bhangra now a commercially popular genre in India, largely due to the influence of the singer Daler Mehndi, Sagoo has felt safe to return to producing bhangra albums for Indian release. He has gone from creating music mainly for an "ethnic" market within Britain to being a global pop star whose largest market and fan base is urban India.

One magazine chose the metaphor of the airport to describe Sagoo's transnational music: "If Bally Sagoo were an airport, he'd be JFK with a welcome message saying 'Give me your Madonnas, your Jackos, your Springsteens and I shall transform them.'"[52] This recalls Iain Chambers use of the airport as emblematic of nomadism: "With its shopping malls, restaurants, banks, post-offices, phones, bars, video games, television chairs and security guards, it is a miniaturised city. As a simulated metropolis it is inhabited by a community of modern nomads: a collective metaphor of cosmopolitan existence where the pleasure of travel is not only to arrive, but also not to be in any particular place."[53] The imaginary travel of musicians like Apache Indian and Sagoo has been translated into real travel. These musicians have nomadic careers. If there have always been communication networks between Britain, the subcontinent, and other parts of the South Asian diaspora that have bypassed mainstream or dominant media channels, many of these channels have become integrated into the networks of transnational media corporations.

Rage and South Asian Salvation: Militant Raps

Another return to South Asia as homeland in the diasporic imaginary can be found in the work of the black-Asian hip-hop duo Fun^da^mental. The group appropriates Hindi film music but to a radically different effect. The string arrangements of Bollywood add an epic, grandiose dimension to the soundscape of dense hip-hop beats. Fun^da^mental was given the tag of the "Asian Public Enemy" by a lazy music press because of its polemics. In one respect, Fun^da^mental is like that rap group: it does "bring the noise." The density of the layered production seems modeled on the barrage of sounds found on the Bomb Squad's early productions for Public Enemy. Where Bally Sagoo's remixes are as clean and polished as any mainstream dance pop record, Fun^da^mental's noise is busier, a cluttered sound and clamor of voices matching the urgency of the lyrics.

The core of the group is a black Briton, Dave Watts (AKA Impi-D), and the Pakistani-born Aki Nawaz Qureshi (AKA Propa-Gandhi). Guest rappers include Hot Dog and MC Mushtaq. Aki grew up in Bradford and was the drummer in Southern Death Cult, the original early-80s incarnation of the rock group the Cult. He also started the Nation label, which released Fun^da^mental's music through a distribution deal with Beggar's Banquet in the U.K. and Mammoth records in the United States.

Fun^da^mental's work presents an apocalyptic vision of racial violence. The cover of the 1994 album *Seize the Time* (named after Bobby Seale's slogan) shows a clock set to five minutes past twelve. The words "eleven sixty-five" are written on the cover several times. It is too late; forces beyond our control are moving toward inevitable racial conflict. The samples tell the story. Malcolm X says, "If someone lays a hand on you, put him in the cemetery." Farrakhan is looped repeatedly: "You have never seen the wrath of the black man." For Fun^da^mental, the nation is in a state of civil war.

"Dog Tribe," a single from the album, opens with the dissonance of a phone call by a member of the far-right Combat 18 group: "The BNP's got your card marked, you bastards. We're gonna burn your building down, you fuckheads. C-18's watching you, you communist nigga-loving Paki cunts. Fuckin' dickheads, we're gonna hang you for burnin' the British flag. You'll hang from every fuckin' flagpole in Britain for burnin' the Union Jack." On the page these words are incendiary but the sample captures the virulence of the delivery, the acid anger and hatred of the utterance. A vinyl scratching riff introduces a propulsive beat and the repetition of the words "primitive" and "the city." The rap bursts in, warning of militarized skinheads who kill black children and burn Bengalis. Against this tide of violence, MC Mushtaq shouts that blacks and Asians must unite and fight, and die if necessary. The sound is an assault on the senses, dense with Indian drums, flutes, and melodramatic Bollywood string orchestration all superimposed over a militant, almost marching drum pattern and fulsome bass line. The track is a merger of hardcore hip-hop and South Asian elements. Some remixes of "Dog Tribe" remove the lead vocal and BNP phone call, instead sampling a male Indian classical singer whose mournful voice floats into the mix, giving the song a gravity and grace. This version tears the Indian sonic/vocal signifier from its literal meaning or frame of reference within the aesthetic rules of Indian classical music.

The black-and-white video for "Dog Tribe" presents a narrative in which Aki plays an Asian youth who is attacked and beaten up by white youth, then politicized by the failure of the state to protect its citizens. Initially he follows the democratic way. After failing to convince the police to do anything about catching the culprits, he takes a signed petition to his Member of Parliament. Outside the House of Commons he is met with indifference from the MP. This leads him to join a vigilante group to defend the neighborhood's residents from racist violence. The video was banned by the BBC.

Through versions of "blackness," many Brit Asians speak their Muslim identities. In "Mera Mazab" (My Religion), U.S. hip-hop vernacular meets Quranic verse in MC Mushtaq's rhymes. The collective imaginary is not focused on a homeland India but around a transnational Islamic identity. For many young U.K. Muslims, Black America successfully merges Islam with popular culture. Malcolm X is a popular celebrity and a religious icon. Posters of the brother at prayer in the Mecca mosque cover the walls of young Muslim bedrooms. For many Muslim males, African-American Islam is as attractive as the South Asian Islam of their parents' generation. A pan-Islamism generated by student and youth groups constructs solidarity with other Muslims in the United States, Palestine, Bosnia, Chechnya, and Kosovo. Fun^da^mental establishes an affective link between African-Americans and Asians through the cut-up at the beginning of "President Propaganda," which takes Farrakhan samples and splices them to say, "You have the Negro problem / We have the Muslim problem."

This predominantly male militancy is also a reaction against U.K. Islamophobia in the wake of the Rushdie affair and the "ethnic cleansing" of Muslims in Bosnia and Kosovo. In an editorial in *The Spectator* (19 October 1991), Charles Moore voiced this racist prejudice against Muslims: "You can be British without speaking English or being Christian or being white, but nevertheless Britain is basically English-speaking, Christian and white, and if one starts to think that it might become basically urdu-speaking and Muslim and brown, one gets frightened and angry. . . . Because of our obstinate refusal to have enough babies, Western civilisation will start to die at the point when it could have been revived with new blood. Then the hooded hordes will win, and the Koran will be taught, as Gibbon famously imagined, in the schools of Oxford."[54]

In response to this kind of xenophobia, Fun^da^mental aims for calculated shock effect, creating a spectacle to attack white power. The group has had a particular fondness for inverting orientalist semiotics. Early promotional photographs present the members in guerrilla uniform, Aki Nawaz's head wrapped in a Palestinian keffiyah. Is this Third World revolutionary chic or anti-orientalist sartorial statement? Fun^da^mental's CD covers rework the melodramatic and iconic film poster styles of Bollywood to present imposing angry young men with guns and bloodstained clothes, mosques and minarets, crescent moons, and Arabic script, graphically designed to prick the perceptions of Brit/Euro Islamophobia.[55]

The group's music points to the failure of U.K. multiculturalism. In an interview with *The Guardian,* Aki states: "What does 'multi-culturalism' mean? . . . I don't think the Asian community sees any multiculturalism going on. In Bradford, the blacks live in the inner city, and the whites in the suburbs. It's a term that's bandied about by whites who don't really know what it means. A lot of white liberals are patronising—they talk down to you and say you should do things their way. They don't realise that you're now educated and know your history."[56] Fun^da^mental's diagnosis may be accurate but its solution to these racist conditions is a worrying move toward a rhetoric of exclusivism and cultural differentialism, linked to the black nationalist fantasies of Louis Farrakhan and the Nation of Islam. According to this view, there can never be a rapprochement between white and black. We are headed for an apocalyptic racial war. This is not that far removed from the vision of inevitable racial violence in Morrissey's more pathetic "Asian Rut."

However, Fun^da^mental's music is by no means exclusively Islamist. The group brings forward other voices on its recordings. Two guests, the Sri Lankan–British Arthanayake and the Indian Subi Shah, offer other arguments over Aki's music.

Arthanayake's "Fartherland" is a spoken-word piece about the difficulty of finding a place to belong, a subjectivity in which to anchor oneself. Though awkwardly phrased at times, the teenage rap undermines much of Propa-Gandhi, MC Mushtaq, and Impi-D's rabble-rousing on *Seize the Time*. Talking over a minimal hip-hop drum pattern, the writer asks why he must crave to be an "honorary white man." He discusses the different models of cultural and social identity available in multiracist Britain. There are no simple answers to the problem of belonging, no easy ways home. Arthanayake walks through suburbia with gangs of white kids a constant threat. He goes to school where he is taught Eurocentric history and doesn't know his own. But a racialized politics is found to be no solution. There is no promised land or mythical home to which one can return, no way out of unbelonging. In "Fartherland," Arthanayake is skeptical of the patriarchal narratives that seek to empower Asians in Britain.

The masculinity of national and diasporic yearnings is also questioned in another spoken-word piece by Subi Shah called "Mother India." Rather than question the construction of the homeland in gendered and familial terms, "Mother India" reels off a list of Third World women, a litany of role models such as the Prophet Muhammad's wives Khadija and Aisha, subcontinental rulers like Raziya Sultan, Rani Jahnsi, and Benazir Bhutto. Shah ends with a plea to the guys to "respect your mothers, sisters, lovers and daughters," and the Islamic platitude that "beneath your mother's feet lies heaven." While these "positive" images interrupt a history of great men, Shah fails to address the structural oppression of women in South Asian families and communities. For South Asian youth, however, such a message might be a first step in a coming-of-age to feminist consciousness and politics.

Taken as a whole, Fun^da^mental's lyrics have the revolutionary zeal and anger of agit-prop. What might be as *revolutionary* as the group's lyrics is its politics of sound. Kodwo Eshun notes that rock critics tend to argue "as if lyrics are more 'serious' than music, as if sound isn't political in itself."[57] The politics of Fun^da^mental's sound are best illustrated on the album *With Intent to Pervert the Cause of Injustice*, essentially an instrumental version of *Seize the Time*. On the former, the sounds of didgeridoos, harmonium drones, tooth harp, drums of all kinds, and the vocals of Indian classical singers are interspersed with segments of DAT recordings made in South Asia. Aki includes the Sufi Muslim rituals of zhikr in Lahore and Punjabi village musicians using the methods of ethnographic field recording like a postcolonial Alan Lomax. This digitally inscribed travel tries to connect to the subcontinent.

Like Apache Indian, when Fun^da^mental actually went "home" to the subcontinent (Pakistan, in this case), the group encountered problems. Members argued about the relative political correctness of their lodgings. Should they stay in expensive hotels like neo-colonial tourists or the houses of village residents? The group split into two separate groups, Detrimental and Fun^da^mental, partly over this issue. Real travel tends to be much messier than its sonic equivalent.

Fun^da^mental continues to tour internationally and collaborate with artists and activists outside Britain. A global political imaginary examining neo-colonialism beyond the British-South Asian relationship has become more important in its work since *Seize the Time*. The recorded monologue at the end of *With Intent to Pervert the Cause of Injustice* sums up the group's confrontational attitude to the oppressor. Aki lectures that the sperm of the colonizer is splattered on his forehead, and that white children are taught to masturbate over the lies in school history books. The "you," presumably denoting the Western world, is indicted for its amoral economic domination in Africa, Asia, Australia, Canada, and South America. Aki advocates a "by any means necessary" philosophy to fight the power. These polemics are part of the group's self-defense and vigilante politics, which unsettle the celebration of globalism advocated by world music discourse.

When I saw the group in concert in Auckland during the WOMAD (World of Music, Arts, and Dance) festival in 1997, it completely broke the hippy feel-good one-world vibe of the festival. Fun^da^mental's sonic assault was more punk than world beat. The group brought Aotearoan New Zealand Pacifikan rapper Che Fu and DJ DLT on stage to reinforce the link between antiracism in the U.K. and New Zealand. Aki, in white kurta pajama, stomped around the stage, a tabla player and Indian vocalist sang parts of Sufi chants, and a dhol player dressed in a long sherwani coat and turban spun around as he whacked out the thumping rhythms. The group's showmanship draws on orientalist spectacle for Western consumers while subverting its easy consumption, though some white folks might "get off" on the angry-young-man-of-color thing because it allows them a good chance to indulge in liberal self-flagellation.

Fun^da^mental's 1998 album *Erotic Terrorism* follows many of the same thematics and polarized politics of anticolonialism and black nationalism of previous albums, but it extends the group's global imaginary in significant ways. The

Indian movie-poster-style image on the cover shows a blood-splattered South Asian man angrily standing with a rifle in his hands while his female partner stands beside him looking worried. Inside the CD booklet the group has reprinted the entire United Nations' Universal Declaration of Human Rights, superimposed over harrowing black-and-white photographs of torture victims and dead bodies. Aki's monologues in between tracks justify the group's confrontational politics in terms of racism, colonialism, and revolution as a universal condition. Noam Chomsky, Jello Biafra, Farrakhan, and other black nationalist speechmakers are sampled as part of a globally dispersed commentary on racism. Here the historical specificities of Britain or the United States are left behind in a universalizing rhetoric. While these aspects of Fun^da^mental's pedagogical "message" may be forms of what Sanjay Sharma calls a "strategic identity politics," they also tend toward Manichean oppositions and a "Gangsta rap dystopia of the white world." As Sharma admits, the incoherences in the group's ideological positions point to the instability of British Asian identity politics.[58]

Putting the group's racial pedagogy aside for a moment, its institutional operations have been important for many Asian musicians. Aki Nawaz runs the Nation label in London. This record company has been a fertile space for Brit-Asian as well as African and Arab musicians working in different electronic and dance music idioms (best represented on the 1997 compilation . . . *And Still No Hits*). Nation's roster has included the rap group Hustlers HC, consisting of two Sikh rappers from West London. Two of their singles superbly document the collective and personal struggle for Asians in London and the details of U.K. racism in the early 1990s.

Adapting its title from John Carpenter's martial arts comedy *Big Trouble in Little China* (1986), the Hustlers' "Big Trouble in Little Asia" has an epic sweep in its narrative of migration, settlement, and memory. The opening rap addresses the difficulty of reclaiming origins for young Asians in Britain. Neo-colonialism has obscured our histories and made it difficult to construct narratives of our selves and communities. The Hustlers tell us that digging into the past is a mammoth task when the culture of colonialism has devalued your cultural heritage or erased it.

In the 1970s, when I was not much older than the Hustlers, teachers were still reading *Little Black Sambo* to us in the classroom. The Romans and their struggles with Boadicea were defined as our heritage. British history was about the local and national but ignored imperial history. Even when, in 1987, I took a night-school A-level in British economic and social history, the syllabus trawled through a Marxist-inflected version of events from the industrial revolution to the present with hardly a mention of colonialism's role in the development of capitalism or the importation of labor from the former colonies.

"Big Trouble in Little Asia" offers a school lesson about the call to the mother country to work as wage labor, and then the move into small-time entrepreneurial capitalism by some members of the Brit-Asian proletariat. The rhymer confesses that a temporally and spatially distant Asia exists primarily in the realm of the imagination. Instead of traveling to an unreachable subcontinent, the track paints a picture of the Brit-Asian urban neighborhood, a harrowing landscape far from the nostalgic white East End of Morrissey-ville. Youths smoke crack cocaine in Brick Lane on Christmas Day; gangsters tighten their grip on the area; religion and culture wars divide the community. These fissures are aggravated by the Asian "coconut" who betrays the people. The track ends with blood on the streets, as the fascists of the BNP are fought by any means necessary in a battle for territory.

The rap lyrics have been analyzed by a number of academics in the anthology *Dis-orienting Rhythms: The Politics of the New Asian Dance Music,* but these critics pay scant attention to the musical sound itself. Part of the power of "Big Trouble" comes from the smooth jazz-funk music and low-key lyrical delivery, which belie the anger and violence of the subject matter. The two rappers are quiet and restrained. In their London accents, their voices calmly lay out the urban images in a chatty style. This "conversating" is cool and detached, like Snoop Doggy Dogg's delivery, and so heightens the wintry tension of the landscape. The effect also recalls the work of Gil Scott-Heron in "Winter in America" and "The Bottle." Female backing vocals add "Big Trouble, Big Trouble," as if this were a laid-back R&B tune. Every time the rappers mention the track's title, a bitten-off sample of Rakim with "Don't cage me coz I'm the Asian" intervenes. The tune's piano riff is discrete and, in its final coda, turns into a reggae rhythm before it almost immediately comes to a halt.

The music and vocal delivery on the follow-up single "Vigilante" is more aggressive, with military-style hip-hop beats appropriate to the subject matter. The track opens with a sample of the national anthem, "God Save the Queen," which is then muffled to be replaced by a meaty marching-drum pattern. The sparse piano notes echo through the mix, evoking the punctulism of 1970s blaxploitation movie soundtracks. This sound fits the urban "ghetto" scene described here. The rap tone of omnipresent threat owes a lot to the understated power of the Geto Boys' gangsta rap classic "Mind Playing Tricks on Me," which samples material from an Isaac Hayes's soundtrack *Three Guys.*

The Hustlers' voices are more clipped, aggressive, and urgent than their discussion in "Big Trouble in Little Asia." Walking in the city at night, they are worried about the racist thugs who look for Pakis and blackies to hurt. As fictional vigilantes, the Hustlers wonder how many more times an Asian has to die before anything will change. The police are unreliable, so the vigilante is forced to carry a knife for self-defense. The Hustlers name-check well-known victims of racist attacks—Quaddus Ali and the murdered Stephen Lawrence. They describe the politicization of young Asian men who, faced with repeated brutality and police ineffectuality, take the law into their own hands. Defending the community with violence is a necessary action. Asians adopt a range of self-defense tactics and strategies, from neighborhood patrols and martial arts training to the use of weapons and the video monitoring of groups like the Guardian Asians, which surveys the neighborhood and provides evidence for court cases. The law criminalizes the vigilante rather than the racist attacker. The track engages and subverts the media perception of the violent Asian, arguing that the vigilante is a figure of discipline and self-control. There is a psychological toll on the vigilante. The controlled anger is always in danger of erupting into violence; the vigilante may have to take to the gun. Silence and anger are presented as yin and yang. The track's power also comes from the flavor of its rap style, in particular its appropriation of a gangsta rap trope—the fear of the bogey man, a scary guy out to get you.

The Kaliphz, named after the leaders of the Islamic empire, hail from Rochdale, near Manchester. Like the Hustlers' "Vigilante," their single "Hang 'em High" (1994) draws on the techniques of rap—in particular, the subgenre known as horrorcore. As practiced by the rap supergroup the Gravediggaz, horrorcore consists of outlandish and often quite amusing scenarios of urban dystopia, blood and gore, psycho killers, and explicit ultra-violence. The Kaliphz use many of the style's cinematic effects to transform the U.K. streets into a battlefield. The track begins with the words, "Ashes to ashes, dust to dust," in homage to the similarly accented spoken intro of a 1972 reggae instrumental by the Crystallites entitled "Undertaker's Burial." In this spaghetti-western-influenced track, the speaker orders a number of coffins from the undertaker for the men he's going to kill. The Kaliphz launch into a gleeful revenge fantasy that sees racists being stabbed and hung. "An eye for an eye, a tooth for a tooth," is repeated in the chorus. With such Old Testament retribution, the rap rejects Gandhi's pacifism, instead spitting threats of violence in the form of fists, kicks, daggers, axes, guns, and crucifixion at the British National Party and the Ku Klux Klan of Tennessee. The sleeve for the twelve-inch single features a cartoon of a skinhead and a hooded KKK member hanging limply from a giant letter K with the word "Kaliphz" inscribed below it. The violence of fascism has been returned and displaced with South Asian violence. In the sleeve notes, the Kaliphz state that "'Hang 'em High' was written to honor the memory of Kelso Cochran, Eustace Pryce, Joy Gardner, Siddik Dada, Mohd. Sarwar, Turan Pekoz, Ali Ibrahim, Steven [*sic*] Lawrence, Rolan Adamo, Sohan Sanghera, Fiaz Mirza, Colin Roach, Pandcharam Sahitharan, Sher Singh Sagoo,

Aziz Miah and Ahmed Sheik, and all the other victims of racial injustice and murder." In memorializing these names, the Kaliphz also invite the listener to contact their anti-Nazi organization Pride of Kolor, based in Manchester.

Nineties Asians would not stand and be beaten. Against the stereotype of the passive immigrant, Asians are "massive not passive," in the words of Asian Dub Foundation, another group that began recording for Nation Records in the early 90s. ADF's music reflects the politicization of this period in response to fascist activity in the East End. The first concert the group played was a benefit for Quaddus Ali at the Hackney Empire. ADF has campaigned and released a single supporting the release of Satpal Ram, who is serving a life sentence for using a work knife to defend himself against a 1986 knife attack by a white racist in a Birmingham restaurant. Both men suffered stab wounds but the white man died after refusing medical treatment.

ADF was set up in 1993 as a sound system at a music-and-technology workshop in Farringdon, in the shadow of the City's commercial towers. Community Music was organized by improvisational, experimental musician John Stevens. Its philosophy promoted a collective approach to music. ADF's 1998 Virgin album *Rafi's Revenge* closes with a thundering "Tribute to John Stevens" in which the group's rapper/toaster, a processed, hiccupped Master D, exhorts, "e-e-e-encourage the massive to become their own creator." The workshop coordinator and bass player, Aniruddha Das, AKA Dr. Das, his fellow youth worker DJ John Pandit (Pandit G) on turntables, and the teenage rapper Deedar Zaman (Master D) formed the sound system. Zaman had been associated with the Joi Bangla sound system, one of the first Asian "sounds" in the mid-80s. Steve Chandra Savale (Chandrasonic), a guitarist from Birmingham, joined the group in 1994 after a stint in the ambient electronic group Higher Intelligence Agency. Another DJ, Sun-J, was brought in to adapt the technology so that the sound system could function as a live band. All ADF members are involved in aspects of computer programming for the band/sound system.

The group, its press kits, and its website describe ADF as "Asian punk junglists." Chandrasonic's aggressive, slashing, fast guitar sounds punky, but the affinity with punk has more to do with an attitude to politics and music production using the new technology than allegiance to a musical idiom. Chandra says: "It's the low technology vibe as well. You know the first thing that punk did was throw out the ideas to spend six months in the studio producing one track and to need the latest technology. The idea of punk music was to make good music and to use what original resources you have, which relates to dub as well."[59]

ADF incorporates the snickety chikketty drum break-beats of jungle, but the sound's foundations are dub bass lines with Master D's breakneck rapping in both

Jamaican Patois and London English accents, samples of Bollywood strings, harmonium drones, Indian classical flute and violin, folk drums, and electronic sequencers. Chandrasonic tunes his guitar like a sitar. Dr. Das says that the group uses "some principles of Indian music that have come down through thousands of years but we're applying technology to it."[60]

If Hustlers HC voice the problem of recovering history and distant origins in South Asia, ADF's memory work finds models for contemporary Brit-Asian activism in the subcontinental colonial and postcolonial past. The cover of their debut album *Facts and Fictions* (1995) makes this explicit with photographs of turbaned Indian freedom fighters superimposed on a colonial map of Asia. The track "Rebel Warrior" (1995) revives the memory of Nazrul Islam, the Bengali Bidrohi, or Poet of Rebellion, in the 1920s and 1930s. Islam was a radical nationalist imprisoned by the British for sedition. He was also an actor and musician whose gramophone records of Muslim and Hindu devotional music were popular in Bengal. "Ami Bidrohi / I am a rebel warrior," chants Master D in an anthemic appropriation of Islam's militancy for London-based activism.

The 1998 album *Rafi's Revenge* also features a song about Indian nationalist heroism. "Assassin" celebrates another Indian freedom fighter jailed and executed by the British. The lyrics voice the righteous rage of anticolonial revenge against General Dyer, the purifying power of the bullet and martyrdom. Even though the assassin might hang in Pentonville prison, death will return him to the land of his ancestors. For ADF, the turf battles on British soil are a continuation of the anticolonial struggle. Another album track, "Naxalite," takes its name from the violent revolutionary communist movement in the Naxalbari district in rural West Bengal during the late 60s and early 70s, but the lyrics might be just as applicable to London in the 90s. West Bengal tactics are filtered through Bob Marley's Rastafarian vocabulary ("Iron like a lion from Zion") and transposed to U.K. urban territory. Such memorialization mobilizes antiracism in Britain. Like Fun^da^mental, Hustlers HC, and the Kaliphz, ADF argues that this fight must be carried out "by any means necessary." Its raps often read like Indian elementary-school illustrated histories of freedom fighters.

I have to confess that when some of the militant sounds of ADF, Fun^da^mental, and Hustlers HC were released in the early 90s, I could have been described as the kind of "skeptical man" Master D has no truck with in the lyrics to "Naxalite." While the instrumental sounds of these Nation acts were novel, rich in their hybridized textures and ominous sonic affect, the lyrics were full of naive and anthemic slogans. The tone of anger celebrated violence as somehow *in itself* a purifying gesture against the oppressor, essential for a decolonized psychic wholeness. ADF and Fun^da^mental's politics seemed to be defined by strict dichotomies. I

understood the antiracist polemics and strategies for defense, but the assertion of
identity was too straightforward. The ambiguities and ambivalences of being British
and Asian were flattened out in the desire to create a sorted, right-on politically
correct identity. The arguments of some of the music seemed too clear cut. One
had to get with the program or get lost.

In the early 1980s I had turned against the ideological straitjacket of punk because it was too literal and lacked sensuality. Admittedly the work of Hustlers
HC seemed nuanced and shaded with doubt, but much of this militant rap hec-
tored the listener with "truths" and "radical" banalities. The music had little room
for notions of pleasure not bound by its verbal message. The politics were also
primarily about young men, defined by the homosociality of Asian lads on the
street. These Asians had to be "dead hard" to counter the image of the passive
Asian. This Asian was the anti-skinhead. This militant Asian was also a subject
as narrowly defined by racism as was *his* passive counterpart.

Doubtless ADF would, like any punk rockers worth their salt, have called me
a middle-class wanker who had lost touch with the realities of racism on the
streets. And yes, I was listening and writing from the vantage point of graduate
school in Austin, in faraway Tejas. So I went to London for Christmas vacation
1993 to visit my family and do some doctoral research on ADF and their fellow
travelers.

In Tottenham Court Road, I saw Mike Leigh's *Naked;* "The end is nigh, the
game is up," says the film's homeless Mancunian migrant and misogynist motor-
mouth, Johnny (played by David Thewlis). Tricky's "Aftermath" in its hip-hop
blues version played on the radio. The damp, cold city was charged with pre-
millennial tension. On Christmas Eve, I accompanied my brother to the Jum-
mah prayers at the Regent's Park Mosque, an act of curiosity and solidarity rather
than faith. Bosnian Muslim refugees were begging outside the masjid. Students
in groups such as Hizbet Tehrir distributed pamphlets advocating modesty in dress
for young women and girls, chiding their parents' generation for slackness in religious practice, and encouraging a manly, militarized discipline of the body and
collective that suggested the strategies of brown-shirted youth and Shiv Sainiks.

In the news media, the authoritarianism of the British state seemed to herald
a disunited Kingdom in Fortress Europe. The government decreed that broad-
casters could not allow listeners and viewers to hear the voice of any member of
the IRA or its political wing, Sinn Fein. A black woman, Joy Gardner, died from
suffocation after police officers gagged her as they attempted to enforce her de-
portation. Passengers who had just arrived on a flight from Jamaica to visit friends
and relatives for Christmas were held in a detention center on the grounds that
some of them had given false U.K. addresses. Seventeen-year-old Quaddus Ali

lay in a coma months after being kicked repeatedly in broad daylight by white youths. The British National Party's Derek Beackon had recently been elected to a local council seat in east London.

The five white youths who had killed the black Londoner Stephen Lawrence in South London in April 1993 would go free. Police surveillance material later recorded them at home, but it was found to be insufficient evidence for a guilty verdict: "If I was going to kill myself do you know what I'd do? I'd go and kill every black cunt, every Paki, every copper. Every mug that I know, I'm telling ya. I'm not talking about the people I love and care for. I'm talking about the people I don't like. I'm telling ya. . . . I'd go down Catford and places like that, I'm letting you know, with two sub-machine guns and I'm telling ya, I'd take one of them, skin the black cunt alive, mate, torture him, set him alight. . . . I'd blow their two legs and arms off and say 'Go on, you can swim home now.'"[61] These white men were not members of any far-right political organization. But the virulence of their race hate echoed the Combat 18 phone call sampled by Fun^da^mental on "Dog Tribe." The revenge scenarios in the Hustlers' "Vigilante" and the Kaliphz' "Hang 'em High" seemed like further violent echoes of white racism.

Much of my research into popular music had involved delving into my own memories and thinking about how music *occupied* these recollections. During this holiday visit to London in late 1993–early 94, I was struck by how similar the political and cultural climate was to that of the late 1970s and early 1980s. Fascist skinheads were on the streets; the number of racist attacks had multiplied; Britain was still fighting a colonial war against Irish Republicans. The machinery of the state was as repressive as it had ever been. At the Virgin megastore in the West End I bought a copy of Cornershop's recently released *Lock, Stock and Barrel* EP, which on its cover featured an entry from Jon Savage's diary, reproduced in his history of punk, *England's Dreaming*: "25.3.78: It is maintained by this writer that everyone involved with Rock 'n' Roll as a mass medium has an enormous responsibility in our unstable and worsening political situation—with various forms of totalitarianism threatening—and that this responsibility is not always, is in fact rarely realized or undertaken." The visit to London brought into relief why I'd left England, reminded me that I still hadn't "gotten over" the nation.

One reason I'd "jumped ship" was the reactionary identity politics engendered by England. I had once believed in these false solutions. As a child I had simultaneously craved the impossible white skin and hated whiteness. As a young man I was often ready to retreat into a Muslim identity, a sense of belonging to a community that wasn't defined by geography. Islam didn't require that I be 100 percent Pakistani, which my halting Urdu prevented. The Shariah law was broader and greater than mere national affinities. I was part of a global Islamscape.

Like the Jihad-warrior mirror-image of the skinhead, I wanted to throw a brick at all the bastards who shouted "Paki" at me in school and in the streets. I yearned to shatter the windows of those shop owners who had given me that "what-do-*you*-want" look. My anger, like sexual desire, was sublimated in following the codes of Islamic practice. If you are constructed as the other, one option is to embrace otherness and forget you were ever English.

But Islam failed me. Family and acquaintances increasingly sounded like apologists for contemporary Islamism's regressive politics—its patriarchal law, sexual repression, and the anti-Semitism lurking behind what was ostensibly a critique of Zionism. The South Asian bourgeois ideology of the family and the peculiarities of its psychological structures amplified my disaffection. Why should I have to choose between two dead-end options: English cultural whiteness or Islamism?

It was John Lydon who sang that "anger is an energy," a sentiment assiduously advocated by other punk ideologues. But anger can also hollow you inside, gnaw away the spirit. Asian Dub Foundation, Hustlers HC, and Fun^da^mental are to be admired for channeling their rage into music, transforming it to work in institutions and organizations. Their angry Brit-Asian music is, in some ways, like Tipu Sultan's tiger, now stashed with the other imperial loot in the Victoria and Albert Museum. Part painted sculpture of a tiger and a white man, part musical machine, when the organ keyboard inside the body of the tiger is played, it simulates both the animal's roar and the cry of the European being devoured. Of course, the contours of this music's anger varies from my Brit-Asian rage in some ways. The members of these bands probably haven't felt the same "culture conflict" as I have because they grew up in communities that were not almost exclusively white; they went to school and worked alongside other Brit Asians, African-Caribbeans, British Chinese, as well as white English.

These Brit-Asian sounds demonstrate the continuing power of a politics of representation in popular music against the postmodernist claims of some dance-floor theorists. Words have not lost their meaning. These musical tracks tell hidden stories and serve as funky pedagogy for young people, even if their "politics" are sometimes narrowly defined and programmatic.

I still have some reservations about this *militant* music's politics. Violence may be necessary in specific contexts; sometimes, as Woody Allen points out in *Manhattan,* the most direct and effective action is to take a baseball bat and go after the fascists. But some of this militant music veers close to a celebration of violent acts as purifying and essential moments toward a liberated postcolonial subjectivity. This seems to head for the same impasse as Fanon in *The Wretched of the Earth,* an all-or-nothing praxis of racial/ethnic redemption within a masculinist politics. Against such an option, I would hope that there are other positions in the space between the passive Asian stereotype and his other brother, the militant Asian.

Racism and antiracism are not the only things that define Brit-Asian identities. Little in the work of Fun^da^mental or ADF examines the fissures and regressive politics *within* Brit-Asian communities or between black and Asian communities; that would be too much like hanging out dirty laundry for the white folks. The politics of these musicians also ignores or glazes over issues of gender and sexuality. Race/ethnicity and less explicitly class are the master categories of their analysis.

The issue of gender in the Brit-Asian communities is addressed by the guitar rock group Echobelly, whose music also articulates anger but in a markedly different style from the boy ploys of Fun^da^mental and ADF. The lead vocalist and lyric writer, Sonya Aurora Madan, was born in India, moved with her parents to Britain at the age of three, and grew up in the suburbs of West London.

On the debut album, *Everybody's Got One* (1994), Madan tempts the wrath of both white liberals and Asian patriarchs when she wails "Give Her a Gun": "It's about empowerment for Muslim women and it's a volatile lyric, but deliberately so. When I wrote it the anger and the expression of that anger was more important to me than what I should or shouldn't be saying, but now I am aware that I could be shot by a fundamentalist Muslim or skinhead!"[62] The sharp "Father, Ruler, King, Computer" (inspired by Germaine Greer's *The Female Eunuch*) remonstrates against South Asian forms of patriarchal law. Madan launches into some jagged guitar-backed vitriol as she tells us that she doesn't need a husband to make her whole, in spite of the ideology of marriage in South Asian families and communities. The singer-songwriter claimed success after she received a fan letter from a young Asian woman who was to be married off to someone selected by her family, even though she was in love with an English boyfriend. "Father, Ruler, King, Computer" gave her the strength to confront her parents.

An intervention like Madan's is significant when female relationships and sexuality in the Asian communities are regulated by various forms of cultural fundamentalism. Carol Upadhya argues that South Asians in the diaspora are as responsible as their subcontinental counterparts for promoting an idea of Indian culture that rests on policing of the female body and sexuality.

> This discourse, which is built upon such tropes as Indian "values," the "Indian family system" and "Indian culture," has become central to the construction of Indian identity among the urban middle classes. It is also found in the reconstruction and reification of "Indian culture" by the wealthy NRI [non-resident Indian] set, as

reflected in films depicting ideal family life such as *Hum Apke Hain Kaun*. In this
discourse, Indian society and its "values" are always counterpoised to the decadent
west. However, when pressed, people are rarely able to specify any values other than
those related to control over female sexuality: virginity at marriage, marriage with
partners approved by the family and community, and female chastity and devotion
to husband within marriage (the behaviour of males of course is another story). These
values are presumed to contribute to the solidarity and stability of the family, both
of which distinguish Indian society from the social fragmentation and sexual per-
missiveness (and perversity) of western societies. . . . This image of Indian culture
is promoted especially by NRIs, who embrace every advantage of life in the west but
jealously guard their daughters from straying and scour India for virginal brides for
their sons, and in so doing claim that they are upholding Indian "tradition"—whatever else they may be doing in other spheres of life.[63]

For many older South Asians in Britain, pop music represents if not exemplifies
the worst of Western vices.

Brit-Asian women often have to cope with the conservative double-whammy
of *sharam* and *izzat*. Literally "shame," sharam is a sense of modesty and self-
respect. Izzat suggests "dignity," a sense of honor, the maintenance of a moral
code that states that a girl or woman must not bring shame to her family. As Sairah
Awan points out: "Asian woman are seen as symbols of their culture, at the core
of family pride, which they have to uphold at all times by retaining modesty, self-
respect and, most importantly, never bringing shame to the family. In Britain,
izzat can still be as strong two or three generations on. With the music industry
enveloped in notoriety and often associated with sex, drugs, and rock and roll, a
woman's *izzat* is definitely at risk."[64] According to Awan, several women DJs,
rappers, and toasters have had to struggle against these ideologies to justify their
involvement in popular music culture. Mariam of the hip-hop and R&B DJ
collective Gangsta Bitchez, Radical Sista, and Ritu are all professional DJs who
initially encountered some resistance from their parents but have subsequently
received support. The singers Pammi and Bindu record on the bhangra scene.
The Voodoo Queens' punky pop has also voiced Asian women's lust, frustration,
and humor. While Brit-Asian women have had to negotiate these freeedoms and
rights with their families and communities, the music business applies other
pressures.

The industry insistently commodifies female sexuality. Early in Echobelly's
career, Madan agreed to appear in a pop magazine fashion spread featuring up-
and-coming British rockers. She sported a Union Jack "England Swings" t-shirt
customized with the scrawled addition "My Home Too." She told the publication: "This T-shirt is a reaction to the BNP. I wanted to make it clear that I won't

be put into a victim role. Nobody's going to kick me out of the country. I want people to know I'll fight these Nazis. For an Asian girl to wear a Union Jack is obviously going to spark discussion. I like to piss people off by taking something that's sacred to them and throwing back the true meaning in their face, like the swastika as a symbol of Asian purity."[65] Lad-oriented magazines like *Loaded* subsequently wanted to harness Madan's semiotic power in the role of exotic "Asian babe," offering her photographic "exposure" in revealing gear.

In a televised debate about racism with Fun^da^mental's Aki Nawaz, Madan's contributions were edited out: "Most of the camera angles were these very mundane, pretty girlie shots where I wasn't saying anything. You could see me and hear Aki's voice. It was typical censorship. I was totally misrepresented, made into an airhead musician."[66] On the one hand, she realizes that her visibility as an Asian woman is important for other Asian women. On the other hand, the burden of representation limits her presence; she doesn't want to have to answer press questions about arranged marriages or become a spokesperson for the "Asian community" every time she is interviewed.

Faced with media regimes of representation that seek to define Brit-Asianness in narrow terms, some musicians prefer invisibility as a strategy. Jyoti Mishra from Derby, an East Midlands town, releases music under the name White Town because he grew up in "predominantly white towns." The electro-pop single "Your Woman" was recorded in his bedroom studio. He chose not to publicize the release with interviews or any photos of himself because he didn't fit the mold of the standard photogenic pop star. The promotional music video for "Your Woman" features a white man and woman enacting the song's battle-of-the-sexes narrative. After BBC Radio One national airplay, the track was a number-one single in 1997.

On the White Town website, Mishra explains that the song was written from several different perspectives: "being a member of an orthodox Trotskyist/Marxist movement (as I was); being a straight guy in love with a lesbian; being a gay guy in love with a straight man; being a straight girl in love with a lying two-timing fake ass marxist."[67] Admittedly, there's no reason that listeners will perceive these different subject positions in the tune, but it's worth considering whether an image of (portly and brown) Mishra in the video, CD sleeve, and other media would have predisposed listeners and viewers to particular interpretations based on their preconceptions of "Asians." Shantanu DuttaAhmed advocates invisibility as a way of evading such audiovisual regimes: "The other is continually implicated in economies of exchange that are attempts to stabilize metropolitan constructions. What I am proposing is the articulation of a politics that provides freedom from this exchange, and that enables the other to occupy a material space from which to reconfigure by leaving that space empty. The other can best be present by being absent, being invisible."[68] If, for example, Farookh Bulsara chose to remain Freddie Mercury of Queen, this decision in itself doesn't make him any less "Asian" than Aki Nawaz or Apache Indian. A similar argument might be applied to the semiotics of sound. If a piece of music features tabla and sitar, is it necessarily *more* Asian than a sounding of Asian experience with noisy electric guitars?

Everybody Needs a Bosom for a Pillow: The Recovery of Brit-Asian Childhoods

Much of the recent Brit-Asian music excavates childhoods. Echobelly's "Call Me Names" dredges up the very common and painful Brit-Asian memory of regular abuse in the school playground. Sonya Madan voices the sentiments of a child who has arrived in England, wants to make friends, learn, and assimilate. The other kids hurl abuse at her. She tries again, desperately scrubbing away at her brown skin so she can be just like the other kids. In the chorus, she wonders if this is the same for everyone or if there's something uniquely wrong with her.

The guitars come crashing in after the second chorus of "why do they call me names?" The double tracking/overdubbing of Madan's voice seems to echo her split subjectivity. The instrumental break in the middle of the recording includes the sounds of children's voices (reminiscent of the crying children in Lou Reed's melodramatically effective "The Kids," from his album *Berlin*). Throughout the second half of the song Madan asks the same question. The word "Why" is stretched out into a child's wailing tearful cry. She whispers, wails, and almost yells the words, trying every way possible to get an answer, to understand her rejection. The track captures the desperate self-doubt of the Brit-Asian kid's rejection.

"Call Me Names" is an instance in which story and emotion uncover the ordinariness of English racism. When I first heard the song, the shock of recognition was exhilarating. For many of us, the school has provided the mythical set pieces of U.K. race hate. For example, Nitin Sawhney recalls: "I remember walking home from school and there'd be guys from the British National Party driving in vans and a guy shouting out 'paki' all the way to my front door. I remember those experiences vividly, so it's ten times more important for me to make the statement very strongly of who I am and where my heritage is, because I don't want any misunderstandings of it."[69]

Music retrieves a childhood repressed, unspoken, unsounded in mainstream

British media. We grew up with the pressure to assimilate into whiteness. As kids we reacted against our cultural traditions, which sometimes became reified as the diasporic experience of our migrant parents made them often fix aspects of South Asianness. We rejected the call to the old country by drawing on black culture, which seemed more dynamic and contemporary, less "traditional." Whiteness and blackness had a public profile in U.K. culture while our Asianness was marginalized. Many Brit-Asian tracks by musicians now in their twenties and thirties directly and indirectly come to terms with the ways we were "Asian" in the U.K.

The recordings of Cornershop illustrate the return to these hybridized childhoods. Like Fun^da^mental, Hustlers HC, Asian Dub Foundation, and Echobelly, Cornershop emerged in the context of early 90s antiracism. The group's moniker comes from the general name of the neighborhood all-purpose grocery store. Many of these small businesses are owned and operated by South Asian families. The open-all-hours cornershop is one of the recognizably and stereotypically Asian spaces in the urban neighborhood.

Led by the singer-songwriter Tjinder Singh and the guitarist Ben Ayres, Cornershop released its first EP on "curry-colored" vinyl on the independent label Wiija in 1993. *In the Days of Ford Cortina* is a look back at the 1970s in the form of "shambling" guitar rock riddled with Indian instruments. "Waterlogged" takes the piss out of the racially stereotyped images of 1970s television, for example, the "natives" of *It Ain't Half Hot, Mum,* a sitcom about a British army song-and-dance troupe stationed in India during World War II. Against this Raj nostalgia, Singh juxtaposes the images of Mahatma Gandhi and Huggy Bear, the sartorially slick black police informant in the television cop show *Starsky and Hutch.* In contrast to the limited repertoire of South Asian images in the media, Singh yearns to "put pen to paper like Hanif Kureishi" and "get laid like Sammy and Rosie." The guitar white noise, reverb, moody Indian flute, and sitar rock riffs of "Hanif Kureishi scene" are the abrasive accompaniment for the travails of an interracial romance in which the protagonist is only fancied because of his "fashionable shade."

The opening and closing tracks on the group's second album, *Woman's Gotta Have It* (1995), are two versions of "6 am Jullandar Shere," a track that offers a return to the Punjabi city that is quite different from Apache Indian's travel. Cornershop's journey takes the form of a long guitar drone, sitar, percussion, and the ambient noise of Jullandar City streets. Singh's Punjabi vocals, processed to sound like a lo-fi Indian recording using a "vintage" microphone, suggest the embarrassment of being out of place when Brit Asians return to their origins. His ironic perspectives extend to the practice of re-placing Western appropriations of Indianness. The group has cut a Punjabi version of the Beatles' sitar-y "Norwegian Wood" and collaborated with sutra exponent Allen Ginsberg, mixing a poem recited in his New York City apartment and a wedding brass band in India, both recorded on digital audio tape.

The group's 1997 single "Brimful of Asha," Singh's tribute to Asha Bhosle, recounts a childhood of listening on a Ferguson mono radio–cassette player to Hindi film playback singers like Bhosle (chorus motif: "brimful of Asha on the 45"), Lata Mangeshkar and Mohammad Rafi with their huge orchestras, as well as reggae records on the Trojan label, the French singer Jacques Dutronc, and the "Bolan Boogie" of glam rockers T. Rex.

The track is an interesting example of how sound studio techniques regulate the representation of Brit Asians as much as the visual technologies of cinema, television, and video. "Brimful of Asha" was promoted with a colorful video in which a young black girl sits in her 1950s/1960s retro room surrounded by scores of Cornershop records. The members of the group appear as moving images on the record sleeves. Singh's knowing wink to the commodity fetishism of record collecting and its relationship to South Asian identity took its Velvet Underground "Sweet Jane" guitar riff to the lower reaches of the British singles charts.

The single was then remixed by Norman Cook of Fatboy Slim fame. Beefier drums were added to make the track more danceable, and Singh's voice was speeded up considerably. This remix version went to number one. The title of Cornershop's 1997 album *When I Was Born for the 7th Time,* from which "Brimful of Asha" is taken, plays on notions of Hindu reincarnation and suggests how South Asian subjectivities in the media are mutable, reborn, their shape and development dependent on technologies of representation and processes of commodification. Singh appears in a childhood photograph on the album's inner sleeve clutching his radio–cassette player firmly to his chest. "Brimful of Asha" includes the catchy chorus line, "Everybody needs a bosom for a pillow." At the end of the song Singh confesses, "mine's on the RPM." These records have been a source of comfort, offering the child the security and solace of the mother/home.

This was one way popular music worked on me, staving off an inner war, as I became more able to listen to the different sounds of myself in a compilation of sounds. These fragments of self inhabited white songs and black songs, pop's images, and the rituals of playing records and making tapes. The songs didn't simply reflect my identity, they also shaped yearning. Records did for me what books did for bell hooks: "They were the places I could bring the broken bits and pieces of myself and put them together again, the places where I could dream alternative realities, possible futures. They let me know firsthand that if the mind was to be the site of resistance, only the imagination could make it so. To imagine, then, was a way to begin the process of transforming reality. All that we cannot imagine will never come into being."[70] Music was compensation, escape, and possibility.

In our house in Ilkley, West Yorkshire, my parents played Hindi film pop, folk songs, qawwalis, and khayal. Visiting musicians from India and Pakistan would sometimes perform all-night sessions. I was into blues, soul, and post-punk Indie, not Indian classical music, which was a foreign code. Hindi film music was simply tacky. The music center in my bedroom battled with my parents' flashier hi-fi system in the living room, Western and Eastern sounds filling the house with an argumentative sound mix. While I didn't appreciate Indian music, its sounds are ingrained in my audio-memory. I still don't understand its syntax or many of its lyrics but listening to it physically relaxes me, puts me into a childhood place of the familiar. Home is where the harmonium is. It was background music when we were kids, so it now carries the ambience of "home." I think a similar process is going on with many Brit-Asian musicians who incorporate South Asian music in their recordings. Sampling and citation from parental record collections bring alive the music they grew up with in the home. These techniques provide a form of rapprochement with the past and the first generation of migrants and settlers.

Such a return to childhood via memory is explicit in the sleeve notes of the album *Star Rise* (1997), a collection of remixes of Nusrat Fateh Ali Khan and Michael Brook recordings by artists associated with the "Asian Underground." In the sleeve notes each musician brings a brief account of his own biographical narrative to a reworking of the "traditional" sound of Nusrat, the late qawwali singer. Asian Dub Foundation, for example, profess to be "inspired by its questioning, rebellious nature and Nusrat's soaring spiritual dialogues." On the other hand, Nitin Sawhney regards Nusrat as "the embodiment of soul and passion in music." Aki Nawaz of Fun^da^mental presents a series of dialogues I recognize from my own Yorkshire past:

The scene: Aki pogoing to the Clash in his and the rest of the family's bedroom in Bradford in 1977.

Dad: Oi, turn that rubbish off, it's crap!
Aki: But Dad it's punk, it's different, it's new, it breaks all the traditions of politics and music.
Dad: Listen son, traditions have been broken for centuries in Asia. You should check out your musical heritage—there's people like Nusrat blah blah blah etc.

Aki thinks: Old codger, me dad thinks he knows music. Asian music, what??? Sounds
        crap!!!

12 years later:

 Aki thinks: Bloody 'ell, me dad was right. There's some amazin' stuff about.

3 years later:
Scene: Aki on the phone to Real World

Aki: Yeah yeah, of course I'd love to remix Nusrat, it'd be an honour. FEE?
            I'll do it for nowt, oh ok fine, I'll do it for that then.

The rest is all about the past, manipulating it, exploiting it and gettin' it heard.

The tabla player and producer Talvin Singh writes that, "Nusrat Khan Sahib
is for me the father figure of Sufi qawwali music. His performances are enhanced
with 'childlike purity,' which in turn invoke my own memories of growing up
within this musical environment." Imran Khan, a journalist, sums up the remix
project in terms of childhood memories: "Nusrat Fateh Ali Khan is one of the
world's leading voices. Listening to him always takes me back to my childhood
and hearing my father's tapes. Now the thought of some of Britain's best young
Asian artists collaborating with him gives me such a great buzz. This is our generation's way of saying 'respect due.'" Remixing Nusrat is a way to return to familial space, an act of creative memory-work, as well as a technologically mediated dialogue with musical tradition.[71]

Even in their digital reworkings of the qawwali master, Brit-Asian musicians
have markedly different attitudes to tradition. On Canada's *New Music* television program, in a segment about the project, the members of Earthtribe argued
that they would never cut and splice Nusrat's vocal phrases, since they respected
the sanctity of the devotional words. On the other hand, Asian Dub Foundation asserted the importance of bringing out the aggressive energy of Khan's performance. ADF add jungle beats and dissonant electric guitar noise to its mix.
Chandrasonic blew a raspberry at criticisms that the purity of the authentic qawwali sound had been desecrated in this misreading or translation.

Traveling with the Asian Underground

The "Asian Underground" represented by some of the artists on the Nusrat Fateh
Ali Khan remix project was a loose conglomeration of musicians recording in the
late 1990s. Talvin Singh is responsible for coining the term, the latest industry
and media buzzword for Brit-Asian music influenced by electronic dance genres,

but with a recognizable South Asian element. Not all of the musicians are Brit Asian. There is no underground scene as such, just a number of disparate artists collected on compilations labeled with the tag. Singh began a Monday-night club called Anokha in London's West End in 1996, DJ-ing a mix of new Brit-Asian beats and South Asian sounds. Singh's label Omni, through Island, released *Anokha: Soundz of the Asian Underground* in 1997, which first took the phrase into pop currency. Singh's canny business sense brought Brit-Asian musicians a higher profile in the industry and media.

Like every music biz buzzword, this might prove to have a very short shelf life, but it has increased the visibility and fashionability of Brit-Asian music. The "New Asian Kool" was a phrase from the early 1990s that made new Brit-Asian music user-friendly to the rock press, even though it sounded like a brand of cigarette or soda drink. "Asian Underground" signifies a measure of street credibility—there's something happening but you don't know what it is, Mr. Jones, so get with the subterranean sounds in the heart of the deterritorialized Ellowen Deeowen.

Here, for example, is the rhapsodizing sleeve note from a compilation called *Eastern Uprising: Dance Music from the Asian Underground* (Sony, 1997):

> These are the state of the nation sounds being produced by a new breed of urbanite Asian. Freed from the dead end of industrial employment, liberated from convention and able to juggle duality and pluralism with more skill than a pre-coke Maradonna, the new young guns go by the sleek sobriquet of "Desi," meaning homegrown and authentic. The artists and recordings featured here represent a celebration of the emergence of a new, peculiarly British form of music. This is the first documentary evidence of the growing bands of groove-fixated shapeshifters, troubadours and jongleurs who rule the roosts in metropolitan Britain. It won't be the last. Welcome to Eastern Uprising, the Music of the Asian Underground.

It is worth noting that the writer makes analogies with the European musicians of the past, rather than with the gurus, ustads, classical artists, and folk musicians of the subcontinent. The paragraph also taps into the common assumption that Asians used to be passive and now after thirty years in Britain are rising up and cool, unlike their parents' generation.

On the album's sleeve are photographs of shops and Indian female showroom dummies in saris, clasping their hands in the namaste greeting. Brit Asians are represented primarily as aspects of postindustrial commerce, the product of Thatcher's enterprise culture. In fact, many of the sleeves for Brit-Asian releases feature the shop window with showroom dummies, though some of these may be drawing ironic attention to the commodification of subcontinental culture.

Like their Brit-Asian predecessors, the Asian Underground continues to mobilize the trope of travel through digital technology. The electronic "ambient" textures of the music suggest space and new-age travel. The *Anokha* compilation contains two such journeys by State of Bengal (Sam Zaman), whose group name breaks down the border between Indian West Bengal and Bangladesh. "Flight IC408" is a track named after an Indian Airlines flight from Bombay to Calcutta and brings Bengali flutes, 1960s soul guitar, a reggae bass line, jungle breakbeats, and the cut-up, hiccupy voice of a Hindi film–style female singer into the mix. The opening spoken-word sample is taken from a female flight attendant's and a pilot's announcements of the flight's details. Another dance track, "Chittagong Chill," invokes the Bangladeshi city, spelling out "B to the B to the B to the E, to the N, to the G, to the A, to the L" in its rap-like chorus. The sleeve notes for State of Bengal's 1999 album *Visual Audio* extend the notion of travel: "Welcome to the world of the State of Bengal, the way in which he paints a picture formed from incidents, variable degrees of emotions, the eruption of the senses to a picturisation and in the end a sculpture of sounds. The audio you are about to encounter is his journey, the translation is the music."

If music is increasingly *seen,* conceived in visual terms, the digital revolution has encouraged a discourse of space in academic and journalistic writing about popular music; that is, sound is increasingly discussed in spatial rather than temporal terms. The mix is described by critics in fluid spatial metaphors. According to David Toop, we inhabit "an ocean of sound" of "aether talk, ambient sound and imaginary worlds."[72] Discourses of globalization and the "worlding" of music have regenerated critical interest in sonic travel through musical technologies, in particular the tropes of various forms of fascination with and desire for other people and places articulated in musical "exotica."[73]

Talvin Singh describes his music in cartographic terms: "My music is like an ocean. That's why the ambient textures are there in every track. The Indian movie is there as well, not by music, but by fantasy."[74] Singh was trained in classical tabla in India. His first album and Mercury Prize–winner, *OK* (Omni, 1998), was recorded in Madras, Bombay, Japan, and his Calcutta Cyber Studio in London. The album sleeve consists of an image of the elephant-headed god Ganesh suspended over a Power Macintosh monitor with a tabla attached to it. Here there is no contradiction between the new technologies and centuries-old traditions. Singh has customized his tabla into what he calls tablatronics, with electronic pickups that allow the sound to be amplified and altered for recording and live performance.

OK sounds like a global map. "Sutrix" consists of the chant "Dil ki baat hon-thon pé" (the heart's words are on my lips) by a female vocalist, a bebop jazzy jungle break-beat, and various electronic squeaks and tweeks. "Mombasstic" begins with an ambient Indian drone of the tampoura and features Jamaican Patois DJ-style, a muted Miles Davis–type trumpet, and a relaxed dub reggae bass line. This über-hybridization makes connections back to Miles Davis's own appropriations of Indian music in his early 1970s album *On the Corner.* Singh's title suggests the Kenyan city Mombassa, in many respects itself an Indian city, and is also reminiscent of reggae DJ Shaggy's "Boombasstic." The track even samples a telephone call that sounds like a discussion of Internet business/e-commerce.

OK includes female singers from the Japanese island of Okinawa. Various "Indian" voices also inhabit the soundscape: an electronic computer voice speaks in Hindi; lads on an Indian street wind each other up; a U.S. accent discusses Hindu myth. The track "Decca" begins with an Indian-accented voice that recounts a version of another myth, "the true story of ecstasy," of "how Shiva and Parvati went to the top of Mount Kailash and were ten thousand years in union. We call this first position naaaasty [in an African-American accent]!" Decca refers to the Deccan region of India but also suggests the name of one of Britain's oldest record companies. The mapping seems most explicit with the track "Disser/Point.Mento.B," which is comprised of an ambient electronic wash and a yearning electric violin theme that gives it the feel of a lush melancholic piece from an old Bollywood film or Ennio Morricone soundtrack. The title of the track itself reads like a complex coordinate on a musical map.

Another group, Black Star Liner, embodies travel in its name, taken from Marcus Garvey's doomed "Back to Africa" shipping line. The group's negotiation of "home" incorporates a polyglot of musical elements. Choque Hosein, an Asian of Trinidadian descent raised in Leeds, fronts the group and live on stage drops "ironic snatches of Pulp, Oasis, Beatles and even Queen tunes into his own songs like a verbal sampler."[75] Copyright infringement issues restrict the extent of Hosein's verbal sampling on Black Star Liner recordings. The group's 1998 album *Bengali Bantam Youth Experience* features musical citations and influences from reggae, electro funk, hip-hop, easy listening Indian restaurant music, and the *filmi* textures of Bollywood, John Barry, and Ennio Morricone. The album seems the most *self-consciously* playful example of the new Brit-Asian music hybridity. It doesn't so much travel back to South Asia as articulate the global elements into something uniquely British and metropolitan. For example, with its Hindi spoken-word interjections, the cut "Low BMW" is a funky ode to young (male) Asians who drive around British cities in BMWs equipped with booming bass systems. The track recalls the Los Angeles group War's black-Latino funk hit "Low Rider," which also sounded out the *subaltern* mobilities of the Western metropolis.

Nitin Sawhney's 1999 album *Beyond Skin* seems the most explicit Brit-Asian recording yet to deal with the *ur*-themes of our displacement and yearning for home/abroad. Songs such as "Letting Go," "Homelands," "The Pilgrim," "Tides," "Immigrant," "Anthem without Nation," "Nostalgia," and the title track, like Talvin Singh's own topographic journeys, chart a South Asian transnational imaginary.

The album begins with a sample of the Hindu nationalist Bharatiya Janata Party leader and Indian prime minister Atal Vajpayee announcing India's five nuclear tests at the Pokharan site in western India on 11 May 1998. This track, "Broken Skin," ironically pays homage to the Moog-synth coda of the funk group Kool and the Gang's "Summer Madness." The broken skin of the land is described in the album's closing spoken-word sample: the American journalist Edward R. Murrow reads Robert Oppenheimer's account of the first atom bomb explosion, in which he repeats the words of the Hindu deity Vishnu, "Now I am become death, the destroyer of worlds." In between these interconnected Indian and North American moments more than a half century apart, the album intermittently throws up samples of BBC Radio reports about the Pokharan tests and the French nuclear testing in the Pacific. These fragments of reportage explode the serenity of sections of Indian classical music, Latin jazz, a polyglot of male and female voices, Hindi film string passages, jazz rap, and breakbeats.

The track "Immigrant" begins with Sawhney's father describing how the British recruited Indian workers for the "mother country" with stories and images of a land of plenty. In the sleeve note for the album, Sawhney writes: "I believe in Hindu philosophy/I am not religious/I am a pacifist/I am a British Asian/My identity and my history are defined only by myself—beyond politics, beyond nationality, beyond religion and beyond skin." The statement of purpose ends on an impossible note. Politics, the dreams of nations, the legacies of religion stick to our skins. They cannot be shed easily.

Brit-Asian music uses digital recording technologies to map the local, national, and transnational with multiple perspectives. Its politics of location share common concerns with history and tradition. However, the notion of tradition is multi-accented for South Asians brought up in the U.K., both a blessing and a curse. We draw upon South Asian histories in contemporary cultural forms. However, the members of the first generation of migrants have created their own imaginaries of South Asia, invented traditions that sometimes return to their homelands, as if history and culture were frozen in the 1960s or 1970s. These often conservative versions of South Asianness are invented traditions invoked to police the behavior of the second generation. Then again, some second-generation Brit Asians with their own "invented traditions" are more politically reactionary than their parents. Traditions are also invoked to define second-generation Brit

Asians as inauthentic in both England and the subcontinent. Our deracinated interpretation of the subcontinent is often chided for its incorrectness, though I would argue that our translations might involve sometimes productive misreadings of South Asian traditions and cultural forms.

Many of the musicians discussed in this chapter have, for example, incorporated the dramatic effects and affect of Bollywood to create distinct emotional registers in the U.K. Such active interpretation and selective use of the South Asia's hegemonic media institution and popular tradition reveal more complicated political, social, and cultural processes than the somewhat nostalgic point of view argued by Ziauddin Sardar:

> In Britain, the Indian cinema has sown the seeds of discord and fissures within the Asian community and denied it the possibility of developing a common language of self-description and the evolution of new symbols and ideals that could serve as signposts towards shaping a new identity. It has trapped the British Asian consciousness within a cycle of formulaic conventions that serve as a substitute for genuine dynamic tradition and ease the pain and frustrations of a loss of belonging. The cyclical retellings offer no possibility of a new kind of becoming, a means towards a new vision of the past, present or future. A community that can only articulate the nature of its own perplexity through the formulas of potboiling melodrama, and hear it all said for them in meaningless lyrics of rent-a-tune songs, is a lobotomized community. It has not only reduced its historic, cultural and personal identity to an absurdity, diminished its art and language, but also abandoned the pursuit of great ideas.[76]

The use of Bollywood by Apache Indian, Bally Sagoo, Talvin Singh, and many musicians associated with the Asian Underground hardly demonstrates the cultural production of a "lobotomized community." Like many Brit Asians of the generation older than these musicians, Sardar betrays a yearning for a Brit-Asian identity defined primarily by the U.K.–South Asia axis. But for many young Brit Asians, Hollywood, the Wu-Tang Clan, Bob Marley, Kraftwerk, Aqua, and Kurt Cobain matter as much as or more than Nusrat Fateh Ali Khan, the poet Ghalib, or Bollywood film stars.

Transnational media will continue to play an important role in the construction of cultural memory and identity, extending and accelerating modernity's technological mediation of everyday life. In the so-called information age, images and sounds circulate almost instantly through global networks. This traffic is regulated by nation-states and private businesses, and not all citizens will have equal access to these networks; but if technologies like photography, the telephone, cassette recordings, and video have kept Brit Asians *in touch*, connected to families and communities across the diaspora, and helped them to make sense of history and geography, digital technologies like samplers and the Internet will continue these processes and reshape them to some extent, at the very least in speed and scope. These new aspects of the digitally mediated public sphere may be both progressive and regressive; their political value as modes of communication and aesthetic forms cannot be predicted and is not determined by the limits of the technologies themselves. For example, the diasporic discourse on a large number of websites devoted to South Asian topics demonstrates that the imaginaries of virtual communities are as likely to articulate the regressive communalism of South Asian realpolitik as to offer progressive political imaginations and imaginaries.

Conclusion

England Inglan Inglistan

The transformations of digitization have generated prognoses as anxious as those rendered when the telegraph, cinema, radio, and television began to alter communication and our cognitive landscapes. In "Media, Matter, and Migrants," a chapter in *Writing Diaspora,* Rey Chow argues that the digital threatens memory: "When everything is computed in the form of numbers and figures, and when sense perceptions such as sight and sound are increasingly mixed up in electronic reproductions so that their traditional differentiation no longer 'makes sense' to us, the notion of the medium, together with the memory and sensuality that it signifies, gradually disappears."[1] The phonographic record could store only finite time in its grooves. According to Chow, digitization allows for potentially infinite storage and thereby erases the need to capture a *particular* time. More and more sounds and images from the now digitally archived past are available at our fingertips. We inhabit an everlasting present of the perfect sound and image, without the audio or visual reproduction decaying in any way. The distinction between the original and its reproduction dissolves. And so *the need to preserve* disappears since every sound and image remains exactly the same forever. In the case of music, Chow believes that historicity disappears because sounds and images from different temporalities and spatialities can be assembled to create a new whole. A musical track made of samples and loops from other recordings is a hyperreal assembly of sonic signs, rearranged and processed in a machine environment. It never "happened" as a musical performance in real time.

Chow's stance follows a strand of postmodernist pessimism found in the work of Jean Baudrillard and Paul Virilio. This judges that media technologies have contracted and compressed time and space, creating a "politics of speed" and "aesthetics of disappearance." Mediated culture induces a kind of communication vertigo: narrative breaks down, and we are immersed in a postmodern nonsense of surfaces and floating signifiers.

Jim Collins rightly suggests that such dystopian visions, rather like cyberpunk fictions, depend on "thoroughly modernist notions of subjectivity and cybernetics to describe life in the twenty-first century," with "futuristic visions conceptualized in terms of overload and saturation, formulations which were the product of the first hysterical reactions to information technologies."[2] "Overload" and "saturation" fail to cover the extent to which technologies have already been domesticated in their integration with our bodies and subjectivities. People have been remixed and rewired by media technologies, but in these processes we have learned to make sense in contexts and developed a measure of agency in grounding media signifiers. We are not drowning in the glut of stuff, the noise of popular mediated culture.

Those of us who have grown up immersed in the audiovisual/digital media are attuned to use them to orient ourselves in particular locations. We invest them with value through forms of vernacular theory about culture. Consumers don't control the economy of signs and commodities, but neither does capital entirely determine value. The meaning of these commodity-signs changes as they circulate. As Appadurai writes, things "move in and out of the commodity state" in various ways;[3] their value is not fixed. On the subject of cultural value, Collins writes: "in the age of digital reproduction *and digital access,* aura has everything to do with the projection of value *onto* recordings. . . . the category of *presence* must be rethought in reference to the circumstances of decoding, namely, the ways in which listeners' age, race, sexual preferences determine *which* live recordings are to be valued, *when* CD technology is a matter of cultural airlifting and when it's simply a matter of recycling the same old kitsch."[4]

I don't wish to argue that minority or subcultural forms of appropriation are the politically righteous forms of consumption to be set against the negative consumer practices of the rest of *the people.* Instead, we must pay attention to the complex modalities of popular music's use-value across the range of activities centered on music. "If social relations are constituted in cultural practice," as Simon Frith writes, "then our sense of identity and difference is established *in the processes of discrimination.*"[5]

Talking and writing about music invest it with value. Elvis Costello may have stated that "writing about music is like dancing about architecture," but we still feel compelled to fill in the gap, to pin down the sounds in the material world. Steven Feld reminds us that "music has a fundamentally social life. It is made to be engaged—practically and symbolically, individually and communally—as symbolic entity."[6] According to Frith, "people talk about 'music' in ways which make little sense of how they listen to it."[7] However, people need to talk about it, and they consciously and unconsciously bring to bear conceptual schemes in order to articulate music's aesthetics, affect, feeling, and function. As Feld notes,

> the common structures of verbalization tell us something about the nature of inter-pretation and the possibilities for speech about music. One engages and places an item or event in meaningful social space through ongoing interpretive moves. These moves do not fix or freeze a single meaning; meaning is emergent and changeable in relation to various combinations of moves made by specifically situated speakers. Interview data confirms both the importance of lexical and discourse metaphors for verbally expressing something about musical experience and its prevalence in repre-senting such abstractions as value, identity, and world sense.[8]

In *Sounds English* I have examined the words of musicians, academics, jour-nalists, listeners, and fans—the producers and consumers of music, the partici-pants in musical culture. I have dealt with the range of metaphors of situated-ness and the languages and discourses used to make sense of music. I've considered some of the recurring questions in popular music discourse, such as youth, race, gender and sexuality, industry, technology, and notions of authenticity related to these concepts. I have acknowledged the critical question of music's political economy although the economics of production has not been my central focus.

The pivotal question underlying this book (and one inextricably bound up with the popular music studies concepts above) is: How does popular music culture partake of and participate in notions of a constantly changing and contested sense of the national in England?

My own specifically situated interpretation of popular music and the national has drawn on academic and popular forms of knowledge. The voice of *Sounds English* is located somewhere within, between, and across those of a teacher, a journalist, a radio DJ, and a fan. These are not separate identities and creative spaces but are dialogically engaged with each other. I've attempted to check the possible indulgences inherent in such a self-reflexive exercise. At times I've wanted to disappear into the mix, other times expose myself. The final compromise—the self in the text—may be awkwardly defined but is a consequence of an on-going difficulty with—even suspicion of—identity politics.

It is vital to think through the question of difference, to place gender, sexual-ity, race/ethnicity on the same terrain as class in any critical/cultural/political analysis; it's also important to bring forth hidden histories, to "represent," as the hip-hoppers state. In *Sounds English* I have attempted to "re-vision" (and "re-sound") the nation with these imperatives. But I also register an anxiety about essentialist notions of identity. At the same time, I must caution that the notion of the "hybrid" can become as fixed a category as its essentialist nemesis. A politics of identity may not necessarily translate from the subjective to the collective, and hybridity can be as regressive as any other normative identity, as well as an ideological tool for globalized capitalism.[9]

Music and the discourse *about it* help to mark the contours of the local, national, and transnational as overlapping concepts, not simply set against or beside each other as distinct categories. We should be less concerned with the ontological status of the local/national/global than with the techniques of their production, and the politics of these techniques. To claim a fixity, an immutable difference, *or* a complete disappearance of any difference between the local, national, and transnational is to deny how the same space is constructed in multiple but overlapping versions run through with conflict and social injustice.

The Smiths' Manchester is quite distinct from that lived and imagined by A Guy Called Gerald or Barry Adamson. Morrissey's East End contrasts sharply with Asian Dub Foundation's version of the neighborhood. London sounds like different cities if you compare the Pet Shop Boys' versions with the Hustlers HC's recordings, though these versions register the different effects of related economic, social, and political conditions.

Landscapes are shaped by forms of desire, articulated in the music of these artists, and the myriad interpretations of their work. These desires may be centered on the racialized or sexualized body, drug-induced fantasies of pleasure, paranoid phantasmagoria, various combinations of the above, or other elements. While not steeped in psychoanalytic methodologies, *Sounds English* has explored some of the psychic aspects of "Englishness" suggested in recent English music. The spaces of the nation are imagined and real, aspects of spatiality that are hard to separate.

Social realism and ethnography have been the hegemonic modes of representing England and Britain. As a qualified critique of this tendency, my emphasis on *imagined* notions of place risks a lack of empirical detail, an attention to the *real* nuts and bolts of British politics, economics, and society. Media fictions, sonic or otherwise, are not the whole story. They are embedded in social relations, activated in certain ways depending on subjects and contexts. My turn to recorded music, films, videos, and novels to make sense of England may come from my racial/ethnic alienation from the *real* England. Even when I was there, I wasn't quite there. It was easier to feel and understand life through records, films, and television programs. They gave you, in that phrase of Raymond Williams, "resources of hope," tools to move forward in the real world.

As I now live in Aotearoa/New Zealand, I'm aware that a set of imagined ideas about "the mother country" still shapes this island nation's postcolonial longings. I lived in England for some of the years covered by *Sounds English* but have seen it from a position of double displacement since I left in 1988. This book was inevitably colored by the distant "postcolonial" perspectives provided by the United States, Aotearoa, and India, where it was written, and where ideas of England and Englishness have their own idiosyncratic resonances. Pop music's mobility in commodity form has enabled me not just to remember the *real* nation, but to reconstruct England *through* its sounds and images. Landscape is always invested with particular histories. There are other ways to map a small island off the coast of continental Europe.

Notes

Introduction

1. Jacqueline Rose, *States of Fantasy* (Oxford: Clarendon Press, 1996), 67.

2. Michel Foucault, "Film and Popular Memory: Cahiers du Cinéma/Extracts," *Edinburgh '77 Magazine* (1977): 21–22.

3. Tom Nairn, *The Enchanted Glass: Britain and Its Monarchy* (London: Radius, 1988), 86.

4. Patrick Wright, *On Living in an Old Country: The National Past in Contemporary Britain* (London: Verso, 1985), 143.

5. Raphael Samuel, *Theatres of Memory* (London: Verso, 1994), 114.

6. George Lipsitz, *Time Passages: Collective Memory and American Popular Culture* (Minneapolis: University of Minnesota Press, 1990), 5.

7. Jon Savage, "The Simple Things You All See Are Complicated," in *The Faber Book of Pop,* ed. Hanif Kureishi and Jon Savage (London: Faber and Faber, 1995), xxx.

8. Jon Stratton and Ien Ang, "On the Impossibility of a Global Cultural Studies: 'British' Cultural Studies in an 'International' Frame," in *Stuart Hall: Critical Dialogues in Cultural Studies,* ed. David Morley and Kuan-Hsing Chen (London: Routledge, 1996), 384.

9. Diana Jeater, "Roast Beef and Reggae Music: The Passing of Whiteness," *New Formations* 18 (Winter 1992): 111.

10. Jeremy Gilbert, "White Light/White Heat: *Jouissance* beyond Gender in the Velvet Underground," in *Living through Pop,* ed. Andrew Blake (London: Routledge, 1999), 31–48.

11. See Steven Vertovec, "Conceiving and Researching Transnationalism," in *Ethnic and Racial Studies* 22, no. 2 (Mar. 1999): 447–62.

12. Paul Willemen, "The National," in *Looks and Frictions: Essays in Cultural Studies and Film Theory* (London: British Film Institute, 1994), 210.

13. Ibid., 209.

14. Ibid., 210.

15. Anne McClintock, "Family Feuds: Gender, Nationalism and the Family," *Feminist Review* 44 (Summer 1993): 67.

16. Catherine Hall, "Missionary Stories: Gender and Ethnicity in England in the 1830s and 1840s," in *Cultural Studies,* ed. Lawrence Grossberg, Cary Nelson, Paula Treichler (New York: Routledge, 1992) 270–71.

17. Anne McClintock, *Imperial Leather: Race, Gender and Sexuality in the Colonial Contest* (London: Routledge, 1995), 5.

18. Salman Rushdie, *Imaginary Homelands* (London: Viking Penguin, 1983), 116.

19. Eve Sedgwick, "The Age of Wilde," in *Nationalisms and Sexualities,* ed. Andrew Parker, Mary Russo, Dorris Sommer, and Patricia Yaeger (London: Routledge, 1992), 241.

20. Simon Frith, "Anglo-America and Its Discontents," *Cultural Studies* 5, no. 3 (Oct. 1991): 268.

21. Arjun Appadurai, *Modernity at Large: Cultural Dimensions of Globalization* (Minneapolis: University of Minnesota Press, 1996), 182.

22. Ibid., 31.

23. Benedict Anderson, *Imagined Communities: Reflections on the Origins and Spread of Nationalism* (New York: Verso, 1983), 6, 7.

24. Ibid., 46.

25. Slavoj Zizek, *Tarrying with the Negative: Kant, Hegel and the Critique of Ideology* (Durham, N.C.: Duke University Press, 1993), 202.

26. Arjun Appadurai, "Full Attachment," in *Public Culture* 10, no. 2 (1998): 445–46.

27. Zizek, *Tarrying with the Negative,* 201.

28. For the two sides of this debate, see Nicholas Garnham, "Political Economy and Cultural Studies: Reconciliation or Divorce?" and Lawrence Grossberg, "Cultural Studies vs. Political Economy: Is Anybody Else Bored with This Debate," in *Cultural Theory and Popular Culture: A Reader,* ed. John Storey, 2d ed. (Hemel Hampstead, Eng.: Prentice Hall, 1998), 600–612 and 613–24, respectively. For an attempt at a rapprochement, but one that is still more sympathetic to the critical political economy line, see Douglas Kellner, "Overcoming the Divide: Cultural Studies and Political Economy," in *Cultural Studies in Question,* ed. Marjorie Ferguson and Peter Golding (Sage: London, 1997), 102–20.

29. Gilbert, "White Light/White Heat," 34.

30. Simon Frith and Jon Savage, "Pearls and Swine: Intellectuals and the Mass Media," in *The Clubcultures Reader: Readings in Popular Cultural Studies,* ed. Steve Redhead with Derek Wynne, Justin O'Connor (Oxford: Blackwell, 1997), 7–17.

31. Simon Frith, *Performing Rites: On the Value of Popular Music* (Cambridge, Mass.: Harvard University Press, 1996), 20.

32. Ibid., 48.

33. See, for example, Giles Smith, *Lost in Music* (London: Picador, 1995); Wayne Koestenbaum, *The Queen's Throat: Opera, Homosexuality and the Mystery of Desire* (New York: Vintage, 1994); Nick Hornby, *High Fidelity* (London: Indigo, 1996).

34. Jim Collins, *Architectures of Excess: Cultural Life in the Information Age* (London: Routledge, 1995), 217–18.

35. Simon Frith, "The Cultural Study of Popular Music," in Grossberg et al., *Cultural Studies,* 179–80.

36. Dick Hebdige, *Hiding in the Light: On Images and Things* (London: Routledge, 1989), 11.

37. Rose, *States of Fantasy,* 2.

38. Stratton and Ang, "On the Impossibility of a Global Cultural Studies," 384.

Chapter 1: The Last Truly British People You Will Ever Know

1. *New Musical Express,* 22 Aug. 1992.

2. Bill Buford, *Among the Thugs* (New York: Vintage, 1991), 131.

3. Satnam Virdee, "Racial Harassment," in Tariq Modood et al., *Ethnic Minorities in Britain: Diversity and Disadvantage* (London: Policy Studies Institute, 1997), 259–89.

4. Tony Parsons, *Dispatches from the Front Line of Popular Culture* (London: Virgin, 1994), 93 (first quote), 96 (second quote).

5. Geoff Eley, "Distant Voices, Still Lives: The Family Is a Dangerous Place: Memory, Gender, and the Image of the Working Class," in *Revisioning History: Film and the Construction of a New Past,* ed. Robert A. Rosenstone (Princeton: Princeton University Press, 1996), 17.

6. Valerie Walkerdine, "Subject to Change without Notice: Psychology, Postmodernity and the Popular," in *Cultural Studies and Communications,* ed. James Curran, David Morley, and Valerie Walkerdine (London: Arnold, 1996), 111.

7. Eley, "Distant Voices, Still Lives," 25.

8. Homi Bhabha, "The Other Question," in *Contemporary Postcolonial Theory: A Reader,* ed. Padmini Mongia (New Delhi: Oxford University Press, 1997), 37.

9. For further discussion of this theme, see Michael Billig, *Banal Nationalism* (London: Sage, 1995).

10. Georgina Born, "Music Policy, Aesthetics, and Social Difference," in *Rock and Popular Music: Policy, Institutions and Politics,* ed. Tony Bennett, Simon Frith, and Lawrence Grossberg (London: Routledge, 1993), 272 (first quote), 282 (second quote). See also Keith Negus, *Music Genres and Corporate Cultures* (London: Routledge, 1999), 19–20. Negus's thesis is that industry produces culture but culture also produces industry: "I have adopted the term 'culture produces an industry' to stress that production does not take place simply 'within' a corporate environment structured according to the requirements of capitalist production or organizational formulae, but in relation to broader culture formations and practices that are within neither the control nor the understanding of the company. This idea acknowledges the critique of production put by those who argue that the industry and media cannot simply determine the meaning of musical products, and assumes that these may be used and appropriated in various ways by musicians and groups of consumers."

11. Marcia Landy, *Cinematic Uses of the Past* (Minneapolis: University of Minnesota Press, 1996), 191–94.

12. Lawrence Grossberg, "Is There a Fan in the House?: The Affective Sensibility of Fandom," in *The Adoring Audience: Fan Culture and Popular Media*, ed. Lisa A. Lewis (London: Routledge, 1992), 56–57 (first quote), 59 (second and third quotes), 60 (fourth quote).

13. Dave Laing, "Rock Anxieties and New Music Networks," in *Back to Reality?: Social Experience and Cultural Studies*, ed. Angela McRobbie (Manchester, Eng.: Manchester University Press, 1997), 121.

14. Neil Nehring, *Popular Music, Gender, and Postmodernism: Anger Is an Energy* (London: Sage, 1997), 49.

15. A memorable photograph by Nick Knight taken in the early 1980s shows a skinhead facing an elderly gray-bearded Pakistani Muslim man and giving him the Nazi salute. They stand just a few feet away from each other, alone on a piece of urban wasteland. The caption notes that the Pakistani returned the salute a few minutes later. See Nick Knight, *Skinhead* (London: Omnibus, 1982).

16. Carolyn Steedman, "Landscape for a Good Woman," in *Truth, Dare or Promise: Girls Growing Up in the 1950s*, ed. Liz Heron (London: Virago, 1985), 122.

17. Annette Kuhn, *Family Secrets* (London: Verso, 1995), 107.

18. Steve Redhead, *The End-of-the-Century Party: Youth and Pop towards 2000* (Manchester, Eng.: Manchester University Press, 1990), 88–89.

19. Michel Foucault, "Technologies of the Self," in *Technologies of the Self: A Seminar with Michel Foucault*, ed. L. H. Martin, H. Gutman, P. Hutton (London: Tavistock, 1988), 18. Also quoted in Elspeth Probyn, *Sexing the Self* (London: Routledge, 1993), 115.

20. John Williams, *I-D* 163 (Apr. 1997, quoted in *Logic Bomb: Transmissions from the Edge of Style Culture* (London: Serpent's Tail, 1998), 154. Flip was a London-based store that sold secondhand retro American clothing. For example, you could buy a pair of Levi's someone might have worn in Cleveland many years before.

21. Simon Reynolds, *Blissed Out: The Raptures of Rock* (London: Serpent's Tail, 1988), 24. For more on New Pop, see Dave Rimmer, *Like Punk Never Happened: Culture Club and the New Pop* (London: Faber and Faber, 1985), and Dave Hill, *Designer Boys and Material Girls* (Poole: Blandford Press, 1986).

22. Will Straw, "Popular Music and Postmodernism in the 1980s," in *Sound and Vision: The Music Video Reader*, ed. Simon Frith, Andrew Goodwin, Lawrence Grossberg (London: Routledge, 1993), 6.

23. Simon Frith, "Towards an Aesthetics of Popular Music," in *Music and Society: The Politics of Composition, Performance and Reception*, ed. Richard Leppert and Susan McClary (Cambridge: Cambridge University Press, 1992 edition), 136–37.

24. Redhead, *End-of-the-Century Party*, 13–14; see also Colin McCabe, "Broken English," in *Futures for English*, ed. McCabe (Manchester, Eng.: Manchester University Press, 1988), 9.

25. Jeremy Gilbert, "Soundtrack to an Uncivil Society: Rave Culture, the Criminal Justice Act and the Politics of Modernity," *New Formations* 31 (Summer 1996): 15.

26. Ibid., 19.

27. Quoted in Keith Negus, *Producing Pop* (London: Edward Arnold, 1992), 73.

28. Negus, *Producing Pop*, 72–73.

29. Richard A. Peterson, *Creating Country Music: Fabricating Authenticity* (Chicago: University of Chicago, 1997), 6.

30. Martin Stokes, "Introduction: Ethnicity, Identity and Music," in *Ethnicity, Identity and Music: The Musical Construction of Space*, ed. Stokes (Oxford, Eng.: Berg, 1994), 7.

31. See Timothy Taylor, *Global Pop: World Music, World Markets* (London: Routledge, 1997), 21–22; Stokes, "Introduction."

32. See Tom Gallagher, Michael Campbell, Murdo Gillies, eds., *The Smiths: All Men Have Secrets* (London: Virgin, 1995).

33. Hugo Young, *One of Us* (London: Macmillan, 1991), 317.

34. Jon Savage, "The Escape Artist," *Village Voice Rock and Roll Quarterly* (Summer 1989): 8.

35. See Richard Dyer, Christine Geraghty, Marion Jordan, Terry Lovell, Richard Patterson, and John Stewart, *Coronation Street* (London: BFI, 1981).

36. See Richard Hoggart, *The Uses of Literacy* (London: Penguin, 1992).

37. The Justified Ancients of Mu Mu, "It's Grim Up North" (KLF CD, 1992), sleeve notes.

38. The audio sample of Cicely Courtneidge singing "Take Me Back to Dear Old Blighty" takes fans of the Smiths back to its source in Bryan Forbes's 1962 film *The L-Shaped Room*. Courtneidge plays Mavis, a forgotten wartime performer and lesbian now living in a rented room in a run-down boardinghouse. She revives the song one Christmas, surrounded by the generally unhappy younger tenants of these seedy lodgings. The story centers on a young unmarried woman (played by Leslie Caron) who is pregnant with a married man's baby.

39. Susan Stewart, *On Longing: Narratives of the Miniature, the Gigantic, the Souvenir, the Collection* (Durham, N.C.: Duke University Press, 1993), 167–68.

40. Carolyn Steedman, *Landscape for a Good Woman: A Story of Two Lives* (London: Virago, 1986), 16.

41. Kuhn, *Family Secrets*, 102.

42. Beatrix Campbell, *Wigan Pier Revisited: Poverty and Politics in the 80s* (London: Virago, 1984).

43. John Hill, *Sex, Class and Realism: British Film 1956–1963* (London: BFI, 1986), 5 (includes Macmillan quote).

44. Ibid., 10.

45. Matthew Collin, with John Godfrey, *Altered State: The Story of Ecstasy Culture and Acid House* (London: Serpent's Tail, 1997), 6–7.

46. Catherine McDermott, *Street Style: British Design in the 80s* (New York: Rizzoli, 1987), 10.

47. Campbell, *Wigan Pier Revisited,* 226–27.

48. Emlyn Williams, *Beyond Belief: A Chronicle of a Murder and Its Detection* (New York: Random House, 1967).

49. Joan Smith, "Does She Belong in This Company?" *The Independent,* 26 Nov. 1995, 17; John Diamond, "Mad or Bad? Playing Cat and Mouse with Myra," *Evening Standard,* 20 Dec. 1995, 43.

50. Gordon Burn, *Alma* (New York: Houghton Mifflin, 1991), 163.

51. Ibid., 200–205.

52. Tara Fitzgerald, "UK Gallery's 'Sick' Portrait of Killer Sparks Fury," 16 Sept. 1998, Reuters.

53. Jacqueline Rose, "Margaret Thatcher and Ruth Ellis," *New Formations* 6 (Winter 1988): 3, 10.

54. The 1985 film *Dance with a Stranger* adopts the visual style of film noir rather than kitchen-sink realism to represent Ruth Ellis more sympathetically.

55. Rose, "Margaret Thatcher and Ruth Ellis," 3.

56. Ibid., 20.

57. Ibid., 18–19.

58. Ibid., 5.

59. Iain Sinclair, *Lights Out for the Territory* (London: Granta, 1997), 89.

60. See Sarah Franklin, Celia Lury, and Jackie Stacey, eds., *Off-Centre: Feminism and Cultural Studies* (London: Harper Collins, 1991); and Mary Desjardins, "Free from the Apron Strings: Representations of Mothers in the Maternal British State," in *Fires Were Started: British Cinema and Thatcherism,* ed. Lester Friedman (Minneapolis: University of Minnesota Press, 1993), 130–44.

61. Jacqueline Rose, *Why War?—Psychoanalysis, Politics, and the Return to Melanie Klein* (Oxford: Blackwell, 1993), 74.

62. Ibid., 75.

63. Quoted in Helene Wong, "Planet Bollywood," *New Zealand Listener,* 29 Apr. 2000, 36.

64. Quoted in *The Face,* Mar. 1990, 64.

65. See Seth Koven, "From Rough Lads to Hooligans: Boy Life, National Culture and Social Reform," in Parker et al., *Nationalisms and Sexualities,* 365–91.

66. Richard Dyer, *Heavenly Bodies* (London: British Film Institute/Macmillan, 1987), 154.

67. Andy Medhurst, "That Special Thrill: *Brief Encounter,* Homosexuality and Authorship," *Screen* 32, no. 2 (Summer 1991): 204.

68. Al Wiesel, "Safe Sex Idol," *QW,* 29 Nov. 1992, 33.

69. Quoted in *New Musical Express,* 22 Aug. 1992, 15.

70. Phil Cohen, "Nineteenth-Century Jungles," in *Imagining Cities: Scripts, Signs, Memory,* ed. Sallie Westwood and John Williams (London: Routledge, 1997), 83.

71. Leon Hunt, *British Low Culture: From Safari Suits to Sexploitation* (London: Routledge, 1998), 81–82.

72. Dick Hebdige, *Subculture: The Meaning of Style* (London: Methuen, 1979), 58.

73. Pete Fowler, "The Emergence of the Skinhead," in Kureishi and Savage, *Faber Book of Pop,* 379.

74. John Clarke, "The Skinheads and the Magical Recovery of Community," in *Resistance Through Rituals: Youth Subcultures in Post-War Britain,* ed. Stuart Hall and Tony Jefferson (London: Routledge, 1993), 102.

75. Philip Cohen, "The Perversions of Inheritance: Studies in the Making of Multi-Racist Britain," in *Multi-Racist Britain,* ed. Philip Cohen and Harbajan S. Bains (London: Macmillan, 1988), 83.

76. See the excellent discussion of cartoonish Oi! punk and the "degeneration of the punk rock dialectic" in more loathsome fascist skinhead bands like Skrewdriver, in Stewart Home, *Cranked Up Really High: An Inside Account of Punk Rock* (London: Codex, 1995), 81–92.

77. Knight, *Skinhead,* 83.

78. Clarke, "Skinheads and the Magical Recovery," 99.

79. Paul Du Noyer, "The Seventies: Rebellion, Revival and Survival," in *Cool Cats: Twenty-five Years of Rock 'n' Roll Style,* ed. Tony Stewart (New York: Delilah Press, 1982), 104.

80. See Hebdige, *Hiding in the Light,* 22.

81. David Muggleton, "The Post-Subculturalist," in Redhead, *Clubcultures Reader,* 201.

82. John King, *The Football Factory* (London: Vintage, 1997), 53.

83. Armond White, "Anglocentric: Morrissey," *Village Voice,* 1 Sept. 1992, 70.

84. King, *Football Factory,* 116.

85. The writer Jimmy McGovern focused his righteous anger about the Hillsborough affair in the drama *Inquest,* but its more "incoherent" working-class anger and its racialized aspects are more visceral in the *Cracker* story.

86. Paul Smith, *Millennial Dreams: Contemporary Culture and Capital in the North* (London: Verso, 1997), 118.

87. See Klaus Theweleit, *Male Fantasies Volume 2: Male Bodies—Psychoanalyzing the White Terror* (Minneapolis: University of Minnesota Press, 1989).

88. Zizek, *Tarrying with the Negative,* 214.

89. Quoted in Jo Slee, *Peepholism: Into the Art of Morrissey* (London: Sidgwick and Jackson, 1994), 159.

90. Ibid., 159.

91. *The Guardian,* early Feb. 1995.

92. Barnor Hesse, "White Governmentality," in Westwood and Williams, *Imagining Cities,* 97.

93. Julian Evans, "The Object of Love," *Guardian Weekend,* 26 Feb. 1994, 11.

94. Claude Lévi-Strauss, *The View from Afar* (New York: Basic Books, 1985), 23.

95. Parsons, *Dispatches from the Front Line,* 95.

96. Ibid.

97. Wright, *On Living in an Old Country,* 243.

98. Nick Kent, "The Deep End," interview in *The Face,* Mar. 1990, 57.

99. Jesus Martin-Barbero, "Communication from Culture: The Crisis of the National and the Emergence of the Popular," *Media, Culture and Society* 10 (1988): 459.

100. Jonathan Wilson, "A Very English Story," *New Yorker,* Mar. 1995.

101. Andrew Harrison, "We'd Rather Jack," *Select,* Apr. 1993, 67.

102. See Martin Cloonan, "State of the Nation: 'Englishness,' Pop, and Politics in the Mid-1990s," *Popular Music and Society* 21, no. 2 (Summer 1997): 47–71.

103. Simon Reynolds, "Britpop" (first published in *Frieze,* late 1995) at <http://members.aol.com/blissout/britpop.htm>, site accessed 4 July 1997; see also Jon Savage, "The Boys' Club," *The Guardian,* 4 July 1997, 2–4.

104. Gilbert, "Soundtrack to an Uncivil Society," 20.

105. See David Hesmondhalgh, "Indie: The Institutional Politics and Aesthetics of a Popular Music Genre," *Cultural Studies* 13, no. 1 (Summer 1999): 34–61.

106. See Caroline Sullivan, "Blurred Vision," *The Guardian,* 10 Nov. 1994, 2–4.

107. Sean Campbell, "Britpop: The Importance of Being Irish, or, the Relevance of Ethnicity for Understanding Second-Generation Irish Musicians in England," paper presented at "Changing Sounds: New Directions and Configurations in Popular Music," conference of the International Association for Popular Music, Sydney, 9–13 July 1999. See also Jon Savage, *Time Travels* (London: Chatto and Windus, 1996), 392–94.

108. Savage, *Time Travels,* 393; Savage, "The Boys' Club," 2.

109. Steve Sweeney-Turner, "'Genre Sluts': Blur, Camp, and Postmodern 'Englishness,'" at <http://www.leeds.ac.uk/music/DeptInfo/Staff/SST/blur.html>, site accessed 5 July 1997.

110. Lawrence Grossberg, "Is Anybody Listening? Does Anybody Care?: On Talking about the State of Rock," in *Microphone Fiends: Youth Music and Youth Culture,* ed. Andrew Ross and Tricia Rose (London: Routledge, 1994), 41–58.

111. Ibid., 55.

112. Susan McClary "Same as It Ever Was: Youth Culture and Music," in Ross and Rose, *Microphone Fiends,* 33.

113. See Laura Lee Davies, "Velocity Girls: Indie, New Lads, Old Values," in *Girls! Girls! Girls!: Essays on Women and Music,* ed. Sarah Cooper (New York: New York University Press, 1996), 124–34. I must confess, with Davies, that the Smiths allowed me as a fan to work through a "little-boy-lost" syndrome, but, in my defense, I would argue that these feelings were also shaped by a specifically racialized experience in Britain.

114. See Jon Savage, "Lads and Lasses: Fantasy Football," in Savage, *Time Travels,* 388–90.

115. See Robert Miklitsch, "Rock 'N' Theory: Autobiography, Cultural Studies and the Death of Rock," at <http://jefferson.village.virginia.edu/pmc/text-only/issue.199/9.2miklitsch.txt>, site accessed 20 Nov. 1999.

116. Will Straw, "Systems of Articulation, Logics of Change: Communities and Scenes in Popular Music," *Cultural Studies* 5 (1991): 385.

117. Ibid., 369.

Chapter 2: U.K. Public Limited Company

1. See Frith, "Anglo-America and Its Discontents," 263–69; and Laing, "Rock Anxieties and New Music Networks," 116–32.

2. Corrina Sturmer, "MTV's Europe: An Imaginary Continent," in *Channels of Resistance: Global Television and Local Empowerment,* ed. Tony Dowmunt (London: BFI/Channel 4, 1993), 50–66.

3. See the discussion in Sheryl Garratt, "Martians in Moscow," *The Face,* Sept. 1993, 98–105.

4. Derek Jarman, *The Last of England* (London: Constable, 1987), 99.

5. Quoted in Chris Heath, *Pet Shop Boys, Literally* (London: Viking, 1990), 124.

6. Quoted in *Blitz,* Apr. 1991, 42. Neil Tennant was executive producer on the Red Hot CD compilation project *Twentieth Century Blues: The Songs of Noël Coward* (EMI 1998).

7. Michael Bracewell, *England Is Mine* (London: Harper Collins, 1998), 45.

8. Lawrence Driscoll, "The Rose Revived: Derek Jarman and the English Tradition," in *By Angels Driven: The Films of Derek Jarman,* ed. Chris Lippard (Westport, Conn.: Greenwood Press, 1996), 66.

9. Bracewell, *England Is Mine,* 44.

10. Alison Light, *Forever England: Femininity, Literature and Conservatism between the Wars* (London: Routledge, 1991), 19.

11. The recent publication of Philip Larkin's letters, which exposed him as both a racist and misogynist, and the literary controversy over the prestigious Booker Prize have brought to a head a crisis in the definition of "English" literature, during a period when the Conservatives pressed forward their national curriculum in English and history. On the Larkin issue, see Lisa Jardine, "Saxon Violence," *The Guardian,* Arts section, 8 Dec. 1992, 4. Jardine refers to Terry Eagleton's inaugural lecture as professor of English in which he describes the traditional canon of English literature as increasingly an ancient monument, a cultural Stonehenge, saying professors of English "might as well hand over responsibility for its preservation to the National Trust right now."

12. Quoted in Laura Di Michele, "Autobiography and the Structure of Feeling in *Border Country,*" in *Views beyond the Border Country: Raymond Williams and Cultural Politics,* ed. Dennis D. Dworkin and Leslie G. Roman (London: Routledge, 1993), 29–30.

13. See Eve Kosofsky Sedgwick, *The Epistemology of the Closet* (London: Harvester Wheatsheaf, 1991).

14. See Will Straw, "Organized Disorder: The Changing Space of the Record Shop," in Redhead, *Clubcultures Reader,* 57–65.

15. See Stan Hawkins, "The Pet Shop Boys: Musicology, Masculinity and Banality," in *Sexing the Groove: Popular Music and Gender,* ed. Sheila Whiteley (London: Blackwell, 1998), 118–33.

16. Heath, *Pet Shop Boys, Literally,* and idem, *Pet Shop Boys versus America* (London: Penguin, 1994).

17. Hebdige, *Hiding in the Light,* 175.

18. Ibid., 36.

19. See Hesmondhalgh, "Indie," 34–61.

20. David Buxton, "Rock Stars and Consumer Discipline," in *On Record: Rock, Pop and the Written Word,* ed. Simon Frith and Andrew Goodwin (New York: Pantheon, 1990), 434.

21. Andrew Goodwin, *Dancing in the Distraction Factory: Music Television and Popular Culture* (Minneapolis: University of Minnesota Press, 1991), 104. See also Deena Weinstein, "Art versus Commerce: Deconstructing a (Useful) Romantic Illusion," in *Stars Don't Stand Still in the Sky: Music and Myth,* ed. Karen Kelly and Evelyn McDonnell (New York: Routledge and Dia Center for the Arts, 1999), 57–69.

22. Jonathan Dollimore, *Sexual Dissidence* (Oxford: Oxford University Press, 1990), 322–23.

23. Ibid., 323; Ann Powers, "Camp Counselors," *Village Voice,* 2 Nov. 1993, 73.

24. Joseph Bristow, "Homophobia/misogyny: Sexual Fears, Sexual Definitions," in *Coming on Strong: Gay Politics and Culture,* ed. Simon Shepherd and Mick Wallis (London: Unwin Hyman, 1989), 67–68.

25. Joe Clark, "In and Out with the Pet Shop Boys," *Outweek,* 8 May 1991, 52–53.

26. John Gill, *Queer Noises* (London: Cassell, 1995), 9.

27. Simon Watney, "How to Have Sax in an Epidemic: Simon Watney on the Pet Shop Boys," *Art Forum International,* Nov. 1993, 8–9.

28. David Benedict and John Lyttle, "Moving into the Mainstream," *The Independent,* 27 Nov. 1995, 2.

29. Alexander Doty, *Making Things Perfectly Queer: Interpreting Mass Culture* (Minneapolis: University of Minnesota Press, 1993), 3.

30. Pamela Robertson, *Guilty Pleasures: Feminist Camp from Mae West to Madonna* (Durham, N.C.: Duke University Press, 1996), 9.

31. Quoted in Paul Burston, "Honestly," *Attitude,* Apr. 1994.

32. Quoted in *Bay Windows,* 28 Sept. 1996; and *Gay Times,* June 1997.

33. John Urry, *Consuming Places* (London: Routledge, 1995), 133.

34. Jonathan Culler, "Semiotics of Tourism," *American Journal of Semiotics* 1, nos. 1–2 (1981): 127–40.

35. John Taylor, *A Dream of England* (New York: St. Martin's, 1993), 241. See also *Critical Decade: Black British Photography in the 80s,* special edition, *Ten.8* 2, no. 3 (Spring 1992); and Susan Kismaric, *British Photography from the Thatcher Years* (New York: Museum of Modern Art, 1990).

36. Michel de Certeau, "Walking in the City," in *The Cultural Studies Reader,* ed. Simon During (London: Routledge, 1994), 152–53.

37. Michel de Certeau, *The Practice of Everyday Life* (Berkeley: University of California Press, 1984), 93.

38. John Durham Peters, "Exile, Nomadism and Diaspora: The Stakes of Mobility in the Western Canon," in *The Home and the World,* ed. Hamid Naficy (London: Routledge, 1999), 33.

39. Steve Pile, *The Body and the City: Psychoanalysis, Space and Subjectivity* (London: Routledge, 1996), 226.

40. Frank Mort, "The Politics of Consumption," in *New Times: The Changing Face of Politics in the 1990s,* ed. Stuart Hall and Martin Jacques (London: Lawrence and Wishart, 1989), 170.

41. Ibid., 166.

42. See Jim McGuigan, *Cultural Populism* (London: Routledge, 1992).

43. See Christopher Norris, "Old Themes for New Times: Postmodernism, Theory and Cultural Politics," *New Formations* 18 (Winter 1992): 1–24.

44. See Robert Miklitsch, *From Hegel to Madonna: Towards a General Economy of "Commodity Fetishism"* (Albany: State University of New York Press, 1998).

45. Michael Warner, "Introduction," *Fear of a Queer Planet: Queer Politics and Social Theory,* ed. Michael Warner (Minneapolis: University of Minnesota Press, 1993), xxxi.

46. Simon Frith, "Pet Shop Boys: The Divine Commodity," *Village Voice Rock and Roll Quarterly* (Spring 1988): 148.

47. Walter Hughes, "In the Empire of the Beat: Discipline and Disco," in Ross and Rose, *Microphone Fiends,* 155.

48. Derek Jarman, *Modern Nature* (London: Penguin, 1994), 57. The Pet Shop Boys' "King's Cross" seems also to prophesy the King's Cross underground railway fire disaster, which occurred soon after the release of the song.

49. Frederic Jameson, *Postmodernism, or the Cultural Logic of Late Capitalism* (London: Verso, 1991), 364–65.

50. Patrick Wright, *A Journey through Ruins: A Keyhole Portrait of British Postwar Life and Culture* (London: Flamingo, 1993).

51. Paul Gilroy, "Climbing the Racial Mountain: A Conversation with Isaac Julien," in his *Small Acts: Thoughts on the Politics of Black Cultures* (London: Serpent's Tail, 1993), 167.

52. Alan Hollinghurst, *The Swimming-Pool Library* (New York: Vintage, 1988), 6.

53. Neil Bartlett, *Who Was That Man?* (London: Serpent's Tail, 1988), xx.

54. Ibid., 229–30.

55. Simon Watney, *Policing Desire: Pornography, AIDS and the Media,* 2d ed. (Minneapolis: University of Minnesota Press, 1989), 7.

56. Jarman, *The Last of England,* 54.

57. Simon Watney, *Practices of Freedom* (Durham, N.C.: Duke University Press, 1995), xxi.

58. Hughes, "In the Empire of the Beat," 155.

59. Quoted in Nairn, *The Enchanted Glass,* 86.

60. Nairn, *The Enchanted Glass,* 87.

61. For discussion of this issue, see Jacqueline Rose, "The Cult of Celebrity," *New Formations* 36 (1999): 9–20.

62. Kuhn, *Family Secrets,* 81.

63. See Lauren Berlant and Elizabeth Freeman, "Queer Nationality," in Warner, *Fear of a Queer Planet,* 193–229.

64. The PSB album *Nightlife* (Parlophone 1999) continues to mine the generic tropes of 1970s Disco music.

Chapter 3: E Is for England

1. For a history of the influential machinery, see Chris Kempster, ed., *History of House* (London: Penguin, Castle Communications, The Mix, 1996). The best book on rave and dance-floor culture is Jane Bussmann, *Once in a Lifetime: The Crazy Days of Acid House and Afterwards* (London: Virgin, 1998).

2. Darren Reynolds, *Soul Underground,* Apr. 1988, 16.

3. See Melissa Harrison, ed., *High Society: The Real Voices of Club Culture* (London: Piatkus Books, 1998).

4. Hari Kunzru, "Raving," *London Review of Books,* 22 May 1997.

5. Ibid.; see also Sarah Champion, ed., *Disco Biscuits: New Fiction from the Chemical Generation* (London: Sceptre, 1997).

6. Simon Reynolds, *Energy Flash: A Journey through Rave Music and Dance Culture* (London: Picador, 1998).

7. See Sheryl Garratt, *Adventures in Wonderland: A Decade of Club Culture* (London: Headline, 1998).

8. Ibid., 99.

9. Simon Reynolds, "Rave Culture: Living Dream or Living Death?" in Redhead, *Clubcultures Reader,* 105–6.

10. Collin and Godfrey, *Altered State,* 8.

11. Germaine Greer, *Oz* magazine, Nov. 1969, reprinted in Kureishi and Savage, *Faber Book of Pop,* 342.

12. Susan McClary, "Same as It Ever Was: Youth Culture and Music," in Ross and Rose, *Microphone Fiends,* 32–33.

13. Ibid., 33.

14. See Will Straw, "Sizing Up Record Collections: Gender and Connoisseurship in Rock Music Culture," in Whiteley, *Sexing the Groove,* 3–16.

15. See Jon Savage, "The Sound of the Crowd," in Kelly and McDonnell, *Stars Don't Stand Still in the Sky,* 145–51.

16. Richard Dyer, "In Defense of Disco," in Frith and Goodwin, *On Record,* 410.

17. Hughes, "In the Empire of the Beat," 148.

18. Ibid., 151.

19. Angela McRobbie, "Shut Up and Dance: Youth Culture and Changing Modes of Femininity," *Cultural Studies* 7, no. 3 (Oct. 1993): 422.

20. Maria Pini, "Cyborgs, Nomads and the Raving Feminine," in *Dance in the City,* ed. Helen Thomas (New York: St. Martin's, 1997), 118.

21. Sadie Plant, *Writing on Drugs* (London: Faber and Faber, 1999), 167–68.

22. Pini, "Cyborgs, Nomads and the Raving Feminine," 125.

23. See Antonio Melechi, "The Ecstasy of Disappearance," in *Rave Off: Politics and*

Deviance in Contemporary Youth Culture, ed. Steve Redhead (Aldershot, Eng.: Avebury, 1993), 29–40.

24. See Maria Pini, "Women and the Early British Rave Scene," in McRobbie, *Back to Reality?* 152–69.

25. See Mary Anna Wright, "The Great British Ecstasy Revolution," in *DiY Culture: Party and Protest in Nineties Britain,* ed. George McKay (London: Verso, 1998), 228–41.

26. Hillegonda Rietveld, "Repetitive Beats: Free Parties and the Politics of Contemporary DiY Dance Culture in Britain," in McKay, *DiY Culture,* 264.

27. Grossberg, "Is Anybody Listening?" 56; Reynolds, "Rave Culture," 107.

28. See Andrew O'Hagan, *Observer Life,* 9 Oct. 1994, reprinted in Kureishi and Savage, *Faber Book of Pop,* 806–13.

29. See, for example, Nicholas Saunders, *Ecstasy Reconsidered* (London: N. Saunders, 1997).

30. See Geoffrey O'Brien, "Burt Bacharach Comes Back," *New York Review of Books,* 6 May 1999, 46–52.

31. Joseph Lanza, *Elevator Music: A Surreal History of Muzak, Easy-listening, and Other Moodsong* (New York: Picador, 1995), 2.

32. See Dylan Jones, *Easy!: The Lexicon of Lounge* (London: Pavilion, 1997).

33. Jacques Attali, *Noise: The Political Economy of Music,* trans. Brian Massumi (Minneapolis: University of Minnesota Press, 1985), 11.

34. Alexei Monroe, "Thinking about Mutation: Genres in 1990s Electronica," in Blake, *Living through Pop,* 155.

35. Ibid., 153.

36. Sarah Thornton, *Club Cultures* (London: Polity Press, 1995), 115.

37. Drew Hemment, "e is for ekstasis," *New Formations* 31 (Summer 1996): 35; see also Gilles Deleuze and Félix Guattari, "What Is a Minor Literature?" in *Out There: Marginalization and Contemporary Cultures,* ed. Russell Ferguson et al. (New York and Cambridge, Mass.: The New Museum of Contemporary Art and Massachusetts Institute of Technology, 1990), 59–69.

38. See Hemment, "e is for ekstasis," 36–38.

39. See Michael Keith and Steve Pile, "Introduction Part 1: The Politics of Place," in *Place and the Politics of Identity,* ed. Michael Keith and Steve Pile (London: Routledge, 1993), 1–21.

40. Reynolds, "Rave Culture," 110; Irvine Welsh, on *Face to Face,* BBC2 Television, 27 Nov. 1995.

41. See John Hutnyk, "Repetitive Beatings or Criminal Justice?" in *Dis-Orienting Rhythms: The Politics of the New Asian Dance Music,* ed. Sanjay Sharma, John Hutnyk, and Ashwani Sharma (London: Zed Books, 1996), 156–89.

42. Gilbert, "Soundtrack to an Uncivil Society," 17.

43. See George McKay, *Senseless Acts of Beauty: Cultures of Resistance since the Sixties* (London: Verso, 1996).

44. See Hakim Bey, *T.A.Z.: The Temporary Autonomous Zone, Ontological Anarchy, Poetic Terrorism* (Brooklyn, N.Y.: Autonomedia, 1991).

45. Kodwo Eshun, "Outing the In-Crowd," *The Wire,* New Year 1993, 40.

46. Hemment, "e is for ekstasis," 37.

47. See Alberto Melucci, *Nomads of the Present: Social Movements and Individual Needs in Contemporary Society,* ed. John Keane and Paul Mier (London: Hutchinson Radius, 1989); Ernesto Laclau and Chantal Mouffe, *Hegemony and Socialist Strategy: Towards a Radical Democratic Politics,* trans. Winston Moore and Paul Cammack (London: Verso, 1985); Ernesto Laclau, *New Reflections on the Revolution of Our Time* (London: Verso, 1990).

48. Gilbert, "Soundtrack to an Uncivil Society," 18.

49. See George McKay, "DiY Culture: Notes towards an Intro," in McKay, *DiY Culture,* 41–44.

50. Peter Gartside, "Bypassing Politics? A Critical Look at DiY Culture," in *Young Britain: Politics, Pleasures and Predicaments,* ed. Jonathan Rutherford (London: Lawrence and Wishart, 1998), 71.

51. See Kevin Hetherington, "Vanloads of Uproarious Humanity: New Age Travellers and the Utopics of the Countryside," in *Cool Places: Geographies of Youth Cultures,* ed. Tracey Skelton and Gill Valentine (London: Routledge, 1998), 328–41.

52. Gartside, "Bypassing Politics?," 68.

53. See Angela McRobbie, "Thinking with Music," in Kelly and McDonnell, *Stars Don't Stand Still in the Sky,* 40.

Chapter 4: Black Whole Styles

1. Reynolds, *Blissed Out,* 174.

2. Frank Owen and Carlo McCormick, "Out of Your Head: The New Transcendence" *Village Voice Rock and Roll Quarterly* 4, no. 3 (Fall 1991): 8.

3. Reynolds, *Blissed Out,* 174–75.

4. Jon Pareles, "Dance Music Marries the Machine," *New York Times,* 8 Mar. 1992, H31 and H39.

5. Ross Harley, "Beat in the System," in Bennett et al., *Rock and Popular Music,* 222.

6. Quoted by Richard C. Green and Monique Guillory, "Question of a 'Soulful' Style: Interview with Paul Gilroy," in *Soul: Black Power, Politics, and Pleasure,* ed. Monique Guillory and Richard C. Green (New York: New York University Press, 1998), 253–54.

7. Louis Chude-Sokei, "The Sound of Culture: Dread Discourse and Jamaican Sound Systems," in *Language, Rhythm, and Sound: Black Popular Cultures into the Twenty-first Century,* ed. Joseph K. Adjaye and Adrianne R. Andrews (Pittsburgh: University of Pittsburgh Press, 1997), 201.

8. Paul Gilroy, *There Ain't No Black in the Union Jack: The Cultural Politics of Race and Nation* (Chicago: University of Chicago Press, 1987), 210.

9. In the reggae world, the DJ is the person who rhymes over the records while the selector spins the records on the turntables, whereas in American dance music parlance, e.g., in hip-hop, the DJ designates the person who spins the records, while the MC or

rapper rhymes over the music. These categorizations have been imported to British dance music culture.

10. Paul Gilroy, "Cultural Studies and Ethnic Absolutism," in Grossberg et al., *Cultural Studies*, 193.

11. James Clifford, *Routes: Travel and Translation in the Late Twentieth Century* (Berkeley: University of California Press, 1997), 252.

12. Avtar Brah, *Cartographies of Diaspora: Contesting Identities* (London: Routledge, 1996), 183.

13. Edouard Glissant, *Caribbean Discourse* (Charlottesville: University Press of Virginia, 1989), 62; Walter Benjamin, "Theses on the Philosophy of History," in his *Illuminations* (New York: Schocken, 1969), 253–64.

14. Barnor Hesse, "Black to Front and Black Again," in Keith and Pile, *Place and the Politics of Identity*, 169. See also Michael Hanchard, "Afro-Modernity: Temporality, Politics and the African Diaspora," *Public Culture* 11, no. 1 (1999): 245–68.

15. Paul Gilroy, *The Black Atlantic: Modernity and Double Consciousness* (Cambridge, Mass.: Harvard University Press, 1993), 198.

16. Vijay Mishra, "The Diasporic Imaginary: Theorizing the Indian Diaspora," *Textual Practice* 10, no. 3 (1996): 443.

17. Gilroy, *Black Atlantic*, 6.

18. James A. Snead, "Repetition as a Figure of Black Culture," in Ferguson et al., *Out There*, 220.

19. Ibid.

20. See Tricia Rose, "Soul Sonic Forces: Technology, Orality, and Black Cultural Practice in Rap Music," in *Sounding Off!: Music as Subversion/Resistance/Revolution*, ed. Ron Sakolsky and Fred Wei-Han Ho (Brooklyn: Autonomedia, 1995), 97–107.

21. Chude-Sokei, "The Sound of Culture," 185.

22. See Dick Hebdige, *Cut 'n' Mix: Culture, Identity and Caribbean Music* (London: Comedia, 1987).

23. Paul Willis, with S. Jones, J. Canaan, G. Hurd, *Common Culture: Symbolic Work at Play in the Everyday Cultures of the Young* (Milton Keynes, Eng.: Open University Press, 1990), 72.

24. Steve Barrow and Peter Dalton, *Reggae: The Rough Guide* (London: Rough Guides, 1997), 199–228.

25. Luke Ehrlich, "X-Ray Music: The Volatile History of Dub," in *Reggae International*, ed. Stephen Davis and Peter Simon (New York: R and B Books, 1982), 106.

26. William Gibson, *Neuromancer* (New York: Ace Books, 1984), 104.

27. Chude-Sokei, "The Sound of Culture," 192.

28. David Toop, *The Rap Attack II: African Rap to Global Hip Hop* (London: Pluto Press, 1995), 191.

29. See Paul Gilroy, "It Ain't Where You're From, It's Where You're At: The Dialectics of Diaspora Identification," in Gilroy, *Small Acts*, 120–45.

30. Gilroy, *Black Atlantic,* 105–6.

31. Gilroy, *Small Acts,* 12.

32. Paul Gilroy, "After the Love Has Gone: Bio-politics and Etho-poetics in the Black Public Sphere," in McRobbie, *Back to Reality?* 88.

33. Quoted in Green and Guillory, "Question of a 'Soulful' Style," 259.

34. Ibid., 264.

35. Stuart Hall, "Black and White in Television," in *Remote Control: Dilemmas of Black Intervention in British Film and TV,* ed. June Givanni (London: British Film Institute, 1995), 15.

36. Simon Frith, "Youth/Music/Television," in Frith et al., *Sound and Vision,* 77–78.

37. Paul Gilroy, "Intervention for What? Black TV and the Impossibility of Politics," in Givanni, *Remote Control,* 35.

38. Paul Gilroy, "Exer(or)cising Power: Black Bodies in the Black Public Sphere," in Thomas, *Dance in the City,* 23. Gilroy wonders whether "the relative decline of dance in black popular culture and the curiously unmourned disappearance of breaking may have been connected to the negative impact of video technologies on expressive forms that had previously been sound rather than vision-based and which were absolutely inseparable from the dance cultures in which they were embedded?" (22).

39. Iain Chambers, "Maps, Movies, Musics and Memory," in *The Cinematic City,* ed. David B. Clarke (London: Routledge, 1997), 232.

40. See Gilroy, "After the Love Has Gone," 93–94.

41. Steve Wurtzler, "She Sang Live, but the Microphone Was Turned Off: The Live, the Recorded, and the *Subject* of Representation," in *Sound Theory/Sound Practice,* ed. Rick Altman (New York: American Film Institute/Routledge, 1992), 103.

42. Paul Théberge, *Any Sound You Can Imagine: Making Music/Consuming Technology* (Middletown, Conn.: Wesleyan University Press, 1997), 188.

43. Ibid., 206.

44. See Andrew Goodwin, "Rationalization and Democratization in the New Technologies of Popular Music," in *Popular Music and Communication,* ed. James Lull (London: Sage, 1992), 75–100.

45. Paul Gilroy, "Modern Tones," in his *Rhapsodies in Black: Art of the Harlem Renaissance,* exh. cat. (London: Hayward Gallery/University of California Press, 1997), 108.

46. Tricia Rose, *Black Noise: Rap Music and Black Culture in Contemporary America* (Middletown, Conn.: Wesleyan University Press, 1994), 84–85.

47. Quoted in Mark Dery, "Black to the Future: Interviews with Samuel R. Delany, Greg Tate, and Tricia Rose," in *Flame Wars: The Discourse of Cyberculture,* ed. Mark Dery (Durham, N.C.: Duke University Press, 1994), 211.

48. Ibid., 193.

49. Kodwo Eshun, *More Brilliant Than the Sun: Adventures in Sonic Fiction* (London: Quartet, 1998), 00[-006].

50. See John Corbett, "Brothers from Another Planet: The Space Madness of Lee

'Scratch' Perry, Sun Ra, and George Clinton," in his *Extended Play: Sounding Off from John Cage to Dr. Funkenstein* (Durham, N.C.: Duke University Press, 1994), 7–31.

51. Ian Penman, "Tricky," *The Wire*, Dec. 1994, 38.

52. Eshun, *More Brilliant*, A[192].

53. Ibid., A[193].

54. Ibid., oo[-003].

55. Ibid., oo[-004]. See also Greg Tate, *Flyboy in the Buttermilk: Essays on Contemporary America* (New York: Simon and Schuster, 1992).

56. Quoted in the *Village Voice*, 30 Jan. 1996, 59.

57. Phil Johnson, *Straight outa Bristol: Massive Attack, Portishead, Tricky and the Roots of Trip-Hop* (London: Sceptre, 1997), 40–44; see also George Lipsitz, *Dangerous Crossroads: Popular Music, Postmodernism, and the Poetics of Place* (London: Verso, 1994), and *Bristol Vibes*, Rubert Gabriel's short 1996 film documenting twenty-four hours in the life of Bristol, particularly its Afro-Caribbean inhabitants, using reggae dub by Henry and Louis, the soul of Smith and Mighty, and the jungle/drum'n'bass of Roni Size and DJ Krust.

58. See Johnson, *Straight outa Bristol*, 89–128.

59. William Shaw, "Surprise Attack," in *Details*, Feb. 1995, 123.

60. The video for one song, "Teardrop," with vocals by Elizabeth Fraser, even features a computer-generated lipsynching baby inside a womb.

61. Quoted in Johnson, *Straight outa Bristol*, 116.

62. Rose, *Black Noise*, 9–12.

63. Quoted in Sean O'Hagan, "Go West," *The Face*, Aug. 1994, 59.

64. Johnson, *Straight outa Bristol*, 120.

65. Quoted in O'Hagan, "Go West," 59.

66. Quoted in *Musician*, Aug. 1998.

67. Quoted at <http://www.hauntedink.com/tricky/>, accessed 4 Aug. 1999.

68. Penman, "Tricky," 38.

69. Quoted in Johnson, *Straight outa Bristol*, 135–36.

70. Quoted in *Musician*, Aug. 1998.

71. Quoted in Sean O'Hagan, "Uneasy Listening," *Observer Review*, 22 Oct. 1995, 11.

72. Ibid.

73. Greg Kot, "Shoot from the Hip Hop," *Chicago Tribune*, 15 Sept. 1995.

74. Mark Sinker, "Music as Film," in *Celluloid Jukebox: Popular Music and the Movies since the 50s*, ed. Jonathan Romney and Adrian Sutton (London: BFI, 1995), 116.

75. Frantz Fanon, *Black Skin, White Masks* (New York: Grove Press, 1969), 112.

76. Martin James, *State of Bass: Jungle, the Story So Far* (London: Boxtree, 1997), 6; Kodwo Eshun, in the film *The Last Angel of History*, John Akomfrah/Black Audio Collective, 1994.

77. Simon Reynolds, "Jungle Fever," in *Details*, Jan. 1994.

78. Quoted in Neil Strauss, "It's a Jungle Out There," *New York Times*, 22 Sept. 1994.

79. Quoted in Aidin Vaziri, "Welcome to the Jungle: Inside the Vibe of the U.K.'s Latest Underground Trends," at <http://www.breaks.com>, accessed May 1996.

80. Matthew Collin, *Observer Sunday Magazine,* June 1994, quoted at <http://www.breaks.com>, accessed May 1996.

81. James, *State of Bass,* 29–30.

82. Simon Reynolds, "Sounds of Blackness," *The Wire,* June 1995, 34.

83. Reynolds, *Energy Flash,* xvii.

84. Reynolds, "Sounds of Blackness," 35.

85. For a scathing critique of Reynolds from two Brit-Asian soul-boys, see Koushik and Partha Banerjea, "Psyche and Soul: A View from the 'South,'" in Sharma et al., *Dis-orienting Rhythms,* 123–24.

86. Tony Herrington, "Editor's Idea," *The Wire,* June 1995, 4.

87. Quoted in Stephen Jewell, "A Guy Called Gerald," *Pavement* Feb./Mar. 1997, 29.

88. Quoted in Tim Barr, "Concrete Jungle," in Kempster, *History of House,* 148.

89. Martin James, "Origins of a Sound," *Future Music,* Mar. 1998, 66.

90. Ibid., 63.

91. See, for example, Martin James, "Goldie," *Mixmag,* Oct. 1994.

92. Quoted in Matthew Collin interview with Goldie in *Mixmag,* Sept. 1997, at <http://www.techno.de/mixmag/97.09/Goldie.a.html>, accessed Sept. 1997.

93. Ibid.

94. Forrest Green III, "Rumble in the Jungle," *Detroit Metro Times,* 18–24 Mar., 16.

95. Quoted in Sarah Davis, "Roni Size," at <http://www.futurenet.com/musiciansnet/Hitech/People/Size/size1.html>, accessed Oct. 1997.

96. Paul Gilroy, "Analogues of Morning, Mourning the Analog," in Kelly and McDonnell, *Stars Don't Stand Still in the Sky,* 267.

97. Ibid., 262.

98. Neil Lazarus, "Is a Counterculture of Modernity a Theory of Modernity?" *Diaspora* 4, no. 3 (1995): 337.

99. Chude-Sokei, "The Sound of Culture," 200–201.

100. See the lively discussion of British Asian soul-boy culture in Banerjea and Banerjea, "Psyche and Soul," and of Jungle's South Asian resonances in Koushik Banerjea and Jatinder Barn, "Versioning Terror: Jallianwala Bagh and the Jungle," both in Sharma et al., *Dis-Orienting Rhythms,* 105–24 and 193–216, respectively.

Chapter 5: Asia Massive

1. Quoted in Prasad Bidaye, "Long Way from Home: South Asian Traditions Meet the Future," *Exclaim!* Nov. 1998, <http://www.shmooze.net/pwcasual/exclaim/index2.html>, accessed Nov. 1998.

2. See the discussion in Steven Vertovec, "Three Meanings of 'Diaspora,' Exemplified among South Asian Religions," *Diaspora* 6, no. 3 (1997): 277–99.

3. Quoted at <http://www.soz92awx/musik/dj/interview/adfinterview.html>, accessed 1996.

4. Lucy O'Brien, *She Bop: The Definitive History of Women in Rock, Pop and Soul* (London: Penguin, 1996), 352.

5. See Steven Feld, "From Schizophrenia to Schismogenesis: On the Discourses and Commodification Practices of 'World Music' and 'World Beat,'" in *Music Grooves,* ed. Charles Keil and Steven Feld (Chicago: University of Chicago Press, 1994), 270; James Barrett, "World Music, Nation and Postcolonialism," *Cultural Studies* 10, no. 2 (1996): 237–47; Martin Roberts, "'World Music' and the Global Cultural Economy," *Diaspora* 2, no. 2 (1992): 228–42; Tony Mitchell, *Popular Music and Local Identity: Rock, Pop and Rap in Europe and Oceania* (London: Leicester University Press, 1996); John Hutnyk, "Adorno at WOMAD: South Asian Crossover and the Limits of Hybridity Talk," in *Debating Cultural Hybridity,* ed. Pnina Werbner and Tariq Modood (London: Zed Books, 1997), 106–36; Andrew Goodwin and Joe Gore, "World Beat and the Cultural Imperialism Debate," in Sakolsky and Ho, *Sounding Off!,* 121–31.

6. Arjun Appadurai, "Disjuncture and Difference in the Global Cultural Economy," *Public Culture* 2, no. 2 (Spring 1990): 5.

7. Georgina Born, "Afterword," in Bennett et al., *Rock and Popular Music,* 286.

8. Brah, *Cartographies of Diaspora,* 192–94.

9. Quoted in Lee Harpin, "Birmingham: Ragga and Roots," *The Face,* Sept. 1994, 149.

10. Raminder Kaur and Virinder S. Kalra, "New Paths for South Asian Identity and Musical Creativity," in Sharma et al., *Dis-Orienting Rhythms,* 223–24.

11. Kobena Mercer, "Black Art and the Burden of Representation," *Third Text* 10 (1990): 77.

12. Virinder S. Kalra, John Hutnyk, and Sanjay Sharma, "Re-Sounding (Anti)Racism, or Concordant Politics? Revolutionary Antecedents," in Sharma et al., *Dis-Orienting Rhythms,* 125–27; Gilroy, *There Ain't No Black in the Union Jack,* 131–35.

13. Greil Marcus, *Lipstick Traces: A Secret History of the Twentieth Century* (Cambridge, Mass.: Harvard University Press, 1989), 444–45.

14. Kalra et al., "Re-Sounding (Anti)Racism," 135–37.

15. Kobena Mercer, "Recoding Narratives of Race and Nation," in *Black Film/British Cinema,* ICA Documents 7, ed. Mercer (London: ICA/BFI, 1989), 6.

16. Stuart Hall, "New Ethnicities," in Mercer, *Black Film/British Cinema,* 27–29.

17. Ibid., 27.

18. Stuart Hall, "Old and New Identities, Old and New Ethnicities," in *Culture, Globalization and the World System,* ed. A. D. King (London: Macmillan, 1991), 56.

19. Tariq Modood, "'Difference,' Cultural Racism and Anti-racism," in Werbner and Modood, *Debating Cultural Hybridity,* 170.

20. Sanjay Sharma, "Noisy Asians or 'Asian Noise'?" in Sharma et al., *Dis-Orienting Rhythms,* 40.

21. Aziz Al-Azmeh, *Islams and Modernities* (London: Verso, 1993), 9.

22. The Muslim Parliament is just one British Muslim organization and by no means represents a number of other British Muslim umbrella groups such as the United Kingdom Action Committee on Islamic Affairs (UKACIA), the Union of Muslim Organisations, and the Council of Imams and Mosques, themselves representing various predominantly Sunni Muslim traditions and doctrines. See Yunus Samad, "Imagining a British Muslim Identification," in *Muslim European Youth: Reproducing Ethnicity, Religion, Culture,* ed. Steven Vertovec and Alisdair Rogers (Aldershot, Eng.: Ashgate, 1998), 59–101.

23. Homi Bhabha, "DissemiNation: Time, Narrative, and the Margins of the Modern Nation," in *Nation and Narration,* ed. Homi Bhabha (London: Routledge, 1990), 303.

24. Ibid., 313–14.

25. Homi Bhabha, *The Location of Culture* (London: Routledge, 1994), 114.

26. Ibid., 38.

27. Jonathan Rutherford, "The Third Space: Interview with Homi Bhabha," in *Identity, Community, Culture, Difference,* ed. Rutherford (London: Lawrence and Wishart, 1990), 211.

28. See Robert Young, *Colonial Desire: Hybridity in Theory, Culture, and Race* (London: Routledge, 1995).

29. Aijaz Ahmed, "The Politics of Literary Postcoloniality," *Race and Class* 36, no. 3 (1995): 17.

30. Jonathan Friedman, "Global Crises, the Struggle for Cultural Hybridity and Intellectual Porkbarrelling: Cosmopolitans versus Locals, Ethnics and Nationals in an Era of De-hegemonisation," in Werbner and Modood, *Debating Cultural Hybridity,* 75.

31. See Ulf Hannerz, "Cosmopolitans and Locals in World Culture," in *Global Culture: Nationalism, Globalization and Modernity,* ed. Mike Featherstone (London: Sage, 1990), 237–51.

32. Bhabha, *Location of Culture,* 219.

33. Smadar Lavie, "Blow Ups in the Borderzones: Third World Israeli Authors' Gropings for Home," *New Formations* 18 (Winter 1992): 92–93; Gloria Anzaldua, *Borderlands/La Frontera* (San Francisco: Spinsters/Aunt Lute Books, 1987), 79.

34. Bidaye, "Long Way from Home."

35. Dick Hebdige, "After the Masses," in Hall and Jacques, *New Times,* 92.

36. Andrew Smith, "Some Like It Kool," *Sunday Times,* 10 June 1994.

37. Ibid.

38. Gayatri Gopinath, "'Bombay, U.K., Yuba City': Bhangra Music and the Engendering of Diaspora," *Diaspora* 4, no. 3 1995: 309.

39. Salman Rushdie, *The Satanic Verses* (London: Viking Penguin, 1989), 291–92.

40. Bhabha, *Location of Culture,* 228.

41. Timothy Brennan, *Salman Rushdie and the Third World: Myths of the Nation* (New York: St. Martin's, 1990), 164.

42. Quoted in *I-D* 124 (Jan. 1994): 11.

43. For a discussion of language, see Ben Rampton, *Crossing: Language and Ethnicity among Adolescents* (Harlow, Eng.: Longman, 1995); for a discussion of syncretism and

transculturalism in youth culture, see Les Back, *New Ethnicities and Urban Culture: Racisms and Multiculture in Young Lives* (London: UCL Press, 1996).

44. See a musicological analysis of "Arranged Marriage" in Taylor, *Global Pop*, 159–63.

45. Gopinath, "'Bombay, U.K., Yuba City,'" 310.

46. O. P. Malik, "Make Way for the Indian," at <http://yucc.yorku.ca/home/sanraj/apachi.html>, accessed 19 Sept. 1995.

47. For a discussion of the problematic subcontinental homecomings of Apache Indian and Fun^da^mental, see Mitchell, *Popular Music and Local Identity*, 60–67.

48. Quoted in "The King of New Asian Kool," at <http://www.c2.org/Connect/issues/1/sagoo.html>, accessed 19 Sept. 1995.

49. Simon Reynolds, "Out of the Cornershop into the Charts," *The Observer*, 7 Aug. 1994, 8.

50. Ibid.

51. See Ashish Rajadhyaksha and Paul Willemen, *Encylopaedia of Indian Cinema* (New Delhi: Oxford University Press, 1995).

52. "The King of New Asian Kool."

53. Iain Chambers, *Border Dialogues: Journeys in Postmodernity* (London: Routledge, 1990), 57–58.

54. Quoted in Runnymede Trust, *Islamophobia: Its Features and Dangers*, a consultation paper by the Commission on British Muslims and Islamophobia (1997), 11.

55. See also the Islam-obsessed work of Bryn Jones under the recording name Muslim Gauze.

56. Quoted in Caroline Sullivan, "Islam with Attitude," *The Guardian*, 17 June 1994, T12.

57. Kodwo Eshun, "Rebels without a Pause," *I-D* 124 (Jan. 1994): 27.

58. Sharma, "Noisy Asians or 'Asian Noise'?," 51–54.

59. Quoted at <http://www.soz92awx/musik/dj/interview/adfinterview.html>, accessed Aug. 1996.

60. Ibid.

61. Quoted in Brian Cathcart, "The Case of Stephen Lawrence," *France: The Outsider*, special issue, *Granta* 59 (Autumn 1997): 172.

62. Quoted in Liz Evans, *Women, Sex and Rock 'n' Roll: In Their Own Words* (London: Pandora, 1994), 234.

63. Carol Upadhya, "'Fire' and the Hindu Right," *Economic and Political Weekly*, 12 Dec. 1998, 3176–77.

64. Sairah Awan, "Full of Eastern Promise: South Asian Women in Music," in Cooper, *Girls! Girls! Girls!: Essays on Women and Music*, 102.

65. *Vox*, Apr. 1994.

66. Quoted in Amy Raphael, "Not Just an Asian Babe," *The Guardian*, 24 Aug. 1994, T9.

67. Quoted on the White Town website at <http://www.white-town.com>, accessed Aug. 1998.

68. Shantanu DuttaAhmed, "Border Crossings: Retrieval and Erasure of the Self as

Other," in *Between the Lines: South Asians and Postcoloniality,* ed. Deepika Bahri and Mary Vasudeva (Philadelphia: Temple University Press, 1996), 347.

69. Quoted in Bidaye, "Long Way from Home."

70. bell hooks, "Narratives of Struggle," in *Critical Fictions: The Politics of Imaginative Writing,* ed. Philomena Mariani (Seattle: Bay Press, 1991), 54–55.

71. See sleeve notes for Nusrat Fatah Ali Khan and Michael Brook, *Star Rise* (Real World 1997).

72. See David Toop, *Ocean of Sound: Aether Talk, Ambient Sound and Imaginary Worlds* (London: Serpent's Tail, 1995).

73. See David Toop, *Exotica* (London: Serpent's Tail, 1999); Philip Hayward, ed., *Widening the Horizon: Post-War Popular Music* (Sydney: John Libbey/Perfect Best Publications, 1999).

74. Singh quoted in *Kris World,* Singapore Airlines in-flight magazine, Nov. 1998, 10.

75. Stephen Jewell, "Wise Up!: Black Star Liner," *Real Groove,* July 1999, 18.

76. Ziauddin Sardar, "Dilip Kumar Made Me Do it," in *The Secret Politics of Our Desires: Innocence, Culpability and Indian Popular Cinema,* ed. Ashis Nandy (New Delhi: Oxford University Press, 1998), 70–71.

Conclusion

1. Rey Chow, *Writing Diaspora: Tactics of Intervention in Contemporary Cultural Studies* (Bloomington: Indiana University Press, 1993), 168.

2. Collins, *Architectures of Excess,* 12.

3. Arjun Appadurai, "Introduction: Commodities and the Politics of Value," in *The Social Life of Things: Commodities in Cultural Perspective,* ed. Arjun Appadurai (New York: Cambridge University Press, 1986), 13.

4. Collins, *Architectures of Excess,* 23.

5. Frith, *Performing Rites,* 18.

6. Keil and Feld, *Music Grooves,* 77.

7. Simon Frith, "Adam Smith and Music," *New Formations* (Winter 1992): 82–83.

8. Keil and Feld, *Music Grooves,* 93.

9. See Alberto Moreiras, "Hybridity and Double Consciousness," *Cultural Studies* 13, no. 3 (1999): 373–407.

Selected Discography

Adamson, Barry. *As Above So Below.* Mute (1998).

———. *Moss Side Story.* Mute CD Stumm 53 (1988).

———. *The Negro inside Me.* Mute 61610-2 (1993).

———. *Oedipus Schmoedipus.* Mute 9019-2 (1996).

———. *Soul Murder.* Mute Stumm 105 (1992).

———. *The Taming of the Shrewd.* CD Mute 97 (1989).

Apache Indian. *No Reservations.* Island IMCD215-514 112-2 (1993).

Asian Dub Foundation. *Facts and Fictions.* Nation NAT58LP (1995).

———. *Rafi's Revenge.* FFRR 556006-2 (1998).

Black Star Liner. *Bengali Bantam Youth Experience.* Warner Music (1998).

Blur. *Parklife.* Food (1994).

Cornershop. *When I Was Born for the 7th Time.* Wiija WIJCD1065 (1997).

———. *Woman's Gotta Have It.* Wiija WIJ45CD (1995).

Echobelly. *Everybody's Got One.* Fauve FAUV 3CD (1994).

Fun^da^mental. *Erotic Terrorism.* Nation (1998).

———. *Seize the Time.* Nation NATCD33 (1994).

Goldie. *Timeless.* FFRR/Metalheadz 828646-2 (1995).

A Guy Called Gerald. *Black Secret Technology.* Juice Box 5 019148606222 (1995).

The Justified Ancients of Mu Mu. "It's Grim Up North." KLF Communications, JAMS 028CD.

Kaliphz. "Hang 'em High." SEmtExt/FFRR KAX3 (1994).

Khan, Nusrat Fateh Ali, and Michael Brook, remixed. *Star Rise.* Real World (1997).

Massive Attack. *Blue Lines*. Virgin Records America 86228 2 (1991).

———. *Mezzanine*. Circa/VIRGIN UK WBRCDX4 (1998).

———. *Protection*. Circa/Virgin UK WBRCD2 (1994).

Massive Attack vs. Mad Professor. *No Protection*. Circa/Virgin UK WBRCD 3.

Morrissey. *Kill Uncle*. EMI CSD 3789 (1991).

———. *Viva Hate*. EMI CSD 3787 (1988).

———. *Your Arsenal*. EMI CSD 3790 (1992).

Oasis. *(What's the Story) Morning Glory?* Sony (1994).

Pet Shop Boys. *Actually*. EMI ELJ-46872 (1987).

———. *Behavior*. EMI USA CDP-7-94310-2 (1990).

———. *Bilingual*. Atlantic US 82915-2 (1996).

———. *Discography*. EMI USA CDP-7-97097-2 (1991).

———. *Nightlife*. Parlophone/Sire 31086-2 (1999).

———. *Very*. EMI USA E2-89721 (1993).

Pulp. *Different Class*. Island 524165-2 (1995).

Roni Size/Reprazent. *New Forms*. Talkin' Loud 534933-2 (1997).

Sagoo, Bally. *Bollywood Flashback*. Sony (1994).

Singh, Talvin. *OK*. Island/Omni ILPSD 8075/5x4559-1 (1998).

The Smiths. *Hatful of Hollow*. Rough Trade, Rough 76 (1984).

———. *Louder Than Bombs*. Sire 925569-2 (1987).

———. *Meat Is Murder*. Rough Trade, Rough 81 (1985).

———. *The Queen Is Dead*. Rough Trade, Rough 96 (1986).

———. *The Smiths*. Rough Trade, Rough 61 (1983).

The Specials. "Ghost Town." Chrysalis 12" X-13075 (1981).

Tricky. *Angels with Dirty Faces*. Island 524520-2 (1998).

———. *Maxinquaye*. 4th and Broadway/Island BRLP610 (1995).

———. *Pre-Millennium Tension*. Island 314-524302-2 (1996).

Tricky, with DJ Muggs and Grease. *Juxtapose*. Universal/Island 546552-2 (1999).

Various Artists. *. . . And Still No Hits: The Nation Records Story So Far*. Nation NRCD1100 (1997).

Various Artists. *Anokha: Soundz of the Asian Underground*. Quango/Omni 314-524341-2 (1997).

Various Artists. *Flux Trax: 18 Classic Techno Cuts*. EXP CD001 (1995).

Various Artists. *Jungle Book: Intelligent Minds of Jungle, Volume 1*. Reinforce/Rivet CD 006 (1995).

Various Artists. *Music Box: A New Era in Drum and Bass Compiled by Roni Size.* Full Cycle FYCCD01 (1996).

Various Artists. *Routes from the Jungle: Escape Velocity, Volume 1.* Circa/Virgin VTDCD 46 (1995).

Various Artists. *This Is . . . Jungle.* Ultrasound USCD1 (1994).

Index

Nabeel Zuberi is Lecturer in Film, Television, and Media Studies at the University of Auckland, New Zealand.

Typeset in 10.5/13 Adobe Garamond
with Veljovik display
Designed by Dennis Roberts
Composed by W. L. Ridenour
at the University of Illinois Press
Manufactured by Thomson-Shore, Inc.

University of Illinois Press
1325 South Oak Street
Champaign, IL 61820-6903
www.press.uillinois.edu